Israel's KINGS

A Devotional Study of Kings and Chronicles 

Warren Henderson

Israel's Kings – A Devotional Study of Kings and Chronicles

By Warren Henderson

Cover Design by Benjamin Bredeweg

Published by Warren A. Henderson
3769 Indiana Road
Pomona, KS 66076

Editing/Proofreading: Marilyn MacMullen, Dan Macy, and David Lindstrom

Perfect Bound ISBN: 978-1-939770-54-7
eBook ISBN: 978-1-939770-55-4

ORDERING INFORMATION:
Copies of *Israel's Kings* are available through www.amazon.com/shops/*hendersonpublishing* or www.order@gospelfolio.com (1-800-952-2382) or various online retailers.

Table of Contents

Other Books by the Author

A Heart for God – A Devotional Study of Kings and Chronicles
Afterlife – What Will It Be Like?
Answer the Call – Finding Life's Purpose
Be Holy and Come Near– A Devotional Study of Leviticus
Behold the Saviour
Be Angry and Sin Not
Conquest and the Life of Rest – A Devotional Study of Joshua
Door of Hope – A Devotional Study of the Minor Prophets
Exploring the Pauline Epistles
Forsaken, Forgotten, and Forgiven – A Devotional Study of Jeremiah
Glories Seen & Unseen
Hallowed Be Thy Name – Revering Christ in a Casual World
Hiding God – The Ambition of World Religion
In Search of God – A Quest for Truth
Infidelity and Loyalty – A Devotional Study of Ezekiel and Daniel
Knowing the All-Knowing
Managing Anger God's Way
Mind Frames – Where Life's Battle Is Won or Lost
Out of Egypt – A Devotional Study of Exodus
Overcoming Your Bully
Passing the Torch – Mentoring the Next Generation For Christ
Relativity and Redemption – A Devotional Study of Judges and Ruth
Revive Us Again – A Devotional Study of Ezra, Nehemiah, and Esther
Seeds of Destiny – A Devotional Study of Genesis
Sorrow and Comfort – A Devotional Study of Isaiah
The Beginning of Wisdom – A Devotional Study of Job, Psalms, Proverbs, Ecclesiastes, and Song of Solomon
The Bible: Myth or Divine Truth?
The Evil Nexus – Are You Aiding the Enemy?
The Fruitful Bough – Affirming Biblical Manhood
The Fruitful Vine – Celebrating Biblical Womanhood
The Hope of Glory – A Preview of Things to Come
The Kings – A Devotional Study of Kings and Chronicles
The Olive Plants – Raising Spiritual Children
Your Home the Birthing Place of Heaven

Preface

Kings and Chronicles cover the era of Israel's kings, which spans almost four centuries. Kings picks up with the last days of David, while Chronicles commences with the death of Saul, Israel's first king. Chronicles follows only the Davidic dynasty; references to Israel's kings occur only as a necessary part of the narrative.

The writers of Kings and Chronicles had different objectives. The writer of Chronicles intended to encourage disheartened Jews returning from Babylon to regain their identity as Jehovah's covenant people and to rebuild His temple. Kings highlights the ministry of God's prophets laboring among His idolatrous and wayward people. William Kelly surmises that "Kings is the book of responsibility, Chronicles of God's providence."[1]

Unlike Chronicles which puts a positive spin on Jewish history, Kings unashamedly emphasizes the consequences of disobeying God. The prophet's perspective in Kings upholds God's sovereignty over Israel and His covenant faithfulness despite her disobedience, idolatry, and propensity for seeking foreign alliances. Throughout Israel's history, God judges the wicked and rewards the faithful, but regardless of what Israel does, He proves His covenantal love to them. Consequently, even His stern judgments are tempered with mercy to ensure all His purposes are accomplished for those He loves.

Chronicles evaluates Judah's kings on how well they maintain David's zeal for worshiping Jehovah at His sanctuary, rather than on the basis of personal characteristics or accomplishments. Although David's son Solomon built the temple, it is his father's affections and sincerity that become the measuring stick for all future kings in his dynasty. Only Hezekiah and Josiah are honored with accolades of being like David in his zeal for God.

Israel's Kings is a "commentary style" devotional which upholds the glories of Christ while exploring the books of 1 and 2 Kings and 1 and 2 Chronicles within the context of the whole of Scripture. Because much of the material in Kings and Chronicles overlaps, the devotions are placed in chronological order as kings sit on their respective thrones. I have endeavored to include in this book some principal gleanings from other writers. *Israel's Kings* contains dozens of brief devotions. This format allows the reader to use the book either as a daily devotional or as a reference for deeper study.

— Warren Henderson

Overview of Kings and Chronicles

The Author

The Jews considered Kings to belong to the portion of Scripture termed the "prophets," while Chronicles was placed with Psalms, Proverbs, and other books referred to as the "writings." Jewish tradition points to the prophet Jeremiah as the author of Kings, and the scribe Ezra the historian of Chronicles.

Kings: *Kings*, like *Samue*l, and *Chronicles*, was split into two parts when the Greek Septuagint was translated in the third century B.C. This was done to make the scroll size more manageable. The tenor of *Kings* is the prophet's perspective, "the wages of sin is death." Jewish tradition, the writing style, and the content of the book indicate that Jeremiah was likely the author. James Catron comments to the sources of information available to Jeremiah, if he is the author of the book:

> Jeremiah used three sources to compile the record: the acts of Solomon (1 Kgs. 11:41), the chronicles (diaries) of the kings of Israel (see 1 Kgs. 14:19), and the chronicles (diaries) of the kings of Judah (1 Kgs. 14:29). Jeremiah lived at the end of the kingdom and probably wrote Kings shortly after the destruction of Jerusalem (2 Kgs. 25) in 586 B.C.[2]

Chronicles: Jewish tradition ascribes authorship to the priest-scribe Ezra, who would have had the knowledge and skill to produce such a work. Unlike the general populace, a priest would have access to extensive genealogical information as shown in the first nine chapters. The fact that the first two verses of Ezra are the same as the last two verses of 2 Chronicles further supports this view. The writing style and emphasis of Ezra is also similar to that of Chronicles.

Date

Kings: The closing section of 2 Kings covers the fall of Jerusalem, so the writer would have penned his historical account after 586 B.C. Because the author does not mention Jewish captives returning from Babylon, we can safely conclude that *Kings* was written before 536 B.C. This would have been the timeframe that Jeremiah could have penned the book.

Chronicles: The historian clearly lived after the fall of Jerusalem, as that tragic event is described at the close of his volume. If Ezra was the writer, he would have penned this book in the mid-fifth century B.C. (about 125 years after the destruction of Jerusalem by the Babylonian Empire).

Theme

Kings: The writer begins with the glorious reign of Solomon and his construction of God's temple in Jerusalem, and closes his historical record with the last Judean king, Zedekiah, and the fall of Jerusalem. This history spans four centuries. The book highlights the ministry of God's prophets laboring among His wayward and idolatrous people. Unlike Chronicles which puts a positive perspective on Jewish history to encourage a disheartened people, Kings unashamedly emphasizes the repercussions of disobeying God.

The prophet's focus is the sovereignty of God over Israel. Jehovah is able to uphold His covenants with Israel despite her disobedience, her idolatry, and her propensity to seek foreign alliances. While the Lord judges the wicked and rewards the faithful (e.g., Hezekiah and Josiah), He always upholds His covenant people with tempered mercy to ensure all His purposes are accomplished. The writer typically mentions the parents' names of various kings and the specifics of each reign. More importantly, the historian addresses each king's relationship with God, as shown in his attitude towards God's Law, His temple, and the prophetic messages received.

Chronicles: The Jews originally referred to this book as "The Words of Days." Jerome understood the book to be a chronicle of Jewish history and named it so in his Latin translation (the Vulgate) in the fourth century A.D. First Chronicles retells the story of King David and Second Chronicles the reigns of Solomon and the remaining kings of Judah from the most positive perspective. The writer is seeking to encourage disillusioned and struggling Jews after the devastating Babylonian captivity. Where Kings focuses on Israel's royal history, Chronicles emphasizes the historical nature of Israel's worship. Although the Israelites first worshiped Jehovah at a tabernacle and then later at a temple in Jerusalem, the writer's central focus on the Ark of the Lord (symbolizing God's presence) is always maintained.

The historian desires to help his countrymen regain the spiritual perspective that they were Jehovah's chosen people and His Law and covenants were for them alone. He especially highlights the Davidic covenant and continuing dynasty and God's providential care for Israel. This explains why the writer does not concentrate on Israel's evil kings (other than in association with David's dynasty) and also why he omits from Chronicles certain negative aspects recorded in 2 Samuel and Kings. For example, David's sin with Bathsheba, Adonijah's attempt to seize the kingdom, and many of the negative aspects of Solomon's latter years are absent from the account. The book of Chronicles affirms a truth that we can still rejoice in today: despite days of ruin, God is always faithful to bring about what He promises.

Contrasting Chronology

The reigns of David and Solomon each lasted forty years. Shortly after Solomon's death in 931 B.C., the kingdom split and Jeroboam became the king of Israel, with the ten northern tribes following him, while Solomon's son Rehoboam became king of Judah. The last king of Judah was Zedekiah who was taken to Babylon as a blinded prisoner after the fall of Jerusalem in 586 B.C. This means that the era of Judean kings actually lasted about 325 years. Yet, according to the narrative, the sum total span of all Judah's kings was about 388 years.

There are three explanations for this apparent discrepancy. First, several of the kings were coregents with their fathers, so there was an overlap of years in which both kings ruled. Second, Israel initially used a nonaccession-year system of referring to the reigns of their kings through the ninth century, then switched to an accession-year reckoning during the reign of Jehoash. Judah began with an accession-year reckoning, but switched to a non-accession method in the mid-ninth century, and then went back again to the original format in the mid-eighth century.[3] Third, Israel's calendar year began in the spring with the first month of the religious calendar; however, Judah, as influenced by Babylon, referred to the seventh month of the religious calendar as their New Year (Rosh Hashana). This calendar tradition continues among the Jews to this day.

Outline

1 Kings

David's Final Days: 1:1-2:11
The Reign of Solomon: 2:12-11:43
A Divided Kingdom: 12:1-14:31
Kings of Judah and Israel to Ahab: 15:1-16:27
The Reign of Ahab: 16:28-22:39
The Reigns of Jehoshaphat and Ahaziah: 22:40-53

2 Kings

Elijah's Final Days: 1:1-2:11
The Ministry of Elisha: 2:12-8:15
Kings of Judah and Israel until Assyrian Invasion: 8:16-17:41
Kings of Judah until Babylonian Invasion: 18:1-25:30

1 Chronicles

Genealogies from Adam: 1:1-9:44
Saul's Final Days: 10:1-15
The Reign of David: 11:1-29:30

2 Chronicles

The Reign of Solomon: 1:1-9:31
The Kingdom of Judah: 10:1-36:23

The Kings and Prophets of Two Kingdoms

Judah's Kings	Israel's Kings	Chronicles	Kings	Prophets	Date (B.C.)
Saul	Saul	bk.1/ch.10			1050-1010
David	David	1/11-29	1bk./1-2ch.		
	1010-970				
Solomon	Solomon	2/1-9	1/1-11		970-931
Rehoboam		2/10-12	1/12, 14	Shemaiah	931-913
	Jeroboam I	2/10	1/12-14	Ahijah/unnamed	931-910
Abijah (Abijam)		2/13	1/15	Shemaiah	913-911
Asa		2/14-16	1/15	Hanani	911-870
	Nadab		1/15		910-909
	Baasha		1/16	Jehu	909-886
	Elah		1/16		886-885
	Zimri		1/16	Micaiah/Elijah	885
	Omri (& Tibni)		1/16	Micaiah/Elijah	885-874*
	Ahab	2/18	1/17-22	Micaiah/Elijah	874-853
Jehoshaphat		2/17-20	1/22	Micaiah	870-848*
	Ahaziah		1/22, 2/1	Elisha	853-852
	Joram (Jehoram)		2/3	Elisha	852-841
Jehoram (Joram)		2/21	2/8		848-841*
	Jehu		2/9-10	Elisha	841-814
Ahaziah (Azariah)		2/22	2/8-9		841
Athaliah (queen)		2/22-23	2/11		841-835
Joash (Jehoash)		2/23-24	2/11-12	Joel	835-796
	Jehoahaz		2/13		814-798
	Jehoash (Joash)		2/13-14		798-782
Amaziah		2/25	2/14		796-767
	Jeroboam II		2/14	Jonah/Amos/Hosea	782-753*
Azariah (Uzziah)		2/26	2/15	Isaiah/Micah	767-740*
	Zechariah		2/15	Amos/Hosea	753-752
	Shallum		2/15	Amos/Hosea	752
	Menahem		2/15	Amos/Hosea	752-742
	Pekahiah		2/15	Amos/Hosea	742-740
Jotham		2/27	2/15	Isaiah/Micah	740-732*
	Pekah		2/15		740-732*
Ahaz		2/28	2/16	Isaiah/Micah	732-716

Israel's Kings

* Indicates co-regency with previous king.

Judah's Kings	Israel's Kings	Chronicles	Kings	Prophets	Date (B.C.)
	Hoshea		2/17		732-721
Hezekiah		2/29-32	2/18-20	Isaiah/Micah	716-687
Manasseh		2/33	2/21		687-642*
Amon		2/33	2/21		642-640
Josiah		2/34-35	2/22-23	Jeremiah,	640-608
Jehoahaz (Shallum)		2/36	2/23	Zephaniah,	608
Jehoiakim (Eliakim)		2/36	2/23-24	Habakkuk,	608-597
Jehoiachin (Jeconiah)		2/36	2/23-24	Ezekiel,	597
Zedekiah (Mattaniah)		2/36	2/23-24	and Daniel	597-586

* Indicates co-regency with previous king.

Devotions in Kings and Chronicles

Introduction

The last book in the Hebrew Bible is *Chronicles*, so named by Jerome in his Latin translation; however, the Jews refer to *Chronicles* as "The Words of Days." The Jews commonly attribute the authorship of Chronicles to Ezra the scribe and, thus, place its writing during the latter portion of the Babylonian captivity and the initial stages of the Persian Empire. Regardless of his identity, the writer's focus was to awaken a small, struggling community of exiled Jews to their heritage in Jehovah. They had lost their perspective of being God's covenant people, His chosen people on earth. They should have been elated with their unique identification.

The Hebrew Bible arranges the Old Testament differently than our Bibles, though the content is the same. Chronicles is placed at the end of the Hebrew Bible, which would provide a seamless transition to Matthew, the first book of the New Testament. Chronicles contains the genealogies of Israel up to that point; the gospel of Matthew opens with a series of Davidic genealogies that provide the remaining connections to Christ. The Lord Jesus affirmed the arrangement of the Hebrew Bible by referring to the spirit of rebellion (in them) that had shed the blood of His righteous saints from Abel (Gen. 4) to Zacharias, the son of Barachias (2 Chron. 24). In short, the Chronicles-Matthew genealogical connection should serve to point the Jews to their coming Messiah.

The opening sentence of Matthew introduces that book's theme and explains its placement: *"The book of the generation of Jesus Christ, the Son of David, the Son of Abraham."* The principal topic of this gospel account is the direct fulfillment of the Davidic and Abrahamic covenants through Christ. These were unilateral covenants that God made with David and Abraham but until that time had never been completely fulfilled. For the Jews, the hope of permanent royalty from *a man after God's own heart* and the acquisition of the promised blessing, originally committed to *the friend of God*, were paramount.

The genealogy of Matthew 1 serves as proof to the Jews that Jesus, through Joseph, was a direct descendant of David and, thus, the legal and rightful heir to David's throne. So as not to distract from his theme of covenant fulfillment, Matthew begins with Abraham, not Adam, in his rendition of Christ's genealogy. Luke's genealogy of Christ (Luke 3), however, is for a different purpose. Luke upholds Christ as the "Son of man," or more specifically, the "Son of Adam." In so doing, Luke shows Christ to be the "Last Adam," God's replacement representative of righteousness, and the literal fulfillment of the prophecy that Messiah would come from the *"seed of a woman"* (Gen. 3:15-16). God thought it critical for mankind to understand that Messiah would not be of the seed of fallen man, although His royal lineage would be established through a man, Joseph, back to David through Solomon. The pair of New Testament genealogies accomplishes this: Luke focuses our attention upon the Lord's humanity derived from Mary through the power of the Holy Spirit, while Matthew demonstrates Christ's official authority through Joseph.

In summary, the Hebrew Bible concludes with genealogies from Adam up to the time in which God invoked 400 years of silence toward His rebellious covenant people. This prophetic hush was broken with the announcement of the Savior's coming to earth. In Matthew 1, the genealogy picks up again after centuries of silence and leads the Jews to their much-anticipated and predicted Messiah, the Lord Jesus Christ. He would be the literal fulfillment of God's promise to David: *"I will establish the throne of His kingdom forever"* (2 Sam. 7:13). Matthew provides the culmination of the story which Chronicles only partially disclosed, and bridges the remaining gap between the first Adam and the last Adam, who would restore righteousness and rule forever.

The prophet Jeremiah referred to the coming Messiah as the Righteous Branch of David (23:5; 33:15). God had promised that one of David's descendants would sit on his throne forever (2 Sam. 7:16). His authority would not be limited merely to Judah and Israel, but He would govern all the earth (Jer. 23:5-6). This future Jewish Deliverer would be a righteous and a just King, and would sprout up as a branch from the loins of David. This means that accurate Jewish genealogies would be crucial to authenticate Messiah's identity.

The genealogies in Chronicles maintain the important distinction between the line of kings through Judah and David, and the generations of high priests through Aaron and Eleazar. This was necessary to preserve the uniqueness of Christ's own ministry as Israel's king and high priest. No man could fulfill both offices until Christ came. Priests had to be from the tribe of Levi (Lev. 8-9) and kings from Judah, as Jacob had prophesied (Gen. 49:10). Prior to the Law which formalized this arrangement, there was one who briefly appeared to prophetically typify Israel's future Messiah, who would hold both offices: *"Then Melchizedek king of Salem brought out bread and wine; he was the priest of God Most High"* (Gen. 14:18). The writer of Hebrews affirms that Christ was the king-priest after the order of Melchizedek (Heb. 7:11).

Chronicles calls the Jews to remember the Levitical priesthood, which represented them before God; to recall the glorious kingdom of David; and to anticipate the even more spectacular one to come. The extensive genealogies in 1 Chronicles 1-9 provide the means of connecting the Jews in Ezra's day to their forefathers, and paves the way for their connection to their future Messiah; *"so all Israel were reckoned by genealogies"* (9:1).

Consequently, the first nine chapters contain the longest concentration of genealogies in the Bible and can be summarized as follows:

Adam to Jacob (1:1-2:2)
The Tribe of Judah (2:3-4:23)
The Tribe of Simeon (4:24-43)
The Transjordan Tribes (5)
The Tribe of Levi (6)
Six Other Tribes (7-8, 9:35-44)
The Inhabitants of Jerusalem (9:1-34)

Understanding Apparent Discrepancies

In comparing the lists of genealogies in the next eight chapters with parallel accounts elsewhere in Scripture, we do well to remember the following principles in evaluating what appears to be a discrepancy:

1. Some men have more than one name.
2. The spelling of some names changed over the years.

3. Some names are omitted because the men died early or childless.
4. The Hebrew word *ben* can be translated son, grandson, or great-grandson.
5. Some names are left out because they do not serve the historian's purpose.[4]

Contrasting 2 Samuel with 1 Chronicles

Both 2 Samuel and 1 Chronicles center on David's rise to power and his reign over Israel. However, as both writers have a different perspective and goal, both books contain unique content. For example, the writer of Chronicles (likely Ezra) did not include: David's long power struggle before being recognized as Israel's king (2 Sam. 1-4), nor the story of Mephibosheth (2 Sam. 9), nor the consequences to David and his family resulting from his sin with Bathsheba (2 Sam. 11-23).

Likewise, there is content in 1 Chronicles not found in 2 Samuel, namely: the genealogies of Israel (1 Chron. 1-9), the extensive details of David bringing the Ark to Jerusalem (1 Chron. 13-16), and David's reorganization of religious and civil affairs and his stockpiling of resources for temple construction (1 Chron. 22-29).

The Genealogy From Adam to David

1 Chronicles 1-3

Most of us are not going to get too excited about reading a long list of names of people who died two to four thousand years ago. With that said, there are a number of interesting points and applications embedded within Jewish genealogies which we can benefit from.

1 Chronicles 1

Chapter 1 contains the genealogies of: Adam to Noah (1 Chron. 1:1-7); Noah's three sons (1 Chron. 1:5-23); Shem to Abraham (1 Chron. 1:24-28); Abraham's sons through Hagar, Keturah, and Sarah (1 Chron. 1:29-34); and Esau's descendants and royal lineage in Edom (1 Chron. 1:35-54).

The twelve sons of Ishmael are listed in verses 29-31. We recall that the Lord met distressed, fleeing, and pregnant Hagar in the wilderness and promised her that she would have a son (Gen. 16:7). She was to call his name "Ishmael" and his descendants would become a great nation. A few years later, God promised Abraham that He would bless his son Ishmael and that he would have twelve sons and be the father of a great nation (Gen 17:20). The genealogy contained in this chapter verifies that the Lord honored His promises to both Abraham and Hagar – Ishmael had twelve sons and fathered the Arab people.

1 Chronicles 2

Chapter 2 lists the twelve sons of Jacob, the son of Isaac. After affirming His promise to Abraham concerning Ishmael, the Lord said, *"But My covenant I will establish with Isaac, whom Sarah shall bear to you at this set time next year"* (Gen. 17:21). Isaac was born, just as the Lord said, and later he would have twin sons through Rebekah: Esau and Jacob. God confirmed His covenant with Jacob, who became the father of the nation of Israel. The next three chapters carefully trace the

Messianic line (the One God would use to fulfill all His promises to Abraham) through the tribe of Judah to David (1 Chron. 2:1-4:23). Jacob had previously prophesied that the Messiah would come from Judah (Gen. 49:10).

The historian notes that three sons, Er, Onan, and Shelah, were born to Judah by the daughter of Shua, the Canaanitess (1 Chron. 2:3). Er and Onan were struck down by the Lord because they were wicked men (Gen. 38:6-10). Through deception, Judah fathered the twins Perez and Zerah through Er's and Onan's widow Tamar (1 Chron. 2:4). Interestingly, the grandson of Zerah was Achan, who transgressed concerning the accursed things of Jericho and brought destruction to himself and his family (1 Chron. 2:5-7). In short, one son of Tamar (Zerah) led to cursing and God's judgment against Israel, while her other son, Perez, being in the lineage of Messiah, would bring blessing to Israel. For that reason, the genealogical information follows the line of blessing, not the line of cursing.

David's brothers and sisters (Zeruiah and Abigail) are identified (1 Chron. 2:13-17). Interestingly, none of David's seven brothers had any significant place in his government. (One of David's brothers apparently died at a young age and was not included in the number in verse 15 – though originally David was the youngest of eight sons of Jesse; 1 Sam. 16:10-11, 17:12.) However, the three sons of Zeruiah (Abishai, Joab, and Asahel) and Amasa, the son of Abigail, were important in David's administration; all were warriors.

Young Asahel was killed by Abner in battle, Abishai and Asahel are listed with David's mighty men, and Joab was the leader of David's army for much of his reign. After the rebellion of Absalom, David replaced Joab with Amasa (who had sided with Absalom) but Joab, not approving of the king's decision, murdered his cousin Amasa. He was apparently conceived out of wedlock to an Ishmaelite named Jithra (Jether), an Israelite proselyte (2 Sam. 17:25; 1 Chron. 2:17). Though Joab was brave and clever, he was not named among David's mighty men because of his self-willed and often cruel behavior.

We also learn something about the faithful Rechabites, whom the prophet Jeremiah will present as a positive example to highlight the waywardness of God's people just prior to the first Babylonian invasion in 605 B.C. (Jer. 35). Like Abraham, the nomadic Rechabites did not live in houses, but were tent-dwellers. For centuries, the Rechabites had honored and obeyed their forefather's teachings as a guide to their simple lifestyle, whereas Israel had ignored God's Law for His children. First Chronicles 2:54-55 informs us that they were descendants of the Kenites who normally dwelt in the wilderness of Negev (1 Sam. 15:6), but had been forced to move to Jerusalem after Nebuchadnezzar threatened the region in 598 B.C. (Jer. 35:11).

1 Chronicles 3

This chapter traces the royal line of David through Zedekiah. The historian records the names of David's six wives while he reigned over Judah in Hebron and the names of the sons born to him there (1 Chron. 3:1-4). After moving to Jerusalem and becoming king of Israel, David took more wives and concubines and had many more children (a number of sons are listed in 1 Chron. 3:5-9).

David's firstborn son Amnon (through Ahinoam) was murdered by David's third son Absalom (through Maacah from Geshur). Absalom took revenge on Amnon for raping his sister Tamar. Absalom was killed by Joab during the Civil War that ensued after his revolt against his father. David's second son, Daniel, born of Abigail, is presumed to have died before reaching adulthood. The psalmist, who joyfully wrote of God's sustaining power, suffered the loss of his first three sons.

We also know that David's first son through Bathsheba died as judgment for David's sin, and later Adonijah perished after rebelling against Solomon, the next king of Israel. Unfortunately, David's mistakes of marrying foreigners and polygamy will be repeated by Solomon. Furthermore, Solomon's many foreign wives will prompt him to worship their false gods, thus angering the Lord.

The chapter concludes by specifically listing the descendants of Jeconiah, whom the prophet Jeremiah pronounced a curse upon (Jer. 22:30). Before leaving Jerusalem, Nebuchadnezzar placed the uncle of Jehoiachin, Zedekiah, on the throne of Judah. He would be the last Judean king from the line of Solomon to reign over Jerusalem and would be subservient to Babylon the entire time. Jeremiah's prophecy concerning Jehoiachin is significant, for God had promised David that one of his descendants would be on his throne forever (2 Sam. 7:12-16), but according to Jeremiah, that descendant could not come through the royal line of Jehoiachin, since Jehoiachin had been cursed by God for his wickedness.

This prophecy is used to magnify the incarnation of the Lord Jesus Christ as Messiah. Joseph, the husband of Mary (the mother of the Lord Jesus), was a descendant of Shealtiel who was the son of Jehoiachin or Jeconiah (1 Chron. 3:17; Matt. 1:12). Therefore, no son of Joseph could sit upon David's throne. Mary, however, was also a descendant of David but through Nathan (Luke 3:24-38). Thus, the son of Mary could fulfill both prophecies if she conceived supernaturally through the power of the Holy Spirit and not by Joseph her husband. Such a child would avoid the curse of Jeconiah, would not be corrupted by the fallen nature inherited from Adam, and would be the rightful heir to the throne of David. Although Jeremiah's prophecies foretold God's dealings with the last four wicked kings of Judah, they also laid the foundation for the future exaltation of the King of kings, the Lord Jesus Christ! May we appreciate these Biblical genealogies and prophecies – they point us unerringly to Christ and the eternal King!

Meditation

> Mercy and truth preserve the king, and by lovingkindness he upholds his throne.
>
> — Solomon (Prov. 20:28)

The Genealogy of the Twelve Tribes – Part 1

1 Chronicles 4-5

1 Chronicles 4

We will consider two particulars in this chapter worthy of our contemplation: the prayer of Jabez and the inclusion of Pharaoh's daughter Bithia within the genealogy of Judah.

Jabez's name means "sorrowful." Apparently, there was some adverse situation or hindering obstacle at the time of Jabez's birth that continued to afflict him afterwards. He desired the Lord to remove whatever it was.

> *And Jabez called on the God of Israel saying, "Oh, that You would bless me indeed, and enlarge my territory, that Your hand would be with me, and that You would keep me from evil, that I may not cause pain!" So God granted him what he requested* (1 Chron. 4:10).

Jabez petitioned the Lord for three things: enlargement of territory, closer intimacy with God, and preservation from evil. The land allotments bestowed on Israel's tribes in the book of Joshua were to pass down from generation to generation within the same tribe. This meant that an individual or clan could not increase their inheritance by buying or stealing from their brethren, but only by engaging and defeating the enemy. Accordingly, the Law prohibited Jabez from gaining land through financial acquisition; he could enlarge his territory through legal conquest (i.e., seizing land from those whom God said should be removed from the Promised Land).

To further advance the Kingdom of God today, believers must do more than entertain each other in conquered territories (i.e., their homes and church buildings). They must be willing to venture out beyond these safe havens and to storm the gates of Hell with the gospel message of Jesus Christ. The Lord is building His Church through the earnest efforts of His people to evangelize the lost. Let us never be satisfied with the status quo – may the Lord enlarge our capacity to serve Him as He enlarges His Church.

Jabez also asked the Lord, *"that Your hand might be with me."* Jabez wanted intimacy and close fellowship with God. And whenever there is someone who desires a closer fellowship with God, the Creator will be eager to reveal Himself in new and meaningful ways. As seen with Enoch years before Jabez, those who walk with God will benefit by God's companionship and protection from evil.

The second noteworthy item is that the daughter of Pharaoh, Bithia, is included in the genealogy of Judah (1 Chron. 4:18). She married Mered. Interestingly, her name means "daughter of Jehovah." Though the daughter of the king of Egypt (having a high position in the pagan world), she departed from Egypt and chose to live among God's people as a worshiper of Jehovah – a child of God. Before coming to Christ, we Gentles (Egyptians, so to speak) *"were dead in trespasses and sins"* and *"once walked according to the course of this world, according to the prince of the power of the air, the spirit who now works in the sons of disobedience, ... and were by nature children of wrath"* (Eph. 2:1-3). Accordingly, we were separated from God and had no part in the blessings promised to Israel through Abraham.

But God, who is rich in mercy, made us alive in Christ to become His children also (John 1:12-13; Eph. 2:4-5). Christ is the fulfillment of the Abrahamic covenant and brought us into the good of it by sealing a new covenant with His own blood. Praise the Lord, Gentile believers are no longer children of the world, the devil, and of wrath, but are children of God, light, and mercy.

The chapter concludes by taking up the genealogy of Jacob's second-born son, Simeon (1 Chron. 4:24-43). Simeon's inheritance was originally within Judah's borders (Josh. 19:9), but over time this more feeble tribe lost its distinction by dispersing within Judah or settling among the northern tribes. As a result, Judah became synonymous with that portion of the Promised Land mainly south of Jerusalem.

1 Chronicles 5

This chapter lists the genealogies of the two and a half tribes that settled in the Transjordan region instead of Canaan. Their specific boundaries are recorded in Joshua 15. The Reubenites settled in the land previously occupied by the Moabites east of the Dead Sea. The tribe of Gad inherited the land directly north of them in the region of Gilead. The half-tribe of Manasseh was granted the region of Bashan, which was directly east of the Sea of Galilee (referred to today as the Golan Heights).

Ironically, these two and a half tribes were the first to obtain their inheritance and also the first tribes to be completely dispossessed of it (1 Chron. 5:6). Why? This group of Israelites would be the first to embrace idolatry, and hence, the first to suffer divine punishment. Pul or Tiglath-Pileser III, the king of Assyria, deported Israelites from the Eastern Plateau in 734-732 B.C.

Even before this invasion, the two and a half tribes had already lost a portion of their inheritance. For example, the Reubenites originally settled in the cities of Nebo and Kiriathaim (Josh. 13:19; Num. 32:37-38). These cities and others in the region, such as Heshbon, were later captured by the Moabites. Heshbon had been the capital city of Sihon, king of the Amorites, until the Israelites conquered it prior to entering Canaan (Num. 21:25-29). The tribe of Reuben rebuilt the city (Num. 32:37-38), but years later Moab recaptured it from Reuben.

It was not Jehovah's intention for the two and a half tribes to settle on the eastern side of the Jordan when the Hebrew nation first entered into Canaan, but He permitted it in response to their request. They had assumed that what God had for them in Canaan could not be better than the rich pasturelands they already knew existed on the eastern plateau. Apparently, their lusting for what was outside of God's will eventually led them into idolatry, which then resulted in the loss of their inheritance.

Straying from God's presence and His best for us will always leave us miserable and wanting. We are people of like passion, and are capable of committing the same costly mistake, trading Gilgal for Gilead. May God's people today learn from this important lesson: continued lusting for what is beyond the will of God invariably leads to sin, the loss of God's blessings and fellowship, and finally to destruction (Jas. 1:14-15).

Meditation

An affection which is not inspired by the Lord will soon be transformed into lust. Samson is not alone in the history of man in failing in this regard. Delilah is still cutting the hair of men today!

— Watchman Nee

Though selfishness hath defiled the whole man, yet sensual pleasure is the chief part of its interest, and, therefore, by the senses it commonly works; and these are the doors and windows by which iniquity enters into the soul.

— Richard Baxter

The Genealogy of the Twelve Tribes – Part 2

1 Chronicles 6

First Chronicles 6 covers the lineage of Jacob's third son Levi whose three sons were Gershom, Kohath, and Merari. Their genealogies are recorded in verses 16-30. The first fifteen verses deal with the line of the high priest through Aaron, a descendent of Kohath.

The Proper High Priestly Line (1 Chron. 6:1-15)

Twice in this chapter the Holy Spirit lists the high priests between Aaron and Zadok (1 Chron. 6:3-8, 50-53). Note that the name of the fourteenth judge of Israel, Eli, is missing from the roster. Being from the lineage of Aaron's son Ithamar, Eli and those who followed him were not eligible to be high priests, though they assumed that office. Years later, David recognized Zadok as high priest, from the line of Eleazar, Aaron's other son whom God chose to be high priest. For several years, Abiathar, a descendant of Eli remained high priest with Zadok. Solomon removed Abiathar from office after he conspired with Solomon's half-brother Adonijah to seize the throne when David was ailing (1 Kgs. 2:27). By this action God's judgment against the house of Eli as pronounced by both an unnamed prophet (1 Sam. 2) and again by young Samuel (1 Sam. 3) was completed.

The Sons of Korah (1 Chron. 6:16-30)

Samuel's parents and the dramatic circumstances that led to his conception and birth are revealed in 1 Samuel 1. Samuel's father, Elkanah, resided within the mountainous region of Ephraim in the town of Ramah (1 Sam. 1:1). Elkanah's genealogy (1 Chron. 6:22-37) indicates that he was the son of Jeroham, a descendant of the Levite Korah, who rebelled with others against the Aaronic priesthood in Numbers 16 (Jude 11). Though disengaged from active religious service, Elkanah's existence verifies the validity of Moses' statement after Korah and his household was judged: *"Nevertheless the children of Korah did not die"* (Num. 26:11).

Korah's sons were not self-assertive and chose to side with the Lord, rather than with their father when the call for separation came. This decision not only saved them from death, but is also honored in the Psalms. David wrote twenty of the psalms in Book 2 (Psalms 51-70), and seven of these are ascribed to or dedicated to "the sons of Korah" (Psalms 42, 44-49).

Understanding what happened in Numbers 16 gives much more meaning to Psalm 84:10: *"For a day in thy courts is better than a thousand. I had rather be a door keeper in the house of my God than to dwell in the tents of wickedness."* Indeed, descendants of Korah's sons Assir, Elkanah, and Ebiasaph went on to serve the Lord in the tabernacle and then at the temple in Jerusalem (1 Chron. 6:22-30). David actually appointed some of Korah's descendants as musicians to sing before the tabernacle once the Ark rested in Jerusalem until the temple was built almost forty years later (1 Chron. 6:37).

Paul instructs children to honor and obey their parents *"in the Lord"* (Eph. 6:1-4). The stipulation phrase, *"in the Lord,"* implies children are to serve their parents as unto the Lord in matters of righteousness, but not in matters of sin. The sons of Korah chose to stand with the Lord, rather than to side with their father who was rebelling against God's expressed will, and, for that reason, they were spared judgment and then honored by the Lord.

Songs of Praise (1 Chron. 6:31-48)

The first mention of singing in Scripture is in Exodus 15, where the redeemed Israelites sang the song of Moses after Jehovah delivered them from Egypt and Pharaoh's army by providing a passage through the Red Sea. *"Then Moses and the children of Israel sang this song to the Lord,"* the lyrics of which were recorded in Exodus 15:1-18. Then Miriam, Moses' sister, led the women in jubilant singing to the Lord (Ex. 15:21).

However, a few chapters later, Moses brought God's Law down from Mount Sinai. This had a stifling effect on Israel's singing because the Law saddled the conscience with guilt and burdened the people with hundreds of commands to obey. This difficulty continued for several hundred years until God brought David, a man after His own heart, into Israel's economy. David taught God's people that God's Law was a reflection of God's holy character and therefore should be delighted in and that His people should rejoice in the Lord, for His ways of salvation were beyond their understanding. Such joy should naturally be expressed in song, which explains why David wrote and strummed so many of the melodious lyrics preserved in Scripture. John Heading writes:

> David was the first to have an exercise concerning the song of praise. He was a man after God's own heart to fulfill His will (Acts 13:22), and as such he was exercised about many things, such as the ark, Mount Zion, the temple, and the service of song; afterwards others followed in his steps. He was a man raised on high, anointed of God and the sweet psalmist of Israel, who owned that the Spirit spoke by him and that His word was in his tongue (2 Sam. 23:1-2). Today God has raised us up with Christ, and we are enabled by the Spirit to express the true song of worship that glorifies Him.[5]

Given David's passion for music and prolific composition of spiritual songs, it should be no surprise that he appointed singers to offer praise to the Lord at the tabernacle (1 Chron. 6:31-48, 25:1-8). Although each of Levi's three sons fathered specific clans of Levites which had their distinct duties within Israel's religious economy, all Levites could praise God in song. All three Levitical clans were involved with praising the Lord in song: the lineage of three songmasters follows: Heman, the Kohathite (1 Chron. 6:33-38), Asaph, the Gershomite (1 Chron. 6:39-43), and Ethan, the Merarite (1 Chron. 6:44-47). Heman authored Psalm 88 and was a descendant of Israel's fifteenth judge, Samuel (1 Chron. 6:28). A number of Psalms are associated with Asaph; he wrote eleven of the seventeen psalms in Book 3 of the Psalms (e.g., Ps. 73-83). Ethan penned Psalm 89.

Although each Levite had his specific function to perform, all were permitted to sing before the Lord. Likewise, in the Church Age all those born again have unique spiritual gifts to equip them to perform a specific function within the body-life of the Church, but all believers as believer-priests may worship the Lord.

Throughout the ages it has always been appropriate for the redeemed to sing praise to God, but what is offered to the Lord must be true and Spirit-led – *"those who worship Him must worship in spirit and truth"* (John 4:24). Those singing before the Lord *"were instructed in the songs of the Lord"* (1 Chron. 25:7). Likewise today, believers in the Church Age are to *"be filled with the Spirit, speaking to one another in psalms and hymns and spiritual songs, singing and making melody in your heart to the Lord"* (Eph. 5:18-19). *"Let the word of Christ dwell in you richly in all wisdom, teaching and admonishing one another in psalms and hymns and spiritual songs, singing with grace in your hearts to the Lord"* (Col. 3:16-17). The nature of our songs should be grounded in divine truth, God exalting, and human exhorting as enabled by the Holy Spirit! No matter how well we sing, if the lyrics are not true – it cannot please God.

Furthermore, the singers *"served in their office according to their order"* (1 Chron. 6:32). Because of the large number of Levites at that time, David divided God's ministers into twenty-four orders, each division waiting for their opportunity to serve before the Lord.

Likewise, in the Church Age, Paul reminds us that God has set forth divisions (gender roles) of order for the Church to follow also:

> *God is not the author of confusion, but of peace, as in all churches of the saints. Let your women keep silence in the churches: for it is not permitted unto them to speak* (1 Cor. 14:33-34).

> *Every man praying or prophesying, having his head covered, dishonors his head. But every woman who prays or prophesies with her head uncovered dishonors her head, for that is one and the same as if her head were shaved. For if a woman is not covered, let her also be shorn. But if it is shameful for a woman to be shorn or shaved, let her be covered. For a man indeed ought not to cover his head, since he is the image and glory of God; but woman is the glory of man* (1 Cor. 11:4-7).

God's division of responsibility within the Church declares His glory and manifests His wisdom to power and principalities in high places (Eph. 3:10). The visual ministry of the sisters in concealing competing glories (1 Cor. 11:2-16) and that of the audible leading ministry of the brothers reveal God's glory; therefore, *"let all things be done decently and in order"* (1 Cor. 14:40).

Lost Priestly Cities (1 Chron. 6:54-81)

As recorded in Joshua 21, God desired his Levites to be evenly dispersed in forty-eight cities throughout Canaan and the Transjordan region. This would ensure that those seeking the counsel of His word would have to travel no more than a day's journey. The Merarites received twelve priestly cities in the territories of Zebulun, Reuben, and Gad (Josh. 21:34-40). Bezer in the eastern pasture lands of Reuben would also be a City of Refuge (Josh. 20:8). In Gad, Ramoth-Gilead was to be a City of Refuge. Golan in Bashan was a City of Refuge in Manasseh's territory.

Unfortunately, some of these Levitical cities were still under enemy control, and the Levites, not being warriors themselves, and apparently not receiving much assistance from the other tribes, did not do well in driving out the pagans from their possessions. In time, some of these priestly cities were lost, and sadly, the Levites were forced to relocate. This explains why the list of Levitical cities is shorter in 1 Chronicles 6:54-81 and why some of the names have changed. Levitical cities such as Beth Shemesh (1 Sam. 6:13-15), Jattir (1 Sam. 30:27), and Anathoth (Jer. 1:1) did not exist in Joshua's day.

Meditation

> The best, most beautiful, and most perfect way that we have of expressing a sweet concord of mind to each other is by music.
>
> — Jonathan Edwards

> Music is one of the fairest and most glorious gifts of God, to which Satan is a bitter enemy, for it removes from the heart the weight of sorrow, and the fascination of evil thoughts.
>
> — Martin Luther

The Genealogy of the Twelve Tribes – Part 3

1 Chronicles 7:1-9:34

The genealogies of the remaining tribes of Israel are presented in the next two chapters: Issachar (1 Chron. 7:1-5), Benjamin (1 Chron. 7:6-12), Naphtali (1 Chron. 7:13), Manasseh west of the Jordan (1 Chron. 7:14-19), Ephraim (1 Chron. 7:20-29), Asher (1 Chron. 7:30-40), and Benjamin again (1 Chron. 8). In 1 Chronicles 7, Benjamin is treated as one of the tribes among the people, but in the next chapter his lineage is duplicated to indicate connection with Israel's first king, Saul.

1 Chronicles 7

In the preceding chapters no numbers were associated with the tribal listings, but numbers are noted five times in the genealogies contained within 1 Chronicles 7 (i.e., vv. 5, 7, 9, 11, 40). Recall that the tribe of Benjamin was reduced to 600 men after the Civil War recorded in Judges 19. They had regained much strength and now numbered 22,034 mighty men of valor (1 Chron. 7:7).

The four sons of Naphtali were called the "sons of Bilhah" after Naphtali's mother (v. 13). Bilhah, formerly Rachel's handmaiden, became Jacob's concubine and bore him two sons, Naphtali and Dan.

The descendants of the tribe of Manasseh west of the Jordan River are then listed (1 Chron. 7:14-19; those living in the Transjordan were cited in 1 Chron. 5:23-24). Of special mention is the genealogy of Zelophehad, who had no sons, but five daughters: Mahlah, Noah, Hoglah, Milcah, and Tirzah (1 Chron. 7:15; Num. 26:33). Israel's wilderness years were often marked by unbelief and corruption, but the genuine faith of the daughters of Zelophehad refreshed God's heart. They knew that Canaan would be taken as God had promised and they wanted an inheritance in their father's name. They pleaded with Moses, arguing that their father had not been among the conspirators of Korah's rebellion, and Moses granted their request. When the inheritance of Canaan was dispersed among the tribes years later, Joshua and Eleazar assigned an inheritance to Zelophehad's daughters in his name (Josh. 17:4-6). Beginning in Numbers 27, the names of Zelophehad's daughters are recorded three times in Scripture as a testimony of how God rewarded their faith.

The lineage of Ephraim is then traced to highlight the spiritual exploits of one of the Lord's most trusted and faithful servants – Joshua (1 Chron. 7:20-29).

Lastly, the four sons of Asher and their sister Serah are listed (1 Chron. 7:30-40; Gen. 46:17). Many of their descendants were mighty leaders and men of valor.

1 Chronicles 8

The Northern Kingdom composed of ten tribes fell to the Assyrian Empire in 722 B.C. Many Israelites at that time were slaughtered and many more were taken away into captivity. The Southern Kingdom was mainly comprised of the tribe of Judah (as the weaker tribe of Simeon and portions of Benjamin had been absorbed within Judah's borders) and various Levites and priests dwelling in Judah's territory. The majority of the Israelites exiled from the Northern Kingdom were never permitted to return to their homeland. However, tens of thousands of Jews, descendants of the Israelites from the Southern Kingdom, did return to Israel after their seventy-year captivity in Babylon which concluded in 538/537 B.C.

This explains why the historian devotes more space to the genealogies of Jews returning to Israel than those Israelites of the Northern Kingdom, who remained displaced. This is likely why the writer does not mention the tribes of Dan and Zebulun in his record, but instead focuses his audience's attention on the tribe of Benjamin (1 Chron. 8:1-28).

The chapter concludes with the lineage of Saul, a Benjamite and the first king of Israel (1 Chron. 8:29-40). Although Saul had four sons, only Jonathan, David's beloved friend, is mentioned here. David showed kindness to Jonathan's crippled son Mephibosheth (called Merib-Baal in 1 Chron. 8:34). He was invited to eat at the king's table forever, and in time became the lone surviving male descendant of Saul.

1 Chronicles 9

Verse 1 summarizes the previous eight chapters: *"So all Israel was recorded by genealogies, and indeed, they were inscribed in the book of the kings of Israel. But Judah was carried away captive to Babylon because of their unfaithfulness"* (1 Chron. 9:1). We sense that the genealogies in the previous chapters represent a small portion of the tribal lineages maintained by the kings of Israel and Judah.

The information in Chronicles does not generally deal with the Jewish genealogies after the Babylonian captivity. However, this chapter does mentions key families, mainly among the priests, Levites, and porters (gate keepers) who returned to Jerusalem to rebuild the temple under Zerubbabel's leadership and then later with Nehemiah to rebuild the city's wall (1 Chron. 9:1-34). The returnees recorded in Ezra 2 and Nehemiah 7 supplement the register contained in this chapter. These survivors represent God's purposes in dealing with Israel. He was starting again with His people after their idolatry was purged by severe chastening.

The historian then closes this chapter by again mentioning the lineage of Saul in order to properly preface the historical narrative of Israel's first king in the next chapter. The fuller details of Saul's anointing, reign, relentless pursuit of David, and his death are recorded in 1 Samuel 9-31.

Meditation

There's a time, there's a time
Both for sowing and for reaping there's a time.
Time for losing, time for gain,
Time for joy and time for pain,
Every purpose under heaven has a time.

There are times, there are days,
Weeks and months we cannot understand God's ways.
If for years we fail to scan
What is his eternal plan,
We'll remember that He can, all the time.

— Diane Ball

Saul's Beginning and End

1 Chronicles 9:35-10:14

Saul's Beginning (1 Chron. 9:35-44)

The historical portion of the book commences in 1 Chronicles 9:35 by again noting the genealogy of King Saul. God, in His anger, chose Saul as Israel's first king to teach His people the consequences of rejecting Him (Hos. 13:11). The fact that Saul's genealogy appears twice in Chronicles is notable (i.e., in 1 Chron. 8, and then from Saul's grandfather forward in 1 Chron. 9:35-44).

In contrast, the lineage of David, Israel's next king, is presented only once in Chronicles (though it appears again in Ruth 4, Matthew 1, and Luke 3). Given that the genealogy of the high priests was presented twice to highlight their importance in Israel's religious economy, perhaps Saul's lineage is twice mentioned to highlight the devastating effect that a carnal king had on Israel's prosperity. The working of the flesh, especially in Israel's king, limited God's blessing to His people and also corrupted their representation of Him to the nations. The same is true today.

In their carnality, Israel desired a human king to rule over them, instead of the Lord, so they would be like other nations. Saul was a man of the flesh, and his forty-year self-serving reign over Israel brought misery to God's covenant people and persecution to those who had God's approval. Saul's self-exalting rule prepared the people to readily welcome a man after God's own heart to succeed him, David. As Paul points out later, the contrast of these two kings was sovereignly designed to both reprove His people for their sin and to excite them about their coming Messiah, whom David typified (Acts 13:21-23).

Saul's End (1 Chron. 10:1-14)

The historian now reviews the events leading up to the death of Saul (also recorded in 1 Samuel 31). After gathering their forces at

Aphek, the Philistines moved north and then east in an attempt to secure the Jezreel Valley. The objective was to first cut off Saul from the northern tribes and then to seize control of Galilee. This tactic forced Saul to move down from the more defensible hill country and to engage the Philistines in the southern Plain of Esdraelon. This gave the Philistines, who had more soldiers and war-chariots, the advantage.

Saul had already been told by Samuel that he would die in this battle (1 Sam. 28:19); David also foretold that this would be the way Saul would perish (1 Sam. 26:10). The day of God's retribution had arrived and Saul would answer for sparing the Amalekites, intruding on the priesthood, spilling the blood of the innocent priests and their families at Nob, and for relentlessly pursuing innocent David for eight years.

The Philistine army moved south from Shunem to engage Saul and his troops coming north into the Jezreel Valley from the fountain at Jezreel. Israel's army quickly fell into disarray, was repelled, and driven back. The Jews did not widely use the bow as the Philistines did, so when the ranks of Israel's army drew near for hand-to-hand conflict, they were battered by volleys of arrows from Philistine archers as soon as they came within range. As a result, Israel's army fell into chaos before the clashing swords could ever be heard. This is why David, while later lamenting the death of Jonathan, commanded that the children of Judah be taught the skill of archery (2 Sam. 1:18).

Many soldiers perished as Israel's army retreated up the southern slopes of Gilboa (1 Chron. 10:1). The Philistines followed hard after Saul and his sons (1 Chron. 10:2). Apparently, Jonathan, Abinadab, and Malchishua were quickly slain by enemy archers and the king also *"was wounded by the archers"* (1 Chron. 10:3; 1 Sam. 31:3 says that Saul was "severely wounded"). The language suggests that Saul was struck by more than one arrow. The only son of Saul to survive this battle was Ishbosheth, whose name means "the man of shame." But as expected, his very survival would later perpetuate the awful dishonor that fell upon the house of Saul.

Preferring not to die at the hands of his enemy, Saul commanded his armorbearer: *"Draw your sword, and thrust me through with it, lest these uncircumcised men come and thrust me through and abuse me"* (1 Chron. 10:4). Even at the threshold of death, Saul's self-righteous heart despised the uncircumcised Philistines, but his spiritual vitality was no better than theirs.

Apparently, the armorbearer drew his sword, but was afraid to strike down his king, for he was answerable for the king's life. Saul then took the drawn sword and positioned it in such a way that he could fall on it, and so he ended his life. Seeing that the king was dead, his armorbearer took back his sword from Saul's body and also fell on it, killing himself (1 Chron. 10:5). He was a loyal bodyguard who, though declining to kill his king, did not refuse to die with him. The king, his three sons, and his armorbearer all perished on the same day (1 Chron. 10:6).

Seeing that Saul and his sons had perished, and Israel's army was soundly defeated, the Jews in the Jezreel Valley fled for their lives and the Philistines moved into their cities (1 Chron. 10:7). The next day, while the Philistines were stripping valuables from the slain Israelites, they discovered the bodies of Saul and his three sons on Mount Gilboa (1 Chron. 10:8). They cut off Saul's head and stripped off his armor and sent both to pagan temples throughout Philistia as trophies of victory (1 Chron. 10:9). Though the text does not specifically state this, the Philistines probably cut off and paraded the heads of Saul's sons also. Saul's armor was placed in the temple of Ashtaroth (sometimes called Ashtoreth, Asherah, or Astarte), but his body and the bodies of his sons were fastened to the wall of Beth Shan as a public spectacle (1 Chron. 10:10). This also indicates that the Philistines had captured and occupied Beth Shan and likely other Jewish cities extending eastward to the Jordan.

News came to the men of Jabesh Gilead of the disgraceful way the Philistines had treated Saul's body (1 Chron. 10:11). The thought of their king, who had previously saved them from Ammonites (1 Sam. 11), having no proper burial and the birds of prey feasting on their rotting corpses was more than they could bear. The valiant men of Jabesh then traveled to Beth Shan after dark, took down all four bodies from the wall, and then carried the bodies back to Jabesh where they burned them (1 Chron. 10:12). Cremation was not a normal practice in the Jewish culture, but was used here because the bodies were badly mutilated.

These brave men accomplished quite a feat. They crossed the Jordan River and journeyed through a narrow upland passage some twelve miles to retrieve the four headless bodies, which were probably guarded, and then they carried the bodies back the same route all in one night. After the bodies were burned, they collected all the bones and buried them under a tamarisk tree at Jabesh. Then they fasted seven days.

Meditation

> The nature of Christ's salvation is woefully misrepresented by some present-day evangelists. They announce a Savior from hell rather than a Savior from sin. And that is why so many are fatally deceived, for there are multitudes who wish to escape the Lake of Fire who have no desire to be delivered from their carnality and worldliness.
>
> — A. W. Pink

> If I see aright, the cross of popular evangelicalism is not the cross of the New Testament. It is, rather, a new bright ornament upon the bosom of a self-assured and carnal Christianity. The old cross slew men; the new cross entertains them. The old cross condemned; the new cross amuses. The old cross destroyed confidence in the flesh; the new cross encourages it.
>
> — A. W. Tozer

King David and His Mighty Men

1 Chronicles 11-12

David Becomes King of Israel (1 Chron. 11:1-3)

After Saul's death, David returned to Israel from Ziklag and reigned in Hebron over the tribe of Judah for seven and a half years. Afterwards the tribes of the Northern Kingdom came to Hebron to anoint David king over all Israel; this fulfilled the prophetic anointing of David by Samuel (1 Sam. 16:1-13). The parallel account of this event is found in 2 Samuel 5:1-5. Israel realized that David had been called by God to rule over them and that, even when Saul was king, it was David who was actively shepherding them. Those who have been divinely called to shepherd God's people will be compelled to do the work whether they have been formally recognized or not. Like the northern tribes, God's people usually recognize in time what God has put in place (Acts 20:28; 1 Tim. 3:1).

The City of David (1 Chron. 11:4-9)

With the divided tribes of Israel now united under one king, David recognized that the seat of government must be further north than Hebron, but not too far from Judah. With this in mind, David set his sights on capturing the stronghold at Zion (Jerusalem) in Benjamin's territory, which the Jebusites had occupied for centuries. Of the five high places on which the future city of Jerusalem would be built (Zion, Akra, Bezetha, Moriah, and Ophel), only Zion to the south was inhabited at this time. The Jebusites' fortification there was so impregnable that they taunted David by telling him that they could put blind and lame men on their battlements to keep him out (2 Sam. 5:6-16) and by saying, *"You shall not come in here!"* (1 Chron. 11:4-5).

Although the Jebusites did not believe that David could overcome them, he conquered their fortification and renamed it "the City of David" (1 Chron. 11:7). The historian then describes how David accomplished this. The king discovered that the underground shaft supplying water to the city was vulnerable to attack, so he put out a challenge to his men: *"Whoever climbs up by way of the water shaft and defeats the Jebusites ... he shall be chief and captain"* (1 Chron. 11:6; 2 Sam. 5:8).

Apparently, a small group of David's men (led by Joab) was able to navigate the water shaft, enter the city undetected, and open the gates to allow David's main force to enter the city. By this superb feat, carnal Joab earned the privilege of leading David's army.

After the victory, David moved from Hebron to the City of David. He began fortifying his new stronghold by leveling and filling in areas between the hills (Zion and Ophel) and then erecting retaining walls and embankments to protect the city especially from the Jebusites in the north (1 Chron. 11:8; 2 Sam. 5:9). Jamieson, Fausset, and Brown describe David's construction efforts:

> David built round about from [the] Millo and inward – probably a row of stone bastions placed on the northern side of Mount Zion, and built by David to secure himself on that side from the Jebusites, who still lived in the lower part of the city. The house of Millo was, perhaps, the principal corner-tower of that fortified wall. Such was the small beginning of Jerusalem.[6]

David had accomplished what no Jew had been able to do since Israel entered Canaan under Joshua's leadership. He had removed the Jebusites from Zion (Josh. 15:63)! The feat gained him much notoriety throughout Israel – everyone knew that *"the Lord God of hosts was with him"* (1 Chron. 11:9).

David's Mighty Men (1 Chron. 11:10-47)

Towards the end of his reign, David identified the men who had contributed most to his kingdom (2 Sam. 23:8-9). Chronicles contains almost an identical account, but varies slightly as the historian provides the names of those men who won David's gratitude earlier in his reign. Missing from the list is David's nephew Joab, who was over the king's army for much of his forty-year reign and was indeed a valiant warrior. Notwithstanding, his name is obviously missing because he killed Absalom and murdered both Abner and Amasa. Although David did not punish Joab, Solomon heeded his father's instructions and, after he succeeded his father and became king of Israel, put Joab to death (1 Kgs. 2:5-6, 28-34).

David divides the names of his faithful warriors into three classes. The three mightiest are listed first (Jashobeam, Eleazar, and Shammah), then the second class (Abishai and Benaiah), and then the third class, "the thirty," over which Asahel was chief.

The first three of David's mighty men are given special recognition above the others: Jashobeam, the son of a Hachmonite (also called Adino), slew three hundred (this number may be eight hundred, per the 2 Sam. 23 account) men at one time with a spear (1 Chron. 11:11). Eleazar, the Ahohite, continued slaying the Philistines in a barley field after his fellow soldiers retreated. When his comrades later returned to strip the slain of valuables, they found Eleazar still gripping his sword; apparently because of weariness his cramped muscles could not release it (1 Chron. 11:12-14). The parallel account in 2 Samuel 23 mentions the third of three mightiest men: Shammah, the Hararite, who stood alone in a field of lentils and slaughtered a great number of Philistines (2 Sam. 23:11-12).

The historian then relates the time when three of David's mighty men came to him while he was encamped in the cave of Adullam, preparing to engage the Philistines located in the Valley of Rephaim (1 Chron. 11:15-19). During the years of Israel's civil war, the Philistines were content to let the Jews kill each other, rather than giving them a reason to unify by attacking the Jewish state. However, after David became king over all the tribes, the Philistines moved quickly to attack David before he could get his government and army fully established. So the Philistines began searching for David's location (2 Sam. 5:17-25). After hearing this, David retreated to his stronghold at the cave of Adullam to seek guidance from the Lord.

The Philistines either had control of David's hometown of Bethlehem or were well-positioned between David and Bethlehem. The king casually expressed his longing for a drink of water from the well in Bethlehem (i.e., he did not intend anyone to take his request seriously). Three men did hear David and desired to please their king. Without conferring with their commander, and at great risk to themselves, they broke through enemy lines, drew water from the well in Bethlehem, and brought it to David.

The king was so overcome by this immense gesture of loyalty that he poured the water out on the ground as a sacrifice to the Lord – it cost too much to drink and thus it was deemed a worthy offering. Perhaps David also felt foolish for uttering thoughtless words of a self-indulgent nature that risked the lives of his highly esteemed men. In either case, David would not gratify himself knowing the peril that his soldiers had placed themselves in to retrieve the fresh water for their king.

David then names two more illustrious warriors (1 Chron. 11:20-25). Abishai, Joab's brother, was apparently the commander of the three men just mentioned. On one occasion, he lifted up his spear and slew three hundred opponents. Abishai was the one who, in holy zeal, wanted to slay both David's nemeses, Saul and Shimei, but was prevented from doing so by David. Benaiah, the son of Jehoiada, killed two lion-like warriors from Moab, slew a lion in a pit on a snowy day, and killed an Egyptian with his own spear (having only a staff). David appointed Benaiah over his guard. These two men were more honorable than those listed next, but yet did not attain to the outstanding status of the first three mentioned (1 Chron. 11:10-12).

The remaining "thirty" (or thirty-seven in 2 Samuel 23, or forty-seven in 1 Chron. 11) mighty men are then listed (1 Chron. 11:26-47). William MacDonald explains the numbering of the "thirty" in the final listing of David's mighty men:

> The number "thirty" may have been a technical term, like "the twelve" for the apostles, even if one or more were not always there. It could also be quite literal, but the extra men beyond thirty may have been replacements for those who died in battle, such as Uriah the Hittite, a valiant man in the list and Bathsheba's husband.[7]

Just as the expression "the twelve tribes of Israel" refers to the collective of all Jewish tribes (in actuality there were thirteen), the "thirty" represented David's elite soldiers (the actual number varied through David's reign).

David's "thirty" mighty men included: Asahel, Elhanan, Shammoth, Elika, Helez, Ira, Abiezer, Sibbechai, Ilai, Maharai, Heled, Ittai, Benaiah, Hurai, Abiel, Azmaveth, Eliahba, Jonathan, Ahiam, Eliphal, Hepher, Ahijah, Hezro, Naarai, Joel, Mibhar, Zelek, Naharai, Ira, Gareb, Uriah, Zabad, Adina, Hanan, Joshaphat, Uzzia, Shama, Jeiel, Jediael, Joha, Eliel, Jeribai, Joshaviah, Ithmah, Eliel, Oged, and Jaasiel. Some of David's mighty men, like Uriah the Hittite (1 Chron. 11:31), were not Jewish by birth. Some were even from Ammon and

Moab, but all were completely loyal to David nonetheless (1 Chron. 11:39, 46).

David's Army Grows (1 Chron. 12:1-22)

David first fled to Gath to escape Saul, but then departed Philistia altogether and took up residence in the cave of Adullam (1 Sam. 22:1). The cave of Adullam is located about twelve miles southwest of Bethlehem. After hearing that David was at Adullam, his brethren left Bethlehem to be with him (they probably feared Saul's tyranny also). They were not the only ones. Many who were in debt and oppressed by Saul also flocked to David. The cave was a shelter from oppression, separated from wickedness; hence, anyone willing to identify with the rejected king was welcome. David's ranks quickly swelled and he became captain over four hundred men (1 Sam. 22:2).

About five or six years after this David would again depart for Philistia to escape Saul. At that time, Achish, the king of Gath, gave David the town of Ziklag to live in. David had 600 soldiers with him at Ziklag (1 Chron. 12:1; 1 Sam. 27:2). Many of these men were archers and stone hurlers and could skillfully shoot arrows or sling stones with either hand (1 Chron. 12:2).

The chronologer then lists the names of those who were with David or soon joined him while in Philistia: from the tribe of Benjamin (even some of Saul's brethren; 1 Chron. 12:3-7), from the tribe of Gad (1 Chron. 12:8-15), then others from Benjamin and Judah (1 Chron. 12:16-18), and then, about the time David had agreed to fight with the Philistines against Saul, some from the tribe of Manasseh defected to David also (1 Chron. 12:19-21). We gain the sense that David's ranks rapidly enlarged while he was in Philistia waiting for Saul's death so that he could return to Israel and become king: *"For at that time they came to David day by day to help him, until it was a great army, like the army of God"* (1 Chron. 12:22).

David's Army at Hebron (1 Chron. 12:23-40)

Second Samuel 1 informs us that David learned of Saul's death three days after he and his men returned to Ziklag (after slaughtering the Amalekites). Though he was their archrival, David and his men grieved for Saul, and also for his sons and their countrymen killed in battle against the Philistines. With Saul removed from office, David inquired of the Lord if he should dwell in a city in Judah (2 Sam. 2:1-3). The Lord instructed David to return to Judah and to reside in Hebron. Hebron was about eighteen miles northeast of Ziklag and there would be many loyal to David residing in the vicinity. The thirty-year-old king then took his two wives, Ahinoam and Abigail, to Hebron and his men brought their families there also.

The elders of Judah afterwards anointed David as their king (2 Sam. 2:4). To emphasize David's growing strength and the diminishing of Saul's house, the historian notes how David's army continued to grow during the seven and a half years he ruled from Hebron. The final two years of this period were marked by Civil War which ended with the death of Saul's last remaining son, Ishbosheth. Afterwards, the northern tribes anointed David as king (2 Sam. 5:1-3) and ranks of soldiers from all the tribes joined David's army. Remarkably, the greatest influx of soldiers came from the two and a half tribes settled in the Transjordan and not from Judah, Simeon, and Benjamin who had previously been more sympathetic to David's cause.

The writer then provides this synopsis:

> *All these men of war, who could keep ranks, came to Hebron with a loyal heart, to make David king over all Israel; and all the rest of Israel were of one mind to make David king. And they were there with David three days, eating and drinking, for their brethren had prepared for them. Moreover those who were near to them, from as far away as Issachar and Zebulun and Naphtali, were bringing food on donkeys and camels, on mules and oxen -- provisions of flour and cakes of figs and cakes of raisins, wine and oil and oxen and sheep abundantly, for there was joy in Israel* (1 Chron. 12:38-40).

This is a lovely scene – all Israel is gathered around their divinely appointed king who is consumed with zeal for God. There was much rejoicing, feasting, and merrymaking, for the dark days of a self-honoring, disobedient king were past. Israel would now benefit from a godly shepherd-king who loved the Lord with all his heart and also knew how to care for His sheep!

Meditation

In the secret of His presence how my soul delights to hide!
Oh, how precious are the lessons which I learn at Jesus' side!
Earthly cares can never vex me, neither trials lay me low;
For when Satan comes to tempt me, to the secret place I go.
When my soul is faint and thirsty, beneath the shadow of His wing,
There is cool and pleasant shelter, and a fresh and crystal spring.

— Ellen Gorch

David's Reign and the Ark

1 Chronicles 13-14

The thematic development of the Old Testament rests on two prophecies uttered by Moses on the eve of Israel entering into the Promised Land. The first pertains to the place that God would choose to place His name (Deut. 12:5), and the second to the king that God would choose to represent Him there (Deut. 17:14-15). After the Church Age, Israel's Messiah, God's chosen king, will completely fulfill the Abrahamic covenant at this specific location (Gen. 12:1-3). The place Jehovah chose was Mount Zion in Jerusalem (Ps. 78:68, 87:2) and the king He selected was David (Ps. 78:70), from whose kingly line would come the Lord Jesus Christ. Both prophetic components, which are so needful for Israel's survival and blessing, now converge in the text before us!

David Seeks to Bring the Ark to Jerusalem (1 Chron. 13:1-8)

What David does next indicates to us what was most on his heart – not his kingdom, but God's throne; he wanted to bring the Ark to Zion and assemble Israel before the Lord. Other than a passing reference in 1 Samuel 14, the Ark of the Lord has not been mentioned since it was brought to Abinadab's home about seventy years earlier. David selected thirty thousand choice men throughout Israel to accompany him to "Baale Judah" to bring the Ark of *"the Lord of Hosts, who dwells between the cherubim"* back to the City of David (1 Chron. 13:1-5; 2 Sam. 6:1-2). Baale Judah was situated on a hill about ten miles west of the City of David; the city is also known as Kirjath-Baal (Josh. 15:60) and Kirjath-Jearim (1 Chron. 13:6; 1 Sam. 6:21).

The Ark was carried out of Abinadab's home and placed on a new cart (1 Chron. 13:7). Despite the emotional ferver of this occasion, this is our first indication that trouble was ahead. David should have known God's thoughts concerning transporting His Ark and have followed them. Instead, he permits those serving God to adopt the ways of the world in the matter (i.e., to repeat the method the Philistines used to return the Ark to Israel years earlier). The Philistines were not judged for their actions because they were not Jehovah's covenant people and did not know better – but Israel had no excuse. Whenever God's people tread a religious path previously blazed by worldlings, they will always do damage to their own souls.

Jehovah had previously commanded that the Ark be moved by staves and be carried by the Kohathites:

> *And when Aaron and his sons have finished covering the sanctuary and all the furnishings of the sanctuary, when the camp is set to go, then the sons of Kohath shall come to carry them; but they shall not touch any holy thing, lest they die. These are the things in the tabernacle of meeting which the sons of Kohath are to carry* (Num. 4:15).

Two sons of Abinadab, Uzza (Uzzah) and Ahio, were guiding the cart (Uzzah was on the cart and Ahio was leading the oxen; 2 Sam. 6:4). Accompanying the Ark was joyful musical procession; David and the people were playing various stringed instruments and percussion pieces (1 Chron. 13:8; 2 Sam. 6:5). When the cart came to Chidon's (Nachon's) threshing floor, the oxen stumbled, and Uzzah put out his hand to steady the Ark (1 Chron. 13:9).

Recall that the Ark had been carried from Mount Sinai to Canaan – an arduous thirty-nine-year journey – on the shoulders of the Levites and not once does Scripture record that they stumbled. Even though we may not understand why God demands what He does, or we may think there is a better way to do what He commands, it will always be best for us to obey what He says to do. Sometimes things are right only because God says they are and we must rest in His wisdom in such matters. The Lord will enable us to do what He wants us to do and will impede everything else. The Ark should have been carried by holy Levites, not transported on a cart pulled by beasts.

Uzzah apparently felt the Ark needed to be safeguarded, as if God were not sufficient to protect what was His. But his casual act of touching what was most holy to God only underscored the fact that Israel was dishonoring the Lord by what they were doing. Uzzah's act aroused the Lord's anger and he was immediately struck dead (1 Chron. 13:10).

Had Uzzah acted with sincere intentions? We are not told; perhaps the Lord saw something in his heart that was offensive and judged it accordingly. For instance, Uzzah may have been showing off his bold familiarity with the Ark to impress the crowd. Regardless of what prompted God's instant wrath against Uzzah, the matter greatly displeased David who genuinely desired to revere God by bringing His Ark to Jerusalem (1 Chron. 13:11). But the king's error was not his zeal, rather his lack of awe for God's sacred things for which He is quite jealous.

David then called the place of judgment *Perez Uzzah*, meaning "outburst against Uzzah." The king said, *"How can the ark of the Lord come to me?"* (1 Chron. 13:12). David was elated about reestablishing proper worship of Jehovah at His central sanctuary. He did not understand why God had acted against him and feared that moving the Ark any further might cost more lives. Sadly, David was doing what the Lord wanted, but in the wrong way. Then he ceased to do what he was supposed to do because God objected to the way he was doing it.

There is a valuable lesson for us to glean from David's response: the believer should discern both the *what* and the *how* in serving the Lord. What is done must be in obedience to Him, and how it is done must reflect His character. The Corinthians learned this painful lesson in observing the Lord's Supper. The local church was obeying the Lord's command to break bread in remembrance of Him, but the believers changed the meeting into something that it was not supposed to be – a drunken and gluttonous love feast (1 Cor. 11:20-34). H. L. Rossier notes that the Corinthian believers were judged accordingly.

> What happened to David here also happened to the Corinthians who had introduced a carnal element at the Lord's table. God could not tolerate such a thing. "On this account many among you are weak and infirm, and a good many are fallen asleep" (1 Cor. 11:30). God was a consuming fire for them, as well as for Uzzah, and we must remember this. David was forced to understand this. The Lord had made a breach *before him against the Philistines* at Baal-perazim; now God's judgment makes a breach *against him*. "He called that place Perez-uzzah [breach of Uzzah]" (1 Chron. 13:11).[8]

Believers should never adopt "the end justifies the means" mentality in the Lord's work or in the worship of the Lord. It is God who sanctifies the means, or the end means nothing. Just as the Levites were to labor to bear up the Ark, Christians are to labor to bear up the name of Christ. There is no easy or secular way of accomplishing this; rather, God's way leads believers into suffering (2 Tim. 3:12) and then into glory (Rom. 8:18).

David later realized his mistake and discerned how the Ark should be properly moved (1 Chron. 15:13). His error reminds us that true worshipers of God must labor in His Word to understand what God has revealed about Himself and how He wants to be revered. The value of our worship relates directly to how we commune with God "in spirit and in truth" (John 4:23-24). Only as the Holy Spirit leads believers in worship that is founded in truth can we offer anything to God that He will appreciate. Expressions of adoration towards God have value only if they affirm what He has already approved. Pious acts with good intentions may look good to others, but if what we do affronts God's character or word, we invite His chastening hand, not His pleasure. This is what David learned from this sorrowful experience – he would wait on the Lord and then only do what had His approval.

The festive procession dispersed and instead of bringing the Ark to the City of David, it was taken into the house of Obed-Edom the Gittite (1 Chron. 13:13). Obed-Edom was a Levite of the family of Merari (1 Chron. 15:18-24; 16:38). It is not likely that the Ark traveled too far from Abinadab's home. The writer tells us that his house was on a hill, meaning that a steep slope may have contributed to the oxen stumbling. The Ark of the Lord remained in his house for three months and the Lord blessed him and his household during that time (1 Chron. 13:14).

David's Prosperity and Posterity Grow in Jerusalem (1 Chron. 14:1-7)

Seeing David's military aptitude, Hiram, the king of Tyre, desired to secure peace with David. His good intentions were demonstrated by supplying cedar trees, carpenters, and masons for the construction of David's new city (1 Chron. 14:1). The long years of Philistine oppression had left Israel in short supply of craftsmen and masons, so Hiram's assistance was greatly appreciated. God would supply everything that David needed to establish his kingdom and David was excited to see the Lord honor His promise to him. The new king realized that his position was not for his own honor, but rather he had been divinely selected for Israel's good (1 Chron. 14:2).

Unfortunately, David took more concubines and wives after moving to Jerusalem from Hebron. More wives also meant more sons and daughters, so the writer paused to list the names of some of the males born to David in Jerusalem: Shammua, Shobab, Nathan, Solomon, Ibhar, Elishua, Elpelet, Nogah, Nepheg, Japhia, Elishama, Beeliada, and Eliphelet (1 Chron. 14:3-6).

Notice that the first four sons in this list were born of Bathsheba (Uriah's wife whom David stole by instigating Uriah's death). Although her first son was judged because of their adultery, two of David and Bathsheba's sons are mentioned in the New Testament in the genealogies of Christ: Luke shows that Mary was a descendant of Nathan (Luke 3:31) and Matthew records that Joseph was a descendant of Solomon (Matt. 1:6). Through sovereign design, the Lord clearly shows that He can extend mercy despite the worst human failures and bring about incredible blessing.

The Philistines Defeated (1 Chron. 14:8-17)

During the years of Israel's civil war the Philistines were content to let the Jews kill each other, rather than giving them a reason to unify by attacking the Jewish state. However, after David became king of all the tribes, the Philistines moved quickly to attack David before he could get his government and army fully established. The Philistines began searching for David's location (1 Chron. 14:8). After hearing this news, David retreated to his stronghold at the cave of Adullam (1 Chron. 11:15) and inquired of the Lord if he should engage the Philistines who had gathered against him in the Valley of Rephaim west of Jerusalem (1 Chron. 14:9-10).

It is at this time that three of David's mighty men broke through the enemy lines to fetch water for David from the well of Bethlehem (1 Chron. 11:16-19). They had overheard David express his desire for a drink of that refreshing water: *"Oh, that someone would give me a drink of water from the well of Bethlehem, which is by the gate!"* Because these men had jeopardized their lives to bring him the water, David could not drink it, but poured it out on the ground to the Lord.

The Lord answered David's request and instructed him to fight the Philistines, for He would ensure his victory (1 Chron. 14:10). After learning that the Lord would be fighting his enemy for him, David engaged the Philistines at Baal Perazim and was triumphant (1 Chron. 14:11). David was quick to give the Lord the credit for the achievement: *"God has broken through my enemies by my hand like a breakthrough of water"* (1 Chron. 14:12). The suddenness of Israel's attack caught the Philistines off guard, which meant that they had no time to collect their images. Adam Clarke writes:

> It was the custom of most nations to carry their gods with them to battle: In imitation of this custom the Israelites once took the ark and lost it in the field (1 Sam. 4).[9]

David's men collected the abandoned images and destroyed them by fire (1 Chron. 14:12; Deut. 7:5, 25). The victory then was not just over the Philistines, but also over their gods. For that reason, David named the place "Baal Perazim," meaning Baal is broken.

After their first defeat, the Philistines deployed a second time in the Valley of Rephaim (1 Chron. 14:13). Again, David inquired of the Lord as to what he should do. The Lord answered David's inquiry:

> *You shall not go up after them; circle around them, and come upon them in front of the mulberry trees. And it shall be, when you hear a sound of marching in the tops of the mulberry trees, then you shall go out to battle, for God has gone out before you to strike the camp of the Philistines* (1 Chron. 14:14-15).

The mulberry trees may have actually been aspen, poplar, or balsam trees, which rustle with the slightest movement and line many of the ravines of southern Palestine. Apparently, the Philistines expected David's attack to be a frontal assault from the south, but God directed him to place his troops on the northern side of the valley. As the Philistines marched by the edge of the tree groves, God would cause a sound to be heard that they would mistake as an army marching against them from the south. For them it was an army they could not see, but for David, it was God marching against the Philistines and his signal to attack his enemy's flank and rear guard.

The sound of marching ahead and David's sudden assault from behind caused the Philistines to panic and David routed them. Because David did exactly what the Lord commanded him to do, the Philistines from Geba (Gibeon) were driven back to Gezer (1 Chron. 14:16). The Philistines were now completely removed from the Judean highlands (1 Chron. 14:17). The Lord was with Israel's king, and when the Lord fights for His people, no power on earth or in heavenly places can oppose them!

Meditation

Who is on the Lord's side? Who will serve the King?
Who will be His helpers, other lives to bring?
Who will leave the world's side? Who will face the foe?
Who is on the Lord's side? Who for Him will go?

Fierce may be the conflict, strong may be the foe,
But the King's own army none can overthrow.
Round His standard ranging victory is secure,
For His truth unchanging makes the triumph sure.

— Frances Ridley Havergal

The Ark Comes to Jerusalem

1 Chronicles 15-16

David Brings the Ark to Jerusalem (1 Chron. 15:1-29)

David was informed that the Lord had blessed Obed-Edom because the Ark resided in his home (2 Sam. 6:12). This showed David that the Lord appreciated Obed-Edom's care of the Ark and that God did not oppose its relocation. So David built a house for himself in the City of David and also *"prepared a place for the ark of God, and pitched a tent for it"* (1 Chron. 15:1). Realizing his earlier mistake, David declared, *"No one may carry the ark of God but the Levites, for the Lord has chosen them to carry the ark of God and to minister before Him forever"* (1 Chron. 15:2). When all was ready, the king again gathered the Jewish nation together to bring the Ark of the Lord to the place that had been prepared for it (1 Chron. 15:3).

David led the nation to fetch the Ark, but this time the Ark was appropriately carried by the Levites. David summoned the chief priests Zadok and Abiathar and all the heads of Levitical households to be present to oversee the carrying of the Ark and related sacrifices. Four family heads from the Kohathites (Uriel, Shemaiah, Eliel, and Amminadab), one leader from the Merarites (Asaiah), and one of the Gershomites (Joel) were assembled to oversee 862 assistants from their related clans (1 Chron. 15:4-10).

David then spoke with the six Levitical clan leaders and the two high priests (1 Chron. 15:11):

> *You are the heads of the fathers' houses of the Levites; sanctify yourselves, you and your brethren, that you may bring up the ark of the Lord God of Israel to the place I have prepared for it. For because you did not do it the first time, the Lord our God broke out against us, because we did not consult Him about the proper order"* (1 Chron. 15:12-13).

The priests and the Levites sanctified themselves and the Levites bore the Ark of God on their shoulders, by its poles, as commanded by the Lord through Moses (1 Chron. 15:14-15).

The location of Obed-Edom's home is not stated, but the initial journey from Kirjath-Jearim would have been less than ten miles from the City of David (1 Chron. 15:25). The priests were presenting burnt offerings of oxen and fattened sheep about every six paces along the route the Ark traveled (2 Sam. 6:13). Exactly what distance this represents is unknown. It is ironic that on their first attempt, they had a new cart (picturing their disobedience), but no sacrifices (i.e., they did not worship), but on their second attempt, they had no cart (they were obedient) and offered many sacrifices to the Lord. As we will see, the difference between failure and success was the people's genuine adoration for God forged in obedience – the same is true today!

The Ark proceeded to Jerusalem with great fanfare and celebration. David also instructed the Levitical leaders Heman, Asaph, and Ethan to appoint musicians to join the great procession and direct their playing and singing (1 Chron. 15:16-22). David appointed four men to go before and behind the Ark to protect it. Apparently seven trumpeters were between these guards (1 Chron. 15:23-24). There were likely two guards in front of the Levites shouldering the Ark and two behind them. No one was to touch the Ark or interfere with the proper order of its journey!

Not only did the priests present many burnt offerings of bulls and rams on makeshift altars as the Ark journeyed along, but the king leading the massive procession was busy honoring the Lord also (1 Chron. 15:26-27): *"David danced before the Lord with all his might; and David was wearing a linen ephod"* (2 Sam. 6:14). The people were ecstatic over the sight; all Israel shouted and the trumpets blasted their blissful approval (1 Chron. 15:28). The psalmist tells us that it is most appropriate for God's people to be cheerful in spirit and joyful in praise before Him:

> *Let Israel rejoice in their Maker;*
> *Let the children of Zion be joyful in their King.*
> *Let them praise His name with the dance;*
> *Let them sing praises to Him with the timbrel and harp.*
> *For the Lord takes pleasure in His people;*
> *He will beautify the humble with salvation* (Ps. 149:2-4).

But not everyone was happy in the Lord that day. Michal had not joined the festive entourage and when she saw David (without his royal attire) leaping and whirling before the Ark as it entered the City of David, she despised him (1 Chron. 15:28).

The Ark Is Placed in the Tabernacle (1 Chron. 16:1-6)

The Ark was set in the tabernacle that David had erected, accompanied by burnt and peace offerings. The Ark alone resided in this tabernacle, as the other furnishings were with the original tabernacle located at Gibeon. David blessed the people and each person received a loaf of bread, a piece of meat, and a cake of raisins (1 Chron. 16:1-3).

Asaph was David's choirmaster at the tabernacle to ensure that proper prayer and praise in association with musical accompaniment was offered to the Lord; the high priest Abiathar labored with Asaph at the site of David's new tabernacle in Jerusalem (1 Chron. 16:4-6).

David's Song of Thanksgiving (1 Chron. 16:7-36)

On the day that the Ark was placed in the new tabernacle in Jerusalem, David delivered a psalm of thanksgiving (1 Chron. 16:8-36) to Asaph and his brethren (1 Chron. 16:7). This hymn of thanksgiving is actually a compilation of several Psalms (1 Chron. 16:8-22 relates to Ps. 105:1-15; 1 Chron. 16:23-33 to Ps. 96:1-13; and 1 Chron. 16:34-36 to Ps. 106:1, 47-48).

Psalm 105 (1 Chron. 16:8-22) commences with a series of exhortations to his fellow countrymen: give thanks to the Lord and call on His name, sing praises to Him and talk of His awe-inspiring works, glory in His name, seek the Lord, and do not forget His faithfulness (1 Chron. 16:8-12). It was appropriate for Israel to remember and praise the Lord, because the Lord had remembered them. Because of His unconditional covenant with Abraham, which was also confirmed with Isaac and then Jacob, Jehovah brought their descendants from Egypt into the Promised Land (1 Chron. 16:13-18). Psalm 105:12-41 then retraces several historical events from the call of Abraham to the wilderness experience of his descendants in order to thank God for His faithfulness to the Jewish nation. However, this song simply acknowledges God's dependability to safeguard and provide for His covenant people (1 Chron. 16:19-22).

In Psalm 96 (1 Chron. 16:23-33) the poet urges those who had experienced God's salvation to *"sing unto the Lord"* not by singing songs of dead rote, but new songs which reflect the soul's joy and enthusiasm over receiving fresh mercies from the Lord day after day (1 Chron. 16:23). Those who have experienced God's salvation have the privilege of declaring His glory and His marvelous doings to the nations, so that they might revere and praise Him also (1 Chron. 16:24). He is their Creator and the One who is above all false gods (1 Chron. 16:25-26). The aura of God's presence saturated His temple with honor, majesty, strength, and beauty (1 Chron. 16:27).

Such a great God should certainly be sought out by His people in the beauty of holiness (i.e., with sins confessed and cleansed) and He should receive from them offerings of praise and gifts befitting of His glory (1 Chron. 16:28-29). In fact, everyone should praise the One who reigns over the world, who will judge in righteousness all peoples and nations (1 Chron. 16:30). Furthermore, all creation should honor the Lord and praise His holy name (1 Chron. 16:31-32). First Chronicles 16:33 previews the Second Advent of Christ to the earth when this will occur and the lament of the redeemed will abruptly cease, for the Lord shall rule in righteousness and peace over all nations, the curses on the earth shall be lifted (Gen. 3:17-19; Rom. 8:20-22), and the whole earth will be full of His glory (Isa. 2:2, 62:1-7)!

As on this notable day, it is a great privilege for the redeemed to sing praises to the Lord day after day in the Church Age also. To do so powerfully reflects the believer's salvation (i.e., it demonstrates the Lord resides within him or her) to a lost world that desperately needs to see Christ. The redeemed must sing, must come before the Lord with appropriate gifts (1 Cor. 16:2; Heb. 13:15-16), and worship Him in the beauty of holiness (1 Cor. 11:27-32)!

David's song of thanksgiving concludes with excerpts from Psalm 106 (1 Chron. 16:34-36). Before his overview of Israel's long, rebellious history, the anonymous psalmist acknowledges two fundamental truths: first, *"give thanks to the Lord, for He is good! For His mercy endures forever"* (Ps. 106:1); second, *"blessed are those who keep justice, and he who does righteousness at all times* (Ps. 106:3)! These two ideas express the theme of the psalm, but David mainly focused on the first principle (1 Chron. 16:34) until the closing of the psalm. Then he pleaded for Israel's complete deliverance from Gentile oppression as promised in the Abrahamic covenant and offered a doxology (1 Chron. 16:35-36): *"Blessed be the Lord God of Israel from everlasting to everlasting! Amen and Amen."* And all the people added their "Amens" also!

Regular Worship Established (1 Chron. 16:37-43)

Asaph and his brothers regularly served with the High Priest Abiathar before the Ark of the Covenant in Jerusalem (1 Chron. 16:37). Obed-Edom with his sixty-eight brethren, including Obed-Edom the son of Jeduthun, and Hosah were gatekeepers there also (1 Chron. 16:38). We learn in 1 Chronicles 16:39 that the previous tabernacle of Moses (with the holy articles, but not the Ark) somehow found its way from Shiloh to a high place in Gibeon. The high priest Zadok labored with Levitical musicians Heman and Jeduthun (Ethan) at Gibeon (1 Chron. 16:40-42).

Apparently, this dual tabernacle situation was tolerated for several years, for King Solomon offered sacrifices at Gibeon years later with God's approval (1 Chron. 21:29). Obviously, the City of David (Jerusalem) was to be Israel's capital and the only proper place for Israel to worship Jehovah, but there was a transitional period for this to be completely realized. All was solidified in Jerusalem after Solomon's construction of Jehovah's temple.

The chapter concludes with David returning to his house after he had blessed the people and sent them home (1 Chron. 16:43). We learn in 2 Samuel 6:21-23 that Michal was waiting to censure David, but instead David rebukes Michal, and announces that she would remain barren the remainder of her life (probably meaning that David would not have marital relations with her again).

David considered himself nothing (2 Sam. 6:21-22); he was vile in God's sight and would gladly debase himself further to ensure he remained self-effacing before the Lord. Therefore, the king had gladly put off his royal apparel (outer garments) to dance before the Ark as it was being carried into Jerusalem. David's behavior was appropriate, for *"no flesh should glory in His presence"* (1 Cor. 1:29-30) and *"the Lord lifts up the humble; He casts the wicked down to the ground"* (Ps. 147:6). The king understood that he must remain low before the Lord to rule over His people with His approval and blessing.

Concerning Michal's charge of indecency against David, the nation saw David without his kingly attire and wearing a linen ephod. This was an unusual sight, but David only set aside his royal glory, not his moral integrity. The king told Michal that his behavior was prompted by joy in the Lord, that there was nothing perverse about his actions. David did not think anything which contributed to the glory of God was too much for him to do.

Meditation

> *Give to the Lord the glory due His name; bring an offering, and come before Him. Oh, worship the Lord in the beauty of holiness* (1 Chron. 16:29)!

Davidic Covenant and His Kingdom

1 Chronicles 17-18

God's Covenant with David (1 Chron. 17:1-14)

The events of this chapter occur a few years after David brought the Ark to Jerusalem and put it in a new tabernacle. By God's hand, David enjoyed rest from all his enemies and was living in the fine house that he had constructed in the City of David. David, who had been forced into a nomadic life for eight years while fleeing Saul's wrath was enjoying his new residence. However, as he contemplated the matter, he did not feel it was appropriate that he should have such a fine home while the Ark was residing in a mere tent.

The king notified the prophet Nathan of his intentions to build God a permanent house among His people, saying, *"See now, I dwell in a house of cedar, but the ark of the covenant of the Lord is under tent curtains"* (1 Chron. 17:1). David wanted the Lord to have a permanent structure, not just a cloth tent to reside in. This sounded good to the prophet Nathan who told David, *"Do all that is in your heart, for God is with you"* (1 Chron. 17:2). However, though Nathan was close to the Lord's thoughts, he did not have perfect discernment concerning God's plans for His temple. Therefore, God gave a word to Nathan that very night to correct his statement to David. Nathan then delivered God's message to David the next day:

> *You shall not build Me a house to dwell in. For I have not dwelt in a house since the time that I brought up Israel, even to this day, but have gone from tent to tent, and from one tabernacle to another. Wherever I have moved about with all Israel, have I ever spoken a word to any of the judges of Israel, whom I commanded to shepherd My people, saying, "Why have you not built Me a house of cedar?" Now therefore, thus shall you say to My servant David, "Thus says the Lord of hosts: 'I took you from the sheepfold, from following the sheep, to be ruler over My people Israel. And I have been with you wherever you have gone, and have cut off all your enemies from*

> *before you, and have made you a name like the name of the great men who are on the earth. Moreover I will appoint a place for My people Israel, and will plant them, that they may dwell in a place of their own and move no more; nor shall the sons of wickedness oppress them anymore, as previously, since the time that I commanded judges to be over My people Israel. Also I will subdue all your enemies. Furthermore I tell you that the Lord will build you a house. And it shall be, when your days are fulfilled, when you must go to be with your fathers, that I will set up your seed after you, who will be of your sons; and I will establish his kingdom. He shall build Me a house, and I will establish his throne forever. I will be his Father, and he shall be My son; and I will not take My mercy away from him, as I took it from him who was before you. And I will establish him in My house and in My kingdom forever; and his throne shall be established forever'"* (1 Chron. 17:4-14).

First, the Lord reminded David that He had dwelt in a tabernacle among His people since the time of the Egyptian Exodus. He had been a traveling God going "from tent to tent." Moses erected a temporary tabernacle for the Lord (Ex. 33:7-11) while a more elaborate tabernacle and furnishings were being fabricated at Mount Sinai (Ex. 40:17). This tent was put up and taken down dozens of times as the Lord journeyed through the wilderness with His wayward people for nearly thirty-nine years. After the Israelites arrived in Canaan, the tabernacle mainly resided at Shiloh, but was moved to Nob and Gibeah also.

The entire message is a lovely reflection of God's grace – He came down from heaven to "walk" alongside His people as they wandered through the wilderness to Canaan. During those years, it was necessary that God's holy things be in a portable tent, but now that the Jews were settled in the land, the time had come for them to construct a permanent temple for Him (1 Chron. 17:5-10).

Second, God promised that David would have a son (Solomon) who would build His temple. David would not be permitted to because he had shed too much blood (1 Chron. 17:11-13). If his son sinned, God promised to chasten him, but with tempered mercy so that David's dynasty would continue. David's life work had been characterized by fighting, not building. Yet, until King Saul, the man of flesh, was removed and Israel's surrounding enemies had been subdued, no temple foundation could have been laid.

David's life ministry was to clear the way for the temple's construction, which would be completed by his son Solomon. In grace, the Lord had taken David out of the obscurity of a sheepfold and raised him up to rule over His people, thus paving the way for his son to build a lasting testimony of Jehovah's presence in Israel, that all nations would note.

Third, God promised David that a new and everlasting dynasty would be established and that one of his descendants (the Messiah) would sit on his throne forever (1 Chron. 17:14). As Psalm 89 confirms, God's covenant with David created a special father/son-like relationship between them, with God vowing to bless and protect David and to make him victorious before his enemies. Although at times God would chasten His covenant people for their rebellion, He would not forget His promise to David of an everlasting dynasty!

David's Praise to God (1 Chron. 17:15-27)

God had revealed to David, not only His great plans for David and Israel, but also how He would honor and exalt Christ. After hearing the marvelous details of God's covenant with him, David was beside himself. He went to the tabernacle and in utter amazement and self-effacement sat before the Lord. In the stillness of the quiet and solitary place, David, overwhelmed by God goodness, was prompted to praise and worship Him:

> *Who am I, O Lord God? And what is my house, that You have brought me this far?And yet this was a small thing in Your sight, O God; and You have also spoken of Your servant's house for a great while to come, and have regarded me according to the rank of a man of high degree, O Lord God. What more can David say to You for the honor of Your servant? For You know Your servant* (1 Chron. 17:16-18).

The scene is a wonderful picture of unhindered communion with God – David sharing his deepest thoughts of appreciation and admiration while sitting before the Lord in complete freedom and confidence. David is contrite before God; he has no thoughts of himself, but rather rejoices in what God is determined to accomplish for him and for Israel. C. H. Mackintosh reminds us that when we lose sight of ourselves before the Lord, our souls are liberated to pour out holy adoration for God and appreciation for His ways:

> This is true worship, and is the very reverse of human religiousness. The former is the acknowledgement of God by the energy of faith; the latter is the setting up of man in the spirit of legalism. No doubt, David would have appeared, to many, a more devoted man when seeking to build a house for the Lord than when sitting in His presence. In the one case, he was trying to do something; in the other, he was apparently doing nothing. It is like the two sisters at Bethany, of whom one would seem, in the judgment of nature, to have been doing all the work, and the other to have been sitting idle. How different are God's thoughts! David sitting before the Lord was in a right position, rather than seeking to build.[10]

David pondered why God had selected him for such honor, a mere shepherd boy, the youngest of his brethren, and from an unknown family in a remote town in Israel. The king also pondered God's many mercies that had taken him from obscurity to the throne. David had survived numerous battles with multiple enemies and diverse hostilities from within Israel to be God's chosen victor.

Overwhelmed by his contemplations, the king affirmed why he was still alive and had been so richly blessed: "*O Lord, for Your servant's sake, and according to Your own heart, You have done all this greatness, in making known all these great things. O Lord, there is none like You, nor is there any God besides You, according to all that we have heard with our ears*" (1 Chron. 17:19-20). All that had happened to David was under his great God's control, to bring Himself glory and to honor His covenant with Abraham – to cling to and bless a nation of his lineage (1 Chron. 17:21-22). God had redeemed a people out of Egypt that would forever be His!

First Chronicles 17 can be summarized by the character of three houses. First, there was David's house that he had built in Jerusalem where he resided with his family (1 Chron. 17:1). Second, there was the Lord's house that was to be built in Jerusalem (1 Chron. 17:4-12). Third, there was the spiritual house of David that was in progress, and would culminate with the coming of Christ, David's descendant (1 Chron. 17:16-27).

David expresses his full agreement with God's plan to build up his house and then asks the Lord to fulfill His word so that His name will be magnified forever: *"The Lord of hosts, the God of Israel, is Israel's God"* (1 Chron. 17:23-27). John Heading observes that "the whole of David's utterance in this chapter can be seen to embrace humiliation (1 Chron. 17:16-18), recollection (1 Chron. 17:19-22), and petitions (1 Chron. 17:23-27).[11] Of course, humble petitions that acknowledge God's past faithfulness and hope in His promises that His name might be glorified are of the highest quality. David enjoyed full communion with the Lord and counted it a great joy to pray in this manner.

In the Church Age, believers also have the opportunity to enjoy unhindered communion with God and to humbly request, in the name of the Lord Jesus Christ, that God will honor Himself by answering our prayers (John 15:16, 16:23-24). May we, like David, rejoice in the amazing providential goodness of God, who has determined to enrich His people for the honor and glory of His name!

David's Kingdom Expands (1 Chron. 18:1-13)

The writer details David's further conquests to solidify his kingdom and the various individuals he appointed to give order to it. David left the holy repose of the Lord's presence to fight His battles with heightened zeal. He now understood that he was to clear a way so that another afterwards could lay the foundation of the Lord's house. First Chronicles 18 to 20 record David's preparatory work to this end. The man of war was to clear the land of enemies, so that his son, enjoying the peace his father had secured, could erect a testimony to Jehovah among the nations. The warring of David's reign would secure the wonderful blessing of Solomon's majestic rule. Solomon's reign would be the apex of Israel's glory until Israel's Messiah returned to achieve so much more!

In God's providential purposes, He called David to be a fighter and Solomon to be a builder – both are essential in the triumphal work of God and therefore represent both advents of Christ. C. H. Mackintosh affirms this typological understanding and reminds us that the Church's hope of glory is also in Christ alone:

> At the cross we behold the stroke of justice falling upon the spotless Victim, and then the Holy Ghost came down to gather men around the person of Him who was raised from the dead, just as David began to gather the hewed stones, and the materials for the joinings of the house, the moment the place of the foundation was settled. The

> Church is the temple of the living God, of which Christ is the chief corner stone. The materials for this building were all provided, and the place of its foundation purchased, in the season of Christ's trouble; for David represents Christ in His sufferings, as Solomon represents Him in His glory. David was the man of war; Solomon represents Him in His glory. David was the man of war; Solomon, the man of rest. David had to grapple with enemies; Solomon was able to say, *"There is neither adversary nor evil occurrence"* (1 Kgs. 5:4). Thus do these two kings shadow forth Him who, by His cross and passion, made ample provision for the building of the temple which shall be manifested in divine order and perfectness in the day of His coming glory.[12]

Having secured the loyalty of his countrymen throughout Israel, David begins purging the pagan inhabitants remaining in Israel and reclaiming lost territory. He begins by conquering the Philistines (1 Chron. 18:1). David took control of the Philistine city Metheg Ammah (i.e., Gath). The city in which, as a younger man, he had become fearful and played the madman to preserve his life was now his! Metheg Ammah means the "bridle of the capital" – David now held the key to power in the region.

The Philistines dwelt directly west of the Judean foothills in Philistia and had been Israel's enemies since Joshua led the Israelites into Canaan (Judg. 3:1-4). During the era of the Judges, the Philistines had repeatedly attempted to expand their dominion by invading Jewish territory. The conflict raged back and forth for hundreds of years until David finally subdued Philistia, a necessity before the temple could be constructed.

Next, David defeated the Moabites, the people of his great-grandmother Ruth. The king commanded that two of every three prisoners be put to death; surviving Moabites then became David's servants and paid him tribute (1 Chron. 18:2).

David then set his sights on the loosely joined Syrian (Aramean) city-states to the north. Israel first attacked Zobah north of Damascus because their king Hadadezer and much of his army were engaged in a campaign to recover territory near the River Euphrates (1 Chron. 18:3). David took one thousand chariots, seven hundred horsemen, and twenty thousand foot soldiers from Hadadezer, and hamstrung all but one hundred chariot horses (1 Chron. 18:4). In song, David alludes to why he did not preserve the bulk of warhorses: *"Some trust in chariots, and some in horses; but we will remember the name of the Lord our God"* (Ps. 20:7). While Gentile armies prized their war-chariots and cavalry, by hamstringing the captured horses David demonstrated that his strength for conquering was solely in the Lord.

The Syrians from Damascus moved to cut off David and his men before they could return to Jerusalem with their spoils of war. This proved to be a serious tactical mistake, for 22,000 Syrians were slain by Israel's army (1 Chron. 18:5). This gave David control of two chief cities in the north, Zobah and Damascus. He placed a Jewish garrison in Damascus (likely in Zobah also) and these vassal state-cities served David and paid him tribute (1 Chron. 18:6).

Why was David so successful in opposing larger and better armed forces? The reason was *"the Lord preserved David wherever he went."* David confiscated Hadadezer's shields of gold and much bronze and brought these metals to Jerusalem – the king was stockpiling construction materials for the temple (1 Chron. 18:7-8). Solomon would use this bronze to fabricate the "the bronze Sea," the Bronze Altar, and the two main pillars at the entrance of the temple.

After Toi, the king of Hamath, heard that David had defeated Hadadezer (his enemy also), he sent his son Joram to congratulate David and to provide him with articles of gold, silver, and bronze (1 Chron. 18:9-10; 2 Sam. 8:9-10). All that David received or confiscated from Moab, Ammon, Philistia, the Syrian cities, and the Amalekites was dedicated to the Lord (1 Chron. 18:11). David's fame became even more notable after slaughtering 18,000 Syrians in the Valley of Salt (south of the Dead Sea); this victory occurred under the leadership of Abishai and Joab (1 Chron. 18:12; Ps. 60; 2 Sam. 8:13).

Eugene H. Merrill explains that there is a textual quandary as to whether those defeated were actually Syrians (2 Sam. 8:13) or Edomites (1 Chron. 8:12):

> Though "Aram" (i.e., "Arameans") is in most Hebrew manuscripts, the Septuagint and some other versions have "Edom," a reading that is also supported by a few Hebrew manuscripts and by 1 Chronicles 18:12. The difference in the original language is only one letter: *d* (as in Edom) and *r* (as in Aram), easily confused in Hebrew. If "Aramean," it may be that the Edomites had solicited Aramean help against Israel. In any event, David again prevailed and brought Edom also under his hegemony.[13]

Whether the Syrians assisted the Edomites or not, Edom's rebellion was subdued and David placed garrisons throughout their land (1 Chron. 8:13). The writer again notes, *"The Lord preserved David wherever he went."* David had a heart for God, knew what God wanted him to accomplish, and God enabled him to do it – thus, he was unstoppable.

David's Administration (1 Chron. 18:14-17)

Israel's king desired that his kingdom be governed by justice and equality (1 Chron. 18:14). The writer then lists chief officers in David's cabinet: Joab commanded Israel's army, Jehoshaphat was David's recorder, Zadok and Abiathar (i.e., Ahimelech's son; see 1 Sam. 22:20) were priests, Shavsha (or Seraiah) the secretary, Benaiah was in charge of the king's security (provided by the Cherethites and the Pelethites), and some of David's sons were chief ministers (1 Chron. 18:15-17).

At this juncture, David maintains Abiathar (a descendant of Aaron's son Ithamar through Eli and Phinehas II) as Israel's high priest, likely because of his long association with David during his fugitive years. Later, Solomon will remove Abiathar from this position and Zadok alone will serve as high priest. Zadok was a descendant of Aaron through Eleazar and Phinehas I, and therefore was of the rightful pedigree to be high priest (he was serving at the old tabernacle located at Gibeah). Solomon's action fulfilled God's judgment against the house of Eli.

Conquest and order marked the expansion of David's kingdom. This would permit glory and blessing to be the main characteristics of his son Solomon's reign. Only through Christ's well-ordered victory at Calvary can we receive the vast goodness of an eternal God, who will exalt His Son over all that He has created. How unimaginable Christ's coming kingdom will be – what will it be like to bask in the splendor and love of God with no distractions, no carnality, no limitations, and no sorrow?

Meditation

> Oh, my soul is all aflame, how I love the precious name,
> Jesus, the King of Glory;
> Unto Him my praise I give, for His kingdom I will live,
> Jesus, the King of Glory.

He who died to set me free, shall my king forever be,
Jesus, the King of Glory;
To His cause I'll ever give, for His kingdom I will live,
Jesus, the King of Glory.

— Charles R. Scoville

David's Kingdom Expands

1 Chronicles 19-20

Ammonites and Syrians Defeated (1 Chron. 19:1-20:3)

Nahash, the king of Ammon, died and David desired to show kindness to his son Hanun because of his father's previous, unspecified generosity to David (1 Chron. 19:1-2). Until this time, Ammon had remained loyal and had not resisted David's efforts to secure the region.

David sent comforters to the land of Ammon to console the new king. As some fifty years had passed since Saul's confrontation with Nahash, the deceased may have been the son of the former Nahash. Regardless, David's gesture represents a lovely picture of the Lord Jesus Christ who extends an offer of lavish grace to "whomsoever will" (not just to His covenant people, but to the Gentiles also). However, as witnessed in the story of Hanun, God's goodness can still be refused.

Certain advisors told Hanun that David's ambassadors were not what they claimed to be, but were spies gathering information for an invasion (1 Chron. 19:3). The young Ammonite king heeded their counsel. Before dismissing David's servants, Hanun's men shaved off half their beards and cut their garments off to an indecent length (1 Chron. 19:4). Barnes summarizes the magnitude of the offense: "Cutting off a person's beard is regarded by the Arabs as an indignity equal to flogging and branding among ourselves. The loss of their long garments, so essential to Oriental dignity, was no less insulting than that of their beards."[14] In the Ancient Near East, a man's beard was held in such high respect that men often swore by their own beards in matters of great importance.

Because the Law prohibited trimming their beards in accordance with pagan practices (Lev. 19:27), Jewish men permitted their beards to grow naturally. This meant that the Ammonites' insult was doubly disconcerting, because the Jews would have to shave the other half of their beards to ensure that their facial hair grew back evenly.

After hearing of their disgraceful experience, David told his emissaries to remain in Jericho until their beards had sufficiently grown back (1 Chron. 19:5). Interestingly, Isaiah will later prophesy Moab's final ignominy and doom, employing a colorful reminder of their shameful deed in this chapter, *"Moab will wail ... on all their heads will be baldness, and every beard cut off"* (Isa. 15:2).

Instead of regretting their mistake of humiliating David's envoy (a declaration of war, so to speak), the Ammonites began soliciting allies to bolster their ranks against David's likely imminent retaliation. The Ammonites used one thousand talents of silver to hire 20,000 Syrian foot soldiers from Beth Rehob and Zoba, 1,000 men from Maacah, and 12,000 from Ish-Tob (1 Chron. 19:6; 2 Sam. 10:6). The Syrian chariot force also included 32,000 units (1 Chron. 19:7). Maacah was in Transjordan just north of Manasseh's territory but south of Mount Hebron. Tob was south of Maacah, about forty miles east of the Jordan River and ten miles south of the Sea of Galilee. Ammon gathered their army and mercenary forces and encamped at Medeba.

After learning of Syria's rebellion (for David had already subdued them; 2 Sam. 8) and that Ammon had secured an alliance with Syria, David sent Joab and all of Israel's mighty men to confront the Syrians and Ammonites (1 Chron. 19:8). The Ammonites put themselves in array to protect the gate of Rabbah (Rabbath), their capital city, while the mercenary forces skirted Israel's army in an outflanking maneuver (1 Chron. 19:9).

When Joab saw that the battle lines were on either side of him, he chose some of Israel's best soldiers and arrayed them against the Syrians, the better warriors (1 Chron. 19:10). The remainder of Israel's army would be commanded by Abishai, Joab's brother, and would engage the Ammonites (1 Chron. 19:11). Joab instructed Abishai:

> *If the Syrians are too strong for me, then you shall help me; but if the people of Ammon are too strong for you, then I will help you. Be of good courage, and let us be strong for our people and for the cities of our God. And may the Lord do what is good in His sight* (1 Chron. 19:12-13).

Basically, Joab told his men to be strong and fight for Israel's honor and for the sake of her cities and that the Lord would do what seemed good to Him. The idea was, "Maybe God will help, maybe He will not;

if He does, we will not refuse His help." Joab is a carnal man and his implied message to his men is the extent of his piety: "Heaven will help those who help themselves."

After the battle began, Joab repelled the Syrians, who then fled before Israel's mighty men (1 Chron. 19:14). This sight demoralized the Ammonite soldiers, who then withdrew from fighting Abishai into their walled city (1 Chron. 19:15). Although Joab was victorious that day, it was a meaningless achievement – the Ammonites were secure in their fortification and the Syrians merely withdrew to regroup again. No one was conquered, just temporarily beaten back.

Joab returned to Jerusalem to inform David of Israel's hollow victory. In type, flesh can never achieve a lasting victory over flesh. Aspirations of change and reformation techniques work only for the weekend; enduring victory over carnal impulses must be gained through the power of the Holy Spirit (Rom. 8:13). David, the one called by God to subdue Israel's enemies and empowered by the Holy Spirit, needed to be leading Israel's army to victory under the Lord's direction, not carnal Joab. David learned that he could not delegate his responsibility to a fleshly man and expect anything but a carnal outcome. The Lord was with David, so he must lead the next assault for there to be a spectacular victory.

The Syrians regrouped and fortified themselves at Helam (2 Sam. 10:16). Hadadezer even brought Syrian soldiers from beyond the Euphrates River to bolster their position at Helam (1 Chron. 19:16). The commander of Hadadezer's army was Shobach. David gathered Israel's full army and led them into battle against the Syrians first; he would not repeat Joab's mistake of getting trapped between two battlefronts (1 Chron. 19:17).

The Syrians fled before Israel who killed 7,000 charioteers (this number may be seven hundred per 2 Sam. 10:18), forty thousand horsemen, and Shobach (1 Chron. 19:18). After witnessing the appalling slaughter of the Syrians, the kings aligned with Hadadezer pursued peace with David and thereby became his servants (1 Chron. 19:19). The Syrians rightly concluded that it would be foolish to assist the Ammonites against Israel again. The following map illustrates the various battles David fought as described in this chapter and the next.[15]

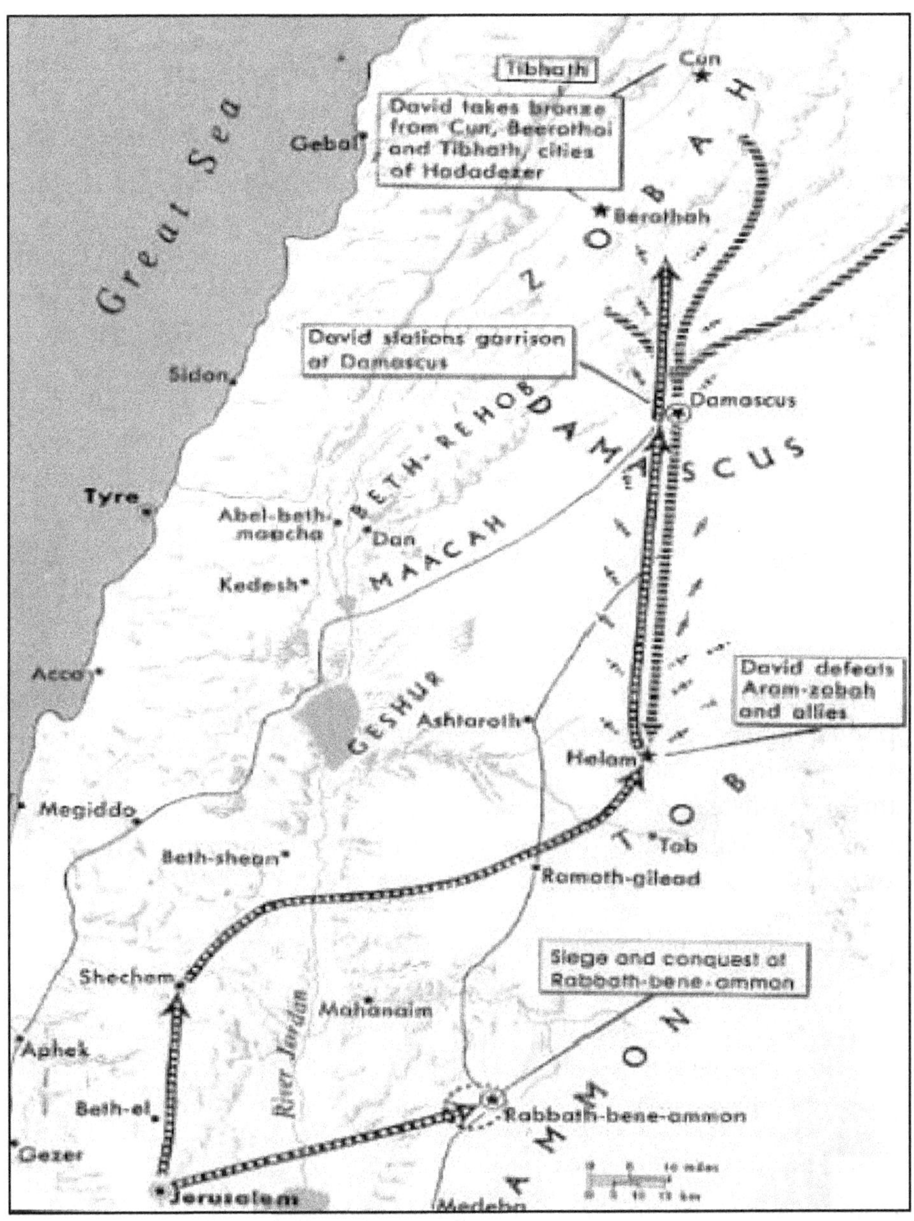

David penned Psalm 21 as an expression of thanksgiving from the congregation for answering their prayers to preserve their king in battle. The historical setting of this psalm seems to have been David's victory over the Ammonites and Syrians in this chapter. On his return the king praises the Lord for displaying His majestic power in battle and for granting him the desire of his heart – the preservation of his life and a complete triumph (Ps. 21:1-6). David affirms the reason his prayer was granted was because he fully trusted in the unfailing love of the Most High (Ps. 21:7). The king is then addressed by the congregation, who state they knew he would be completely victorious over his enemies because he trusted in the Lord (Ps. 21:8-10). They realize God would grant him future victories for the same reason, despite the ongoing efforts of David's enemies to overcome him. The congregation declares they will sing praise to God alone for flexing His might and power on behalf of their king (Ps. 21:11-12).

When God is on our side, every temptation and every conflict can be overcome – if we side with Him! God is with David and David's heart is with the Lord and as a result Israel was unstoppable. Sadly, 2 Samuel 11 reveals that David's heart became entangled in a web of sin at this juncture, which resulted in serious consequences to himself, his family, and the entire nation. Given the positive tenor of the book, and the rapid expansion of David's kingdom, the historian of Chronicles does not mention David's great sin.

After Nathan rebuked David for his sin with Bathsheba and the murder of her husband Uriah, the king repented and was restored to God. Although David had negligently remained in Jerusalem during this time (instead of going to war), Joab had continued his siege efforts against Rabbah, the capital city of Ammon, from the previous year (1 Chron. 20:1). David's general had captured the city's water supply which meant it would soon fall (2 Sam. 12:27). Second Samuel 12:28 informs us that Joab sent word for David to gather Israel's full army and come to Rabbah, so that Joab would not be the one accredited with the victory. This was a noble and loyal gesture by Joab, who often employed carnal methods to accomplish his personal agenda.

David journeyed to Rabbah, and Israel (under Joab's leadership) conquered the city (1 Chron. 20:2). The king's crown, weighing a talent of gold and studded with many precious stones, was removed from the king of Ammon's head and placed on David's. The people of Rabbah and other Ammonite survivors became David's servants (to make bricks, to hew wood, and perhaps to mine) and Israel's army returned to Jerusalem (1 Chron. 20:3).

Philistine Giants Fall (1 Chron. 20:4-8)

The book of Chronicles places the following Philistine battles immediately after the fall of Rabbah and the defeat of the Ammonites. This would place the timing a few years after David's sin with Bathsheba. If this assumption is correct, David would have been in his early fifties.

We learn from 2 Samuel 21 that David led his men into battle again against the Philistines (2 Sam. 21:15). David fought against a giant named Ishbi-Benob, who, with a bronze spear weighing three hundred shekels and a new sword, desired to kill David (2 Sam. 21:16). Seeing that David had become weary and was in trouble, Abishai rescued the king and killed the giant. Although at times Abishai was presumptuous, he did not exhibit the depravity of his brother Joab. Abishai's courage and loyalty to his king is admirable, and confirms why his name is listed among David's mighty men.

Age had affected David more than he realized. His men were determined not to permit their king to return to the battlefield in the future, *"lest you quench the lamp of Israel"* (2 Sam. 21:17). They knew that David was God's anointed and represented His favor on the nation; if David died in battle, the nation would lose hope of God's blessings. The writer of Chronicles does not include David's faintness in fighting the giant in his account, as that would run counter to the tenor of his book. Instead, he tells of three other giants slain by David's mighty men.

During another battle at Gezer (Gob in 2 Sam. 21:18), Sibbechai the Hushathite killed Saph, another son of the Philistine giant from Gath (1 Chron. 20:4; 11:29). During a subsequent altercation at the same location, the Bethlehemite Elhanan (2 Sam. 23:24) killed another giant, Lahmi, the brother of Goliath, whose spear-shaft was like a weaver's beam (1 Chron. 20:5). A fourth giant from the same family had six fingers and six toes and was killed at Gath by David's nephew Jonathan, the son of Shimea (1 Chron. 20:6-7).

It is possible that Goliath had four brothers that were born to one giant residing at Gath and that all were then slain by David or by his near-relatives (1 Chron. 20:8). As the Hebrew word *Rapha* is used to represent the father of these five giants, it may be that all five were merely descendants of the Rephaite family at Gath and may not have been direct siblings. Regardless, they were all remnants of the aboriginal Canaanite giants discovered by Joshua previously and driven out of Hebron by Caleb (Josh. 11:22, 15:14). Their demise fulfilled the prophetic analogy of David taking five stones from the brook on the day he slew the giant Goliath over thirty years earlier (1 Sam. 17:40). Truly, God enables those who will stand as His pilgrims on the victorious ground of Calvary to be triumphant in the land of giants!

Meditation

He who would valiant be against all disaster,
Let him in constancy follow the Master.
There's no discouragement shall make him once relent,
His first avowed intent to be a pilgrim.

Who so beset him round with dismal stories
Do but themselves confound – his strength the more is.
No foes shall stay his might; though he with giants fight,
He will make good his right to be a pilgrim.

Since, Lord, Thou dost defend us with Thy Spirit,
We know we at the end, shall life inherit.
Then fancies flee away! I'll fear not what men say,
I'll labor night and day to be a pilgrim.

— John Bunyan (from
Pilgrim's Progress)

David's Numbering

1 Chronicles 21

Timing

David's kingdom under God's authority and power had expanded rapidly and greatly. The beloved of the Lord had gone in about twenty years from a fugitive in exile to the ruler of Israel who controlled the entire region. God had prospered Israel as He deemed appropriate – that was His business alone and a matter in which David could have no boast. Men normally count their assets to either boast in what they have or to stir up lusting for what they perceive they lack. Yet, at this moment every child of God has what God wants them to have, else they would have more or less than what they presently possess. Gloating over God's blessings is not the same as resting in His sufficiency!

The following story is also recorded in 2 Samuel 24 and likely occurred shortly after David had taken Jerusalem from the Jebusites, but before he erected a new tabernacle in Jerusalem and moved the Ark there. It is quite possible that the "again" in the parallel account in 2 Samuel 24:1 relates to God's judicial three-year famine in 2 Samuel 21 (relating to Saul's slaughter of the Gibeonites). If so, the events in this chapter would fall on the heels of that three-year famine and would have occurred in the first half of David's reign.

The tenor of the passage also affirms this supposition, as the most advantageous opportunity to arouse David's pride would have been when his kingdom was approaching its apex, not after he had learned the immense consequences of personal sin and had been humbled by repeated revolts. If these assumptions are correct, David would have been in his forties, not his late sixties when the events of this chapter unfolded.

David Numbers Israel (1 Chron. 21:1-6)

In 2 Samuel 24:1 we learn that God's anger was aroused against His people, but no particular offense is mentioned. Given the rapid expansion of David's kingdom, they may have been glorying in their king or in their progress. Regardless of what the national sin was, the Lord sought a means of reacquainting His people with His awesomeness and so He instigated a situation which predetermined that David would number Israel and Judah.

Alfred Barnes notes that the Hebrew text literally reads, "For one moved David against them."[16] The "one" is not identified, but would be someone who opposed the interests of David and Israel, and would urge the king to number the people. James informs us that God entices no one to sin, for that would be against His holy character (Jas. 1:13). Rather, God permits the devil (who is more than happy to tempt men to sin against God) to do so, that God's sovereign purposes may be accomplished.

With this understanding and the information in 1 Chronicles 21:1, William MacDonald explains what occurred:

> We learn from 1 Chronicles 21:1 that it was Satan who moved David to take a census of Israel and Judah. Satan *precipitated* it, David *performed* it (because of the pride in his heart), and God *permitted* it. The Septuagint rendering of verse 1 reads "and Satan moved David" rather than "and He moved David."[17]

David ordered Joab to conduct a nationwide census (1 Chron. 21:2), but Joab rebuffed the idea: *"May the Lord make His people a hundred times more than they are. But, my lord the king, are they not all my lord's servants? Why then does my lord require this thing? Why should he be a cause of guilt in Israel?"* (1 Chron. 21:3). For a carnal man, Joab's insight into the offense of numbering Israel is remarkable; in fact, this is one of the wisest statements by Joab recorded in Scripture. He understood that, since David gave no explanation for the numbering of Israel, the command was motivated by pride and vanity and would have dire consequences.

In the Ancient Near East, a census was often a precursor to war, so perhaps David had intentions of expanding his empire beyond God's designs. Or the king may have been tempted to trust in the numbers of his soldiers instead of in the Lord for Israel's security. No matter what

David's specific wrong motive was, Joab knew that all the soldiers on the planet could not offset God's fury.

Nevertheless, David would not heed Joab's or his captain's objections in the matter and they departed from the king to perform the census (1 Chron. 21:4). Moses numbered the men twenty years old and upwards after the Exodus in order to validate the number of ransomed souls; each man paid a half shekel of silver to the Levitical treasury to affirm their past redemption (Ex. 30:12, 38:26). A second numbering occurred in Numbers 1 to determine the number of men able to go to war. Just before entering Canaan thirty-nine years later, Moses again numbered the people in order to determine tribal allotments of land in Canaan (Num. 26). Each of these censuses was commanded by the Lord for a specific purpose, but there was no such command or need for a census in David's time. The ransom money had already been paid, the army was established, and the land allotments had been received.

It took Joab and his captains nine months and twenty days to number all the Israelites from Dan to Beersheba in Canaan and those residing in the Transjordan (2 Sam. 24:5-8). Joab returned to Jerusalem and gave the tally to David: *"All Israel had one million one hundred thousand men who drew the sword, and Judah had four hundred and seventy thousand men who drew the sword"* (1 Chron. 21:5). Joab did not provide a number for the tribes of Levi and Benjamin, *"for the king's word was abominable to Joab"* (v. 6). Apparently, Joab left out these two tribes in his total to ease his own conscience somewhat.

The numbers in this chapter are more specific than figures in 2 Samuel 24. In 1 Chronicles 21 the tally for Judah is more precisely stated at 470,000 (2 Sam. 24 rounds this number to 500,000), but Israel's total of 1.1 million is well above the 2 Sam. 24 figure of 800,000. The discrepancy is explained if David's standing army of 288,000 men (1 Chron. 27:1-15) was added to the 800,000 men associated with Israel (2 Sam. 24:9). In other words, because those in David's standing army had already been numbered off, they did not need to be counted again, and since David already knew their number, Joab did not include them in the 1 Samuel 24 tally.

Even though these are large numbers, the figures still discredited God's promise to Abraham to make Israel increase as the sands of the sea and the stars in the heavens (Gen. 15:2-5). David should have been satisfied with whatever number of Israelites God had deemed best to occupy the Promised Land at that time. The number was what it was, and characterizing it only demeaned God and fueled David's pride.

The Judgment on David's Sin (1 Chron. 21:7-17)

God was displeased with what David had done and therefore struck Israel (1 Chron. 21: 7). With a guilty conscience David then called upon the Lord, *"I have sinned greatly, because I have done this thing; but now, I pray, take away the iniquity of Your servant, for I have done very foolishly"* (1 Chron. 21:8). The Lord responded to David's prayer of confession by sending the prophet Gad to him with a message (1 Chron. 21:9-10). Gad presented the Lord's determination on the matter to the king. David was to choose one of three punishments: seven years of famine, three months of oppression by Israel's enemies, or three days of pestilence (1 Chron. 21:11-12).

David was in great distress – as Israel's king, he understood that his sin would have grave consequences for the entire Jewish nation (1 Chron. 21:13). Having already experienced God's abundant mercy, David chose the pestilence under the hand of God, rather than the rage of his enemies or of nature. The Lord then sent a plague throughout Israel. It apparently began in the outskirts of Israel and then moved towards Jerusalem resulting in seventy thousand deaths (1 Chron. 21:14). This is the most destructive plague ever recorded in Scripture against Israel. During Korah's rebellion against Moses' leadership and God's ordained priesthood, 14,700 died (Num. 16:49). At Baal Peor, 24,000 died by pestilence because of idolatry (Num. 25:9). Whatever the unnamed sin was that had angered the Lord, we gain a sense that it was heinous.

God's judgment from our standpoint seems extreme – seventy thousand deaths because of the king's pride? But, let us remember that David is Israel's king, and that God absolutely hates pride (Prov. 6:17). Further, a proud king stimulates the same in those he rules over. The stubborn attitude in question was also deeply ingrained in David, for at any time in the nine months he could have stopped the census, but he did not. Remember too that the larger emphasis at this juncture was that God's anger was already kindled against Israel (2 Sam. 24:1). So, although it was David's sin that opened the floodgates of wrath, the people as a whole had fully contributed to the deluge.

Just as the destroying angel was preparing to raze Jerusalem, the Lord commanded the angel, *"It is enough; now restrain your hand"* (1 Chron. 21:15). This pause in judgment was because it had already brought about a spirit of repentance in David, thus permitting him to offer public intercession and to obtain divine mercy for Jerusalem. The angel, with sword still unsheathed, then took up a position over Jerusalem above the threshing floor of Ornan (Araunah) the Jebusite. This was Mount Moriah, the historical site where Abraham offered Isaac a millennium earlier (Gen. 22:2).

The destroyer may have been either an angel or "the Angel of the Lord" (preincarnate Christ). Based on other similar situations in Scripture (Ex. 12:29; Num. 22:22), it seems more likely that the one destroying (1 Chron. 21:16), the one exacting justice, was the Angel of the Lord. On judgment day (i.e. at the Great White Throne Judgment), it will be Christ who executes justice on the wicked (John 5:22, 27).

After David saw the angel *"standing between earth and heaven, having in his hand a drawn sword stretched out over Jerusalem"* (1 Chron. 21:16), he and elders wearing sackcloth went to this site and fell on their faces. David pleaded with the Lord, *"Was it not I who commanded the people to be numbered? I am the one who has sinned and done evil indeed; but these sheep, what have they done? Let Your hand, I pray, O Lord my God, be against me and my father's house, but not against Your people that they should be plagued"* (1 Chron. 21:17). David knew his God was characterized by mercy as well as justice, and therefore he wisely put his trust in the Lord and then interceded for the people, even if it meant his own demise. God appreciated both David's comprehension of His character and the king's desire to mediate on behalf of Israel. In response, the Lord sent the prophet Gad to inform David of the appropriate means of atoning for his sin.

The Altar on the Threshing Floor (1 Chron. 21:18-30)

Gad immediately came to David and commanded him to erect an altar to the Lord at a precise location – the threshing floor of Ornan (Araunah) the Jebusite (where the Angel of the Lord was positioned; 1 Chron. 21:18). Ornan saw David and the elders coming and bowed down before the king and inquired why he had come (1 Chron. 21:19-21; 2 Sam. 24:20-21). (Verse 20 informs us that Ornan and his four sons saw the angel there and that Ornan's sons hid themselves, being afraid, but their father continued to thresh wheat.) David responded to his question, *"Grant me the place of this threshing floor, that I may build an altar on it to the Lord. You shall grant it to me at the full price, that the plague may be withdrawn from the people"* (1 Chron. 21:22).

Hearing what was at stake, Ornan immediately offered to give his threshing floor to David, including the oxen for sacrifice, and even the threshing implements and oxen yokes as wood for the fire (1 Chron. 21:23). The threshing implements probably included one or more threshing sleds which were made of wood and had iron teeth (these were dragged over the harvested sheaves of grain). The angel's presence with a drawn sword no doubt further compelled Ornan to want to help David in any way he could to end the plague, even if it meant giving the king everything he had.

However, the king rejected Ornan's kind offer, for the atoning sacrifice must be David's, not Ornan's. David knew that a sacrifice was not truly a sacrifice unless it cost the offerer something: *"No, but I will surely buy it for the full price, for I will not take what is yours for the Lord, nor offer burnt offerings with that which costs me nothing"* (1 Chron. 21:24). So, David bought the threshing floor, the implements, and the oxen for fifty shekels of silver (2 Sam. 24:24) and Ornan's entire property for 600 shekels of gold (1 Chron. 21:25). John Heading observes the giving nature of both David and Ornan as evidence of true repentance and then offers us a practical application:

> A personal price at great cost was necessary to display the fruit of the exercise behind David's repentance. In fact, in maturity, both David and Ornan wanted to offer of his own! For Christians, the cost of service and worship must be ascertained and paid – it means being different from men in the world, and the cost can be seen in 1 Timothy 4:12-16. … God wants each Christian to pay the cost of his own bringing, so David declined Ornan's offer – David always gave of his "own proper good," namely, from his personal possessions (1 Chron. 29:3).[18]

Although the tabernacle was at Gibeon at this time (1 Chron. 21:29-30), the king commanded an altar to be built at that location and he presented burnt offerings and peace offerings on it. We then read how the Lord responded to David's prayer:

> *David built there an altar to the Lord, and offered burnt offerings and peace offerings, and called on the Lord; and He answered him from heaven by fire on the altar of burnt offering. So the Lord commanded the angel and he returned his sword to its sheath* (1 Chron. 21:26-27).

God's fire meant that the Lord had accepted David's offering and heeded the prayers of His people for the land – the plague was permanently ended (1 Chron. 21:28). David chose to put himself in God's hand for three days and to hope in His mercy. His action wonderfully typifies the three days necessary to accomplish the Lord's death, burial, and resurrection so that God could extend mercy to all who will receive His solution for sin. Interestingly, Abraham's testing also lasted three days and God then spared Isaac from being offered on Mount Moriah in response to Abraham's obedience – the proof of his faith (Gen. 22).

The property that David had purchased from Ornan would be the future site of Solomon's temple, Herod's temple, the Jewish tribulation temple, and finally the vast millennial temple which Christ will fill with His glory. C. A. Coates submits that the two greatest events in David's life were the bringing of the Ark to its resting place in Zion and the building of the altar to offer a sacrifice on the threshing floor of Ornan:

> Both these acts were the setting aside of the original order and the institution of something new in the ways of God. They were light given by God as to how He would get His place after the complete breakdown of the system set up by Moses. He would have His will done perfectly by Christ, and something set up to which the ark could be brought as a place of rest. Many scriptures speak of Zion as God's dwelling place. We need to apprehend this before we can take up the thought of the house as built by Solomon. Zion had been the stronghold of the enemy's power, but when taken by David it became the royal city and the resting place of the ark. Zion represents the assembly as the place where the reign of grace is known; … every hostile element has been overcome, so that, under the mighty influence of Christ every heart is pervaded by divine grace. It is the fruit of His triumph here, not in heaven.[19]

In mercy, God, through the circumstances of this chapter, was marking not only the future location of His temple, but indeed the very location in which eternal propitiation for human sin would be achieved (i.e., the location of Golgotha is on the same ridge line). God's provision for communing with Him would not be at Gibeon, where the tabernacle (representing the Law) was pitched, but in Jerusalem, where God's grace for humanity would be shown at Calvary. As already typified in Isaac, Abraham's only begotten son (Heb. 11:17), God's only begotten Son (John 3:16), the Lord Jesus Christ, was destined to be sacrificed at this location. C. H. Mackintosh writes:

> But there was mercy in the midst of wrath. By the threshing floor of Ornan the Jebusite, the angel of the judgment sheathed his sword. *"Then the Angel of the Lord commanded Gad to say to David, that David should go up, and set up an altar unto the Lord in the threshing floor of Ornan the Jebusite."* Here, then, was the place where mercy triumphed, and caused her voice to be heard above the roar of judgment. Here the blood of the victim flowed, and here the foundation of the Lord's house was laid.[20]

As the writer of Hebrews affirms, Christ is our altar, our sacrifice; only in Him can we expect to receive God's mercy and escape His wrath for sin (Heb. 10:10-13). On Ornan's threshing floor God marked the exact spot in which propitiation for humanity's sin would later be achieved (1 Jn. 2:2). At Calvary, God would cause His Son, the Lord Jesus Christ, the sinless Lamb of God, to *"taste death for every man"* (Heb. 2:9). Praise the Lord for His undeserved mercy and grace found only in Christ!

Meditation

Alas, and did my Savior bleed? And did my Sovereign die?
Would He devote that sacred head for such a worm as I?

Was it for sins that I had done He groaned upon the tree?
Amazing pity! Grace unknown! And love beyond degree!

Well might the sun in darkness hide, and shut his glories in,
When Christ, the mighty Maker, died for man, His creature's sin.

— Isaac Watts

Temple Preparations

1 Chronicles 22

The historian then reverts to God's covenant with David and God's choice of David's son (Solomon) to build Him a magnificent house. The king realizes that God has chosen the spot for His future house and the altar of burnt offering – Ornan's threshing floor (1 Chron. 22:1). David discerned: *"Solomon my son is young and inexperienced, and the house to be built for the Lord must be exceedingly magnificent, famous and glorious throughout all countries. I will now make preparation for it"* (1 Chron. 22:5).

Therefore, David, until the time of his death, made preparations for the future construction project by assembling a work force of foreigners in Israel (1 Chron. 21:2) and gathering building materials (1 Chron. 22:3-4). The laborers were Canaanites who should have been destroyed during the days of Joshua, but regrettably were permitted to remain in the land as laborers (Judg. 1:28-33; 1 Kgs. 9:20-21). David stockpiled resources such as iron, bronze, and cedar trees from the Sidonians (1 Chron. 22:3-4).

Before David died, he told his son Solomon that he had desired to build the Lord a temple and why he had not been permitted to do so – because he had been a man of blood (1 Chron. 22:6-8). David had been a great warrior most of his life and had killed many men in battle, and even women and children in raids while in Philistia. It was necessary for David to first secure the region through military action so that Solomon could enjoy a reign of peace in order to concentrate on the construction project (1 Chron. 22:9).

David again told Solomon that the Lord had chosen him to erect the temple that he had desired to build and he asked the Lord to give Solomon wisdom and understanding to accomplish the task (1 Chron. 22:10-12). The king promised that the Lord would sustain Solomon on Israel's throne if he chose to obey the Mosaic Law (1 Chron. 22:13).

Accordingly, David charged his son: *"Be strong and of good courage; do not fear nor be dismayed."*

David then apprised Solomon of his efforts to gather materials and laborers for the construction project (1 Chron. 22:14-16). One hundred thousand talents of gold (3,750 tons), one million talents of silver (37, 500 tons), bronze and iron beyond measure, and an abundance of timber and stone had been set aside for building and furnishing the temple. David's work force included woodsmen, stonecutters, and all types of skillful men for every kind of work (1 Chron. 22:15). Seeing that the needed provisions were available, the king commands his son, *"Arise and begin working, and the Lord be with you"* (1 Chron. 22:16).

The king also urged Israel's leaders to cooperate with Solomon in erecting a temple for Jehovah (1 Chron. 22:17). The Lord had prospered Israel and had quieted all their enemies, so they could focus on the work without being distracted by invaders – this was proof that God was with them and had endorsed the task before them (1 Chron. 22:18).

David concludes his address by exhorting them to *"Set your heart and your soul to seek the Lord your God ... therefore arise and build the sanctuary of the Lord God"* (1 Chron. 22:19). David knew that one's heart had to be right with the Lord before one's hands could render acceptable service to Him!

Several hundred years earlier Moses rebuked his rebellious countrymen saying something similar: *"You will seek the Lord your God, and you will find Him if you seek Him with all your heart and with all your soul"* (Deut. 4:29). God desires to be one with those who will seek Him. Those who seek God – will find Him! Scripture repeatedly offers man an opportunity to search out and commune with God if man will yield to what God wants him to understand and obey: *"You will seek Me and find Me, when you search for Me with all your heart"* (Jer. 29:13). *"The Lord is near to all who call upon Him, to all who call upon Him in truth"* (Ps. 145:18). God provides abundant mercy to those who humbly seek Him with empty hands, which He promises to fill with blessings. It is only when we are in fellowship with God that we can joyfully and profitably serve Him. As C. A. Coates explains, the temple better illustrates the idea of ongoing communion with God than the tabernacle did:

> The temple adds considerably to our conception of the house of God, for in connection with the temple we get the thought of God's house as a dwelling place for men. In the tabernacle there was no provision for men to dwell in God's house; there was not even a seat there for the priests. But in the temple there were chambers which suggest the thought of men dwelling in the house of God. That house was to be not only a place of approach to God but a dwelling place for men. I need not remind you how often this thought is taken up in the Psalms. *"I will dwell in the house of Jehovah for the length of the days"* (Ps. 23:6). *"One thing have I asked of Jehovah, that will I seek after: that I may dwell in the house of Jehovah all the days of my life, to behold the beauty of Jehovah, and to inquire of him in his temple"* (Ps. 27:4). [Also see Ps. 65:4, 84:4] ... I have no doubt that the Lord made reference to the chambers of the temple when He said, *"In My Father's house there are many abodes; were it not so, I had told you: for I go to prepare you a place; and if I go and shall prepare you a place, I am coming again and shall receive you to Myself, that where I am ye also may be"* (John 14:2-3).[21]

Not only was the temple God's permanent dwelling place among His people, but it was where He wanted His people to be also. This will be a reality during the Kingdom Age and, in its fullness, during the Eternal State. Then all believers in God's presence will drink of the river of water of life and eat from the tree of life (Rev. 21-22). *"Behold, the tabernacle of God [speaking of the New Jerusalem] is with men, and He will dwell with them, and they shall be His people. God Himself will be with them and be their God"* (Rev. 21:3). The temple to be built pictured the great city of God, the future dwelling place of all saints!

Meditation

> *I love those who love Me, and those who seek Me diligently will find Me. Riches and honor are with Me, enduring riches and righteousness. My fruit is better than gold, yes, than fine gold, and My revenue than choice silver. I traverse the way of righteousness, in the midst of the paths of justice, that I may cause those who love Me to inherit wealth, that I may fill their treasuries* (Prov. 8:17-21).

Levitical Order and Divisions

1 Chronicles 23-26

Levites Ordered (1 Chron. 23)

As the tabernacle would no longer be moved and would soon be replaced by a temple in Jerusalem, David revised the original duties of the Levites before his death. This required a census of the Levite clans to determine the number of men who were thirty years of age and older, the minimum age for active priestly service (1 Chron. 23:1-3).

Through God's prophets, David was instructed to then organize the 38,000 available Levites into four groups of service (1 Chron. 23:4-5; 2 Chron. 29:25): 24,000 would oversee temple operations, 6,000 would function as officers and judges, 4,000 as gatekeepers, and 4,000 as musicians and singers before the Lord.

The genealogies of the three Levitical clans are then recorded to certify legitimacy of service before the Lord: the Gershonites (1 Chron. 23:7-11), the Kohathites (1 Chron. 23:12-20), and the Merarites (1 Chron. 23:21-23). Obviously, the lineage of the Kohathites referenced Moses and Aaron, the latter and his descendants being entrusted with the priesthood (1 Chron. 23:13).

Next David describes the duties to be performed by the Levites, as God's temporary dwelling place, the tabernacle, would no longer be disassembled, moved, or reassembled in the future (1 Chron. 23:24-27). David also lowered the minimum age of Levitical service from 25 to 20 years of age in order to provide more manpower for all the work that would need to be accomplished relating to the temple (Num. 8:24). The lower age of twenty would also align with Solomon's approximate age when he became king.

The nation of Israel had grown, which meant that even though the tabernacle would not be moved in the future, more laborers would be needed to accomplish the sacrifices, to receive the offerings of the people, to maintain the temple, and to manage its operations. It is noteworthy that 1 Kings 8:8 informs us that the carrying staves (poles) were withdrawn from the Ark once it was placed in the new tabernacle to illustrate the permanence of Jerusalem as its final resting place.

The 6,000 appointed judges were likely dispersed throughout Israel to uphold God's Law and to ensure justice in the land. However, the 24,000 Levites remaining in Jerusalem were to serve in the tabernacle/temple and to assist the priests (1 Chron. 23:28-32).

Twenty-Four Divisions (1 Chron. 24)

David divided both the priests (1 Chron. 24:1-19) and Levites (1 Chron. 24:20-31) into twenty-four households. Each of these twenty-four divisions was then assigned a schedule to serve before the Lord on a rotating basis (1 Chron. 24:4, 19). This meant that each household would serve at the tabernacle/temple about two weeks a year.

The priest Zacharias, the father of John the baptizer, was of the eighth course of priests (of the house of Abijah: 1 Chron. 24:10; Luke 1:5). An angel conversed with Zacharias in the holy place before the Altar of Incense (Luke 1:11). Given how many priests there were in Israel at the time of Christ, it may have been Zacharias' only opportunity to be before the Lord his entire lifetime. But God caused the lot to fall on him because He had a message for the faithful priest – he and his barren wife were going to have a son – the forerunner of the Messiah!

Aaron's youngest two sons, Eleazar and Ithamar, formed the lineage of the priesthood, for his older sons Nadab and Abihu were struck down by the Lord (Lev. 10:1-5). There were sixteen divisions of priests from the former, and eight from the latter (1 Chron. 24:4). *These would be the "officials of the sanctuary and officials of the house of God"* (1 Chron. 24:5).

The twenty-four priestly divisions were determined by lot in the presence of David, the elders, and Zadok and Ahimelech (the two high priests of Israel); the scribe Shemaiah recorded the results (1 Chron. 24:6-19). Ahimelech may refer to Ahimelech's son Abiathar who represented his father here, or Abiathar may have named a son after his father Ahimelech. The same procedure was followed for the twenty-four courses of Levites and the outcome was recorded by Shemaiah (1 Chron. 24:20-31).

The number twenty-four, as implicated in this chapter, is associated with priestly service. The number of Levitical courses of priests is identical to the number of elders before the heavenly throne of the Lamb that John saw (Rev. 4:4). This scene wonderfully pictures the future priestly ministry of the redeemed offering praise, honor, and glory in God's presence forever.

Divisions of Musicians (1 Chron. 25)

God had given David the authority to initiate the priestly service of song before the Lord. First Chronicles 25 lists the singers and musicians who were to perform this sacred service, according to their divisions. These were the sons of Asaph (1 Chron. 25:2), of Jeduthun (or Ethan; 1 Chron. 25:3, 15:17-19), and Heman (1 Chron. 25:4-5). Asasph's name means "one who gathers," Jeduthun denotes "a choir of praise," and Heman's name signifies "faithfulness." The gathering of faithful souls to sing praise to God should characterize the corporate worship of God's people in any dispensation.

The sons of Asaph composed four divisions, the sons of Ethan, six courses, and the sons of Heman, fourteen divisions. In all there were 288 men who were to sing in the house of the Lord when their appointed time arrived. The singers were to be accompanied by cymbals and various stringed instruments, including harps (1 Chron. 25:6-7). The twenty-four courses were again determined by lot and the results recorded in 1 Chronicles 25:8-31.

Divisions of Gatekeepers (1 Chron. 26:1-19)

The divisions of gatekeepers and the gates to which they were assigned by the casting of the lot are set down in this chapter. The first major division related to Meshelemiah – his sons and brethren (Kohathites) compose eighteen divisions. Meshelemiah was in the lineage of Korah and a grandson of Asaph (probably a short spelling for Ebiasaph). He had seven sons who formed seven divisions of gatekeepers (1 Chron. 26:1-3). It is somewhat ironic that these descendants of Korah, the man who attempted to intrude on the Aaronic priesthood (Num. 16), were entrusted with the responsibility of permitting only those fit for worship to enter before the Lord.

The second major division of gatekeepers was related to Obed-Edom (also of the Kohathites). He was blessed of God and had eight sons who formed eight more divisions (1 Chron. 26:4, 8, 15). While it is possible that this is the Obed-Edom who briefly kept the Ark in his home after the Lord struck down Uzziah (1 Chron. 13:14), the last portion of 1 Chronicles 16:38 suggests that this man was the son of Jeduthun (or Ethan, but not a Merarite; 1 Chron. 6:44-47). This conclusion is further substantiated by the fact that the Obed-Edom who kept and protected the Ark before it was brought to Jerusalem went on to be a minister before the Ark in the temple (1 Chron. 15:21, 16:38).

The third major division of gatekeepers was composed of a subdivision of the family of Obed-Edom, headed by Shemaiah. All three branches of the Kohathites mentioned above totaled eighty men (1 Chron. 26:8-9). The Merarite branch of Levites provided thirteen men as headed by Hosah (1 Chron. 26:10-11).

These chief gatekeepers (who would manage the 4,000 total gatekeepers) were assigned their posts by lot (1 Chron. 26:12-13). The East Gate was assigned to Shelemiah, Zechariah was to stand watch at the North Gate (1 Chron. 26:14), Obed-Edom and his son were to man the South Gate and storehouse (1 Chron. 26:15), and Shuppim and Hosah were to oversee the West Gate (1 Chron. 26:16). There were to be twenty-two gatekeepers on duty at any given time (1 Chron. 26:17-19).

The Levitical Treasurers and Administrators (1 Chron. 26:20-32)

Ahijah was in charge of overseeing the temple treasuries which received the tithes, offerings, and redemption money from the people (1 Chron. 26:20). Broadly speaking, the responsibility for managing the temple treasuries was shared by the Gershonites, through the line of Laadan, as headed by the family of Jehieli (1 Chron. 26:21-22), and the Kohathites, through the line of Moses, as headed by Shebuel (1 Chron. 26:23-24).

The portion of the treasury derived from military plunder or the dedicated offerings of past kings and judges was under the jurisdiction of Shelomith, also a descendant of Moses through Eliezer (1 Chron. 26:26-28). The Izharites were responsible for overseeing and protecting the treasury of goods and funds collected from outlying areas of Israel (away from Jerusalem; v. 29). Seventeen hundred men under Hashabiah's leadership served the tribes in Canaan proper, while 2,700 men under Jeriah were to manage the Transjordan region (1 Chron. 26:30, 32). David's orders (1 Chron. 23 through 26) were implemented in the fortieth year of his reign, just a few months before his death (1 Chron. 26:31).

David ordered the service of the Levites (with revised roles) and the priesthood as directed by the Lord. As Paul affirms, our God is a God of order and design: *"For God is not the author of confusion but of peace, as in all the churches of the saints"* (1 Cor. 14:33). God's blessings are enjoyed when we yield to His order of things, but the devil is the author of confusion, sorrow, and suffering.

Meditation

> The very word *authority* has within it the word *author*. An author is someone who creates and possesses a particular work. Insofar as God is the foundation of all authority, He exercises that foundation because He is the author and the owner of His creation. He is the foundation upon which all other authority stands or falls.
>
> — R. C. Sproul

> I am Thy servant to do Thy will, and that will is sweeter to me than position or riches or fame, and I choose it above all things on Earth or in Heaven.
>
> — A.W. Tozer

Military Order and David's Officials

1 Chronicles 27

Standing Army of Twelve Divisions (1 Chron. 27:1-15)

We learn in this chapter that David had a standing army of twelve divisions of 24,000 troops, one division rotating into service each month. The remaining eleven divisions were considered troop reserves and could be summoned into action quickly if needed. The wider populace of men in Israel would be summoned into action if the threat was perceived to be extreme. Each division of 24,000 men (after a father's house) appointed captains of thousands, hundreds, and various officers (1 Chron. 27:1).

The division commanders (many of which were included in David's list of mighty men) were: first, Jashobeam of the children of Perez; second, Dodai and Mikloth; third, Benaiah the priest and mighty among the thirty; fourth, Asahel the brother of Joab; fifth, Shamhuth the Izrahite; sixth, Ira the Tekoite; seventh, Helez the Pelonite; eighth, Sibbechai the Hushathite; ninth, Abiezer the Anathothite of the Benjamites; tenth, Maharai the Netophathite, of the Zarhites; eleventh, Benaiah the Pirathonite, of Ephraim; twelfth, Heldai the Netophathite of Othniel (1 Chron. 27:2-15).

Leaders of Tribes (1 Chron. 27:16-24)

There was also a recognized civil leader for each tribe: Reuben – Eliezer, Simeon – Shephatiah, Levi – Hashabiah (but Zadok was over the priests), Judah – Elihu (one of David's brothers), Issachar – Omri, Zebulun – Ishmaiah, Naphtali – Jerimoth the son of Azriel, Ephraim – Hoshea, over the half-tribe of Manasseh in Canaan – Joel, over the half-tribe of Manasseh in Gilead – Iddo, Benjamin – Jaasiel, Dan – Azarel (1 Chron. 27:16-24).

Why the tribes of Gad and Asher are not in this list is not known; perhaps the information was unavailable to the historian. Regardless, by including Levi and two parts of Manasseh, the picture of twelve tribes describing Israel's completeness is maintained. The above men were the leaders of the tribes of Israel at the end of David's reign.

Although Joab almost completed the census that David ordered, the wrath of God prevented the full number of Israelite men twenty years of age and older (i.e., military age) from being tallied and disclosed (1 Chron. 27:24). Because the thing was distasteful to Joab, he did not number the tribes of Benjamin and Levi when he first reported back to David.

To highlight the faithfulness of God to Israel, instead of David's mistake, the historian puts the matter in a positive light – how David responded afterwards: *"But David did not take the number of those twenty years old and under, because the Lord had said He would multiply Israel like the stars of the heavens"* (1 Chron. 27:23). Indeed, this is what David should have realized before he commanded Joab to number Israel – the number of Israelites is under God's hand of blessing! Praise the Lord, for He is good, but gloating in God's goodness normally leads to pride and then painful consequences.

Other Officials (1 Chron. 27:25-34)

Other officials managed David's property (1 Chron. 27:31). These included: Azmaveth over the king's treasuries, Jehonathan over the storehouses in the field, in the cities, in the villages, and in the fortresses (1 Chron. 27:25). Ezri supervised field workers (1 Chron. 27:26), while Shimei was over the vineyards, and Zabdi managed the wine produced from the vineyards (1 Chron. 27:27). Baal-Hanan was over the olive trees and the sycamore trees in lowlands, while Joash managed the store of oil collected (1 Chron. 27:28). Shitrai managed David's herds in Sharon, but Shaphat was over the valley herds (1 Chron. 27:29). Obil cared for camels, while Jehdeiah was entrusted with the donkeys (1 Chron. 27:30) and Jaziz with the flocks of sheep and goats (1 Chron. 27:31).

Jehonathan, David's uncle, was a wise counselor and scribe for David; Jehiel watched over and cared for the king's sons (1 Chron. 27:32). Ahithophel was the king's counselor, and Hushai the Archite was the king's companion (1 Chron. 27:33). Although the chronologer did not speak of Ahithophel's betrayal during Absalom's revolt (2 Sam. 15:31), he did note that he was succeeded by Jehoiada and Abiathar (1

Chron. 27:34; 2 Sam. 15:35). The roster concludes by acknowledging that David's nephew, Joab, was the general over the king's army.

Whether in matters of temple operation, military fortitude, civil affairs, or managing royal assets, David guided and protected Israel as a good shepherd should; all benefited from his respectful and humble leadership. In matters of administration, David reminds us of the Chief Shepherd, who in a coming day shall appear and put all things on the earth in proper order, such that all in His kingdom will be blessed (1 Pet. 5:4). Then everyone will appreciate the Good Shepherd who laid down His life to save His sheep (John 10:17-18). Thankfully, the Great Shepherd continues to lead, protect, refine, and strengthen His people today in preparation for that day (Heb. 13:20-21).

Meditation

Loving Shepherd of Thy sheep,
Keep Thy lamb, in safety keep;
Nothing can Thy power withstand;
None can pluck me from Thy hand.

Loving Savior, Thou didst give
Thine own life that we might live;
And the hands outstretched to bless,
Bear the cruel nails' impress.

Loving Shepherd, ever near,
Teach Thy lambs Thy voice to hear;
Suffer not our steps to stray,
From the straight and narrow way.

— Jane Elizabeth Leeson

David's Farewell and Solomon's Investiture

1 Kings 1-2; 1 Chronicles 28-29

David Assembles Israel's Leaders (1 Chron. 28)

The elderly and soon departing king assembled all Israel's civil and military leaders (including men of valor), and those who had stewardship of his affairs at Jerusalem (1 Chron. 28:1). David reminded them that he had wanted to build Jehovah a temple, but was prohibited from doing so because he had been a man of war and had shed much blood over his lifetime (1 Chron. 28:2-3). David reiterated that God had promised him an everlasting dynasty on the throne of Judah, and that though he had many sons, the Lord had chosen Solomon to be Israel's next king and the one who would build His temple (1 Chron. 28:4-6). As long as Solomon was steadfast to observe God's Law, Jehovah promised to be a father to him and to establish and greatly bless his kingdom (1 Chron. 28:7).

The king then charges his subjects to seek out and obey God's commandments so that they will be blessed in the land and have it for generations to come as a lasting inheritance (1 Chron. 28:8). Likewise, David charged Solomon to remain loyal to God and faithful to the task that God had given him:

> *As for you, my son Solomon, know the God of your father, and serve Him with a loyal heart and with a willing mind; for the Lord searches all hearts and understands all the intent of the thoughts. If you seek Him, He will be found by you; but if you forsake Him, He will cast you off forever. Consider now, for the Lord has chosen you to build a house for the sanctuary; be strong, and do it* (1 Chron. 28:9-10).

If Solomon departed from the Lord, he would utterly fail to accomplish anything important for God, including the construction of the temple. The charge is reminiscent of the Lord Jesus' parting charge to His disciples: *"I am the vine, you are the branches. He who abides in Me, and I in him, bears much fruit; for without Me you can do nothing"* (John 15:5). David then delivered to his son the divinely inspired plans for the vestibule, the temple with its various treasures, chambers, and holy compartments (1 Chron. 28:11-12). The king also confirmed the divisions of the priests and the Levites for all the work of the service of the house of the Lord, including the articles needed for serving in the temple (1 Chron. 28:13). David then revealed the specific weights of gold and of silver that each of the various holy articles and furnishings for the temple was to have (1 Chron. 28:14-18). David again affirmed that all this information had been received from the Lord (1 Chron. 28:19).

David then issued a final charge to his son Solomon: *"Be strong and of good courage, and do it; do not fear nor be dismayed, for the Lord God – my God – will be with you. He will not leave you nor forsake you, until you have finished all the work for the service of the house of the Lord"* (1 Chron. 28:20). To assist his son in accomplishing this important task of building God's house, David had secured peace throughout the region, had set aside a vast wealth of precious metals and building materials, had delivered God's specifications of all that was to be fashioned and built, and also had assembled a huge workforce of slaves and skilled craftsmen to accomplish the task (1 Chron. 28:21).

Offerings and Praise (1 Chron. 29:1-20)

David then turns to the leaders assembled before him and reminds them that Solomon, the one God had chosen for this massive undertaking, was young and inexperienced and would therefore need their help and cooperation (1 Chron. 29:1). Then the king sought to inspire them to give generously to the construction effort by acknowledging his own contributions to it (1 Chron. 29:2-4). Although everyone already knew that David had collected a vast amount of gold, silver, bronze, iron, wood, onyx stones, other precious stones of various colors, and marble slabs for the construction of the temple, they probably did not know how much David had contributed towards this important enterprise. To inspire others to be generous, he revealed that he has contributed three thousand talents of gold and seven thousand talents of refined silver. He then challenges his audience, *"Who then is willing to consecrate himself this day to the Lord?"* (1 Chron. 29:5).

David's esteemed audience, the Who's Who of Israel, responded generously to their departing king's challenge by significantly contributing to the temple undertaking (1 Chron. 29:6-8): *"five thousand talents and ten thousand darics of gold, ten thousand talents of silver, eighteen thousand talents of bronze, and one hundred thousand talents of iron and whoever had precious stones gave them to the treasury of the house of the Lord."* Seeing their generous spirit and loyalty to the Lord thrilled David's soul and prompted him to pray (1 Chron. 29:9).

In one of David's greatest psalms, he publicly acknowledges God's majesty, omnipotence, and generosity to Israel (1 Chron. 29:10-11). David affirms that no earthly position or possession should distract from honoring the Lord, because everything comes from Him: *"Both riches and honor come from You, and You reign over all. In Your hand is power and might; in Your hand it is to make great and to give strength to all"* (1 Chron. 29:12). Paul reminds the carnal Corinthians of the same truth: *"For who makes you differ from another? And what do you have that you did not receive? Now if you did indeed receive it, why do you boast as if you had not received it?"* (1 Cor. 4:7). Without Christ, the believer is nothing, has nothing, and can do nothing for God (John 15:5). But in Him we inherit all things (Rom. 8:17), rule over all things (2 Tim. 2:12), and can do all things that God endorses (Phil. 4:13). Both David and Paul affirm that believers have no boast, but in the Lord: *"He who glories, let him glory in the Lord"* (1 Cor. 1:31).

The king then expressed his amazement that Jehovah had permitted the Jewish nation to have a special relationship with Him (1 Chron. 29:13-14). He realized that such privileged communion should prompt the Israelites to act as aliens and pilgrims while residing in the world (1 Chron. 29:15).

David then affirmed that the abundance of materials set aside for the construction of the temple was for the Lord and that He would reward those who contributed from a willing heart (1 Chron. 29:16). God delights in the sacrificial giving of His people when they have upright hearts. Accordingly, David rejoiced to see the people follow his example of willingly offering to the Lord of their possessions (1 Chron. 29:17). Because true giving is tied to the moral fabric of the heart, John Heading writes:

> God knew the ultimate reason behind David's giving – the uprightness of his heart. By trying the heart, God tries the nature of what we bring: He knows that where one's treasure is, there is one's heart also. In fact, the moral state of heart corresponds to the nature of the gifts brought; the offerings that God would not accept in Malachi 1:10 arise from lives in sin (Mal. 2:8).[22]

The king then prayed that God would always keep the hearts of His people fixed on Him; he specifically prayed that Solomon would remain loyal to God, and to His Laws, and would build the Lord a house (1 Chron. 29:18-19). David then said to the assembly: *"Now bless the Lord your God."* The people did just that, bowing their heads and prostrating themselves before the Lord (1 Chron. 29:20).

David's Decline and Adonijah's Ambition (1 Kgs. 1)

Because Chronicles centers on the positive aspects of David's kingdom, the writer does not mention David's failing health in his autumn years, nor Adonijah's attempt to seize the throne. Apparently, David, in his frail condition, could not keep warm, so a beautiful young virgin, Abishag, was found to care for David (1 Kgs. 1:1-3). Although Abishag did lie in bed with David to keep him warm, the two did not have sexual relations (1 Kgs. 1:4). Such an intimate association could have been permitted only on the grounds of decency, meaning that Abishag likely had become David's concubine – this status would protect her reputation.

Adonijah, the son of Haggith (born after Absalom) and David's oldest living son, then exalted himself, saying, *"I will be king"* (1 Kgs. 1:5). David did not rebuke or challenge Adonijah's efforts to promote himself before the people (e.g., having chariots, horsemen, and fifty heralds going before him; 1 Kgs. 1:6). Adonijah brought David's deposed general Joab and one of the high priests at that time, Abiathar (in the line of Eli), into his scheming (1 Kgs. 1:7). However, Zadok, the other high priest, Benaiah, one of David's distinguished mighty men and the commander of the eleventh rotational army division, Nathan, the prophet, Shimei, Rei, and the other mighty men who belonged to David were not with Adonijah (1 Kgs. 1:8).

Adonijah invited all the influential men of Judah and his brothers (the king's sons excluding Solomon) to a sacrifice of sheep, oxen, and fattened cattle by the stone of Zoheleth located at the foot of Ophel just east-southeast of Jerusalem (1 Kgs. 1:9). The prophet Nathan, the high priest Zadok, and Benaiah, David's humble and loyal commander, were not invited to the celebration either (1 Kgs. 1:10). Nathan understood the leveraging tactic of that time and realized that if Adonijah became king, those not invited to his feast would be executed; Solomon and his mother Bathsheba were in imminent danger.

Nathan quickly informed Bathsheba of the matter. The two formulated a plan to inform David of what Adonijah was doing and then to remind him that he had already promised that Solomon would be his successor (1 Kgs. 1:11-27). Although this promise to Bathsheba is not recorded in Scripture, David could have uttered it because the Lord had already told him that Solomon would be Israel's next king before he was born (1 Chron. 22:9-10). It would seem that this scenario occurred prior to David's national address just discussed (i.e., 1 Chron. 28 and 29), as David publicly names Solomon as his successor at that time.

The two-stage plan called first for Bathsheba to speak to an apparently bedridden David with Nathan arriving immediately after she departed to establish her claim. After hearing Nathan, David summoned Bathsheba to return. After she arrived, David affirmed by oath that Solomon would be Israel's next king, just as he had previously promised (1 Kgs. 1:28-31).

Having learned of Adonijah's plot, David immediately acted to place Solomon on Israel's throne as king. He tasked Zadok, Nathan, and Benaiah to assemble David's loyal servants and to have Solomon ride his own mule before the people and lead him to the spring of Gihon where he should be anointed as king (1 Kgs. 1:32-33). Then the horn (likely the two silver trumpets) was to be blown and all the people should shout, *"Long live King Solomon!"* (1 Kgs. 1:34). Besides summoning the Israelites to action during the wilderness era, the silver trumpets were blown over sacrifices (Num. 10:10), and on feast days (Num. 29:1; Lev. 23:24). Now a precedent was being set for the silver trumpets to be blown over a newly anointed king.

Following Solomon's anointing David said that his son should be escorted to the throne, for he had *"appointed him to be ruler over Israel and Judah"* (1 Kgs. 1:35). David's servants did all that their king commanded them to do and Solomon became Israel's king (1 Kgs. 1:36-40). Solomon was escorted by the Kerethites and the Pelethites (David's royal bodyguards) under Benaiah's command. Zadok took a horn of oil from the holy tabernacle and carried it to Gihon to anoint Solomon.

Solomon shared a brief coregency with his father David for an unknown period of time (but certainly less than two years). Jamieson, Fausset, and Brown, referring to 2 Samuel 5:5 with 1 Chronicles 29:27, suggest a six-month coregency.[23] The evidence also suggests a short interval since David was in poor health and apparently bedridden at the time of Solomon's first anointing, and he could not attend the ceremony (1 Kgs. 1:48). However, not long afterwards, David became strong enough to address the people concerning Solomon and the temple. Solomon would be anointed a second time after David's death. The second anointing was to publicly recognize his sole rulership of the Jewish nation (1 Chron. 29:22).

Meanwhile Adonijah's guests, just a half mile south of the spring of Gihon, were baffled by the loud commotion coming from Jerusalem and the sounding of a horn (or trumpets). However, Jonathan, the son of the high priest Abiathar, soon arrived bearing the news that David had put Solomon on the throne (1 Kgs. 1:41-48). Previously, Jonathan and Zadok's son Ahimaaz had risked their lives by leaving En-rogel to warn David of Absalom's plans against him. Ironically, a few years later he returns to En-rogel to inform Adonijah that his plot to take the throne has been foiled (Jonathan was not numbered with the rebels).

Realizing that their conspiracy had failed and that now all their lives were in jeopardy, everyone, including Adonijah fled from their feast (1 Kgs. 1:49). Being terrified of Solomon, Adonijah apparently fled to the old tabernacle at Gibeah and took hold of the horns of the bronze altar and pleaded for Solomon to show him mercy (1 Kgs. 1:50-51). Exodus 21:14 implies that the altar was a safe haven until a matter had been fully investigated and decided.

Based on Adonijah's action, Solomon was willing to extend conditional mercy to him: If he proved himself to be a man worthy of mercy, he would receive it, but if he pursued wickedness, he would be executed (1 Kgs. 1:52). Adonijah agreed to Solomon's conditional amnesty, left the altar and came before the king and humbled himself (1 Kgs. 1:53). Solomon honored his promise and granted Adonijah leave, saying, *"Go to your house."*

David's Final Instructions to Solomon (1 Kgs. 2:1-10)

Just before David died, he privately instructed the new king concerning his relationship with God (1 Kgs. 2:1-4) and then concerning three official matters pertaining to others (1 Kgs. 2:5-9). David exhorts his son to walk in the ways of the Lord by keeping His statutes, commandments, judgments, and testimonies as written in the Law of Moses (1 Kgs. 2:3). As Ezra and the Lord Jesus did later, David, in verse 3, affirms that Moses wrote the five books of the Law (Neh. 8:1; Mark 7:10, 12:26). Solomon is warned by his father that his prosperity going forward was contingent on honoring the Lord. He even informs the new king of God's promise to him: *"If your sons take heed to their way, to walk before Me in truth with all their heart and with all their soul ... you shall not lack a man on the throne of Israel"* (1 Kgs. 2:4). The Davidic covenant promised David an everlasting dynasty, an eternal throne, and an eternal kingdom (2 Sam. 7:12-13); however, David warned Solomon that God would still judge the sins of his posterity.

Switching to official matters, David first instructed Solomon to execute Joab for murdering Abner and Amasa during a time of peace (1 Kgs. 2:5-6). These crimes were committed by one under his authority and therefore David was taking responsibility to uphold the righteousness of God's Law. The second decree was for Solomon to show kindness to the sons of Barzillai the Gileadite because of his kind hospitality to David during Absalom's revolt (1 Kgs. 2:7). The third official matter related to Shimei. Although David (after regaining the throne) did not execute Shimei for cursing him, Shimei was guilty of an offense worthy of death (1 Kgs. 2:8-9). David probably chose not to mar the celebratory nature of his return by taking vengeance on those who had opposed and oppressed him during Absolom's rebellion; however, David had not forgotten the offense and Solomon was instructed to pursue a righteous end in the matter.

Solomon Anointed King Again (1 Chron. 29:21-25)

The day after David's proclamation concerning Solomon (1 Chron. 28:9-10), a thousand bulls, a thousand rams, a thousand lambs, with drink offerings, and sacrifices in abundance were offered to the Lord (1 Chron. 29:21). All Israel ate and drank with gladness before the Lord (1 Chron. 29:22).

The last portion of 1 Chronicles 29:22 seems to relate to another national gathering a short time after David's death. Solomon was anointed a second time to illustrate that he was now the sole king of Israel; Zadok also became the sole high priest (1 Chron. 29:23). The Lord prospered Solomon and all Israel submitted to his authority (1 Chron. 29:23-24). Because *"the Lord exalted Solomon exceedingly in the sight of all Israel,"* his royal majesty exceeded that of his father David and of Saul before him (1 Chron. 29:25).

David Dies (1 Kgs. 2:10-12; 1 Chron. 29:26-30)

The historian then summarizes David's forty-year reign (1011-971 B.C.). He ruled over Judah for seven years plus in Hebron and then over the entire nation for thirty-three years in Jerusalem (1 Kgs. 2:11-12). David died at the age of seventy, being *"full of days and riches and honor"* and his son Solomon reigned in his place over a thoroughly established kingdom (1 Chron. 29:28). Three prophets recorded the acts of King David; these are contained in the book of Samuel, in the book of Nathan, and in the book of Gad (1 Chron. 29:29-30). Although the latter two books were eventually lost (i.e., God chose not to preserve them), the historian apparently gleaned from their contents to compose his own work. David was laid to rest with his fathers and was buried in the City of David (1 Kgs. 2:10).

Like Saul before him, and Solomon after him, David reigned over Israel for forty years (seven years plus in Hebron, and thirty-three years in Jerusalem (1 Chron. 29:26-27). In his early years, David did not know that God had chosen Jerusalem as the location to establish His name; however, after learning the mind of God, David moved his home and the political capital of Israel from Hebron to Jerusalem.

Forty is the number of probationary testing in the Bible, as first established by Moses leading Israel through the wilderness for forty years. Saul's forty-year kingship taught Israel about the ills of following the flesh. David then instructed the people how to rightly follow the Lord. Solomon's reign would test the people as to which example of Israel's previous kings they would follow.

David's life had not been without difficulties, but he lived a full life and accomplished many great things for God. Even while fleeing from Saul, God blessed David, built up his warriors, his family, his wealth, and his fame. His life was full because he had a heart for the Lord, which was the reason God chose him in his adolescent years to lead His people.

Judgments Follow David's Death (1 Kgs. 2:13-46)

Adonijah visited Bathsheba, and bemoaned that the kingdom had been taken from him and given to Solomon by the Lord (1 Kgs. 2:13-14). The queen's initial question, "Do you come peaceably?" conveys her apprehension over Adonijah's visit and that caution was warranted. Adonijah's acknowledgment of the matter being "from the Lord" seems to be a pious ploy to settle Bathsheba's anxiety and leverage her to take up his request with her son, the king. As a compensation for his loss, Adonijah asked Bathsheba to petition Solomon to give him the young virgin Abishag for a wife (1 Kgs. 2:15-17). This seemed like a harmless matter to her, so Bathsheba agreed to speak to Solomon (1 Kgs. 2:18).

Solomon greeted his mother with great respect, rising from the throne to meet her, bowing before her, and then seating her at his right hand (1 Kgs. 2:19). This permitted the opportunity for a private conversation, so she presented Adonijah's request to have Abishag as his wife (1 Kgs. 2:20-21). Incensed, Solomon immediately responded, *"Now why do you ask Abishag the Shunammite for Adonijah? Ask for him the kingdom also – for he is my older brother – for him, and for Abiathar the priest, and for Joab the son of Zeruiah"* (v. 22). To give Abishag to Adonijah would be the same as confessing that he had a right to be David's successor, which would then permit him further opportunity to assert himself later. Solomon swore before the Lord that he would not tolerate any exploitation of Israel's throne on which the Lord had put him (1 Kgs. 2:23-24). Adonijah had sealed his doom.

While Bathsheba merely thought of the matter as a matchmaking opportunity between two striking young people, Solomon understood Adonijah's scheming. The king responded forcefully for at least two reasons: first, he had shown Adonijah mercy, but Adonijah had tried to manipulate his authority through the queen mother. Second, and the more serious offense, was the affront to his throne. To protect Abishag's honor, she most certainly had become David's concubine – a legal wife with lesser status. In the Ancient Near East, whoever possessed the deceased king's harem was understood to have his throne also. The previous king's wives were a symbol of royal status. For example, Absalom, understanding this custom, had sexual relations with ten of David's concubines to show the people that he was the new king of Israel. Adonijah had infringed on Solomon's authority on both counts, hence the king ordered Benaiah to immediately execute his half-brother Adonijah, which he did (1 Kgs. 2:25).

Next Solomon dealt with the high priest Abiathar, who had aligned with Adonijah against him. Although deserving death, Solomon chose to banish Abiathar from the priesthood and sentenced him to live in his hometown of Anathoth located about three miles northeast of Jerusalem (1 Kgs. 2:26). The reason the king's judgment was tempered with mercy was because Abiathar had ministered before the Lord and had served David faithfully for nearly 48 years. Being the lone survivor of Saul's slaughter of priests and their families at Nob, Abiathar had joined David during his fugitive years.

Solomon's actions completed that judgment against Eli's house uttered a century earlier by God's prophet and then confirmed by the Lord to Samuel (1 Kgs. 2:27). Zadok, in the rightful line of high priest through Aaron's son Eleazar (then Phineas), became the sole high priest (1 Kgs. 2:35). (Abiathar came through Aaron's son Ithamar.) Zadok was the first high priest to oversee Solomon's temple and his descendants will have an honored position of authority within God's Millennial Temple. Ezekiel affirms that only the priests in the lineage of Zadok will be able to enter the sanctuary of the Millennial Temple to serve the Lord (Ezek. 44:15-16). The Lord indeed rewards faithfulness.

News came to Solomon that Joab had fled to the tabernacle of the Lord and had taken hold of the horns of the Bronze Altar seeking mercy (1 Kgs. 2:28). Joab no doubt was aware that Adonijah had received mercy from the new king by resorting to this tactic previously (1 Kgs. 1:50). The altar was a haven of protection to ensure that someone who had accidently killed another person was not prematurely judged by vengeful kin before receiving a fair trial. However, Joab's crimes were not accidental; he had twice committed premeditated murder and therefore would not receive mercy.

Solomon sent Benaiah to execute Joab, but he would not leave the Bronze Altar when summoned by Benaiah under the king's authority – Joab wanted to die at the altar (1 Kgs. 2:29). Not wanting to slay Joab in the tabernacle courtyard, Benaiah returned to Solomon to receive instruction (1 Kgs. 2:30). The king told his servant to slay Joab where he was to recompense the innocent blood that Joab had shed; then Benaiah was to bury him (1 Kgs. 2:31-32). As king Solomon was accountable to the Lord to avenge murder, and by judging Joab, he was fulfilling his accountability to uphold justice in the Land – the punishment for Joab's crimes would rest on him and his descendants (1 Kgs. 2:33). Benaiah executed Joab and buried him by his own house in the wilderness (1 Kgs. 2:34). Benaiah then became the general over Israel's army (1 Kgs. 2:35).

The last order of judicial business was the judgment of Shimei. Solomon summoned Shimei and affirmed that he deserved to die for his treachery and railing against David, but he would honor his father's decree of mercy as long as Shimei stayed in Jerusalem (1 Kgs. 2:36). Shimei was under house-arrest of sorts, and if he left his jail-city, he would suffer the consequences of his transgressions – death (1 Kgs. 2:37). Shimei agreed to this, but after three years, he journeyed to Achish to retrieve two run-away slaves; Solomon pronounced his sentence after he returned and Benaiah executed him (1 Kgs. 2:38-46). Through snubbing Solomon's offer of mercy, Shimei proved that his heart had not changed; the same evil that slandered David's authority was still lurking in Shimei (1 Kgs. 2:44). Solomon's wisdom in showing mercy and yet testing Shimei absolved him of a vindictive act.

Solomon had followed David's instructions concerning Joab and Shimei, fulfilled God's word concerning Abiathar from the house of Eli, and removed his rebel brother Adonijah. *"Thus the kingdom was established in the hand of Solomon"* (1 Kgs. 2:46). Solomon's pattern of strengthening himself by disposing of those who would hinder him from doing God's will is noteworthy. By removing Adonijah, the king upholds God's governing authority in His *work*, by disposing of Abiathar, Solomon affirmed God-ordained *worship*, by ridding himself of Shimei, the king affirms the necessity of an upright *walk*, and the demise of Joab shows the king's commitment to justice and to avoiding carnal *warfare*.[24] As Paul repeatedly affirms in his epistles, if we want to accomplish great things for the Lord, we also must be God-honoring in our work, our worship, our walk, and our warfare.

Meditation

> In order for a war to be just, three things are necessary. First, the authority of the sovereign. Secondly, a just cause. Thirdly, a rightful intention.
>
> — Thomas Aquinas

Men of authority and influence may promote good morals. Let them in their several stations encourage virtue. Let them favor and take part in any plans which may be formed for the advancement of morality.

— William Wilberforce

Solomon Blessed

1 Kings 3-5; 2 Chronicles 1-2

The Lord had a threefold purpose for Solomon, David's seed: First, to build His temple; second, to inherit an established kingdom so he would be unhindered in accomplishing the first objective; third, to follow and exhibit God's Law and righteousness to those under his rule. On the last point, God would bless Solomon with wisdom and power unconditionally, but other blessings on his kingship would be conditional on Solomon's faithfulness (2 Chron. 1:12). For example, he would enjoy a long life if he was subject to the Lord (1 Kgs. 3:14). Solomon strayed from the Lord in his later years and therefore did not outlive his father in age, but died after a forty-year tenure as Judah's king (971-931 B.C.), being about 59 years of age.

David becomes the spiritual measuring stick for the twenty kings of Judah that follow him. (Israel's kings were all evil to differing degrees, Jehu being the best of the worst.) Seven Judean kings were compared to David's goodness (Solomon, Asa, Jehoshaphat, Joash, Jotham, Hezekiah, and Josiah). However, only Hezekiah and Josiah had a heart for the Lord as David did, and Solomon and Joash withdrew from following the Lord in their later years. Amaziah and Uzziah began in a David-like fashion, but did not finish well, though overall, both were considered good kings. Manasseh was a pagan ruler most of his long tenure, but turned to the Lord after being chastened as a prisoner in Babylon. The remaining ten kings (Rehoboam, Abijah, Jehoram, Ahaziah, Ahaz, Amon, Jehoahaz, Jehoiakim, Jehoiachin, and Zedekiah) were evil and remained evil during their reigns. Only three of Judah's final ten kings were good. Thus, the Southern Kingdom was plunged into spiritual declension and ultimately reaped divine retribution.

The High Places

Before the judgeship of Samuel, the Ark had resided for approximately four centuries in the tabernacle pitched at Shiloh. Those loyal to Jehovah (e.g., Elkanah and Hannah; 1 Sam. 1) worshiped Him there (i.e., at the central sanctuary as decreed by Deuteronomy 12:1-32). But this was not possible after the Ark had been captured by the Philistines, then relocated at Kiriath-Jearim after its return, and then brought by David to the tent in the City of David. During the time that the Ark was separated from the tabernacle (more than a century) the Jews offered their sacrifices on high places throughout Israel (1 Kgs. 3:2). This was tolerated because technically there was no central sanctuary and the patriarchs had previously offered worship to the Lord in the high places. This explains why Solomon also offered sacrifices to Jehovah on the hills of Judah (1 Kgs. 3:3-4).

Obviously, without the Ark, some ceremonies, such as the Day of Atonement, could not be performed at all. Others, such as maintaining a lit Lampstand and presenting weekly show bread in the tabernacle at Nob and then later at Gibeon continued. By erecting the Lord's temple in Jerusalem, the central sanctuary would be again established as the only lawful place to offer the Levitical sacrifices (Lev. 17:3-4). However, offering sacrifices to God on high places remained a traditional practice in Israel until Hezekiah outlawed it almost three centuries later.

In time, Israel began to adopt the pagan customs of the Canaanites who worshiped their gods and goddesses in the high places of Canaan long before the Israelites arrived in the land. El, Baal, Ashtoreth, Dagon, Molech, and Chemosh are a few of their many false deities. Regrettably, the Jews were often enticed through immoral religious practices into committing idolatry at these lofty pagan sites and thereby angering the Lord (Isa. 57:4-5). Even Solomon, after building Jehovah's temple, later established idolatrous high places outside Jerusalem for his foreign wives, and, sadly, he worshiped with them there (1 Kgs. 11:11). This resulted in the decline of the kingdom and a dynasty that would not produce the Messiah. Only Judean kings Hezekiah and Josiah, centuries later, prohibited all worship in the high places of Israel. The proper worship of Jehovah must be accomplished before Him in His sanctuary (originally in the tabernacle and then later in the temple).

Solomon Requests Wisdom (1 Kgs. 3:1-15; 2 Chron. 1:1-13)

At the time of his coronation, Solomon was zealous for the Lord and the Lord was with him (1 Kgs. 3:3). We read that *"Solomon loved the Lord, walking in the statutes of his father David, except that he sacrificed and burned incense at the high places"* (1 Kgs. 1:3). As a result, the Lord strengthened Solomon's kingdom and exalted him exceedingly among the people.

The historian's summary note (1 Kgs. 3:1) concerning Solomon's construction feats and his alliance with Egypt (as sealed by his marriage to Pharaoh's daughter) seems to be chronologically out of place with the initial events of this chapter. The verse reads like a "preface" to alert the reader about things to come. In the negative sense, this union and others with foreign wives corrupted Solomon's purity, but that happens years later (after 1 Kgs. 10). Until the narrative of 1 Kings 11, Solomon typifies the glory and peace of Christ in His kingdom, where David portrays Christ's first advent of conquering evil through righteous faithfulness. This insight helps to explain the typological meaning of Solomon's marriage to Pharaoh's daughter.

Technically, Pharaoh's daughter, being an Egyptian, was not admissible into the stronghold of Zion because the Ark was located there (Deut. 23:7-8). However, temporary accommodations were provided for her until more suitable housing was constructed. This temporary situation pictures the Gentiles in the Church Age whom the Lord espouses in grace (2 Cor. 11:2) – they dwell in the place where the suffering and victorious king had provisionally placed the Ark (i.e., Christ's triumph at Calvary is pictured in the conqueror David).

Actually, Scripture has already revealed another picture of this same symbol. When Joseph was first rejected and then exalted, he took a Gentile bride in Egypt. However, the Ark itself has no connection with Pharaoh's daughter, but symbolizes God's covenant with Israel (Heb. 8:8). (Gentiles are a second benefactor of the New Covenant as explained in Eph. 3; Gentiles were never under the Law – it pertained to Israel only; see Gal. 3.)

After the glorious temple is erected and the Ark is placed in it, the wonders of the Kingdom Age are rightly represented in Solomon's reign of peace and prosperity. Then, Pharaoh's daughter, the wife of Solomon, is moved to a spectacular palace adjoining his. This pictures the Gentiles that survive the Tribulation Period, who are then brought into a position of blessing when Israel is restored to Christ in the Kingdom Age. Gentiles at that time will not have access to the millennial temple as will the Jews, but they will be ecstatic nonetheless about residing in a kingdom full of peace, productivity, and righteousness. As recipients of God's manifold grace, the Gentile nations will gladly worship Israel's Messiah in Jerusalem (Zech. 14:16-21). The glorified Gentile Church will have no such limitation, as their inheritance is beyond the earthly scene – it is Christ Himself.

Returning to the narrative, Solomon gathered the esteemed officers, judges, and leaders of Israel to the original tabernacle of Moses at Gibeon to offer sacrifices at the high place there (the Ark was in David's erected tent in Jerusalem; 1 Kgs. 3:2-4). The hill at Gibeon, "the great high place," was about 600 feet higher than any other hill in the surrounding region. Apparently, a new bronze altar fabricated by Bezalel had been set up there and made ready for the king's sacrifices, and Solomon offered a thousand burnt offerings on the new altar (2 Chron. 1:5-6).

That very night the Lord appeared to Solomon in a dream, and said to him, *"Ask! What shall I give you?"* (1 Kgs. 3:5). Solomon acknowledged God's mercy in first establishing David and then himself in a great kingdom; therefore, he asked the Lord for wisdom to rightly rule over the great multitude that he was responsible for (1 Kgs. 3:8-10). The Lord was delighted to grant Solomon's request. But since Solomon had not asked for riches, honor, the lives of his enemies, or a long life, the Lord promised to give him *"riches and wealth and honor, such as none of the kings have had who were before you, nor shall any after you have the like"* (1 Kgs. 3:11-13). The Lord also added the conditional promise, *"If you walk in My ways, to keep My statutes and My commandments, as your father David walked, then I will lengthen your days"* (1 Kgs. 3:14). Solomon then awoke from the dream and journeyed from Gibeon to Jerusalem and *"stood before the ark of the covenant of the Lord, offered up burnt offerings, offered peace offerings, and made a feast for all his servants"* (1 Kgs. 3:15). The new king obviously did not enter the tabernacle, but stood facing the Ark outside the tent's entrance.

At this time of his life, Solomon loved the Lord and the Lord was with Solomon. However, as previously noted, we are clued in to the cause of Solomon's future downfall in 1 Kings 3:1 – his foreign wives:

"Solomon made a treaty with Pharaoh king of Egypt, and married Pharaoh's daughter; then he brought her to the City of David until he had finished building his own house." The Law prohibited Jewish men from marrying foreign women lest their Jewish families suffer spiritual corruption (Deut. 7:3, Ezra 9:1-11).

Solomon's Wise Judgment (1 Kgs. 3:16-28; 4:29-34)

The astonishing wisdom God granted to Solomon became apparent to all through his judgments. The king's judgments caused his subjects to fear him because they knew *"the wisdom of God was in him to administer justice"* (1 Kgs. 3:28). The historian notes one such instance when two harlots approached the king concerning the custody of a baby, which both claimed to be theirs. Apparently, both women delivered baby boys three days apart, but one of the babies then died during the night. The mother of the deceased child was claiming the living child as her own. But which woman was the true mother of the living child?

Solomon commanded that a sword be brought to him so he could divide the remaining baby in two, giving each woman half. Of course, the true mother was willing to forgo her maternal rights to save the child's life, while the mother of the dead baby was agreeable to Solomon's plan – "divide it." Thus, the true mother was revealed and was consequently rewarded with the custody of her son. Considering the narrative before us, H. L. Rossier observes that in the realm of Christian profession, those who have not found the true object of the heart's focus, Christ, will quickly reveal the falseness of their claims on Christ.

> "Divide it," says the one who is not the mother, yielding to her resentment. One quickly sacrifices Christ when it is a matter of satisfying one's own passions. Only divine wisdom is able to discern *the reality of profession* by the state of the heart. How frequently there is profession without reality! Where are the affections for Christ? Where the devotion which sacrifices even its legitimate advantages and rights for Him? In this passage, it is not a question of natural goodness nor of nobleness of heart, for we are dealing with two harlots. It is a question of ties created by God, of an object given by Him which the soul appreciates. God will never take it away from us; to the contrary, in the trial we shall receive it afresh from His own

hand: *"Give her the living child, and in no wise slay it: she is the mother thereof."*[25]

Indeed, the Lord abundantly rewards those whose true affections center in the Lord. What we truly love and appreciate becomes obvious by what we are willing to sacrifice to safeguard it.

The writer further highlights the king's astute abilities: *"God gave Solomon wisdom and exceedingly great understanding, and largeness of heart like the sand on the seashore"* (1 Kgs. 4:29). His wisdom excelled that of all the men of the East and all the wisdom of Egypt (1 Kgs. 4:30). He was wiser than famed counselors such as Ethan, Heman, Chalcol, and Darda (1 Kgs. 4:31). His knowledge of vegetation, animal life, fish, and birds was world-acclaimed and many from the farthest reaches of civilization came to seek his counsel (1 Kgs. 4:33-34).

Solomon was also a prolific writer. He penned 3,000 proverbs and 105 songs (1 Kgs. 4:32). Many of these proverbs have been preserved in the books of Proverbs and Ecclesiastes. The Song of Solomon is one of the king's 105 songs. The Holy Spirit preserved only a small portion of Solomon's literary works for our benefit, perhaps because he did not walk with the Lord in his autumn years.

Solomon's Military and Economic Power (2 Chron. 1:14-17)

After sacrificing at Gibeon, Solomon returned to Jerusalem and organized his military reserves. He divided four hundred chariots and twelve thousand horsemen among his chariot cities, while also maintaining a strong contingent of both in Jerusalem.

The materials Solomon gathered for his various construction projects (including the temple) was so vast that silver and gold were as common as stones in Jerusalem, and cedar lumber was as abundant as that from sycamore trees in the lowland. Solomon also imported many horses and chariots from Egypt and Keveh and then sold them to the Hittites and Syrians for a handsome profit.

Solomon's Administration (1 Kgs. 4:1-19, 27-28)

King Solomon's cabinet officials included: Azariah the son of Zadok, the priest; Elihoreph and Ahijah, the sons of Shisha, scribes; Jehoshaphat the son of Ahilud, the recorder; Benaiah the son of

Jehoiada, over the army; Zadok and Abiathar (though removed), the priests; Azariah the son of Nathan, over the officers; Zabud the son of Nathan, a priest and the king's friend; Ahishar, over the household; and Adoniram the son of Abda, over the labor force (1 Kgs. 4:1-6).

Solomon also had twelve governors (whose names are listed in verses 8-19) throughout Israel. Each governor was responsible for supplying the king's table one month of the year. They ensured that the king never lacked any supplies; they even brought barley and straw for his horses (1 Kgs. 4:27-28). Since two of the governors listed (Ben-Abinadab and Ahimaaz) married daughters of Solomon, the list of various officials probably reflects key officials throughout Solomon's tenure.

Solomon's Prosperity (1 Kgs. 4:20-26)

The inhabitants of Judah and Israel had become as numerous as the sand by the sea and they rejoiced in their abundance of food and wine (1 Kgs. 4:20). Though not part of Israel's territory, Solomon controlled all the kingdoms from the Euphrates to the land of the Philistines, as far as the border of Egypt; these nations brought him tribute during his reign (1 Kgs. 4:21). Tiphsah was a sizeable town on the west bank of the Euphrates River. Solomon's dominion over the entire region ensured that all those in Judah and Israel would be safe from and unhindered by Gentile oppression – a necessary condition for him to construct the temple (1 Kgs. 4:24-25).

This political situation, however, is not a fulfillment of the Palestinian covenant that God made with Abraham (Gen. 15:18-21), for Israel did not possess all the land within the boundaries affirmed to the patriarch. This prophecy will not be fulfilled until the Kingdom Age, when Christ reigns over Israel on the earth.

The daily provisions required for Solomon's table were incredible: thirty kors (195 bushels) of fine flour, sixty kors (390 bushels) of meal, ten fatted oxen, twenty oxen from the pastures, and one hundred sheep, besides deer, gazelles, roebucks, and fatted fowl (1 Kgs. 4:22-23). In total, the king had forty thousand stalls of horses for his chariots, and twelve thousand horsemen (1 Kgs. 4:26).

Solomon Prepares to Build the Temple (1 Kgs. 5; 2 Chron. 2)

To build Jehovah a temple and himself a house, Solomon conscripted 70,000 men to bear burdens, 80,000 men to quarry stone in the mountains, and 3,600 men to oversee his labor force (1 Kgs. 5:15-16; 2 Chron. 2:1-2). This work force was composed of 153,000 aliens (Canaanites) in the land of Israel as determined by his father David's census (2 Chron. 2:17-18).

Solomon's action further fulfills Noah's prophecy against his wicked son Ham as recorded in Genesis 9: the descendants of Ham's son were the Canaanites. They were an immoral and perverse people (Lev. 18:3, 27) many of whom were destroyed by the Israelites (the descendants of Shem) under the leadership of Joshua (Deut. 20:17-18). Some, like the Gibeonites, became slaves to the Israelites as a result of their trickery (Josh. 9:16-27). Those who survived the Canaan Conquest were levied a tribute of bond service by King Solomon, according to 1 Kings 9:20-22. As Noah acknowledged, it would be through the line of Shem that God's Messiah would come (which Luke verifies; Luke 3:36) and that Ham's descendants would be servants of their brethren (Gen. 9:25).

Besides non-Jewish laborers, Solomon additionally conscripted 30,000 Jewish men to work one month out of every three in the forests of Lebanon (i.e., 10,000 men rotated into service each month; 1 Kings 5:13-14).

Solomon contacted Hiram, king of Tyre, and requested an abundance of cedar, algum, and cypress trees for his construction projects. Solomon informed Hiram that he desired to build Jehovah a house greater than any temple erected for pagan deities, for the heavens could not contain Jehovah, who was greater than all so-called gods (2 Chron. 2:2-5). Because the Phoenicians were well-known for their skillful architecture, Solomon also asked Hiram to supply him with skilled craftsmen, engravers, seamstresses, and woodsmen. In return for Hiram's assistance, Solomon promised to supply an abundance of wine, oil, and food for his laborers (2 Chron. 2:10). These provisions included 20,000 cors (about 125,000 bushels) of ground wheat, 20,000 baths (about 115,000 gallons) of oil and of wine.

Hiram wrote a favorable response to Solomon's request because he knew that the Lord loved His people, had made Solomon king over them, and had also given him wisdom and understanding to accomplish what needed to be built (2 Chron. 2:11-12). Hiram agreed to supply laborers, skilled workers, and timber as Solomon requested in return for wheat, barley, oil, and wine as proposed (2 Chron. 2:13-16). The wood would be cut in Lebanon, transported to Tyre, floated by rafts down the Mediterranean Sea to Joppa, and then Solomon would be responsible for transporting the timber to Jerusalem (2 Chron. 2:16).

The king also commanded that large quarried stones for the temple's foundation, and other costly stones and hewn stones, be prepared at the quarry before being transported to the construction site (2 Kgs. 5:17-18). All stones were *"finished at the quarry, so that no hammer or chisel or any iron tool was heard in the temple while it was being built"* (1 Kgs. 6:7). This meant that the temple was erected quietly. This was quite an engineering feat, but no task is too difficult when the Lord is enabling the work!

David understood from God's covenant with him (2 Sam. 7) that he was to clear the way so that his son could build the Lord's house. In God's providential purposes, He called David to be a fighter and Solomon to be a builder – both are essential in the triumphal work of God and represent both advents of Christ. This is why Solomon in all of his greatness could say: *"The Lord my God has given me rest on every side; there is neither adversary nor evil occurrence"* (1 Kgs. 5:4).

Indeed, King Solomon established the most glorious kingdom in Israel's history. His wealth was so vast that silver became like common stones in Jerusalem; his wisdom was coveted by rulers worldwide (1 Kgs. 10:23-27). Though the splendor of his own monarchy was astounding, Solomon foretells in Psalm 72 an even more spectacular dominion of peace, prosperity, and righteousness – the Millennial Kingdom of Christ (Isa. 11; Rev. 20). The millennial reign of Christ is the theme of Psalm 72 and is a direct answer to the sufferings of Christ at the hands of sinners in Psalm 69, the petition of Christ recorded in Psalm 70, and the restoration of Israel foretold in Psalm 71. The greatest kingdom the world will ever know is yet to come!

Meditation

Blest be our everlasting Lord,
Our Father, God, and King!
Thy sovereign goodness we record,
Thy glorious power we sing.

By Thee the victory is given;
The majesty divine,
And strength, and might, and earth, and Heaven,
And all therein, are Thine.

The kingdom, Lord, is Thine alone,
Who dost Thy right maintain,
And high on Thine eternal throne,
Over men and angels reign.

Riches, as seems good to Thee,
Thou dost, and honor, give;
And kings their power and dignity
Out of Thy hand receive.

— Charles Wesley

Solomon Builds

1 Kings 6-7; 2 Chronicles 3:1-5:1

The Importance of Jerusalem (2 Chron. 3:1)

In Genesis 22:1-2 we read that God commanded Abraham to offer Isaac as a burnt offering on a mount in the land that He would show him. Abraham proved his love for the Lord, and the Lord intervened to stop the sacrifice and to provide a ram to be offered in Isaac's place. Abraham offered the ram *"instead of his son"* (Gen. 22:13). Accordingly, *"Abraham called the name of the place, The-Lord-Will-Provide; as it is said to this day, 'In the Mount of the Lord it shall be provided'"* (Gen. 22:14). This prophecy would be fulfilled over two thousand years later, when just outside of Jerusalem God provided His own Son as a sacrifice for human sin.

A millennium after Abraham's test, David offered a burnt sacrifice to God on a mountain in Moriah to stay a judgment of pestilence against Israel (1 Chron. 21). Pride had lured David to number the men of Israel, and God responded with a disciplinary plague. A generation later, Solomon was to build a spectacular temple on Mount Moriah, the same location that the Lord had appeared to David when he offered the sacrifice to avert the plague (2 Chron. 3:1). Another millennium later, the Lord Jesus Christ was tried and crucified on or near the same location. In a future millennium, the Lord Jesus will reign from Jerusalem, which will then be honored as the religious capital of the world (Zech. 14:16-17).

From Genesis to Revelation, Scripture indicates that the ridge of Moriah at Jerusalem is a special location to the Lord. After the Israelites settled in Canaan, Jerusalem would be formally recognized as the only place that worship was to be offered to Jehovah for as long as the earth exists, except during the Church Age. At present, all believer-priests (Christians) are the temple of God and lift up worship and living sacrifices heavenward to God wherever and whenever they desire (1 Pet. 2:5, 9; Rev. 1:6; Rom. 12:1).

The pattern for God's plan of human redemption was first revealed in Genesis 22. Abraham's saga is so traumatic, yet so awe-inspiring, that our finite minds are captivated as we ponder Calvary from a heavenly perspective of divine anguish. God would judge His innocent and only begotten Son at Calvary, near Jerusalem, for our sin. Only by embracing the Savior's cross at Jerusalem would man find forgiveness and solace for his grieving soul. To the Jew, God declares, *"Zion, you who bring good tidings, get up into the high mountain; O Jerusalem, you who bring good tidings, lift up your voice with strength, lift it up, be not afraid; say to the cities of Judah, 'Behold your God!'"* (Isa. 40:9). Concerning the Gentiles, it was the Lord's will for evangelism to begin at Jerusalem and then to spread to the uttermost parts of the world (Matt. 28:19-20; Acts 1:8).

During the Millennial Kingdom, the message to the world shall be, *"And it shall come to pass that everyone who is left of all the nations which came against Jerusalem shall go up from year to year to worship the King, the Lord of hosts, and to keep the Feast of Tabernacles"* (Zech. 14:16). The Lord ascended into heaven from Jerusalem, and He will return to Jerusalem to establish His earthly kingdom (Acts 1; Zech. 14). From Isaiah 2:1-5 and 66:20 we learn that Jerusalem shall then be the religious center of the world. Christ will reign from there, and all the nations will come there to praise, worship, and learn (Zech. 14:16-21). There will be no war or violence, only peace. All the earth shall see the glory of the Lord Jesus. So great will be the glory of the Lord upon the earth that there will be no need for the sun or moon to illuminate it (Isa. 60:18-20). Though God permitted its destruction several times in its history due to Jewish disobedience, Jerusalem is the location where God chose to tie His name. The Lord wept over the city, suffered in the city, and chastened its inhabitants, but there is a day coming when it will be full of joy and will shine forth the glory of God to all nations!

Construction Begins and Bible Chronology (1 Kgs. 6:12; Chron. 3:2)

Both Chronicles and Kings provide the exact day that Solomon began construction of the temple, but Kings also notes that the work began *"in the four hundred and eightieth year after the children of Israel had come out of the land of Egypt"* (1 Kgs. 6:1). Solomon reigned as king in Israel for forty years, from 971 to 931 B.C. This means that the temple work was initiated in 966 B.C., and 480 years earlier would put the date of the Exodus at 1446 B.C.[26]

The statement in 1 Kings 6:1 enables us to fix the interval of the Judges with more confidence. Working forward from the 1446 B.C. date for the exodus and adding forty years for the wilderness experience, seven years for the Canaan conquest, and a few decades for the elders who outlived Joshua to die, the period of the Judges would have commenced between 1390 and 1350 B.C. If the last elder (being less than twenty years of age at the time of the exodus) lived as long as Joshua (i.e. 110 years), then a date nearer to 1350 seems reasonable. Israel entered into idolatry shortly after this time (Judg. 2:7), thus initiating the cycle of disciplinary action which necessitated the Judges. This evaluation would suggest that the period of the Judges ended with Saul's ascent to the throne in 1050 B.C. and likely lasted between 300 and 340 years.

What about Paul's historical overview in Acts 13:18-21, which specifies 450 years for the era of the Judges? The reference is difficult to reconcile with the previously explained Bible chronology, though various explanations have been suggested. It is possible that Paul is including the years of Jewish oppression in Egypt within the scope of oppression during the time of the Judges. But textually speaking, this rationalization does not hold much merit. A more likely explanation is that Paul is speaking of the total number of years of independent judgeships and related oppressions, instead of absolute chronology, as in Solomon's statement. Because judges had authority over a particular region of Israel, rather than over the entire nation, some judgeships were concurrent. This would mean that the total time of the judges would be less than the cumulative 408 years of judgeships and oppressions recorded in Scripture. If Paul included the nearly forty years that Samuel, the last judge, lived after Saul's ascent to the throne, that would be approximately 450 years (i.e., the era of kings and judges overlapped).

Given the various scriptural references just discussed, a start date of 966 B.C. for Solomon's temple seems appropriate.

Temple Construction (1 Kgs. 6:1-11, 13-36, 7:13-51; 2 Chron. 3:3-5:1)

Stones for the temple were finished at the quarry and then brought to the construction site and fitted together without the hammering and chiseling noise of iron tools (1 Kgs. 6:7). Jamieson, Fausset, and Brown explain the archeological evidence which verifies the related biblical narrative:

> A subterranean quarry has been very recently discovered near Jerusalem, where the temple stones are supposed to have been hewn. There is unequivocal evidence to be found in this quarry that the stones were dressed there, because there are blocks exactly similar in size, as well as in the nature of the stone, to the ancient remains. Thence probably they would be moved on rollers down the Tyropean valley to the very site of the temple. The discovery of the great quarry under Bezetha has shown that these immense stones were excavated, hewn, and fully prepared on the spot, whence they were conveyed on trucks or on rollers down the gently-inclined plane to the site chosen for the temple.[27]

The Jewish historian Josephus states that the summit of the temple mount was leveled with incredible labor in order that the lowest parts might be raised 600 feet, to the same height as the top of the hill upon which the temple foundation would be laid.[28] The temple foundation was 90 feet long and 30 feet wide, with an additional 30 feet on its east side for the portico (2 Chron. 3:3-4; 1 Kgs. 6:3 allots only 15 feet for the porch). The height of the temple was 45 feet, with the portico being 30 feet tall. The holy place was paneled with pine or cypress and covered with gold from Parvaim; this gold veneer was then engraved with figures of palm trees and cherubim (2 Chron. 3:5-7). From inside the temple nothing but gold would have been visible to the priests.

The most holy place of the temple was 30 by 30 feet and its interior was plated with 600 talents of gold (about 23 tons); gold nails were also used as fasteners in this chamber (2 Chron. 3:8-14). The Ark would be placed in this room between two constructed gold cherubim which apparently faced forward. As each cherub had a fifteen-foot wingspan, their wings would have reached to the northern and southern walls and touched in the middle of the room over the Ark. As in the original tabernacle, a veil of four colors (blue, purple, crimson, and white) with woven images of cherubim hung between the most holy place and holy place compartments.

We learn from 1 Kings 6:5-10 that Solomon built three levels of chambers around the walls of the temple. The lowest chamber measured 7.5 feet in width, the middle chamber was 9 feet in width, and the upper chamber was 10.5 feet wide, because "*he made narrow ledges around the outside of the temple, so that the support beams would not be fastened into the walls of the temple*" (1 Kgs. 6:6). The doorway to the middle story was on the right side of the temple, which allowed the priests to access the middle and upper stories by stairs. These rooms were used for storage, to conduct meetings, and to provide living quarters for the priests (1 Kgs. 6:5; 2 Chron. 31:11; Neh. 13:7-9).

We are introduced to a second man bearing the name of Hiram (also spelled Huram) in 1 Kings 7:13. This man is not the king of Tyre (1 Kgs. 5:1), but a master craftsman known for his skill in bronze works. It is interesting to see that works of bronze were crafted by Huram, who was under Solomon's authority, but the narrative says that Solomon made the golden vessels. Obviously, Solomon did not personally craft the gold articles, but it does show that what is connected with service to God belongs under the authority that He has recognized. This ensures proper direction and accountability.

While all our service for the Lord is under Christ's authority, much of what we do is not specifically commanded. However, what is demands a higher diligence of our attention: *"If anyone thinks himself to be a prophet or spiritual, let him acknowledge that the things which I write to you are the commandments of the Lord"* (1 Cor. 14:37). When God has declared His order in Scripture for us to follow, we must be attentive to not compromise any truth for the sake of service. The most advanced and spiritual part of our service will always uphold the headship of Christ as pictured in the gold vessels in the holy place being made by Solomon.

Positioned in front of the temple entrance were two free-standing bronze pillars, referred to as Jachin and Boaz (2 Chron. 3:15-17; 1 Kgs. 7:15-21). Each pillar stood 35 feet tall with their capitals (27 feet without), was nearly six feet in diameter, and had two rows of a hundred engraved pomegranates on its upper portion (2 Chron. 4:13). Each of the two pillars is estimated to have weighed about 89 tons and would have attracted the immediate attention of those visiting the temple.[29]

These are the only two pillars mentioned in the temple and their significance is conveyed in the meanings of their names: Jachin – "He shall establish" and Boaz – "in Him is strength." While both strength and stability were apparent in Solomon's magnificent reign, their fuller fulfillment will occur in the Kingdom Age, when Christ, by His own strength, establishes His own kingdom. Solomon did not initiate his own kingdom, God did for a time and then it faded, but Christ will have the authority and power to both inaugurate and maintain His majestic dominion of peace, prosperity, and righteousness.

The Bronze Altar was fabricated and placed in the courtyard directly in front of the temple. This altar was as large as the most holy place (30 by 30 feet) and was 15 feet high (2 Chron. 4:1).

The Bronze Laver (the Bronze Sea) was fashioned and placed in front of the temple's entrance, but to the south of the Bronze Altar (2 Chron. 4:2-6, 10). It held 2,000 baths (around 12,000 gallons or 50 tons of water) and measured about 7.5 feet in height and 15 feet in diameter (1 Kgs. 7:23-26). The thickness of the rim was a handbreadth (2 Chron. 4:5). If a 3.5 inch-thick casting is assumed, the Laver would have weighed 25 to 30 tons.[30] The Bronze Laver rested on the backs of twelve bronze bulls, three facing each of four directions.

Timothy Paine calculates that the bronze laver with its twelve sculpted bronze bulls would have weighed a bit less than 44 tons. This would mean that the laver (when filled with water) with its twelve supports weighed about 120 tons. Paine also estimates that the bronze altar with its fourteen large castings weighed approximately 270 tons.[31] Obviously, whatever the two Bronze Pillars, the Bronze Altar, and the Bronze Laver with its "bull" supports actually weighed, their incredible size and heaviness presented a tremendous casting challenge that was overcome.

There were also ten smaller brass lavers resting on ten elaborate bronze carts that were 6 feet by 6 feet and 3 feet wide. Five of these laver/carts were positioned on the north and south sides of the temple (1 Kgs. 7:27-39). According to Jewish tradition, water from the huge Bronze Laver was piped through the mouths of the oxen like a faucet to supply water to the portable basins. The priests then used the water in the smaller lavers to wash the burnt offerings (2 Chron. 4:6), and items used for preparing the sacrifices, or purification activities (e.g., washing their hands and feet before entering the temple). The water in the lavers was replaced at least daily.

If one of these smaller lavers was filled with water one foot deep, that would be approximately one ton of water and the supporting structure probably did not weigh any less than that. Napier estimates one full portable laver weighed about two tons.[32] As we inventory all the bronze items about the temple courtyard, their total weight was likely between 500 and 600 tons, which is roughly equivalent to the maximum takeoff weight of the largest commercial aircraft ever built to date (i.e., the A380).

The writer then turns from the items of bronze forged for placement outside the temple to the articles of gold fashioned to reside within the temple. Ten gold lampstands (five against the south wall and five against the north wall) were placed in the holy place of the temple (2 Chron. 4:9). Also, ten gold tables (i.e., identified with the Table of Showbread – "the bread of the Presence") were also placed in the main hall of the temple, five on the north side and five on the south side (2 Chron. 4:8). These were located on the interior side of the lampstands, which were near the north and south walls. The original tabernacle had a single Gold Lampstand (against the south side) and one Table of Showbread (on the north side).

One hundred gold bowls were also placed in this room. The purpose of these bowls is unknown, but was likely connected with the gold vessel that contained a special incense that was set before the Lord, and only He was to enjoy its fragrance (Ex. 30:34-38). Although no specific measurements were given for the sweet spices (stacte and onycha and galbanum), equal amounts of the spices were to be *"beaten small."* Frankincense, which yields a sweet aroma when burned, was to be placed upon the ground incense and set before the Lord (in the most holy place of the original tabernacle).

This special incense speaks of those superb and indescribable qualities that the Father appreciates about His Son, especially those exhibited in the agony of Calvary. The Lampstands proclaim Christ as "the light of the world" and the Tables of Showbread, as *"the bread of life which came down from heaven,"* but these one hundred bowls likely symbolize God's satisfaction in His Son's sacrifice and His delight in His Son's moral excellence. While Solomon fabricated ten lampstands and tables as compared to one each in the original tabernacle, he was guided by the Lord to create one hundred bowls instead of one to convey the Father's utter pleasure in His Son!

The writer then summarizes the work of Huram, the chief fabricator of bronze articles for the temple (2 Chron. 4:11-18). Besides casting the two gigantic pillars, the Bronze Altar, and the Bronze Laver, Huram also fashioned various utensils (e.g., pots, shovels, and sprinkling bowls) which the priests would need in the inner courtyard. The historian also informs us that the larger items were cast in clay molds in the Jordan Valley between Succoth and Zeredah (Zarethan). This meant that these massive bronze articles had to be transported about 45 miles southwest to Jerusalem. That journey also requires an ascent of nearly 3,800 feet. So much bronze was used in all the items that Huram fabricated that there was no attempt to weigh it!

A summary of the gold items furnished by Solomon for the temple (including chains and various decorative items) is then given (2 Chron. 4:19-22). The Gold Altar of Incense is mentioned in 1 Chronicles 4:19 and 1 Kings 6:22, which reads: "*he* [Solomon] *overlaid with gold the entire altar that was by the inner sanctuary*." Although the Golden Altar of Incense was located in the Holy Place, it was really associated with the Ark of the Covenant; thus, the altar is often spoken of as being *"before the Lord"* (Lev. 16:12-14; 1 Kgs. 6:22; Ps. 141:2). However, the Golden Altar had to be separated from the Most Holy Place by a veil so that the priests could frequently burn special incense upon it (Ex. 30:34-38) and also so they could apply sacrificial blood upon its horns to link it with the work of atonement accomplished on the Bronze Altar. Besides the Altar of Incense, Solomon supplied ten Lampstands, ten Tables of Showbread, plus all the gold utensils needed for the priests in the sanctuary (e.g., wick-trimmers, bowls, ladles, censers).

Solomon's Palace (1 Kgs. 7:1-12)

The writer of Kings pauses to note that Solomon was busy constructing his royal palace complex while also erecting the temple. His palace was about four times larger than the temple and required thirteen years to complete, probably because of its size and that the temple work had precedence. Solomon's royal estate was also called "the Palace of the Forest of Lebanon" (1 Kgs. 10:17; Isa. 22:8) because of its vast use of Lebanese cedar.

Solomon's house measured 150 feet by 75 feet and was 45 feet high and had a surrounding porch/walkway with a canopy on pillars over it. The central feature of the king's house was the hall of pillars (1 Kgs.

7:6), which likely served as an armory and display room for the king's 300 gold shields (1 Kgs. 10:17). The Hall of Justice was also attached to the royal palace as was an associated residence for Pharaoh's daughter whom he had married. A great walled courtyard in the middle united all these stone buildings into a huge palace complex.

The Temple Finished (1 Kgs. 6:37-38; 2 Chron. 5:1)

The construction of the temple and its furnishings began in April/May of the fourth year of Solomon's reign (966 B.C.) and was finished in October/November of the eleventh year of his reign (959 B.C.; 1 Kgs. 6:37-38). Hence, the entire construction project took seven and a half years to complete. After Solomon completed building the house of the Lord, he *"brought in the things which his father David had dedicated: the silver and the gold and all the furnishings. And he put them in the treasuries of the house of God"* (2 Chron. 5:1). All was now set to dedicate the temple to the Lord.

Meditation

Pride of man and earthly glory,
Sword and crown betray his trust;
What with care and toil he builds,
Tower and temple fall to dust.
But God's power, hour by hour,
Is my temple and my tower.

— Joachim Neander

The Temple Receives the Ark

1 Kings 8:1-61; 2 Chronicles 5:2-6:42

The Ark Is Brought to the Temple (1 Kgs. 8:1-13; 2 Chron. 5:2-14)

In the seventh month, the temple having been completed and its holy articles in place, Solomon summoned Israel's leaders to Jerusalem to bring the Ark from its tent in the City of David to the temple (2 Chron. 5:2). The Jewish nation gathered with Solomon for a great feast on this festive occasion (2 Chron. 5:3-4). A multitude of sheep and oxen were sacrificed for burnt offerings and peace offerings (2 Chron. 5:6).

The Ark of the Covenant and other holy furnishings in the tabernacle were carried by the Levites to the temple. The Ark is one of the most remarkable objects in Scripture, for, though it was a physical thing, it depicted the actual seat of Jehovah's presence among His people.

The Ark was put in the Most Holy Place under the two gold cherubim (2 Chron. 5:5, 7-9). Because of the frequent moves during the wilderness years, the Ark's carrying poles were to remain in its rings (Ex. 25:15). However, to now show permanence, the poles were removed, but still kept in the Most Holy Place with the Ark. The historian notes that the two stone tablets of the Mosaic Law were the only contents of the Ark at that time (2 Chron. 5:10). What happened to the pot of manna and the rod of Aaron which were placed in the Ark in the days of Moses?

The Ark being brought to Zion, by the victorious King David, pictures the triumphant work that Christ accomplished in His rejection at Calvary. After the Ark is placed in the temple, the glorious splendor of the Millennial Kingdom is reflected in King Solomon's reign of peace and prosperity. This latter event is fulfilled in reality after Israel is ultimately restored to the Lord (i.e., after the Tribulation Period), but until that time Israel will continue to reject their Messiah and to suffer the condemnation demanded by the Law. The pot of manna represents the Bread of Life who came down from heaven to impart eternal life, but was rejected by Israel and hence He returned to heaven (John 6:31-41). Aaron's rod pictures the unfailing and eternal priesthood of Christ which ensures resurrection life, but, being disdained by His own people, He returned to heaven, where He never ceases to be the Great High Priest of the redeemed (Heb. 4:14-15, 9:11-12). This explains why only the Law and not the pot of manna or Aaron's rod were in the Ark.

For this special occasion of bringing the Ark into the temple, the priests did not keep to their divisions assigned by David. Accordingly, a large host of sanctified priests wearing white linen robes accompanied the Ark into the temple (2 Chron. 5:11). Overall, Israel, as led by the priests and the Levites, followed the example of David when he brought the Ark to Jerusalem nearly four decades earlier (2 Sam. 6). *"Those of Asaph and Heman and Jeduthun, with their sons and their brethren"* played cymbals, harps, and lyres and a hundred priests blew trumpets. The priests and Levites sang, *"For He is good, for His mercy endures forever"* (2 Chron. 5:12-13). The religious leaders were acknowledging by this song that Jehovah had established them in the land, but was also blessing and protecting the Jewish nation again.

We then read that *"the house of the Lord was filled with a cloud, so that the priests could not continue ministering because of the cloud; for the glory of the Lord filled the house of God"* (2 Chron. 5:14). As during the wilderness years after the Exodus, Jehovah wanted His people to know that He was residing with them again – a cloud of glory filled the temple. C. A. Coates relates this scene to the future and fuller reality of Christ in glory with all His priests present.

> When we consider the Father's house of John 14 we find that glory dwells there. The Father's house is where the Son is, and He says, "*Father, as to those whom Thou hast given Me, I desire that where I am they also may be with Me, that they may behold My glory which Thou hast given Me, for Thou loved Me before the foundation of the world"* (John 17:24). That is the glory which fills the house. Of old, *"the priests could not stand to do their service because of the cloud"*; the glory absolutely excluded man in the flesh. But now we find a blessed company secured by divine love and in divine righteousness able to behold the glory without a concealing veil.

> The glory that the Father has given to the Son is infinitely great. It is nothing less than the glory of giving effect to all the counsels of divine love. The accomplishment of all the unnumbered thoughts of blessing and grace that filled the heart of God before the foundation of the world, of all the holy counsels which originated in the Father, has been entrusted to the Son. … It is the glory of the Son to bring out and establish the glory of the Father in the fulfillment of all the purposes of His love. That glory fills the abodes of the Father's house, and we are brought there to behold the Father glorified in the Son. Christ's brethren are the companions of His rejection and reproach in this world, but they are also His companions in the circle of ineffable rest and love where He is with the Father, and where His glory appears.[33]

Solomon's Message (1 Kgs. 8:14-21; 2 Chron. 6:1-11)

Speaking to the congregation, Solomon affirmed that he had been obedient to the Lord's command and had built Him a glorious temple. Additionally, the Lord had promised Solomon that He would dwell in it (i.e., within the darkness of the Most Holy Place; 2 Chron. 6:1-2). Then, with the Jewish nation before him, Solomon, following the example of Moses before Israel entered the Promised Land (Deut. 27), blessed his countrymen and called them to covenant renewal (2 Chron. 6:3-11).

The king's message begins by thanking God for choosing David for a lasting dynasty to oversee Israel and for permitting him to build a temple in Jerusalem, the location God had chosen to honor His name (2 Chron. 6:4-6). The word "name" occurs fourteen times in this chapter (more than any other chapter in the Bible) to emphasize that God's presence as shown through His attributes and character would now be evident in Jerusalem.

It was David who had first been burdened to build the Lord a permanent house, but he was prevented from doing so because he had shed much blood as a man of war (2 Chron. 6:7-8). However, God did use David to obtain regional dominance and peace and to accumulate resources for the temple's construction, so that his son Solomon could build the temple unhindered and expediently (2 Chron. 6:9-11).

Solomon's Dedicatory Prayer (1 Kgs. 8:22-53; 2 Chron. 6:12-42)

After blessing the people, the king offered praise to God in a prayer of dedication. Solomon's prayer is the longest prayer recorded in Scripture. He knelt on a specially constructed bronze platform in the center of the temple's outer court and extolled the Lord for being a covenant-keeping God (2 Chron. 6:12-15). Solomon pleads for the Lord to continue showering David's dynasty with love and blessing as the Jewish nation continued to honor His Law (2 Chron. 6:16-17).

The central theme of the king's prayer is contained in 2 Chronicles 6:18-21 and is then expanded in the verses that follow. Solomon extols God's uniqueness, His faithfulness, His boundlessness, and His enduring compassion and concern for His people. Centuries later, the Lord Jesus would instruct His disciples how to address God in prayer by sharing with them a model prayer. Like Solomon's prayer, the Lord began by acknowledging God's holy and sovereign nature: *"Our Father in heaven, Hallowed be Your name. Your kingdom come. Your will be done on earth as it is in heaven"* (Matt. 6:9-10). Admiring God's character, His attributes, and His displayed awesomeness in all that He does is an appropriate way to commence any prayer!

Solomon humbly acknowledges the impossibility of a mere building, even one as grand as the temple just constructed, to contain an omnipresent God who transcends His creation (2 Chron. 6:18). However, the king requested that, though God dwelt in heaven, He would recognize the temple as the focal point of His presence and communion among His people (2 Chron. 6:19-21). For this reason, Solomon faced the temple while praying and asked God to honor the future prayers of His people who also humbly faced the temple to pray (2 Chron. 6:20-21).

David had previously faced the Ark located in the tabernacle while praying (Ps. 5:7). He also sought the Lord in prayer regularly three times a day (evening, morning, and noon; Ps. 55:17). After Solomon's prayer of blessing, the Jewish tradition of kneeling and praying towards the temple in Jerusalem was widely held. For example, even four centuries later, the Jewish captive Daniel had a lifelong practice of facing Jerusalem and praying three times a day – long after the Babylonians had destroyed Solomon's temple (Dan. 6).

Solomon then requested that the temple be known as a place of justice and impartiality in resolving offenses between individuals (2 Chron. 6:22-23). He also requested that after God had chastened His people through military oppression, drought, and disasters, He would hear the prayers of repentance and forgive Israel's waywardness (2 Chron. 6:24-31). Only when Israel was following the Lord would the nations be drawn to Jerusalem to seek Jehovah also.

In 1 Kings 8:11-30, the king is functioning as a priest representing the people to God; in 1 Kings 8:46-53, Solomon speaks as a prophet warning the people and foretelling what will happen to them. Solomon's roles of prophet, priest, and king typify Christ's offices during the Kingdom Age, namely: He is the Great Prophet (Deut. 18:18-29; John 1:1), the Great High Priest (1 Sam. 2:35; Heb. 4:14-16, 9:11-14), and the King of Kings (2 Sam. 7:12-13; Rev. 1:5, 19:16). Only Christ will hold all three offices.

Believing Jehovah to be the only true God who controls human affairs, Solomon then asked the Lord to bestow grace and mercy also to foreigners as well who came to the temple to seek and honor Him (2 Chron. 6:32-33). The king desired, *"That all peoples of the earth may know Your name and fear You, as do Your people"* (2 Chron. 6:33). Solomon's prayer carries a powerful exhortation for the Church today: If the unsaved masses are to be reached for Christ, the Church must rethink its careless attitudes regarding how it represents and proclaims the name of Christ. Deliberate disregard for the Word of God, complacency over sin, and loss of reverence for the Lord's name have degraded the name of Christ throughout the world. The Church desperately needs revival! May we all repent and again esteem Christ above all things, *"that in all things He may have the preeminence"* (Col. 1:18).

The king then petitioned the Lord to bless Israel in battle, but he also recognized that this might not be possible if the Jewish nation digressed and that even Jewish exile was a possibility (2 Chron. 6:34-35). If such divine chastening did occur, Solomon requested that the Lord would forgive repentant Jewish captives and restore them to Himself (2 Chron. 6:36-39).

Solomon then closes his prayer by interceding for God's new resting place (the temple), the priests, His people, and himself, as David's anointed successor (2 Chron. 6:40-41). Specifically, he requested that God would accept his prayer, grant the priests grace to serve Him with joy, and to bless his kingdom because of His love for David. These three requests are admitted from the parallel account in 1 Kings 8, which also records Solomon blessing the people at the conclusion of his prayer (which is not recorded in 2 Chronicles).

Solomon employs a figure of speech called anthropomorphism in 2 Chronicles 6:40 (see Ex. 33:11, 20; Job 34:21; Jas. 5:4 for other examples). Anthropomorphisms poetically assign to an entity or to an inanimate object human attributes in order to better convey the meaning. Solomon uses this devise to emphasize God's emotions in a way that we can better empathize with. Solomon declares: *"Now, my God, I pray, let Your eyes be open and let Your ears be attentive to the prayer made in this place."* The king closes his prayer by pleading with the Lord to be attentive and to honor his prayer because of His loyal love promised to David and his dynasty (2 Chron. 6:42).

Solomon Exhorts and Blesses the Assembly (1 Kgs. 8:54-61)

During his prayer, the king had been kneeling with his hands spread up to heaven while facing towards the temple (1 Kgs. 8:54). After concluding his prayer, he rose to his feet and turned to the people to pronounce a benediction (1 Kgs. 8:55). Chronicles does not record this blessing, perhaps because the historian did not want his audience to be distracted from appreciating God's immediate approval of Solomon's prayer – fire from heaven consumed the sacrifices on the Altar.

Solomon reminded the congregation that God had been faithful in richly blessing them and giving them peace among their enemies as promised by Moses (1 Kgs. 8:56). The king desired that the Lord would inspire his generation to faithfully walk with Him, so that they would be blessed as their forefathers were, and the nations would come to know Jehovah as the one true God (1 Kgs. 8:57-60). Hence, the king implored his countrymen: *"Let your heart therefore be loyal to the Lord our God, to walk in His statutes and keep His commandments, as at this day"* (1 Kgs. 8:61). Sadly, Solomon eventually failed to follow his own warning.

Meditation

We are going to a palace
That is built of gold;
Glory to God, hallelujah!
Where the King in all His splendor
We shall soon behold,
Glory to God, hallelujah!

O, the children of the Lord,
Have a right to shout and sing,
For the way is growing bright,
And our souls are on the wing;
We are going by and by,
To the palace of the King!

— Fanny Crosby

The Temple Dedicated and God Appears to Solomon

1 Kings 8:62-9:28; 2 Chronicles 7

God's Glory Fills the Temple (2 Chron. 7:1-3)

After Solomon finished praying, *"fire came down from heaven and consumed the burnt offering and the sacrifices; and the glory of the Lord filled the temple"* (2 Chron. 7:1). Once again the priests could not enter the temple, because the glory of the Lord had filled His house (2 Chron. 7:2). This visible evidence of God's presence confirmed to everyone that He was pleased with their work; Israel observed a similar phenomenon when Moses dedicated the first tabernacle in the wilderness (Ex. 40:34-35).

This awe-inspiring sight caused the children of Israel to bow down their faces to the ground and worship and praise the Lord, repeating what the priests had earlier sung when the Ark was brought into the Most Holy Place (2 Chron. 5:12-13): *For He is good, for His mercy endures forever."* God shows His favor on the nation when both its leaders and people willingly honor the one good and eternal God.

The Temple Dedicated (1 Kgs. 8:62-66; 2 Chron. 7:4-10)

After fire from heaven consumed the sacrifices, the king led the people in a seven-day dedication ceremony. During this time, both the king and all the people offered sacrifices; Solomon's tally included 22,000 bulls and 120,000 sheep (2 Chron. 7:4-5). Only Burnt Offerings, Meal Offerings, and Peace Offerings were offered at the temple dedication – no Sin or Trespass Offerings were placed on the Bronze Altar.

Some have questioned the accuracy of these numbers, suggesting the number of animals slaughtered is too high. However, Keil and Delitzsch note in the days of Emperor Nero, procurator Cestius directed the priests to count the number of paschal lambs slaughtered at the temple. It was determined that 250,000 lambs were slaughtered during the three-hour afternoon timeframe.[34]

The people stood before the temple as the sacrifices occurred, the Levites played their musical instruments that David had fashioned for praising the Lord, and the priests sounded their trumpets (2 Chron. 7:5-6). Solomon also consecrated the central courtyard for offering sacrifices to the Lord because even the huge Bronze Altar was not sufficient to receive Israel's sacrifices and offerings (2 Chron. 7:7; 1 Kgs. 8:62-65).

The temple dedication feast lasted seven days and included the Day of Atonement; this was followed by the Feast of Tabernacles, which lasted another seven days (2 Chron. 7:8). Solomon released the people on the morning after the "holy convocation" (i.e., on the twenty-third day of the seventh month; 2 Chron. 7:9). The people departed for their tents being *"joyful and glad of heart for the good that the Lord had done for David, for Solomon, and for His people Israel"* (2 Chron. 7:10).

God Appears to Solomon Again (1 Kgs. 9:1-9; 2 Chron. 7:11-22)

Besides the preparatory work of nearly five years, it took Solomon six more years to finish building God's house and another seven years to complete his own palace. It was after these accomplishments (when Solomon was at the apex of his power and wealth) that the Lord appeared to Solomon a second time with a message of assurance, but also of warning (2 Chron. 7:12). During this night visit, the Lord promised His blessing if Solomon continued in His Law, and His judgment if the king erred from it (2 Chron. 7:12-16). If Israel suffered a drought, a plague of locusts, or pestilence, the people were to humble themselves, turning from their wicked ways to seek the Lord. If Israel responded appropriately to His chastening, then God promised to forgive their sins and restore them.

Second Chronicles 7:14 is not only a good theme verse for the entire book, but it also conveys the timeless remedy for sin in any age – our humble repentance prompts spiritual restoration and revival: *"If My people who are called by My name will humble themselves, and pray and seek My face, and turn from their wicked ways, then I will hear from heaven, and will forgive their sin and heal their land."* Although the context of this verse clearly pertains to the nation of Israel, the Church today would benefit much from heeding it.

Second Chronicles 7:16 is not an unconditional promise that Solomon's temple would stand forever, but rather that it would endure as long as Israel walked with the Lord. Generally speaking, over the next four centuries, idolatry would infect Israel so deeply that God's only remedy was to destroy His temple and permit His people to be carried away to Babylon, where paganism originated. This occurred in 586 B.C. when, after a long siege, Jerusalem fell to Babylonian armies and was subsequently destroyed. Through seventy years of captivity, God refined His people, and then restored them to their homeland. Thankfully their idols remained in Babylon.

The Lord promised Solomon that if he continued in righteousness, as his father David did, He would establish his throne and his descendants would also sit on it (2 Chron. 7:17-18). However, if Solomon caused the people to reject His Law and embrace other gods, the Lord promised to uproot His people from the land that He had given them (2 Chron. 7:19-22).

God's name would be sanctified before the nations one way or another; either through His people's obedience and worship or through their judgment and chastening. If the latter occurred, even the nations would understand why God had dealt so severely with His people: *"Because they forsook the Lord God of their fathers, who brought them out of the land of Egypt, and embraced other gods, and worshiped them and served them; therefore He has brought all this calamity on them"* (2 Chron. 7:22). For the present, Israel was walking with the Lord, the Lord's glory had filled the temple, and He was abundantly blessing His people. In reviewing Israel's sad history, this moment was probably the closest thing to the coming Kingdom Age that Israel ever experienced.

Meditation

Come, gather, all tribes and all nations,
To worship Jehovah our king;
O, enter His presence with gladness,
Your tribute of gratitude bring.
O, sing of the wondrous redemption,
The purchase of life for us all;
O, give Him your song and your service
For blessings that momently fall.

— Adaline Hohf Berry

Solomon's Accomplishments, Declension, and Death

1 Kings 9:10-11:43; 2 Chronicles 8-9

Historically speaking, we are privileged to view Israel's political, religious, and economic high-water mark in this portion of Scripture. A new magnificent sanctuary had been erected for Jehovah, national prestige was high, economic prosperity was at its prime, and the grandeur of Solomon's kingdom had gained international attention. The first half of Solomon's reign is outstanding in every way, but his later years will be marked by spiritual declension, and thus Israel's prosperity and strength wane accordingly.

Solomon's Achievements (1 Kgs. 9:10-28; 2 Chron. 8:1-17)

The historian pauses to summarize Solomon's many achievements after about twenty years of rule. The king had built the Lord a magnificent house and completed the royal palace (2 Chron. 8:1-2). He also erected leveling-terraces about Jerusalem so that he could extend the existing wall around the City of David northward to protect the temple and royal palace – this doubled the area of the city (1 Kgs. 9:15). Solomon also conquered Hamath Zobah in the north, built Tadmor in the wilderness, and constructed storage cities in Hamath (2 Chron. 8:3-4). He also made Upper and Lower Beth Horon fortified cities; Baalath and other cities in Israel and Lebanon became sites of storage, chariot cities, or cities of the cavalry (2 Chron. 8:5-6).

Because his friend Hiram had supplied Solomon with cedar and cypress wood and much gold, Solomon gave Hiram twenty cities in northern Galilee (1 Kgs. 9:10-11). However, Hiram expressed his disappointment at this gift because these cities were surrounded by unprofitable land, nevertheless, the king of Tyre sent one hundred and twenty talents of gold to Solomon (1 Kgs. 9:12-14). Richard I. McNeely explains the two different measurements for a talent: "The Babylonian talent was the equivalent of 130 pounds. The Jewish talent, which came later, weighed about 66 pounds."[35] Others suggest that the Hebrew talent at this time weighed 75 pounds.[36] If the latter case is correct, that would mean that Hiram paid Solomon about 4.5 tons of gold. At the time of this writing, that amount of gold would be worth about 168 million U.S. dollars.

Solomon realized that the more he built, the more there was for others to take, hence the king strengthened his kingdom's defenses: *"And this is the reason for the labor force which King Solomon raised: to build the house of the Lord, his own house, the Millo, the wall of Jerusalem, Hazor, Megiddo, and Gezer"* (1 Kgs. 9:15). John Gray suggests that the Millo consisted of filling the valley between the City of David on the southeast hill and Ophel to the northeast.[37] The extension of Jerusalem's fortifications was necessary as both the temple and the royal palace were located north of the old City of David.

The principle fortress cities of Hazor, Megiddo, and Gezer would also be reinforced. Hazor, in the far north, protected the trade routes into Galilee, while Megiddo guarded the fertile Jezreel Valley and important trade corridors through it. Gezer secured the western trade routes from Philistia into the heartland of Solomon's kingdom. Gezer had been inhabited by Canaanites, but was conquered by Egypt's previous Pharaoh, who killed the inhabitants and burned the city (1 Kgs. 9:16). The new Pharaoh gave Gezer to Solomon as part of the dowry for his daughter.

The historian reminds us that the bulk of Solomon's labor force were descendants of the Hittites, Amorites, Perizzites, Hivites, and Jebusites (2 Chron. 8:7-8). Solomon did not enslave his countrymen for his construction endeavors, but rather appointed them various positions of authority to oversee the work, or within his army (2 Chron. 8:9-10). Five hundred and fifty Israelites were to manage the Canaanite laborers to ensure the quality of their work was maintained (1 Kgs. 9:23). Solomon brought Pharaoh's daughter, his wife, up from the City of David to live in the lavish house he had built for her adjoining his own palace, apparently at Millo which had been constructed as a citadel. As a foreigner, it was not appropriate for her to remain in the City of David, because David had brought the Ark into his own house for a time, making his residence a holy place (i.e., sanctified by the Lord's presence; 2 Sam. 6:12; 2 Chron. 8:11; 1 Kgs. 9:24). She would benefit wonderfully because of her association with Solomon, just as Gentiles will benefit from Christ in the Kingdom Age, but God's intimate presence at the temple was reserved for His covenant people alone.

Following the Law of Moses, the king offered daily burnt offerings, weekly Sabbath offerings, and monthly New Moon offerings on the Bronze Altar (2 Chron. 8:12). Additionally, he held the three Feasts of Jehovah that all males were required to attend each year: the Feast of Unleavened Bread, the Feast of Weeks, and the Feast of Tabernacles (2 Chron. 8:13). Solomon also upheld his father David's divisions of the priesthood and Levites (2 Chron. 8:14). The priests served and praised God and the Levites attended to the treasures and functioned as gatekeepers (2 Chron. 8:15).

Solomon also had commercial enterprises situated in Ezion Geber and Elath on the seacoast in southern Edom (2 Chron. 8:17). Using ships and sailors supplied by Hiram, Solomon obtained 450 talents of gold from Ophir through these port cities (2 Chron. 8:18). The ruins at Tell el-Kheleifeh on the northeastern tip of the Gulf of Aqaba (the eastern arm of the Red Sea) may be the remains of the seaport Ezion Geber (this city is also referred to in Num. 33:35; Deut. 2:8).

The Queen of Sheba (1 Kgs. 10:1-13; 2 Chron. 9:1-12)

After hearing of Solomon's fame, the queen of Sheba (Yemen in Arabia) traveled nearly 1,200 miles to test his wisdom with hard questions (2 Chron. 9:1). Solomon's mercantile navy operated along the Arabian coast and would have had contact with this influential Arabian kingdom.

The queen's large caravan brought exceptional spices, gold in abundance, and precious stones as gifts for Solomon (2 Chron. 9:1). Such spectacular presents corroborated her prestige and wealth. The queen spoke with Solomon about all that was in her heart and he explicitly answered all of her questions expertly (2 Chron. 9:2). Her interaction with Solomon was beyond anything she could have imagined. The king's incredible wisdom, immense wealth, enormous table provisions, and the incredible accomplishments were all true. In fact, she concluded that the half had not been told to her (2 Chron. 9:3-6).

One of the things that overwhelmed the Queen of Sheba was seeing Solomon's *"entryway by which he went up to the house of the Lord"* (2 Chron. 9:4). She was stunned to learn that the king had direct and private access to Jehovah's sanctuary. The king did not have to be concerned about his personal protection or public perception when coming before the Lord – he had the expedient opportunity to do so privately at any time. This impressed the queen. Apparently, the gold shields kept in the king's house were formally used when the king entered the temple through this private corridor.

Believers today also have a glorious and protected entrance before the Lord at any time; in fact, they are invited to come boldly to the throne of grace to receive mercy in time of need (Heb. 4:14-16). Christians do not have to travel to temples, shrines, mosques, synagogues, or even church buildings to have immediate access to God. May the lost be envious of the power and peace associated with such communion. Clearly, what believers have in Christ today transcends all Old Testament types and figures. Oh that the lost today might be in awe of our private and direct access to God through Christ (John 14:13-14). As children of God, we are invited to come boldly to God's throne and to receive from our Father the bounty of His love (Heb. 4:14-16) – that should entice others, like the Queen of Sheba, to search out the truth for themselves.

Indeed, the queen acknowledged that Israel was being blessed by God because He had put such a wise king on Israel's throne (2 Chron. 9:7). This realization caused the queen of Sheba to extol Solomon's God:

> *Blessed be the Lord your God, who delighted in you, setting you on His throne to be king for the Lord your God! Because your God has loved Israel, to establish them forever, therefore He made you king over them, to do justice and righteousness* (2 Chron. 9:8).

While clearly a hyperbolic expression of esteem and admiration, we must not forget that whatever might be true of Solomon's kingdom is only a shadow of Christ's glorious kingdom to come. As William Kelly puts it, "There is a deeper glory in the heavens; and we must carefully remember that the same millennial day will see the Church glorified in heaven, and the Jew blessed upon the earth, and the nations also. All will be under Christ."[38]

The queen then gave Solomon all the gifts that she had transported from her homeland: 120 talents of gold (about 4.5 tons), and an abundance of rare spices and precious stones (2 Chron. 9:9). In return,

King Solomon gave to her *"all she desired, whatever she asked, much more than she had brought to the king"* and then she returned to her own country (2 Chron. 9:12). The text concerning the obtaining of gold from Ophir, algum wood, and precious stones through sea trade seems to be out of place in this section. Thomas L. Constable explains why the acquisition of gold and algum wood (perhaps sandlewood) from Ophir may have been included within the narrative detailing the queen of Sheba's visit to meet Solomon:

> These verses, which seem out of place here, may reflect a trade arrangement that resulted from the queen's visit. Ophir may have been close to or a part of the queen's kingdom of Sheba (1 Kgs. 9:28).[39]

Algum wood was black on the outside and ruby red on the inside – it was strong and durable. Solomon used it for the steps of the temple and for constructing musical instruments (1 Kgs. 10:11-12; 2 Chron. 9:10-11).

Solomon's Wealth (1 Kgs. 10:14-29; 2 Chron. 9:13-17)

In addition to the gold Solomon obtained through trade taxes and tolls, he received 666 talents in annual revenue from subservient nations under his rule (2 Chron. 9:13). The governors of these lands and even the kings of Arabia brought gold and silver to Solomon (2 Chron. 9:14). With the gold he received, Solomon made 200 large shields of hammered gold (each shield weighed 600 shekels or about 15 pounds) and 300 shields of hammered gold which each weighed 300 shekels (2 Chron. 9:15-16). These ornamental shields were placed in a fortified location within Solomon's palace complex which was largely made of cedar wood and called "the House of the Forest of Lebanon."

For himself, Solomon fashioned a great throne of ivory and overlaid it with pure gold (2 Chron. 9:17). This golden throne had an attached footstool and six steps with a guardian lion on either side of each step and two more lions – one under each of two armrests (2 Chron. 9:18-19). The writer affirms that no other kingdom had ever had a throne matching the grandeur of Solomon's throne.

All Solomon's drinking vessels were gold, none were silver and these were also stored in the House of the Forest of Lebanon (2 Chron. 9:20). Silver was so plentiful during Solomon's reign that it was considered worthless; silver was as common in Jerusalem as stones (2 Chron. 9:27). The king's ships manned with servants of Hiram returned every three years with gold, silver, ivory, apes, and monkeys (2 Chron. 9:21). King Solomon surpassed all the kings of the earth in riches and wisdom; many kings sought to benefit from the wisdom that God had bestowed to Solomon (2 Chron. 9:22-23). In return, his visitors brought him articles of silver and gold, garments, armor, spices, horses, and mules (2 Chron. 9:24).

Having spoken of Solomon's vast wealth, the historian paused to summarize the king's military strength (2 Chron. 9:25) and his political dominion (2 Chron. 9:26). David had enhanced Israel's infantry from sword- and spear-wielding soldiers to include archers. Solomon further modernized his army to include war-chariots, something that Israel had been without previously. He had four thousand stalls for horses and chariots, and twelve thousand horsemen whom he stationed in the chariot cities throughout Judah and in Jerusalem. Solomon received his horses primarily from Egypt, but also from other lands, such as Keveh (2 Chron. 9:28). His domain included all the kingdoms from the Euphrates River to the east, to the land of the Philistines in the west and as far as Egypt's border in the south.

Solomon's Heart Turns From the Lord (1 Kgs. 11:1-13)

Because the writer sought to encourage the chastened and discouraged Jewish nation to regain their identity as Jehovah's people, Chronicles does not emphasize Solomon's spiritual decline towards the end of his reign. However, the prophet-writer of Kings is not squeamish about mentioning Solomon's declension so that his countrymen will learn that there are always consequences to turning away from the Lord, no matter what your social status might be.

We are informed that Solomon had seven hundred wives and three hundred concubines, many of whom were foreign women from Moab, Ammon, Edom, Sidon, and included some Hittites and Pharaoh's daughter from Egypt (1 Kgs. 11:1, 3). Regrettably, the next king of Judah, Solomon's son Rehoboam born to him by his Ammonite wife Naamah, would pursue wickedness (1 Kgs. 14:21-23). The writer then reiterates that Jewish men were forbidden to marry foreign women (v. 2; 1 Kgs. 11:2; Deut. 7:3-4, 17:17). If Solomon knew that the Law of Moses prohibited Jews from marrying foreigners, why did he do it?

Many commentators believe that Solomon married foreign women to ensure peace with their nations and to obtain intelligence of the state of affairs in those countries. While this is possible, Matthew Henry suggests that the motive behind Solomon's marriages to foreigners was more likely lust: "I rather fear it was because the daughters of Israel were too grave and modest for him, and those foreigners pleased him with the looseness and wantonness of their dress, and air, and conversation."[40] Believers today fall into the same trap when they marry for sensual and not spiritual reasons.

Solomon should have heeded the warning he issued to his sons, that is, to keep away *"from the immoral* (or *"strange"*; KJV) *woman, from the seductress who flatters with her words"* (Prov. 7:5):

> *Now therefore, listen to me, my children; pay attention to the words of my mouth: Do not let your heart turn aside to her ways, do not stray into her paths; for she has cast down many wounded, and all who were slain by her were strong men. Her house is the way to hell, descending to the chambers of death* (Prov. 7:24-27).

The king did not follow his own wisdom, but eventually fell prey to his own lusts. Let us pause to consider the threefold warning Moses extended to future Jewish kings to prevent their spiritual declension:

> *But he shall not multiply horses for himself, nor cause the people to return to Egypt to multiply horses, for the Lord has said to you, "You shall not return that way again." Neither shall he multiply wives for himself, lest his heart turn away; nor shall he greatly multiply silver and gold for himself* (Deut. 17:16-17).

Many warhorses meant that the king was trusting in his own military resources for victory and not the Lord. The danger of many wives was in being emotionally drawn away from the Lord, who was to remain the king's first love. Lastly, much wealth enables sensual appetites and the pursuit of comfort and luxury to go unchecked. How could the wisest man on the earth fail to heed Moses' warnings? Solomon had multiplied horses, and wives, and wealth to himself, all of which caused him to turn away from the Lord. In his autumn years, he trusted in his own strength and wealth and was led by unchecked lust, not by God's word or wisdom. Each of us have a free will to choose to follow God or not. Solomon's life illustrates that we are more inclined to rely on the Lord and obey Him when in lack or distress. It should be no surprise then that the Lord often uses various trials to both mature His people to Christ-likeness and to keep them near to Him.

How should we understand Solomon's warning to his own son regarding not lusting after the immoral (*"the strange,"* KJV) woman, which he mentions several times in Proverbs 5 to 7? Although Solomon did marry many women (including many foreigners), clearly he did not exercise wisdom in that aspect of his life. In time, his many wives turned his heart from the Lord (1 Kgs. 11:4-8).

As in the Song of Solomon and Proverbs 5, the king apparently wants to set the matter straight: God's design for marriage is one man and one woman bound by a covenant for life (Matt. 19:5-6). The central message to his own son, then, is one that married men should heed today: do not lust for what is outside the will of God (i.e., the unchaste woman), but rather seek to be faithful and satisfied with your own wife! May we remember that God's charge throughout Scripture has always been to marry only within God's people and for life (Deut. 7:3-4; Ezra 9; 1 Cor. 7:39).

How sad to read that Solomon's *"heart was not loyal to the Lord his God, as was the heart of his father David"* (1 Kgs. 11:4). The king went after the false deities Ashtoreth and Milcom and did evil in the sight of the Lord (1 Kgs. 11:5-6). He even built high places near Jerusalem for Chemosh (the abomination of Moab) and Molech (the abomination of Ammon, as was Milcom – 1 Kgs. 11:33), and others so that all his foreign wives had a place to worship their pagan deities (1 Kgs. 11:7-8). But Solomon's wickedness did not stop there; he burned incense and sacrificed to the gods of his wives as well.

God had appeared to Solomon twice to personally convey His covenant to him and to warn him against disobedience, especially against committing idolatry (1 Kgs. 11:9-10). Although Solomon had done much to honor the Lord in his early years, his spiritual declension towards the end of his life angered the Lord. Therefore the Lord spoke to Solomon saying:

> *Because you have done this, and have not kept My covenant and My statutes, which I have commanded you, I will surely tear the kingdom away from you and give it to your servant. Nevertheless I will not do it in your days, for the sake of your father David; I will tear it out of the hand of your son. However I will not tear away the whole*

> *kingdom; I will give one tribe to your son for the sake of My servant David, and for the sake of Jerusalem which I have chosen* (1 Kgs. 11:11-13).

Disobedience always has consequences and, though God's judgment was tempered in mercy for David's sake, Solomon would not have an everlasting dynasty in Israel. In fact, the Jewish nation would be divided after Solomon's son was crowned and he would retain only one tribe in Israel. This refers to Benjamin, as the kingly tribe of Judah was a given. Included within Judah's borders was a portion of Simeon (whose original possession was within Judah's borders) and also those Levites loyal to Jehovah. The Northern Kingdom (referred to as the northern ten tribes) included Reuben, Dan, Naphtali, Asher, Gad, Issachar, Zebulun, Ephraim, Manasseh, and portions of Simeon and Levi.

Solomon's Adversaries (1 Kgs. 11:14-40)

Faithful David had militarily secured the region so that Solomon could build the Lord a temple unhindered. Solomon then solidified and fortified the region for the next three decades, but after his spiritual decline, the Lord withdrew his blessing from Solomon and stirred up adversaries to oppose him. Hadad the Edomite, who had escaped Joab's slaughter of the Edomite males during David's reign by fleeing to Egypt, was one such adversary (1 Kgs. 11:16-17). Pharaoh had treated Hadad well in Egypt and had even given him as a wife the sister of his own wife, that is, the sister of Queen Tahpenes (1 Kgs. 11:18-19). His son Genubath was raised in Pharaoh's household among his own sons (1 Kgs. 11:20). After learning of David's and Joab's deaths, Hadad received leave of Pharaoh to return to his homeland of Edom (1 Kgs. 11:21-22).

Another adversary raised up by the Lord against Solomon was Rezon who had previously fled from Hadadezer, the king of Zobah. After David defeated Zobah, Rezon became the leader of a band of raiders in Damascus who, because of their hatred for Israel, continually harassed Solomon (1 Kgs. 11:23-25).

We are then introduced to a third adversary whom God would use to divide the Jewish nation shortly after Solomon's death. His name is Jeroboam, the son of Nebat, an Ephraimite whose mother was a widow named Zeruah (1 Kgs. 11:26). Jewish tradition has it that Nebat was

Shimei; if correct, Zeruah would have become a widow after Solomon executed her husband early in his reign.[41] Solomon noticed that young Jeroboam was a mighty man of valor and industrious; therefore he made him an officer over the labor force tasked with building Millo and repairing and extending the wall of the City of David (1 Kgs. 11:27-28).

The Lord also noticed resourcefulness in Jeroboam and sent the prophet Ahijah to deliver a message to him while he was away from Jerusalem (1 Kgs. 11:29). The prophet met Jeroboam in a field alone and took off a new garment he was wearing and tore it into twelve pieces. He gave ten portions to Jeroboam, explaining that he was tearing the kingdom from Solomon and giving Jeroboam ten tribes to rule over (1 Kgs. 11:30-31). The prophet explained that, for David's sake, the Lord would retain one tribe in the Southern Kingdom to occupy Jerusalem, the place that he had chosen to place His name (1 Kgs. 11:32). Solomon did not realize at that time that his greatest political threat would not be from Edom or Syria, but from the young Israelite he had just placed in a position of authority.

The prophet also explained why this judgment was forthcoming: Solomon had not followed the Lord as his father David had, but rather had led the people into idolatry and to forsake God's Law (1 Kgs. 11:33-34). God promised to be with Jeroboam and to establish him as the king of Israel to rule over the ten northern tribes (1 Kgs. 11:35-37). The Lord then promised to continually bless Jeroboam with an enduring dynasty if he did what was right in His sight by heeding all His commandments, as His servant David did (1 Kgs. 11:38). The Lord revealed that He planned to chasten the descendants of David for their disobedience, but not forever (1 Kgs. 11:39)! Judah would be like a lamp that God would never let burn out; Judah's perpetual existence declared God's choice of a Davidic dynasty to rule over Israel.

Either Jeroboam rebelled against Solomon after hearing the prophecy or Solomon learned of it, for the king sought to kill Jeroboam. Jeroboam, however, fled to safety in Egypt and remained there until the death of Solomon (1 Kgs. 11:40). While the exact date of Jeroboam's flight to Egypt cannot be determined, it certainly was not before Solomon's twenty-fourth year, as the building and fortifying of Millo occurred afterwards. Albert Barnes suggests that archeological information helps us to determine the approximate time that Jeroboam began his exile in Egypt:

> Shishak is the first Pharaoh mentioned in Scripture who can be certainly identified with any known Egyptian monarch. He is the Sheshonk (Sheshonk I) of the monuments, and the Sesonchosis of Manetho. The Egyptian date for his accession is 980 or 983 B.C., which synchronizes, according to the ordinary Hebrew reckoning, with Solomon's 32nd or 35th year. Sheshonk I has left a record of his expedition against Judah, which accords well with what is related of Shishak in 1 Kings 14:25-26 and 2 Chronicles 12:2-4.[42]

This historical information suggests that Jeroboam's exile in Egypt was probably less than five years. Regardless of the timing, Solomon's behavior to thwart the providential plans of God is reminiscent of Saul's efforts to execute his God-appointed successor, David. When a king thinks he can outwit or out-maneuver the designs of his Creator, the worst is yet to come for his kingdom.

Solomon's Death (1 Kgs. 11:41-43; Chron. 9:29-31)

The writer pauses to note that at that time information on Solomon's reign could also be found in the writings of three prophets: Nathan, Ahijah, and Iddo (2 Chron. 9:29). Solomon reigned in Jerusalem over all Israel forty years and was buried in the City of David his father (2 Chron. 9:30). Solomon's son Rehoboam, born to him by his Ammonite wife Naamah, reigned in his place (2 Chron. 9:31).

Solomon began well for the Lord, but finished poorly. Solomon shows us that the possession of wisdom alone does not secure success in life; rather, the individual who rightly applies wisdom is the one who benefits from having wisdom. He would have done well to heed his own counsel while he was walking with the Lord:

> *Let us hear the conclusion of the whole matter: Fear God and keep His commandments, for this is man's all. For God will bring every work into judgment, including every secret thing, whether good or evil* (Eccl. 12:13-14).

Some Judean kings, such as Manasseh, started poorly but finished well. But only a handful, such as Hezekiah and Josiah, started well and finished well. May the Lord help us to learn from Solomon's example: even the wisest person can be drawn away from following the Lord if he pursues power, wealth, and sensual pleasure.

Given this ever present danger, Paul exhorted his spiritual son Timothy: *"You therefore must endure hardship as a good soldier of Jesus Christ. No one engaged in warfare entangles himself with the affairs of this life, that he may please him who enlisted him as a soldier"* (2 Tim. 2:3-4). The Greek verb rendered "entangles" in this passage is in the passive voice, meaning that a good solider does not permit the cares of the world to entangle him! The issue is not that faithful believers desire the things of the world, but these are after them. Believers must continually beat these devices away (like tentacles of an octopus after its prey) in order to remain free to serve the Lord. Because Solomon did not do this, his heart got encumbered with carnal and temporal things instead of with what counted for eternity. May God gives us grace to remain near to Him, to reject the ploys of an ensnaring, wicked world, and to finish well for His honor and glory!

Meditation

Take my life, and let it be
Consecrated, Lord, to Thee;
Take my moments and my days,
Let them flow in ceaseless praise.

Take my silver and my gold;
Not a mite would I withhold;
Take my intellect, and use,
Every power as Thou shalt choose.

Take my will, and make it Thine;
It shall be no longer mine.
Take my heart; it is Thine own;
It shall be Thy royal throne.

— Frances Ridley Havergal

Division of the Kingdom – King Rehoboam

(1 Kgs. 12:1-24, 14:21-31; 2 Chron. 10-12)

Revolt Against Rehoboam (1 Kgs. 12:1-20; 2 Chron. 10)

The entire nation gathered at Shechem to recognize Solomon's son Rehoboam as their king. The elders of the northern tribes (under Ephraim's leadership) had summoned Jeroboam from Egypt to represent them before Rehoboam (1 Kgs. 12:2-5; 2 Chron. 10:1). Jeroboam had previously fled to Egypt during Solomon's reign to escape death, but, knowing the prophecy about to be fulfilled, returned expectantly to Shechem (2 Chron. 10:2-3).

Speaking for the northern tribes, Jeroboam addressed Rehoboam: *"Your father made our yoke heavy; now therefore, lighten the burdensome service of your father and his heavy yoke which he put on us, and we will serve you"* (2 Chron. 10:4). Rehoboam requested three days to consider this proposal. The elders counseled Rehoboam to accept Jeroboam's terms, but his younger friends advised him to show a firm hand, threatening Jeroboam with even harsher conditions than what they had experienced under his father Solomon (2 Chron. 10:5-11).

When Jeroboam and all the people reassembled before Rehoboam on the third day, the king answered them roughly, per the counsel of his friends: *"My father made your yoke heavy, but I will add to it; my father chastised you with whips, but I will chastise you with scourges!"* (2 Chron. 10:12-14). The Hebrew word *`aqrab* may refer to a literal scorpion or figuratively as a scourge or knotted whip depending upon the context of the narrative. Here it is referring to a particularly cruel style of whip, which John Gray describes as a sadistic elaboration of lashes loaded with leather bags stuffed with sand and armed with spikes.[43] Not only did the king not listen to Israel's elders or to the people, but he employed a brutal metaphor which only stirred up more opposition to his throne. Yet, the resulting hostility was of the Lord so that His word through the prophet Ahijah to Jeroboam would be fulfilled (2 Chron. 10:15).

"The ten tribes" now becomes a figurative title for the Israelites not remaining under Judah's rule. As previously mentioned, this included the tribes of Asher, Dan (upper and lower clans), Naphtali, Zebulun, Issachar, Manasseh (clans in Canaan and the Transjordan), Ephraim, Gad, and Reuben. Benjamin was a border tribe and had mixed loyalties, but mainly to Judah. Many Levites returned to Judah after the kingdom divided. Simeon's original possession was within Judah's borders and had largely lost its distinction by this time.

When Jeroboam and all the people saw that the king had rejected their proposal, they rejected him. Those following Jeroboam said, *"What share have we in David? We have no inheritance in the son of Jesse. Every man to your tents, O Israel! Now see to your own house, O David!"* (2 Chron. 10:16). So those of the northern tribes departed to their tents without a king, but Rehoboam reigned over Judah (2 Chron. 10:17).

Of the nineteen kings that would rule over the Northern Kingdom during its 253-year duration, not one turned the people back to worshiping the Lord as prescribed by the Law. King Jehu's efforts to remove idolatry from Israel are commendable, but he still promoted the worship of Jehovah through the religious system established by Jeroboam. In contrast, during the same period, Judah's kings largely followed the religion of Jehovah with approximately 200 years of faithfulness – thus idolatry never became deeply rooted in Judah. Wicked monarchs, such as Rehoboam, Abijah, Joram, Ahaziah, Athaliah, Ahaz, or those who turned evil (like Joash and Amaziah), were in the minority.

While still at Shechem, King Rehoboam ordered Hadoram (also called Adoram; 1 Kgs. 12:18) to collect tax revenue from the children of Israel, but they responded by stoning him (2 Chron. 10:18). It is hard to imagine what motivated Rehoboam to send Hadoram to these discontented insurrectionists, and he was foolish for doing so. The king then realized that his own life was in jeopardy, so he mounted his chariot in haste and bolted to Jerusalem (2 Chron. 10:19).

The historian, writing centuries later, pauses to note that Israel was still in rebellion against the house of David at the time he was penning his work. Even though Israel had likely been carried away by the Assyrians at that time (722 B.C.), they still rejected the idea that a descendant of David should rule over them. This rebellious attitude was still prevalent at the time of Christ and will persist until the Kingdom Age, when He returns to restore and to unite all of Israel's tribes under His rule.

Rehoboam Reigns Over Judah (1 Kgs. 12:21-24; 2 Chron. 11)

Rehoboam departed from Shechem and returned to Jerusalem where he assembled 180,000 warriors to fight against the northern tribes, so that he might restore his kingdom (1 Kgs. 12:21). The Lord summoned the prophet Shemaiah to warn Rehoboam: *"You shall not go up nor fight against your brethren the children of Israel. Let every man return to his house, for this thing is from Me"* (1 Kgs. 12:22-23). Understanding that the division was from the Lord, Rehoboam obeyed the word of the Lord, withdrew from the conflict, and returned home (1 Kgs. 12:24). John Heading derives a practical lesson for us to consider from Rehoboam's loss:

> Rehoboam had a sense of loss – all the other tribes were no longer in his power, and had to be regained at all costs, regardless of the fact that the division was "of God" (2 Chron. 10:15). It is the same in Christendom; God allows divisions and heresies, so *"that they which are approved may be made manifest among you"* (1 Cor. 11:19). But those who love truth must not seek to fight against Christendom; we do not war after the flesh (2 Cor. 10:3) in a carnal manner. God steps in, to guide those who are willing to learn (2 Chron. 11:2-3). God has His men (Shemaiah, in this case) in every place; a "man of God" is one who manifests His ways in life and lip. ... Hence, Shemaiah's message was to "all" leaders, the faithful nation of the south, and the unfaithful of the north.[44]

Though Rehoboam was a proud man who did not heed wise counsel, he was a descendant of David's dynasty and therefore the rightful heir to Israel's throne at that time. Yet, in the providence of God he was permitted to experience loss, which then provided him an opportunity to be affirmed and blessed by God, that is, if he went on with the Lord. Regrettably, Rehoboam did not, and thus never regained the kingdom – he lost the opportunity to be approved by God before others. May we not squander such opportunities when unfair and unrighteous things happen to us!

Shemaiah is one of eight men who are specifically identified as a "man of God" in the Old Testament; others include: Moses (Deut. 33:1; Josh. 14:6), the Preincarnate Christ (Judg. 13:6), the prophet Samuel (1 Sam. 9:6), the prophet Elijah (1 Kgs. 17:18), the prophet Elisha (2 Kgs. 1:9), King David (2 Chron. 8:14), and Igdaliah (Jer. 35:4). Elijah and Elisha will be introduced to us in the following chapters.

Suspecting a possible attack by Jeroboam, Rehoboam quickly built up and fortified cities in defense of Judah: Bethlehem, Etam, Tekoa, Beth Zur, Sochoh, Adullam, Gath, Mareshah, Ziph, Adoraim, Lachish, Azekah, Zorah, Aijalon, and Hebron (2 Chron. 11:5-10). These cities were in the tribal territories of Judah and Benjamin, but since Benjamin had become a small tribe after the Civil War during the time of the judges, it was often associated with Judah in name. Rehoboam placed captains over these fortified strongholds with supplies and weapons (2 Chron. 11:11-12).

Thankfully, most of the priests and Levites would not have anything to do with Jeroboam's religious corruption and decided that it was better to leave their common-lands and possessions and move to Judah to serve the Lord in Jerusalem (1 Kgs. 14:21-24; 2 Chron. 11:13-17). The historian also notes that many families in the northern tribes also wanted to follow the Lord and came to Jerusalem to worship *"the Lord God of their fathers."* After three years, because the people under Rehoboam's leadership walked with the Lord, the Southern Kingdom became very strong.

Rehoboam's Family (2 Chron. 11:18-23)

Rehoboam apparently married Mahalath (the daughter of David's son Jerimoth), then Abihail (the daughter of David's brother Eliah), and then Maachah the granddaughter of Absalom, who became his favorite of his eighteen wives and sixty concubines (2 Chron. 11:18-20). While much of what Rehoboam did was not honoring to the Lord, there is no scriptural evidence that he married foreign women like his father Solomon did. Rather, we do know that Rehoboam chose wives from the extended royal family.

In all, the king was blessed with twenty-eight sons and sixty daughters (2 Chron. 11:21). Rehoboam appointed Abijah the son of

Maachah to be the leader among his brothers because he intended to make him the next king of Judah. Rehoboam acted prudently, by dispersing many of his sons throughout the well-provisioned fortified cities in Judah and Benjamin (2 Chron. 11:22-23).

Egypt Attacks Judah (1 Kgs. 14:21-28; 2 Chron. 12:1-12)

Sadly, Rehoboam led Judah to forsake the Lord in the fourth year of his reign, so the following year the Lord brought Shishak (Sheshonk I), king of Egypt, northward to punish His people for their transgressions the following year (2 Chron. 12:1-2). The writer of Kings details the offense of Judah: *"For they also built for themselves high places, sacred pillars, and wooden images on every high hill and under every green tree"* (1 Kgs. 14:23). Asherah was the Canaanite fertility goddess and Baal was her consort. The sacred stones symbolized male fertility organs. The Asherah poles were also a wooden fertility symbol. Moses identified both pagan symbols as an abomination to the Lord and then he warned his countrymen that God would not bless them in the land unless they maintained religious purity (Deut. 16:20-21).

Pharaoh Shishak brought 1,200 chariots, 60,000 horsemen, and an innumerable number of Egyptian soldiers (including contingencies of the Lubim, the Sukkiim, and the Ethiopians) into Judah. He was successful in capturing many fortified cities in Judah (2 Chron. 12:3-4). The king of Egypt knew of Jerusalem's vast wealth accumulated during the days of Solomon and rightly believed that, without the support of the northern Israelite tribes, he could conquer and despoil Judah. Pharaoh Shishak's invasion into the region (which netted him 156 cities in Judah, Israel, Edom, and Philistia) is recorded on the exterior south wall of the Amon (Amun) Temple in Jarnak, Egypt.[45]

Having captured Jerusalem's peripheral fortification, the colossal army from the south marched towards Jerusalem. The prophet Shemaiah was sent to deliver a message to Rehoboam and Judah's leaders gathered at Jerusalem: *"Thus says the Lord: 'You have forsaken Me, and therefore I also have left you in the hand of Shishak'"* (2 Chron. 12:5). The king and Judah's leaders immediately humbled themselves and declared *"the Lord is righteous"* (2 Chron. 12:6).

After observing their response, the Lord sent Shemaiah again to inform the king and the elders that because they humbled themselves at His Word and acknowledged their own unrighteousness, He would not consume them in wrath. The prophet went on to promise that the Lord would preserve them from destruction, but they would be Shishak's servants (2 Chron. 12:7-8). Indeed, the king of Egypt confiscated the treasure in the house of the Lord and the king's house (2 Chron. 12:9). William MacDonald comments on the ironic nature of Egypt plundering Solomon's wealth:

> Isn't it ironic that Solomon had sought to protect himself from Egypt by marrying Pharaoh's daughter, but within a short time after his death Shishak of Egypt walked off with much of the glitter of Solomon's golden city![46]

Because Shishak carried away the gold shields which Solomon had made, Rehoboam replaced them with bronze shields and entrusted their care to the captains of the guards (2 Chron. 12:10). Hence, whenever the king entered this house, the captains guarding the doorway would bring the shields out of their safe location to display to the king (2 Chron. 12:11). Though there were costly repercussions from Rehoboam's sin, because he humbled himself before the Lord, he and his people were spared destruction. In fact, God blessed the Southern Kingdom afterwards – *"things also went well in Judah"* (2 Chron. 12:12).

Rehoboam's Death (1 Kgs. 14:29-31; 2 Chron. 12:13-16)

Rehoboam was forty-one years old when he became king of Judah. He ruled seventeen years (931-913 B.C.) in the city in which the Lord chose to put his name – Jerusalem. After the despoiling of Jerusalem by Egypt, King Rehoboam strengthened himself, but because he did not prepare his heart to follow after the Lord, his reign was marked by much wickedness. The pride in his heart at the onset of his reign continued to grow and resulted in the decline of his kingdom. This is why he did not enjoy a peaceful tenure; rather, God permitted ongoing conflict between Judah and Israel all the days of his reign. Rehoboam was buried with his fathers in the City of David and his son Abijah (the great-grandson of the rebel Absalom) ruled in his place.

Meditation

> Repentance is as much a mark of a Christian, as faith is. A very little sin, as the world calls it, is a very great sin to a true Christian.
>
> — Charles Spurgeon

Division of the Kingdom – King Jeroboam

(1 Kgs. 12:25-14:20)

Jeroboam's Pagan Religious System (1 Kgs. 12:25-33)

Historically, Shechem has been a place of decision. It is situated between the mountains of Ebal and Gerizim and at the crossroads of central Palestine. It was here centuries earlier that Joshua assembled the Israelites to choose between being blessed by God through obedience or cursed by God for disobedience (Josh. 8:30-35). A few years later, Joshua delivered his final charge to the nation of Israel to follow God at Shechem (Josh. 24). Now Shechem would be built up by Jeroboam as a stronghold to divide Solomon's kingdom (1 Kgs. 12:25). Later, Jeroboam moved Israel's capital to Tirzah (1 Kgs. 14:17) and Omri later built and established Samaria as the royal city of the Northern Kingdom (1 Kgs. 16:23-24).

Jeroboam realized that the Law required all Israelite men to appear at the central sanctuary three times a year for the feasts of Jehovah and that all sacrifices were to be offered by Levitical priests. He feared that if the northern tribes continued to go to Jerusalem for religious reasons, their hearts would be turned back to King Rehoboam in Judah, which would most certainly result in his death (1 Kgs. 12:26-27).

Jeroboam's solution was to devise a rival religious system for the northern tribes to make returning to Jerusalem unnecessary. He fashioned two golden calves and told the people that these were the gods who had brought them out of Egypt (1 Kgs. 12:28). The calves were not intended to replace the worship of Jehovah, but rather introduced a new way of worshiping Him. He then created two religious centers, Bethel in the south and Dan in the far north, and placed one golden calf at each location (1 Kgs. 12:29-30). He also erected shrines on the high places, and made priests from every class of people (i.e., non-Levites; 1 Kgs. 12:31). In order to save his own life, Jeroboam ensnared Israel in a sanitized form of idolatry and caused his countrymen to sin greatly against the Lord. The fact that many within the northern tribes readily embraced Jeroboam's religion reveals how far from the Lord the people already were, even before the kingdom had divided.

Since the Levitical Law required the people to offer sacrifices, to recognize special days, and to attend religious feasts, Jeroboam also ordained such things for the Northern Tribes. He instituted a feast on the fifteenth day of the eighth month, apparently the day the altar at Bethel was placed into service (1 Kgs. 12:32). Sacrifices were offered and incense was burned in honor of the golden calf. This entire idolatrous system was created from the imagination of Jeroboam's heart in an attempt to keep Israel from submitting to Rehoboam (1 Kgs. 12:33).

This situation actually began about three centuries earlier when the tribe of Dan failed to drive out the remaining Amorites from their inheritance after the land allotments were received from Joshua. The Amorites gained strength and took over much of their possession, which caused many of the Danites to move to the far north where they conquered the city of Leshem and claimed it as their new possession (Judg. 19:47). God's best was for them to seize their proper inheritance, but Leshem was within the vast region of land promised to Abraham centuries earlier, so the action was permissible.

Yet, disobedience has its consequences and these northern Danites were the first Israelites in Canaan proper to engage in flagrant idolatry (Judg. 18:30). Now the kingdom was divided, Jeroboam would make the city of Dan one of two pagan worship centers (1 Kgs. 12:29; 2 Kgs. 10:29). Eventually, God used the Assyrians to punish Dan and the other northern tribes – many were slaughtered, and most of the survivors were exiled. In short, the tribe of Dan lost their inheritance twice because of disobedience!

Bethel was the second location where Jeroboam erected a pagan altar and the image of a gold calf to be worshiped (1 Kgs. 12:25-30; Hos. 10:5). Two centuries into the future, the prophet Hosea would warn Judah to avoid the gross sin of her northern sister Israel: *"Though you, Israel, play the harlot, let not Judah offend. Do not come up to Gilgal, nor go up to Beth Aven, nor swear an oath, saying, 'As the Lord lives'"* (Hos. 4:15). The threefold warning "do not come up," "nor go up," "nor swear" is a rhetorical device to accentuate the grossness of Israel's sin in such a way as to rebuke Israel, while also warning Judah. The prophet Hosea acknowledges that Israel made Bethel, meaning "the house of God" (this site was named by Jacob after making a vow to God; Gen. 28:19, 31:13) to become Beth Aven, meaning "the house of wickedness."

The Man of God and His Message (1 Kgs. 13)

The Lord sent an unnamed prophet, a man of God from Judah, to Bethel to rebuke Jeroboam for his idolatry (1 Kgs. 13:1). There are four unnamed individuals in the Old Testament who are acknowledged as being a "man of God": the man who rebuked Eli for his sons' wickedness (1 Sam. 2:27), the man from Judah who rebuked Jeroboam in this chapter, the man who told Ahab that he would have the victory over the Syrians because they mocked God (1 Kgs. 20:28), and the man who told King Amaziah not to hire mercenaries out of Israel to battle Edom (2 Chron. 25:7).

The fact that these men remained unnamed in Scripture suggests that their work for the Lord was more important than the recognition of men. Paul acknowledged that this is a good principle to govern how we serve the Lord: *"And whatever you do in word or deed, do all in the name of the Lord Jesus, giving thanks to God the Father through Him"* (Col. 3:17). Being heavenly-minded ensures our earthly good.

After arriving at Bethel, the man of God found Jeroboam standing by the pagan altar preparing to burn incense. The prophet delivered this message against him and his altar:

> *O altar, altar! Thus says the Lord: "Behold, a child, Josiah by name, shall be born to the house of David; and on you he shall sacrifice the priests of the high places who burn incense on you, and men's bones shall be burned on you." And he gave a sign the same day, saying, "This is the sign which the Lord has spoken: Surely the altar shall split apart, and the ashes on it shall be poured out"* (1 Kgs. 13:2-3).

There were both immediate (as will be soon evident) and future aspects to the prophet's decree. He had foretold the name of a future king and what he would do nearly three centuries before it would happen! Godly Josiah, the king of Judah from 640 to 609 B.C., destroyed the altar at Bethel's shrine and slaughtered the pagan priests there to fulfill this prophecy (2 Kgs. 23:15-20). Ironically, the prophecy was fulfilled about eighty years after the Northern Kingdom fell to the Assyrians.

This message infuriated the king, who stretched out his hand to point to the man he wanted his guards to arrest, but two things immediately happened (1 Kgs. 13:4-5): First, Jeroboam's hand and perhaps his arm immediately withered and became fully paralyzed. Second, as the prophet had just proclaimed, the altar split apart and the ashes poured out of it – this was a sign from God to validate the message of His prophet. The king wisely chose not to resist the prophet further and beseeched him to petition the Lord to restore his hand. The prophet did so and the king's hand was fully restored (1 Kgs. 13:6).

In appreciation, Jeroboam requested that the man of God come to his home so that he could be refreshed and rewarded for healing his hand (1 Kgs. 13:7). Though a kind gesture, the prophet declined the invitation because he had been commanded by the Lord not to eat or drink during his mission into Israel. He also had been commanded to return to Judah a different way than he had arrived at Bethel (1 Kgs. 13:8-9). The prophet said it was better to obey the Lord even if the king offered him half of his kingdom, hence the prophet departed for home a different route (1 Kgs. 13:10). The Lord has no tolerance for false religion, and the people of God are to have no association with it!

The Man of God Dies (1 Kgs. 13:11-34)

So far, the man of God has completely obeyed the Lord and therefore his ministry has been fruitful. He successfully, by God's grace, withstood the most powerful man in Israel and lived to tell about it.

But there was an old prophet living in Bethel, who, through his sons, found out about the prophet's message and what happened at the altar that day (1 Kgs. 13:11). In response to their father's request, they saddled a donkey for him and pointed him in the direction they had seen the Judean prophet heading (1 Kgs. 13:12-13). The old prophet soon found a man resting under the shade of an oak tree and asked him if he was the man of God for Judah. The man affirmed that he was (1 Kgs. 13:14).

The old prophet then invited the Judean prophet to come to his home and eat with him, but he refused, quoting again the instructions he had been given by the Lord (1 Kgs. 13:15-16). Eager to have such an esteemed guest in his home, the old prophet resorted to a falsehood: *"I too am a prophet as you are, and an angel spoke to me by the word of the Lord, saying, 'Bring him back with you to your house, that he may eat bread and drink water'"* (1 Kgs. 13:18). Regrettably, the faithful prophet believed the lie and returned to the old prophet's home and ate bread and drank water in his house (1 Kgs. 13:19).

All too often in Christendom today we hear the same kind of language, "I too am a prophet," being bantered about by professing Christians who want to justify their bad behavior. This lie might be spotted by statements such as: "Well, that is open to interpretation." "Everyone understands the Bible a little differently." "God will not judge me if I am wrong because He knows my heart." Scripture presents God's will in only one way and it is to be understood in only one way.

When Scripture declares the will of God, there is no ambiguity about what God means. For example, we read, *"For this is the will of God, your sanctification: that you should abstain from sexual immorality"* (1 Thess. 4:3-4); yet, carnal people will justify their appetites by saying such things as, "living together before marriage is OK because we plan to get married," or "homosexual relationships are acceptable to God if two people really love each other," or "we can have an 'open marriage' relationship if both spouses agree to it." Fornication is fornication, and is an abomination to God no matter what form it takes. His condemnation of fornicators is equally clear: no fornicator will inherit the kingdom of God (i.e. go to heaven; Eph. 5:5), and all fornicators will be cast into the Lake of Fire (i.e., hell; Rev. 21:8). This is what God thinks about moral relativity!

Although the old prophet had not spoken for the Lord earlier, God does use him to deliver a message of judgment against the Judean prophet now. God can use whomever or whatever he desires to express His mind. He used the false prophet Balaam to bless Israel, and Balaam's donkey to rebuke its master. God spoke powerfully through Jonah to the Ninevites even when Jonah's will was not conformed to God's. Now speaking for the Lord, the old prophet told his companion that because he had not obeyed God's word, he would not be buried in the tomb of his fathers (1 Kgs. 13:20-22). This message implied that his death was imminent – he would not make it home.

The old prophet then saddled his donkey for the Judean prophet and sent him on his way, but as he was journeying back to Judah, a lion slew him on the side of the road (1 Kgs. 13:23-24). A lion attacking a lone traveler was a real danger in those days, but to show that the death of the prophet was divine judgment instead of a naturally occurring event, both the lion and the donkey stood by the dead man's body (1 Kgs. 13:25). Onlookers saw this sight and reported it to the old prophet, who affirmed that God had fulfilled His word. Then, after his sons saddled a second donkey, he arrived at the peculiar and unsettling scene (1 Kgs. 13:26-27).

The old prophet found the lion and donkey still standing by the corpse of the man of God. Furthermore, he observed that the lion had not eaten the corpse nor torn the donkey, and that the donkey was not afraid of the lion (1 Kgs. 13:28). He placed the man's corpse on the donkey and brought him back to Bethel, where he mourned the death of the man of God and buried him in his own tomb (1 Kgs. 13:29-30). The old prophet requested that his sons bury him alongside the man of God and proclaimed that his prophecy to Jeroboam concerning the pagan shrines and high places in Samaria would surely come to pass (1 Kgs. 13:31-32).

Regrettably, this godly Judean prophet had rejected the flattery and reward of a wicked king only to succumb to the lying tongue of a fellow prophet. We know that children of the devil are pernicious to the children of God, so we expect malicious behavior from them (John 15:18-19). We know that Satan's false prophets use crafty speech and can conjure up unusual signs to deceive God's people from following the truth (e.g. Moses' contest with Pharaoh's magicians). Paul acknowledged that the same dark practices continued in his day (2 Cor. 11:13-15). So, we too should expect such deception from the enemy, but oh how wretched it is when God's people, because of selfish motives and pride, deceive their brethren away from the path of righteousness.

The child of God is to seek the truth (2 Tim. 2:15), rejoice in the truth (1 Cor. 13:6), speak the truth (1 Tim. 2:7), and abide in the truth (Jas. 5:19-20). As Paul affirmed, the believer *"can do nothing against the truth, but for the truth"* (2 Cor. 13:8). Genuine truth is eternally certain, and to the extent possible, believers must know it, hold to it, and live it out in order to honor the Lord; living a lie will never glorify the God of truth: *If you abide in My word, you are My disciples indeed. And you shall know the truth, and the truth shall make you free* (John 8:31-32).

Jeroboam did not heed the Lord's word and sign through his prophet, but rather returned to his evil of sanctifying a non-Levitical priesthood and leading the northern tribes deeper into idolatry (1 Kgs. 13:33). Because of his great sin, God promised to completely destroy the house of Jeroboam (1 Kgs. 13:34).

Judgment on the House of Jeroboam (1 Kgs. 14:1-20)

Jeroboam sent his wife to the prophet Ahijah in Shiloh to receive news concerning their son Abijah who had become quite ill (1 Kgs. 14:1-2). Jeroboam told his wife to disguise herself and to take the old and nearly blind prophet ten loaves of bread, some cakes, and a jar of honey (1 Kgs. 14:3-4). This same prophet had first confirmed his kingship long ago.

Shiloh was located about ten miles south of Shechem (the capital city of Israel) and within Ephraim's territory. Tirzah, where Jeroboam's son was located in this story, was about three miles northeast of Shechem on the north side of Mount Ebal. Obviously, if God could reveal news to Ahijah about Jeroboam's son, he could also be informed about the identity of the messenger, Jeroboam's wife. Therefore, the reason for the disguise was not to dupe the prophet, but to ensure that the people (i.e., "they") under Jeroboam's rule were not aware that Jeroboam's wife was seeking counsel from a prophet of Jehovah. That would prove the ineptness of his own priests and prophets and would undermine his religion.

The Lord told Ahijah all about his imminent visitor so that, when she arrived, he greeted her properly and delivered God's message to be repeated to Jeroboam (1 Kgs. 14:5):

> *Come in, wife of Jeroboam. Why do you pretend to be another person? For I have been sent to you with bad news. Go, tell Jeroboam, "Thus says the Lord God of Israel: 'Because I exalted you from among the people, and made you ruler over My people Israel, and tore the kingdom away from the house of David, and gave it to you; and yet you have not been as My servant David, who kept My commandments and who followed Me with all his heart, to do only what was right in My eyes; but you have done more evil than all who were before you, for you have gone and made for yourself other gods and molded images to provoke Me to anger, and have cast Me behind your back – therefore behold! I will bring disaster on the house of Jeroboam, and will cut off from Jeroboam every male in Israel, bond and free; I will take away the remnant of the house of Jeroboam, as one takes away refuse until it is all gone. The dogs shall eat whoever*

> *belongs to Jeroboam and dies in the city, and the birds of the air shall eat whoever dies in the field; for the Lord has spoken!'"* (1 Kgs. 14:6-11).

When Ahijah originally gave Jeroboam the ten pieces of a new garment to confirm his rule over the northern tribes, he was told that God would be with him if he followed David's example of loyalty (1 Kgs. 11:29-33). He did not, but rather caused Israel to sin greatly against the Lord. Therefore, the kingdom would be taken from him and his household would be completely destroyed.

Ahijah then told Jeroboam's wife to return to her own house, for when her feet entered Shechem, her son would die (1 Kgs. 14:12). The prophet said that all Israel would mourn his death (1 Kgs. 14:13). Because there was something good in the child, in the Lord's sight, he would be the only one in Jeroboam's house to receive a decent burial (1 Kgs. 14:13).

The prophet then decreed that God would raise up another king of Israel who would completely cut off the house of Jeroboam because he had provoked the Lord to anger by promoting idolatry in the land (1 Kgs. 14:14). Additionally, Ahijah foretold that, because Israel had provoked God's anger by her idolatry, He would "strike Israel," "uproot Israel" and "scatter them beyond the River" (1 Kgs. 14:15-16). The language is strong and predicted the fall of the Northern Kingdom and the mass exile of Israelites; yet, the Lord would not forever cast away His wayward people. God's unconditional promise to Abraham ensured that his descendants would be blessed forever in the Promised Land and would be free from Gentile oppression (Gen. 12:2-3). This meant the best was yet to come!

There is no evidence that Jeroboam's wife even spoke in the presence of the prophet. Instead, God gave her a message to deliver to her husband. She quickly departed and returned to Tirzah, likely the next day as this would have been about a fifteen-mile journey detouring around Mount Ebal back to Tirzah (1 Kgs. 14:17). Just as the prophet had predicted, when she came to the threshold of the house, the child died and all Israel mourned for him and buried him (1 Kgs. 14:18).

Interestingly, Tirzah was the name of one of Zelophehad's faithful daughters who was granted an inheritance in Manasseh's territory because her father had no sons (Num. 26:33). The Hebrew word translated Tirzah means "she is my delight." Sadly, the city named after the one who had previously delighted the Lord had now become the center of contempt and rebellion for the things of God. The man of God in the previous chapter had foretold the fate of Jeroboam's corrupt religious system, and Ahijah had now foretold the doom of Jeroboam's dynasty.

Jeroboam was not a strong leader and because he led the people away from the Lord, he was not helped, but punished by Jehovah. As a result, much of Israel's regional dominance gained by David and Solomon was lost during Jeroboam's reign. Thomas L. Constable summarizes the lost regions:

> This lost area included the land around Damascus to the north. In the southwest the Philistines repossessed some of their former territory and grew stronger (1 Kgs. 15:27). On the east Moab was apparently lost. Ironically, Jeroboam's protector in Egypt (1 Kgs. 11:40), Shishak (Sheshonk I), invaded Judah (1 Kgs. 14:25) during Jeroboam's reign. This resulted in heavy damage and widespread destruction. Jeroboam was also defeated by King Abijah of Judah (2 Chron. 13:13-20). Israel suffered both in military strength and in territorial holdings during Jeroboam's reign.[47]

The writer notes that, at the time of his writing, the acts of Jeroboam could be found in *"the book of the chronicles of the kings of Israel."* Information regarding eighteen kings of Israel and fourteen kings of Judah (but in the annals of the kings of Judah) are said to be recorded in these official documents. These important historical texts were probably kept in the royal archives, but were eventually lost.

Jeroboam died and was buried with his fathers; he reigned over Israel for twenty-two years (931-910 B.C.; 1 Kgs. 14:20). His son Nadab reigned in his place (1 Kgs. 14:20). Jeroboam was the first of nine wicked dynasties that would rule over Israel in the next two centuries.

Meditation

> Truth is so obscure in these times, and falsehood so established, that, unless we love the truth, we cannot know it.
>
> — Blaise Pascal

A man may imagine things that are false, but he can only understand things that are true, for if the things be false, the apprehension of them is not understanding.

— Isaac Newton

King Abijah of Judah

1 Kings 15:1-8; 2 Chronicles 13

Rehoboam's son Abijah (Abijam) became the king of Judah in the eighteenth year of King Jeroboam's reign, but ruled for only three years (913-911 B.C.; 2 Chron. 13:1-2). The outcome of marrying foreign women in David's and Solomon's tenures becomes apparent in the first two kings of Judah (i.e., after Solomon's death). Rehoboam was the son of an Ammonite and Abijah's mother was Maachah the granddaughter of Absalom (Abishalom), whose mother was a Geshurite (1 Kgs. 15:2; 2 Sam. 3:3). Therefore, King Abijah was actually more Gentile than Jew, bloodline wise.

The old adage "like father like son" describes Abijah well, for *"he walked in all the sins of his father, which he had done before him; his heart was not loyal to the Lord his God"* (1 Kgs. 15:3). Abijah did not abandon the Lord, but he did tolerate idolatry in his kingdom. He did not embrace such apostasy outright, but rather suffered from spiritual complacency, a slinking disposition affecting much of the Church today. Yet, complacency inevitably leads to compromise, which eventually results in carnality. Despite Abijah's lack of loyalty, God did not snuff out the dynasty of David because of His covenant with him; rather, He permitted Abijah to father a son (Asa) who would be "a lamp in Jerusalem" and establish Jerusalem for God's glory (1 Kgs. 15:4).

As during the days of Rehoboam, the warring between Israel and Judah continued into Abijah's reign. On one particular confrontation, Abijah placed 400,000 choice warriors in battle array against 800,000 men of valor from Israel under Jeroboam's command (2 Chron. 13:3). On the eve of battle, the prophet Abijah delivered a message to Jeroboam and his men from Mount Zemariam (2 Chron. 13:4). He recounts how Jeroboam rose up against and rebelled against Solomon, even though God had established an eternal covenant with David, meaning that his descendants were destined to rule the Jewish nation (2 Chron. 13:5-7).

Rhetorically speaking, Abijah then asked Jeroboam, even with his vast army and the gold calves (which he fashioned for his gods), if he could resist the will of God (2 Chron. 13:8)? Did he think all the common people who had bribed their way into Jeroboam's pagan priesthood could somehow assist him (2 Chron. 13:9)? He had expelled God's true priests to uphold his own conjured up religious system, but despite having a wicked king, Judah had not forsaken the Lord, His priesthood, His prescribed offerings or sacrifices (2 Chron. 13:10-11).

To illustrate this point, the prophet called Jeroboam's attention to the Levitical priests sounding the silver trumpets as an alarm against him and then warned: *"O children of Israel, do not fight against the Lord God of your fathers, for you shall not prosper!"* (2 Chron. 13:12). From Numbers 10 we learn that the two silver trumpets, fashioned in the days of Moses, were blown by the priests for various reasons, but chiefly to declare the mind of God to His people (Num. 10:3-8). The trumpets were also to be blown when the Jews were appealing to God for assistance, such as on the eve of a battle (Num. 10:9-10). This is how the trumpets were being used in the scene before us. Judah was ceremonially identifying with the Lord and summoning His help in the forthcoming battle (e.g. Num. 31:1-6). The sounding of the trumpets would greatly strengthen the hearts of Judah's warriors because it would remind them that Jehovah was with them on the battlefield.

However, Jeroboam ignored the prophet's message and the blowing of the silver trumpets, and set an ambush for Judah's army. Through an outflanking maneuver Jeroboam was able to put Israel's troops both behind and in front of Judah's army (2 Chron. 13:13-14). Trusting in their God for deliverance, the men of Judah gave a shout to the Lord who immediately struck down Jeroboam and Israel's army (2 Chron. 13:15). Israel then fled before Judah, for God had given them into their hands. Israel suffered 500,000 casualties (2 Chron. 13:16-17).

The outcome of the battle was that Israel was subdued and Judah prevailed *"because they relied on the Lord God of their fathers"* (2 Chron. 13:18). While driving Jeroboam and his tattered army northward, Abijah seized a number of cities from Israel, namely *"Bethel with its villages, Jeshanah with its villages, and Ephrain with its villages"* (2 Chron. 13:19). This defeat was devastating to Jeroboam who never recovered his strength again, for the Lord struck him down afterwards (2 Chron. 13:20).

The historian tells us that Abijah, though inept spiritually, became mighty and that he had fourteen wives, who bore him twenty-two sons and sixteen daughters (2 Chron. 13:21). He also notes that the acts of Abijah were also recorded in the annals of the prophet Iddo (2 Chron. 13:22). After Abijah died, he was buried with his fathers in the City of David and his son Asa reigned in Judah in his place (1 Kgs. 15:8).

Meditation

The battle is the Lord's! Not ours in strength or skill,
But His alone, in sovereign grace, to work His will.
Ours, counting not the cost, unflinching, to obey;
And in His time His holy arm shall win the day.

The battle is the Lord's! The Victor crucified,
Must with the travail of His soul be satisfied.
The powers of hell shall fail, and all God's will be done,
Till every soul whom He has given to Christ be won.

The battle is the Lord's! Stand still, my soul, and view,
The great salvation God has wrought revealed for you.
Then, resting in His might, lift high His triumph song,
For power, dominion, kingdom, strength to Christ belong!

— Margaret Clarkson

King Asa of Judah

1 Kings 15:9-24; 2 Chronicles 14-16

Asa Rules Judah (1 Kgs. 15:9-15; 2 Chron. 14)

Abijah's son Asa ruled Judah and he enjoyed peace for the first ten years of his reign (2 Chron. 14:1). Israel's devastating defeat in the previous chapter subdued the northern tribes, preventing hostility towards Asa for several years (until Baasha became king of Israel). Asa became ruler of Judah in the twentieth year of Jeroboam king of Israel and he reigned forty-one years in Jerusalem (911-870 B.C.; 1 Kgs. 15:10). Abijah had to die before revival could come under Asa. In the same way, believers must reckon, practically speaking, that the old man (who we were in Adam) was crucified with Christ. Only then can we live out the resurrection life of the Last Adam and experience revival in Him.

Both historians write favorably of Asa: *"Asa did what was right in the eyes of the Lord, as did his father David"* (1 Kgs. 15:11). *"Asa did what was good and right in the eyes of the Lord"* (2 Chron. 14:2). Although Asa was not a prophet, a psalmist, a writer, or a conqueror like David, his heart was right with the Lord and he consistently worshiped the Lord as the Law commanded.

Asa is one of five Judean kings who stands out among the rest as being honorable. Judah had suffered three decades of wickedness under her last three kings, so Asa's godly character was a breath of fresh air for the Southern Kingdom. He was zealous for the Lord in his determination to spiritually purify Judah (1 Kgs. 15:12-15; 2 Chron. 14:3-5). He …

- removed the altars of foreign gods at the high places (but not those for Jehovah; 2 Chron. 14:3),
- broke down the sacred pillars and cut down the wood images,
- commanded Judah to seek the Lord and obey His Law,

- removed the pagan high places and incense altars throughout Judah,
- banished the sodomites (i.e., paganized homosexuals) from the land,
- dedicated gold and silver articles to the house of the Lord,
- removed his grandmother from being queen and destroyed her image of Asherah.

The king's reforms were wide sweeping, yet he did permit Jehovah to still be worshiped in the high places instead of at the central sanctuary as required by the Law (1 Kgs. 15:14). His godliness caused his countrymen to follow after the Lord. Accordingly, the Lord blessed Judah with His peace which brought a deep serenity to the land. C. A. Coates comments on the recovery achieved during Asa's reign and what it would typify in the Church Age:

> There was the unsparing judgment of evil and what was idolatrous. He did not follow his father or his grandmother but goes back in principle to David, so that we get dedicated things brought into the house of Jehovah, silver, gold and vessels. The silver speaks of redemption as that which is brought back to God in the value of the death of Christ. Gold expresses our new creation in Christ, and generally, all things of God. Vessels suggest persons dedicated so that God has His portion in them.[48]

Indeed, Christendom today must rediscover the value of Calvary, the necessity of becoming a new creation in Christ, and then a consecrated vessel for His honor and glory!

Besides spiritually renovating the nation, Asa was also industrious. He rebuilt Judah's fortified cities, many of which fell to Pharaoh Shishak during his grandfather's reign (2 Chron. 14:6-7). He also expanded Judah's military. His army included 300,000 from the tribe of Judah who carried shields and spears, and 280,000 from Benjamin who carried shields and bows. All were mighty men of valor (2 Chron. 14:8).

It was not long before Asa's robust army was needed to defend Judah from Ethiopia, which had an invasion force of one million soldiers and 300 war-chariots (2 Chron. 14:9). The Ethiopians were led by Zerah and came to Maresha. Asa responded by putting his troops in array before Zerah in the Valley of Zephathan about 25 miles southwest of Jerusalem (2 Chron. 14:10). This was a bold position, as it gave the enemy the ability to use their war-chariots in the flat terrain in the valley. However, Asa's boast was not in his military might, for though the enemy's soldiers numbered twice his, he cried out to the Lord not to let men prevail against him:

> *Lord, it is nothing for You to help, whether with many or with those who have no power; help us, O Lord our God, for we rest on You, and in Your name we go against this multitude. O Lord, You are our God; do not let man prevail against You!"* (2 Chron. 14:11).

Israel's confidence that a superior opposition is irrelevant if the Lord fights your battles resulted in many outstanding victories throughout the nation's history. Jonathan conveyed this conviction to his armorbearer in 1 Samuel 14, and David did to Saul before facing Goliath in 1 Samuel 17. Consequently, the faith of these young men prompted the Lord's help to overcome their opponents and then encouraged others to exercise faith such that a great slaughter of the enemy resulted.

Asa's faith also inspired such a miraculous outcome, for Zerah was defeated by the Lord and Asa's army pursued the retreating Ethiopians and massacred them as far as Gerar (2 Chron. 14:12-13). They also defeated and plundered all the cities around Gerar, because the fear of the Lord came upon the Philistines likewise (2 Chron. 14:14). The spoil (including much livestock and camels) from the Ethiopian army and the cities in the region of Gerar was "exceedingly much" (2 Chron. 14:15).

Asa Reforms Judah (2 Chron. 15)

The Holy Spirit prompted the prophet Azariah (mentioned in Scripture only here) to deliver a message to Asa and his victorious army (2 Chron. 15:1):

> *The Lord is with you while you are with Him. If you seek Him, He will be found by you; but if you forsake Him, He will forsake you. For a long time Israel has been without the true God, without a teaching priest, and without law; but when in their trouble they turned to the Lord God of Israel, and sought Him, He was found by them. And in those times there was no peace to the one who went out, nor to the*

> *one who came in, but great turmoil was on all the inhabitants of the lands. So nation was destroyed by nation, and city by city, for God troubled them with every adversity. But you, be strong and do not let your hands be weak, for your work shall be rewarded!* (2 Chron. 15:2-7).

Another prophet named Obed apparently conveyed a similar message to Asa, which encouraged him to be relentless in getting abominable idols out of Judah, Benjamin, and even out of the cities which he had taken in the mountains of Ephraim (probably referring to the previous victory of his father Abijah; 2 Chron. 15:8). He also restored the altar of the Lord that was before the vestibule of the Lord.

Simeon was a smaller tribe situated within Judah's borders and was mostly absorbed into Judah and by this time had lost their distinction. After the kingdom split following Solomon's death, some from Simeon migrated northward and re-settled in Ephraim and Manasseh (2 Chron. 34:6). Now, seeing that the Lord was with Asa, many from Ephraim, Manasseh, and Simeon came over to him (2 Chron. 15:9). These gathered with the men of Judah and Benjamin on the third month in the fifteenth year of Asa's reign to offer sacrifices to the Lord and to feast together (2 Chron. 15:10). Seven hundred bulls and 7,000 sheep from the spoil of the Ethiopians were offered to the Lord (2 Chron. 15:11).

With such a large congregation gathered before the Lord, Asa used the opportunity for covenant renewal. The people promised the Lord, on the penalty of death, to seek the Lord God of their fathers with all their heart and with all their soul (2 Chron. 15:12-14). Such widespread aspiration to wholeheartedly follow the Lord did not occur often in Israel's history, but when it did occur, a delighted God was prompted to bless His people. Sadly, the northern tribes remained idolatrous at this time. Judah rejoiced in their oath to God, who in turn gave them peace.

Asa's Treaty with Syria (1 Kgs 15:16-22; 2 Chron. 16:1-10)

The narrative states that in the thirty-sixth year of Asa's reign, Baasha king of Israel withstood Judah. He began fortifying the city of Ramah in Benjamin's territory as a staging area from which to attack Judah. However, the timing of these events cannot be correct as Baasha would have died long before Asa's thirty-sixth year as Judah's king. Most commentators agree that there is a copyist's error and the numbers 35 (2 Chron. 15:19) and 36 (2 Chron. 16:1) should either be 15/16 (as suggested by Keil and Archer) or 25/26 (as preferred by Edersheim).

Ramah, Samuel's hometown, was situated about five miles north of Jerusalem and seven miles south of Bethel. Baasha believed that his presence in Ramah, on the main highland route north and south, would prevent Israelites of the northern tribes from visiting Jerusalem and identifying with King Asa (2 Chron. 16:1).

After Asa became aware of Baasha's military buildup, he took silver and gold from the temple and the king's treasury and sent it to Ben-Hadad king of Syria who was residing in Damascus (2 Chron. 16:2). The purpose of the bribe was to prompt Ben-Hadad to break his treaty with Israel, so that Baasha would withdraw from Judah's northern border (2 Chron. 16:3). Regrettably, Asa did not call on the Lord to deliver Judah as he had done when facing the threat of the Ethiopians, but rather relied on his own ingenuity and strategy to resolve the threat.

Asa did persuade Ben-Hadad to enter into an alliance with Judah against Israel. He then began attacking cities in northern Israel; this caused Baasha to withdraw from Ramah in the far south to defend this new threat from the north (2 Chron. 16:4-5). Asa then dismantled Baasha's fortification in Ramah and used the lumber and stones to fortify Geba (Gibeah) and Mizpah (the former being two miles west of Ramah and the latter, two miles northwest of Ramah; 2 Chron. 16:6). As a result, Judah had two strongholds just south of Israel's border to prevent any further military buildup on Judah's border.

While Asa's plan did resolve the ominous situation, the Lord was not honored by it. Defrauding God to enrich those who oppose Him will always earn God's rebuke. Nor should believers today use what the Lord has graciously given us (time, money, resources, spiritual gifts, intellect, etc.) to strengthen the devil's rebellion against the Lord. Asa had valued Syria's assistance above the Lord's help, so He sent the prophet Hanani to rebuke the king (2 Chron. 16:7-9).

During times of spiritual declension, the Lord multiplies His prophets to warn and rebuke wayward kings. Jeroboam's idolatry was first rebuked by an unnamed prophet (1 Kgs. 13:1-10), and then the king was warned twice by the prophet Ahijah (1 Kgs. 11:29, 14:1-18). Shemaiah was sent to Rehoboam in order to persuade the angry king not to fight his northern brethren (1 Kgs. 12:22). After God gave Judah victory over the Ethiopians, the prophet Azariah was summoned to implore King Asa to restore proper worship of Jehovah in the land (2 Chron. 15:1-8). Now, Hanani has been called to prophesy against Asa who had paid Ben-Hadad, the king of Syria, to help him fight Baasha, the king of Israel (2 Chron. 16:7).

Hanani reminded Asa how the Lord had previously overcome the Ethiopians, a much greater threat to Judah than Israel had been. The prophet also reminded Asa that Syria was his true enemy, but through his manipulation of the circumstances, he had strengthened Syria. The king should have relied on the One whose eyes *"run to and fro throughout the whole earth,"* and who longs *"to show Himself strong on behalf of those whose heart is loyal to Him"* (2 Chron. 16:9). Finally, Hanani told Asa that because he had behaved foolishly, he would suffer wars during the remainder of his reign. Asa was enraged by Hanani's message. He imprisoned the prophet and also oppressed some of the people afterwards (2 Chron. 16:10).

Most of Asa's long reign was marked by faithfulness and devotion, and the Lord consequently prospered Judah under his leadership. However, in his final years, Asa became proud and the nation suffered. Concerning the Syrians, the king traded a short-term benefit for a long-term detriment. This is a common mistake of time-dependent creatures who are guided by their natural impulses; we cannot see the beginning from the end as God does, which is why we need His wisdom and power in our affairs.

Hanani reminded Asa of a truth that the writer of Hebrews would also declare – it just is not possible to hide anything from the Lord: "*There is no creature hidden from His sight, but all things are naked and open to the eyes of Him to whom we must give account"* (Heb. 4:13). The Lord is omniscient and only a self-righteous man thinks he can avoid being seen, being caught, and being judged for his sin (Rom. 2:1-4). No one can hide from the Lord or escape His jurisdiction, *"for the eyes of the Lord run to and fro throughout the whole earth, to show Himself strong on behalf of those whose heart is loyal to Him"* (2 Chron. 16:9). Let us therefore be found among this loyal company, rather than seeking help from the Syrians.

Asa's Illness and Death (1 Kings 15:23-24; 2 Chron. 16:11-14)

Asa became severely diseased in his feet in the thirty-ninth year of his reign (2 Chron. 16:12). This may have been a disciplinary measure to teach Asa the necessity of relying on the Lord. Though Asa was a godly king and the Lord had wonderfully prospered every area of his kingdom, he sadly did not seek the Lord to cure his disease, but rather only his physicians (2 Chron. 16:12). After two years Asa succumbed to his illness and was buried with his fathers in the City of David (2 Chron. 16:13).

Asa ruled Judah during the reigns of seven kings of Israel (representing four dynasties). He was a beloved king and did much good for Judah. Accordingly, the people *"laid him in the bed which was filled with spices and various ingredients prepared in a mixture of ointments. They made a very great burning for him"* (2 Chron. 16:14). Asa was one of the few kings of Judah who began well and ended well because he remained devoted to the Lord throughout his forty-one-year reign in Jerusalem. Although he did not seek the Lord against the Syrians or in his illness, he still finished devoted to the Lord!

Meditation

> Stopping at third adds no more to the score than striking out. It doesn't matter how well you start if you fail to finish.
>
> — Billy Sunday

> Nothing paralyzes our lives like the attitude that things can never change. We need to remind ourselves that God can change things. Outlook determines outcome. If we see only the problems, we will be defeated; but if we see the possibilities in the problems, we can have victory.
>
> — Warren Wiersbe

Kings Nadab, Baasha, Elah, Zimri, and Omir of Israel

1 Kings 15:25-16:28

One of the measures of a healthy society is stable leadership, something wayward Israel generally lacked throughout their history. During Asa's reign in Judah, a number of kings seized Israel's throne in quick succession, largely through insurrection, which ended in the assassination of the previous king.

Nadab (1 Kgs. 15:25-31)

Jeroboam's son Nadab ruled Israel after his father's death. He ruled Israel for only two years (910-909 B.C.), which coincided with the first two years of King Asa's reign in Judah. Nadab continued the evil policies of his father, which had plunged Israel into gross idolatry. Nadab put the Philistine town of Gibbethon, located between Ekron and Gezer, under siege to conquer it. Baasha took advantage of the situation (i.e., the bulk of Israel's army was not nearby) and assassinated Nadab to seize the throne of Israel.

To ensure that there would be no rivals from the house of Jeroboam, Baasha *"killed all the house of Jeroboam. He did not leave to Jeroboam anyone that breathed"* (1 Kgs. 15:29). This slaughter fulfilled the judgment of God pronounced by the prophet Ahijah against Jeroboam for leading Israel away from the Lord. Nadab's death ended the siege; Gibbethon was never captured. Because he did not honor Jehovah, the Lord brought Jeroboam's dynasty to an end in its second generation.

Baasha (1 Kgs. 15:32-16:7)

The historian introduces Baasha by stating that he and Asa were in constant conflict, which was mild at first, but grew increasingly hostile throughout Baasha's twenty-four-year reign (909-886 B.C.). Though having the third longest reign in Israel, the brevity of the narrative would suggest a lackluster performance, marked by the continuation of Jeroboam's religious policies and conflict with Asa.

The Lord directed the prophet Jehu (not to be confused with Israel's later king), the son of Hanani (who may be the prophet imprisoned by Asa years later), to deliver a rebuke to Baasha:

> *Inasmuch as I lifted you out of the dust and made you ruler over My people Israel, and you have walked in the way of Jeroboam, and have made My people Israel sin, to provoke Me to anger with their sins, surely I will take away the posterity of Baasha and the posterity of his house, and I will make your house like the house of Jeroboam the son of Nebat. The dogs shall eat whoever belongs to Baasha and dies in the city, and the birds of the air shall eat whoever dies in the fields* (1 Kgs. 16:2-4).

The Lord had lifted up Baasha from a low social position to execute His foretold judgment on the dynasty of Jeroboam and to become the king of Israel. Although Baasha was God's chosen instrument of judgment, he had acted on his own behalf, rather than upholding the righteousness of God in the matter. Therefore, the Lord held him accountable for the slaughter, even though He had previously decreed the destruction of Jeroboam's house. Consequently, the prophet promised that many of Baasha's descendants would not receive a proper burial, but would be eaten by birds and wild dogs – such a thing was appalling to the Israelite mind.

Baasha's judgment is an important reminder to believers that only good deeds performed in the power of the Holy Spirit (i.e., void of selfish motives) please the Lord and are rewardable (1 Cor. 3:11-15). All else is wood, hay, and stubble and will be burned up at the Judgment Seat of Christ. And standing before the Lord in all His glory, we will be glad to see such filthiness ascend in smoke!

Baasha died and was buried with his fathers in Tirzah. His son Elah became the king of Israel. Jehu's prophetic words would be fulfilled during his short reign.

Elah (1 Kgs. 16:9-14)

Elah continued the evil of his predecessors. He ruled two years (886-885 B.C.) from Tirzah (near Shechem) without any notable accomplishments. While drunk, he was murdered by Zimri, a commander over half of Elah's war-chariots. Zimri completely destroyed Elah's household and even those associated with the family to prevent retaliation for his coup. As foretold by the prophet Jehu, Israel's second dynasty had come to an abrupt end.

Zimri (1 Kgs. 16:15-20)

Zimri's attempts to prevent retaliation for his treason in the murder of King Elah proved to be insufficient. After Israel's army, gathered against Gibbethon, heard that Zimri had killed their king, they appointed Omri as their commander. They departed to attack Zimri at Tirzah. Seeing that the city had fallen, Zimri went into the royal citadel and committed suicide by setting fire to it. He reigned only seven days after taking the throne of Israel, during the twenty-seventh year of Asa's rule over Judah (885 B.C.). God judged idolatrous Zimri for his sin.

Omri (1 Kgs. 16:21-28)

Israel then suffered a divided kingdom, as half of the people followed Tibni the son of Ginath and half followed Omri. However, in the sixth year, Omri prevailed and Tibni died (he was likely executed). Since Omri had control of the military, it is mystery as to why it took several years for him to suppress the opposition. Regardless, Omri became the unchallenged king of Israel in the thirty-first year of Asa's reign and ruled over the Northern Kingdom for twelve years (885-874 B.C.).

Omri bought the hill of Samaria for two talents of silver; then he built the city of Samaria on it. Apparently, Omri named the new city after Shemer, the previous owner of the property. The historian then notes that *"Omri did evil in the eyes of the Lord, and did worse than all who were before him"* (1 Kgs. 16:25). The king not only walked in the evil ways of Jeroboam (who developed a corrupt religion to solidify his kingdom), but he also delighted in provoking God to anger through unrestrained idolatry.

Arguably, Omri was the strongest king of Israel up to this time. Not only did he fortify himself against possible attack from Assyria in the northeast, but he also led a successful campaign against Moab in the southeast. His victory is recorded on the Moabite Stone. He also formalized an alliance with the Phoenicians through marriage: the daughter of the Phoenician king Ethbaal, Jezebel, was given to Omri's son Ahab in marriage. Through this ill-advised marital union, Baal worship would be popularized in the Northern Kingdom.

Omri ruled from Tirzah six years and then from Samaria six more years. After his death, Omri was buried with his fathers in Samaria and his son Ahab ruled Israel. Since the Northern Kingdom originated under Jeroboam sixty years previously, Israel suffered two coups resulting in three dynasty changes, and one civil war. Living on a sin-cursed planet is demanding, but it is even harder without the Lord!

Meditation

> The best form of government is that which is most likely to prevent the greatest sum of evil.
>
> — James Monroe

> He who passively accepts evil is as much involved in it as he who helps to perpetrate it. He who accepts evil without protesting against it is really cooperating with it.
>
> — Martin Luther King, Jr.

King Ahab and the Prophet Elijah – Part 1

1 Kings 16:28-17:24

Ahab Is King of Israel (1 Kgs. 16:29-34)

Ahab became the king of Israel after his father Omri's death in the thirty-eighth year of Asa's reign over Judah; he ruled Israel for twenty-two years from Samaria (874-853 B.C.; 1 Kgs. 16:29). Omri was more wicked than any king before him, and Ahab was more evil than his father (1 Kgs. 16:30). Ahab even married a flagrant Baal worshiper named Jezebel, the daughter of Ethbaal, king of Sidon (1 Kgs. 16:31). He erected a temple and an altar for Baal in Samaria, the new capital city of Israel (1 Kgs. 16:32). A specially crafted wooden idol was placed in this temple to honor Baal.

Moses had told Israel why a single idolater should not be tolerated in the land: because just one person secretly practicing paganism could become a poisonous root that corrupts the entire nation (Deut. 29:18). Ahab's marriage to Jezebel demonstrates this warning to be valid, for she popularized in the Northern Kingdom the worship of the Canaanite fertility gods Baal and Ashtaroth. Under her wicked influence, Ahab *"did more to provoke the Lord God of Israel to anger than all the kings of Israel that were before him"* (1 Kgs. 16:33).

Probably to preface the upcoming narrative of Ahab's brazen rebellion and its consequences, the historian adds a historical note about a man who did not heed the curse Joshua had placed on Jericho: *"In his days Hiel of Bethel built Jericho. He laid its foundation with Abiram his firstborn, and with his youngest son Segub he set up its gates, according to the word of the Lord, which He had spoken through Joshua the son of Nun"* (1 Kgs. 16:34). Joshua had put a curse on the ruins of Jericho: any man attempting to fortify Jericho would lose his oldest son when the foundation was laid, and, if the construction continued, his youngest son would die when the gates were set in place (Josh. 6:26).

This curse was meant to keep the Benjamites from refortifying Jericho after they settled in that region. We now learn that it was not until the reign of evil Ahab over apostate Israel that Hiel the Bethelite attempted to rebuild the walls of Jericho. It cost him the lives of his two sons Abiram and Segub. Although the Jews had dwelt in the area of Jericho before this time, Hiel made the first attempt to restore Jericho as a walled city. No doubt the direct fulfillment of Joshua's five-hundred-year-old curse served as a warning to Ahab that rebellion against God's revealed Word would not be tolerated – stern judgment would come.

The Prophet Elijah's Drought (1 Kgs. 17:1-7)

As previously mentioned, God sent a steady stream of godly prophets to Israel's wicked leaders to warn of the consequences of rejecting God's Law. In this chapter we are introduced to one of the premier prophets of the Old Testament, Elijah the Tishbite from Gilead (a town just east of the Jordan River). His ministry was consistent with the meaning of his name, "my God Jehovah is He." Elijah was called to the challenging ministry of upholding the name of Jehovah before an idolatrous people.

There is no record of the Lord speaking to Elijah prior to his encounter with Ahab. But James tells us that Elijah spoke much with God before being used by Him in ministry: *"Elijah was a man with a nature like ours, and he prayed earnestly that it would not rain; and it did not rain on the land for three years and six months"* (Jas. 5:17). Elijah shows us that before believers can engage in effective public service, they first must have private exercise before God in prayer. Ministry that profits others must commence in this fashion, otherwise we do not experience and learn from the Lord what is necessary to mature our faith. Ministry not fostered in prayer is merely an academic exercise which will lack God's power and will stymie our spiritual growth. Before Elijah ever set foot in the palace of the wicked, he had first mourned and lamented Israel's state before God's holy throne. C. H. Mackintosh summarizes Elijah's resource as a faithful servant of the Lord (and ours too):

> Prayer; patient, persevering prayer; secret communion with God; deep and real exercise of soul in His presence, where alone we can arrive at a true estimate of ourselves, and things around us: and not only so,

> but also obtain spiritual power to act for God amongst our brethren, toward the world without. … But how often are we deceived by the mere form of prayer – with the formal utterance of words which have no reality in them. There are many who make a kind of god of prayer – many who let their very prayers get between their souls and the God of prayer. This is a great snare. We should always take care that our prayers are the natural outflow of the Spirit within us, and not of the mere superstitious performance of what we think ought to be done.[49]

Elijah was a godly man who was emboldened to confront the king because he keenly felt the scorn Ahab had caused to Jehovah's name. But before he could exert a powerful influence on others, he first had to seek the Lord privately to escape himself, that is, his own expectations and fleshly devices. His time in God's presence purged whatever would hinder his zeal for God or would divert him from God's purposes. As a result of effectual praying, Elijah was strengthened in his inner man to endure the hardships to come.

Whether Elijah was called directly by God as a prophet, or brought into that office because of his zeal for God (like Phineas into the high priesthood) we are not told. Regardless, Elijah abruptly faced the king and announced: *"As the Lord God of Israel lives, before whom I stand, there shall not be dew nor rain these years, except at my word"* (1 Kgs. 17:1). This was a bold move, which would normally have resulted in Elijah's arrest, but no doubt the court was somewhat stunned by his curt decree and by Elijah's prompt departure. The long drought would be the first of seven miracles instigated by Elijah to declare the power of Jehovah's name to depraved Israel.

The Lord then spoke to His brave prophet and directed him to go to a safe location at the Brook Cherith on the east side of the Jordan River (1 Kgs. 17:2-3). There the prophet would have plenty of water to drink and the Lord promised to airlift food to Elijah by ravens (1 Kgs. 17:4). Cherith feeds the Jordan River some 15 miles north of where the Jabbok meets the Jordan. The Lord was directing Elijah to some hidden recess in the Gilead uplands along the Cherith which Elijah would have been familiar with from his earlier days.

We know that Elijah spent time in fervent prayer before engaging in a brief public ministry and then God directed him back into private communion with Him again. There are two important applications that we pause to consider here. First, our time of secret training should far exceed our time in public ministry. Second, powerful ministry requires little of man and much of God; Elijah's entire message took approximately five seconds to deliver, but had a three-and-a-half-year impact! Elijah's time alone with the Lord taught him to keep low before his God. It is when we are before the Lord that we learn the necessity of keeping our flesh out of the Lord's work, and how to rely on God alone to do it.

Elijah obeyed *"the word of the Lord"* and journeyed to Cherith. There the ravens brought him bread and meat morning and evening until the brook dried up because of the drought (1 Kgs. 17:5-7). As was often the case for prophets, Elijah drank from his own ministry and suffered with God's covenant people in their rebellion, though he was not personally a part of it.

Elijah and the Widow at Zarephath (1 Kgs. 17:8-24)

After the brook dried up, *"the word of the Lord"* again came to Elijah. Elijah, who had no resources of his own, had to be completely reliant on the Lord's care and His word to carry him through the deep trial. Dependence and obedience always mark those God uses to exalt His name! How could Elijah later charge his countrymen at Carmel, *"If the Lord be God, follow Him,"* if he himself was rebellious to God's word? Such a challenge is effective only if issued in proven sincerity.

The Lord commanded His prophet to travel about ninety miles north-northwest to the town of Zarephath (1 Kgs. 17:9). (This Phoenician town was located about eight miles south of Sidon and fourteen miles north of Tyre.) The Lord also informed Elijah that He had commanded a widow in that town to care for him. Luke 4:25 indicates that Elijah stayed in Israel (in Gilead) for the first six months of the drought and then remained at Zarephath for the next three years.

The Lord's instructions would have been distasteful to Elijah for several reasons. First, it was a long journey requiring nearly a week and he was without water. Second, the Lord was directing him to reside with unclean people (Gentiles) and in a pagan town. Third, his journey would take him through northern Israel, the jurisdiction of Ahab, who wanted to find and kill him. Fourth, living with a poor Sidonian widow did not sound very appealing; no doubt she was barely surviving the drought, and an added guest would be a huge burden for her. Additionally, she was a Gentile.

Despite all the reasonable objections Elijah might have had, he chose to obey the Lord. One of the lovely things about the providential care of the Lord is that He is quite able to chasten an entire nation for rebellion, while also benefitting and edifying individuals through the same experience. God was as concerned about refining His prophet as He was about dealing with idolatrous Israel. He also was concerned about a poor Gentile widow in Zarephath who also needed to experience His goodness and mercy. It is then no accident that Elijah's new home, Zarephath, means "refinement." The Lord would use the lowliest means, unclean birds and an unclean woman (a poor Gentile widow) to both provide for and teach His prophet important lessons.

When Elijah arrived at the gate of Zarephath, he found a widow gathering a few sticks with which to kindle a fire. He called her and asked, *"Please bring me a little water in a cup, that I may drink"* (1 Kgs. 17:10). As she was departing to get the water, Elijah added, *"Please bring me a morsel of bread in your hand"* (1 Kgs. 17:11). The harsh living conditions caused by the drought are evident in Elijah's meager request for *a little* water and *a morsel* of bread.

The woman's response to Elijah indicates some level of discernment as to his identity:

> *As the Lord your God lives, I do not have bread, only a handful of flour in a bin, and a little oil in a jar; and see, I am gathering a couple of sticks that I may go in and prepare it for myself and my son, that we may eat it, and die* (1 Kgs. 17:12).

While Elijah's attire and facial hair would have certainly identified him as Israelite, she had already been told by the Lord that he was coming and that she was to care for him, although she had no idea how. Her situation was desperate; the sum of her provisions included a handful of flour and a little oil. It was just enough to bake one cake over a small fire kindled by the few twigs she had gathered. The widow believed that this would be her and her son's last meal and then they would die of starvation. However, the Lord had an entirely different plan for her future, as Elijah then explained to her:

> *Do not fear; go and do as you have said, but make me a small cake from it first, and bring it to me; and afterward make some for yourself and your son. For thus says the Lord God of Israel: "The bin of flour*

> *shall not be used up, nor shall the jar of oil run dry, until the day the Lord sends rain on the earth"* (1 Kgs. 17:13-14).

Notice how Elijah demanded that the bread and water be dispersed: "*first – me*" and "*afterward – yourself and your son.*" In other words, Elijah was representing God's claim over the last of her resources. If she yielded to God's word, then He would bless all of them! The widow had a choice to make: would she trust the word of a man she had just met whose God she did not know with all the food she had remaining in her house? The Lord had shown her that His word was reliable by foretelling her of Elijah's arrival. Perhaps she reasoned that she did not have anything to lose by doing what Elijah said. After all, one meager meal would not change the outcome of their impending starvation anyway. Whatever her reasoning, she chose to obey the prophet's word and give him the last of her provisions.

What a surprise it must have been to return to the barrel afterwards to find flour in it and also oil in the jar. She then made bread for herself and her son to eat. And such was her experience during the entire drought – she scraped the bottom of the barrel for their daily food and poured out the oil in the jar, but neither the barrel nor the jar remained empty (1 Kgs. 17:15-16). The Lord did not fill the barrel or the jar, for then she would not have had the daily thrill of discovering God's new and daily provision for them. Day by day she was learning about Jehovah from Elijah and through experiencing His goodness.

After many days, the Lord permitted another challenge in the life of the widow to demonstrate His majesty and authority over creation; the widow's son became seriously ill and died (1 Kgs. 17:17). She charged Elijah harshly over the matter: *"What have I to do with you, O man of God? Have you come to me to bring my sin to remembrance, and to kill my son?"* (1 Kgs. 17:18). Because she referred to a particular sin brought to memory by the death of her son, and not her sins in general, it is possible that she had committed a similar abhorrent sin previously (e.g., sacrificing a child to Baal in an attempt to resolve their difficulties).

Earlier the Lord had put His claim on all the remaining meal and oil she possessed. Now He lays claim to the most precious object of her affections – her only child. If God had merely provided for the widow's daily needs through the long famine, the widow would not have been prompted to consider her sin. The Lord knows how best to reach us where we are and to lay claim to what will make us aware of our need and His solution for it.

Through her agony, the widow would learn what we also must realize to be most blessed: God alone is to be our first love and our only confidence in life. Those redeemed by Christ's blood are His – body, soul, and spirit (1 Cor. 6:19-20). The only reason that God permits us to live today is to bring Him glory (i.e., to make Him look good; Rev. 4:11). If we lose sight of this objective, what we do for the remainder of our earthly sojourn will have no value for eternity. As we observe the death of the widow's son, may we realize God's claim on us too and never permit our affections for another (spouse, child, parent, friend, etc.) to obstruct our obedience and devotion to Christ!

The widow had already experienced the recent painful loss of her husband (for her son was young), and through harsh circumstances the deaths of one or more children (one possibly through pagan ritual, and the other while ministering to Jehovah's prophet). The widow might have easily concluded that Jehovah was no better than the gods of her people and so there was no reason for her to continue living. But both assumptions would shortly be proven erroneous. She would learn that Elijah was a true "man of God." He is one of eight named men and four unnamed men in the Bible to be referred to as a "man of God" (1 Kgs. 17:18). His successor, Elisha, is another (2 Kgs. 2:9).

Elijah told the widow to give him her son. He took him from her arms to an upper chamber and laid him on his own bed (1 Kgs. 17:19). Then the perplexed prophet cried out to the Lord asking why He had killed the widow's son. Then he requested that the Lord let the child's soul come back to him (1 Kgs. 17:20-21). Elijah petitioned the Lord three times on the matter, each time stretching his body out over the child (1 Kgs. 17:22). Elijah's faith is astounding in that he is requesting the Lord to do something never witnessed before – resurrection. The Lord had promised to sustain him through the widow's hand for the duration of the entire drought; therefore, it was imperative that she have a reason to keep living. We may not understand why God does what He does, but we must realize that He is the only One who can overcome all our difficulties regardless – Elijah knows this.

This is the kind of faith that pleases God, for it rests in God's attributes, His character, and His word (Heb. 11:6). Abraham exercised such faith when he was willing to sacrifice his son Isaac at Moriah (Gen. 22). Since Isaac was the only son of promise, Abraham believed that God would have to raise Isaac from the dead if he struck him down as commanded, because God had to keep His word (Heb. 11:19).

Indeed, the Lord honored Elijah's request and the soul of the child returned to the little body and the child revived. What a joy it was for the prophet to lead the child downstairs and give him to his grieving mother saying, *"See, your son lives!"* (1 Kgs. 17:23). The prophet was inferring, "See, nothing is too hard for Jehovah, my God, and He can be your God also!" The elated mother then affirmed, *"Now by this I know that you are a man of God, and that the word of the Lord in your mouth is the truth"* (1 Kgs. 17:24). Apparently, the daily miracle of flour and oil was not enough to cause her to fully trust Elijah's God. However, after losing what was most precious to her, her son, and then having him restored to her, she no longer had any doubts. Indeed, Elijah served the God of resurrection power. Likewise, the miracle of resurrection power is witnessed today through sharing the gospel of Jesus Christ with those dead in sin.

Meditation

> Faith certainly tells us what the senses do not, but not the contrary of what they see; it is above, not against them.
>
> — Blaise Pascal

King Ahab and the Prophet Elijah – Part 2

1 Kings 18

Elijah's Message to Ahab (1 Kgs. 18:1-18)

In the third year of the drought, the Lord directed Elijah to deliver a message to King Ahab – the drought was coming to an end (1 Kgs. 18:1). Previously, the Lord had commanded Elijah to *"get away from here ... and hide by the Brook Cherith"* (1 Kgs. 17:3). Now the Lord instructed His prophet, *"Go, present yourself to Ahab"* (1 Kgs. 18:1). Elijah's example here is one we should follow, whether going or coming, showing or hiding – the Lord should be obeyed no matter the cost. As a result, Elijah understands his course in life, while bewildered Obadiah must be pointed in the right way by the one openly walking with the Lord.

Apparently the famine was exceptionally severe in Samaria and threatened to wipe out all the livestock in the land (1 Kgs. 18:2). Ahab summoned the steward of his household affairs, Obadiah, and tasked him to search everywhere for brooks, springs, and any remaining grass that might preserve their livestock, horses, and mules (1 Kgs. 18:3, 5). Ahab would also scout out the land, but in a different direction (1 Kgs. 18:6).

Though his master was entrenched in idolatry, Obadiah still feared the Lord greatly. He risked his life by secretly caring for and hiding one hundred of the Lord's prophets in two caves (1 Kgs. 18:4, 13). This was to protect them from Jezebel's slaughter of Jehovah's prophets. Obadiah's deeds honored his name, which means "a servant of the Lord." Matthew Henry considers Obadiah's unusual testimony:

> It was strange that so wicked a man as Ahab would prefer him to it [his position] and continue him in it; certainly it was because he was a man of celebrated honesty, industry, and ingenuity, and one in whom he could repose a confidence, whose eyes he could trust as much as his own, as appears here (1 Kgs. 18:5). Joseph and Daniel were

> preferred because there were none so fit as they for the places they were preferred to. Notice that those who profess religion should study to recommend themselves to the esteem even of those that are without by their integrity, fidelity, and application to business.
>
> It was strange that so good a man as Obadiah would accept of preferment in a court so addicted to idolatry and all manner of wickedness. ... Obadiah would not have accepted the place if he could not have had it without bowing the knee to Baal, nor was Ahab so impolitic as to exclude those from offices that were fit to serve him, merely because they would not join with him in his devotions. That man that is true to his God will be faithful to his prince. Obadiah therefore, could, with a good conscience, enjoy the place, and therefore would not decline it, nor give it up, though he foresaw he could not do the good he desired to do in it.[50]

Because of his connection with Israel's wicked throne, Obadiah served the Lord secretly, for he feared Ahab and Jezebel. While admirable to some degree, we must realize the limitations that such an association will impose in accomplishing great feats for God. C. H. Mackintosh explains this truth by comparing the ministries of Obadiah and Elijah:

> Hence, while Elijah was boldly confronting Ahab, and openly serving the Lord, Obadiah was openly serving Ahab, and stealthily serving the Lord, While Elijah was breathing the holy atmosphere of Jehovah's presence, Obadiah was breathing the polluted atmosphere of Ahab's wicked court. While Elijah was receiving his daily supplies from the hand of the God of Israel, Obadiah was ranging the country in search of grass for Ahab's horses. Truly a most striking contrast! And is there not at this moment many an Obadiah similarly occupied? Is there not many a God-fearing man sharing, in common with the children of this world, its death and misery, and laboring in cooperation with them to avert its impending ruin?[51]

We know that believers are to remain in their callings and where God places them in the world (Matt. 13:36-43; 1 Cor. 7:20, 12:18). Yet, the more believers openly associate with worldlings instead of with the Lord, their potential to represent Him and accomplish great things in His name is also diminished. For this reason, God used Obadiah to do some good, and Elijah to do much good.

Obadiah must have headed north from Samaria, because he suddenly met Elijah traveling southward from Zarephath. Obadiah recognized Elijah and fell on his face in disbelief (1 Kgs. 18:7). The prophet had a message for Obadiah's master; he was to return to Ahab and tell him that Elijah wanted to meet with him (1 Kgs. 18:8).

Obadiah did not want to deliver this message to Ahab because the king had unsuccessfully searched Israel and the surrounding kingdoms to locate Elijah (1 Kgs. 18:10). Ahab's steward feared that if he told his master that "Elijah was here" but then God directed the prophet elsewhere, the king would hold Obadiah responsible and kill him (1 Kgs. 18:9, 11-14). No doubt, his life was already in peril because of his secret care for Jehovah's prophets. Yet Obadiah was a God-fearing man from his youth, so when Elijah vowed in the name of the Lord that he would present himself before Ahab that very day, Obadiah agreed to deliver Elijah's message (1 Kgs. 18:15).

Ahab did come to meet Elijah and, when he saw him, said, *"Is that you, O troubler of Israel?"* (1 Kgs. 18:16-17). Ahab was distressed over the consequences of his sin, but not grieved because of it, so the prophet set the matter straight and challenged Ahab to a contest on Carmel:

> *I have not troubled Israel, but you and your father's house have, in that you have forsaken the commandments of the Lord and have followed the Baals. Now therefore, send and gather all Israel to me on Mount Carmel, the four hundred and fifty prophets of Baal, and the four hundred prophets of Asherah, who eat at Jezebel's table* (1 Kgs. 18:18-19).

The nation could not continue much longer under the circumstances of the drought, so Ahab accepted Elijah's challenge. Elijah was not the troublemaker of Israel, but in faithful obedience to God's word would stand against the one who was – Ahab. We see the same dynamic occurring today when a believer is willing to speak out against the life-strangling false doctrine and human traditions which have crept into the Church. The one causing the unrest is regarded by those settled in corrupt religion as a "troubler" of the Church. As we shall soon witness, fire fell from heaven on the water-soaked, sacrifice-laden altar on Carmel to prove God's authority and power to His covenant people.

May the Holy Spirit raise up many more such *troublers* today that the power and authority of Jesus Christ might be known in His Church.

Victory on Mount Carmel (1 Kgs. 18:20-40)

Ahab summoned Israel and the 450 prophets of Baal to come to Mount Carmel for the showdown; however, Jezebel's 400 prophets of Asherah remained with her in Jezreel (1 Kgs. 18:20). Elijah reproved the people, *"How long will you falter between two opinions? If the Lord is God, follow Him; but if Baal, follow him,"* but the people did not answer him (1 Kgs. 18:21). Elijah then pointed out that he was outnumbered 450 to 1 by the prophets of Baal, so he was going to offer them more than a fair test to prove who ruled Israel – Baal or Jehovah (1 Kgs. 18:22).

Elijah then suggested that Baal's prophets prepare an altar, a bull for sacrifice, and then call on Baal to bring fire down from heaven to consume the sacrifice – no human was to put fire to the wood (1 Kgs. 18:23). Elijah would do the same in the name of Jehovah. The one who answered from heaven with fire would be proven to be the God of Israel; all the people agreed to the terms of the contest (1 Kgs. 18:24). Elijah then confirmed the rules of the challenge to the prophets of Baal and even gave them first choice of the two bulls to be offered (1 Kgs. 18:25).

The prophets of Baal finished their altar, put their sacrifice on it and began calling on Baal to honor their request of sending fire down from heaven to consume their sacrifice (1 Kgs. 18:26). The prophets implored Baal all morning, but there was no answer, so they began leaping about their altar to entice Baal to respond. At noon Elijah mocked them: *"Cry aloud, for he is a god; either he is meditating, or he is busy, or he is on a journey, or perhaps he is sleeping and must be awakened"* (1 Kgs. 18:27).

The ridicule of Elijah prompted the prophets of Baal to cry out all the louder as they cut themselves with knives and lances until the blood gushed out (1 Kgs. 18:28). Cutting oneself to indicate remorse (such as in a funeral procession) or to show devotion to one's god was a pagan practice. However, Jehovah expressly forbade the Israelites to mark, tattoo, or cut their flesh for such purposes (Lev. 19:28). His people were to be a holy people; they were not to adopt the practices of a wicked world. Why does God find such changes to one's appearance offensive? God designed and created each of us the way we are; thus, it stands to reason that desiring to change what God has made without His permission is a form of rebellion. Every individual is a unique expression of His wisdom and sovereign purpose. Should we be changing what God has put in place?

Five to six hours of chanting, crying, and cutting had not caused Baal to do anything; therefore, at the time of the evening sacrifice Elijah called the people to come near to him (1 Kgs. 18:29-30). The people had probably moved away from the altar of Baal because of the bloody and grotesque scene. Elijah then repaired a broken down altar of the Lord that was there by putting in place twelve stones, to represent the tribes of Jacob whom God called Israel (1 Kgs. 18:31). The prophet's calling the people and rebuilding the altar, after Baal fail to act, illustrated that all Israel could be unified and could again enjoy communion with God, if they would only realize the futility of their idolatry and return to Jehovah.

Elijah then carved a trench about the altar deep enough to hold two seahs or about four gallons (1 Kgs. 18:32). Next, Elijah put the wood in order, divided the bull, and put portions of it on the wood. He then instructed the people to fill four waterpots with water and pour each over the sacrifice on the wood (1 Kgs. 18:33). It would require a significant effort to go down to the Brook Kishon and then carry the water back up the mount. But the people obeyed Elijah, who then commanded them to do it a second and then a third time (1 Kgs. 18:34).

In all, twelve waterpots of water were emptied on the sacrifice. The water ran down the sacrifice and altar such that it filled the trench around it (1 Kgs. 18:35). This was done to further accentuate the miracle that Jehovah was about to perform, as it is not reasonable to soak a sacrifice for a burnt offering with water. What God was about to do would defy several physical laws governing nature.

Elijah then publicly called out to the Lord, so all the people would know who was responding to his request:

> *Lord God of Abraham, Isaac, and Israel, let it be known this day that You are God in Israel and I am Your servant, and that I have done all these things at Your word. Hear me, O Lord, hear me, that this people may know that You are the Lord God, and that You have turned their hearts back to You again.* (1 Kgs. 18:36-37).

Commenting on this scene and on Elijah's serene prayer of faith, H. L. Rossier writes:

> Completely separated from the evil that surrounds him, Elijah is not in the least taken up with himself nor desirous of personal recognition. He stands before the Lord, hears His word, obeys Him, lives in dependence upon Him in every detail. He depends upon God for sustenance, to bring grace to the nations, to resist the enemy, to bear witness, to exercise divine power in holding back or in giving rain, but above all else, to cause fire to fall from heaven upon the burnt offering and to judge the world. He waits upon the Lord, walks with Him, and, like Enoch, will be caught up into glory. The word of the Lord, the angel of the Lord, and the Lord Himself all speak to Elijah; as for himself, he speaks to God and God listens to him. Elijah is *a friend of God* (1 Kgs. 8:38, 44, 17:22).[52]

Unlike Baal who was unavailable, Jehovah heard his prophet and immediately responded to Elijah's prayer. Fire came down from heaven and consumed not just the sacrifice and wood, but also the stones, the dust, and the water in the trench (1 Kgs. 18:38). When the people saw this spectacular miracle, they immediately fell on their faces and declared, *"The Lord, He is God! The Lord, He is God!"* (1 Kgs. 18:39). After hearing their profession of Jehovah as God, it was time to deal with the phony prophets. Elijah commanded that the prophets of Baal be seized, taken down to the Brook Kishon and executed – all 450 prophets of Baal were killed (1 Kgs. 18:40). Just hours earlier the people would have been frightened to offend a prophet of Baal, but after realizing that Jehovah was God, they did not fear the one proven to be weaker than Jehovah.

The Drought Ends (1 Kgs. 18:41-46)

Elijah then told Ahab to eat and drink without delay, for there was an abundance of rain coming (1 Kgs. 18:41). Ahab did so while Elijah journeyed to the top of Carmel. There he bowed down on his knees and put his face to the ground and asked his servant to look towards the sea to determine if there was a storm coming (1 Kgs. 18:42). The servant responded, *"There is nothing"* (1 Kgs. 18:43). Elijah told his servant to look towards the sea six more times, and on the seventh time he said, *"There is a cloud, as small as a man's hand, rising out of the sea!"*

Elijah told his servant to quickly go to Ahab and warn him to mount his chariot and get off the mountain before the rain prevented his return to Jezreel (1 Kgs. 18:44).

His servant departed and delivered this message to Ahab. In the meantime the sky blackened, the wind blew, and heavy rain began to pour down on the mount. Ahab heeded the prophet's warning and rode ahead of the storm back to Jezreel (almost 25 miles to the east-southeast of Mount Carmel; 1 Kgs. 18:45). The hand of the Lord came upon Elijah and he girded up his loins and ran to Jezreel, arriving at the city's entrance before Ahab did (1 Kgs. 18:46).

To demonstrate God's power, Elijah had commanded a long drought, foretold its end, called fire down from heaven to consume a sacrifice, and ran a marathon at a speed faster than a chariot drawn by horses. For three and a half years Elijah had suffered along with Israel because of their idolatry, but now, through awesome demonstrations of God's power, the people knew that Jehovah was the true God of Israel. Elijah journeyed to Jezreel to see if what he wanted most would happen – revival in Israel. Would the revival that started at Carmel spread throughout Israel?

Meditation

> If we will do God's work in God's way at God's time with God's power, we shall have God's blessing.
>
> — Leonard Ravenhill

> A true revival means nothing less than a revolution, casting out the spirit of worldliness and selfishness, and making God and His love triumph in the heart and life.
>
> — Andrew Murray

Elijah Bolts

1 Kings 19:1-18

Elijah was called to be a prophet at a time when Israel was overcome with apostasy. King Ahab and his pagan wife Jezebel from Sidon had popularized the worship of Baal and Ashtaroth. Elijah was outspoken against Israel's wickedness; he wanted the people to repent and to worship Jehovah alone. He informed Ahab that God would chasten His people with a severe drought for their idolatry. Although Elijah suffered along with everyone else during this time, God sustained Elijah through the entire drought. At first, ravens brought food to Elijah at the brook Cherith; later, he boarded with a poor widow and her son who lived in Zarephath.

Three and a half years later, on Mount Carmel, Elijah proved to all the people that Baal was a false God and that Jehovah was the one true God. Only Jehovah brought fire from heaven to consume Elijah's offering along with the water, stones, and dust (1 Kgs. 18:38). After the 450 prophets of Baal were slain, Elijah warned Ahab that rain was coming and urged him to get off the mountain. Elijah then girded his loins and proceeded to run ahead of Ahab's chariot all the way back to Jezreel, some 25 miles (1 Kgs. 18:44-46).

Elijah Flees (1 Kgs. 19:1-8)

Elijah yearned for spiritual revival to sweep through Israel. He waited at Jezreel's gate to see how evil Jezebel would respond to the news about what had happened at Carmel (1 Kgs. 19:1). Amazingly, Ahab takes no leadership role whatsoever in the matter, but merely informs Jezebel about the death of Baal's prophets. He had watched fire come down from heaven in response to Elijah's prayer, had quietly stood by while 450 of his prophets were slain, and then, as foretold by Elijah, witnessed rain fall from heaven, breaking the long drought. It becomes obvious that Ahab is more concerned about the temporal matters than the spiritual ramifications of what has just occurred. True, his prophets were dead, but the drought was over and thus he was content. What was Jehovah or Baal to him, as long as he could eat, drink, and be merry?

Jezebel, on the other hand, was infuriated by the news, and vowed to take Elijah's life within the next twenty-four hours (1 Kgs. 19:2). Her response greatly discouraged Elijah. He had already suffered much in fulfilling his prophetic ministry and now, instead of revival sweeping through Israel, as he had envisioned, there was to be persecution. The text reads, *"when he saw that"* (1 Kgs. 19:3), meaning when he understood the hopeless situation in Israel was not changing, he fled for his life.

Ahab had previously searched all of Israel and many other countries to find and arrest Elijah (1 Kgs. 18:10), so being a wanted man was no new thing for this prophet. In running away, Elijah seemed to be more motivated by discouragement than by fear for his personal well-being. Elijah surmised that his entire ministry had been a failure and that he was the only prophet of God remaining. The situation seemed hopeless and he just wanted to run away and give up. Such a retreat occurs when believers get caught up with their circumstances instead of resting in God and His Word. Elijah had bravely withstood Ahab, his idolatrous countrymen, and 450 false prophets, but now the threat from one woman daunted him. When a man's faith has given way, his own shadow will scare him.

Any of God's people can suffer this type of despair, which I will refer to as "spiritual depression." We all tend to have expectations for our ministries, and when these are not attained, we can become disheartened, even to the point of not wanting to go any further. We forget that God is sovereign over His creation and is working sextillions of situations simultaneously for His glory, meaning that we may be required to suffer so that God may accomplish the greater good within His foreordained design. God's timing, not ours, is always perfect. It is natural for us to want to escape trials before God's best is accomplished in us; however, it is spiritual to wait with God until He either removes the difficulty or removes us from it (Phil. 1:23-25).

The prophet hurried to the far southern border of Judah, Beersheba, and left his servant there (1 Kgs. 19:3). He then journeyed another day south into the Negev desert and, being exhausted and discouraged, rested under a broom tree and asked the Lord that he might die: *"It is enough! Now, Lord, take my life, for I am no better than my fathers!"*

(1 Kgs. 19:4). Although Elijah was not very rational at this point, he was correct on one point – he was no better than his fathers! Though called to be God's prophet, Elijah was flesh and blood, with the same nature as his fathers and, as James declares, us too: *"Elijah was a man with a nature like ours"* (Jas. 5:1). Without experiencing the Lord's mercy and grace, we too are no different than our fathers. When ensnared by despair, we also will be prone to isolate ourselves from God's servants, to collapse under a juniper tree in despondency, or even try to hide in the dark cave of seclusion and self-pity.

The Lord chose to disregard Elijah's prayer because He was not finished with His servant. As the Lord's servants, we are permitted to remain on this earth for only one reason – to do God's bidding and make Him look good! All that we do must be for His glory: *"Whatever you do, do all to the glory of God"* (1 Cor. 10:31). *"For none of us lives to himself, and no one dies to himself. For if we live, we live to the Lord; and if we die, we die to the Lord. Therefore, whether we live or die, we are the Lord's"* (Rom. 14:7-8). Though Elijah was discouraged, it was not his time to die.

Accordingly, the Angel of the Lord ministered to him twice to strengthen him for the long journey down to Mount Horeb (1 Kgs. 19:5-7). William MacDonald observes that God's treatment for severe depression was *"rest; food and drink; more rest; more food and drink."* Of course, being soothed and encouraged by God's word was mixed in with resting the mind and nourishing the body.

At Horeb (Sinai), God would restore His servant Elijah to fruitfulness again – His solution would be to yoke despondent Elijah with younger Elisha in a mentoring relationship. After Elijah ate and drank what was provided for him by the Lord, we read that *"he went in the strength of that food forty days and forty nights as far as Horeb, the mountain of God"* (1 Kgs. 19:8).

Forty Days

The number forty in Scripture represents *probation* and *testing*, which explains its frequent occurrence. The Lord often extended forty-year probationary periods to the Jewish nation to test or prove them. Accordingly, the Israelites were tested in the wilderness forty years (Deut. 8:2-5), then were delivered and had rest during the forty years that Othniel, Barak, and Gideon judged Israel (Judg. 3:11, 5:31, 8:28).

They enjoyed dominion during the forty-year reigns of five kings: David, Solomon, Jeroboam, Jehoash, and Joash (2 Sam. 5:4; 1 Kgs. 11:42; 2 Kgs. 12:1; 2 Chron. 24:1). Another demonstration of forty as the number of probation and testing is found in God's dealings with Nineveh – the prophet Jonah preached that, unless the inhabitants repented, God's judgment would fall on them in forty days (Jonah 3:4).

The first forty-day visit of Moses to Mount Sinai served not only as an opportunity for him to receive the Law, but was also a time of testing for the Israelites: would they be faithful to their newly affirmed covenant with Jehovah? They failed the test, even fashioning and bowing down to a golden calf, and were judged. However, the second time Moses was before the Lord for forty days, the Israelites remained repentant and faithful. They patiently waited for Moses (the only one who could make intercession for them) to descend the mountain and tell them whether or not they had been forgiven.

The Bible also records occasions when individuals went forty days without food or drink through the supernatural care of God: Elijah during his wilderness experience before us (1 Kgs. 19:8), Moses before Jehovah on Mount Horeb (Ex. 34:28), and Christ during His testing in the wilderness (Matt. 4:2). How was this possible? God completely sustained each of them.

Elijah Alone? (1 Kgs. 19:9-18)

In the provision of the Lord's food, Elijah arrived at Mount Horeb and took up residence in a cave. The Lord spoke to Elijah while he was in this cave, *"What are you doing here, Elijah?"* (1 Kgs. 19:9). In his depressed condition, Elijah responded to the Lord as a defeated and isolated warrior of Jehovah: *"I have been very zealous for the Lord God of hosts; for the children of Israel have forsaken Your covenant, torn down Your altars, and killed Your prophets with the sword. I alone am left; and they seek to take my life"* (1 Kgs. 19:10). On Carmel, Elijah had vindicated Jehovah's name in an effort to convert his brethren; at Horeb, Elijah vindicates himself and accuses his brethren.

The same is true today. When a believer disregards his ministry calling and ceases to serve among his brethren, he will invariably exalt himself and accuse others of wrongdoing. It is natural for those who do the least to be critical of those doing the most, but thankfully the latter group has the least amount of time to worry about such criticism. While this situation is emotionally exhausting, it really pales in comparison to when those who have done much for the Lord justify their despondency by blaming everyone else (including the Lord) for their condition.

Before the Lord corrects Elijah's self-focus, He first will remind His prophet, to whom He spoke: *"Go out, and stand on the mountain before the Lord"* (1 Kgs. 19:11). Elijah may have moved towards the entrance of the cave to look out, but he clearly did not exit the cave as commanded. We then read that the Lord passed by, and a powerful wind ripped rocks from the face of the mountain, but the Lord was not in the wind. Then there was an earthquake, but the Lord was also not in the earthquake. Next, fire roared across the mountainside, but the Lord was not in the fire either (1 Kgs. 19:12). Kiel and Delitzsch explain the meanings of these expressions:

> Tempest, earthquake, and fire, which are even more terrible in the awful solitude of the Horeb mountains than in an inhabited land, are signs of the coming of the Lord for judgment (e.g., Ps. 18:8). It was in the midst of such terrible phenomena that the Lord had once come down upon Sinai, to inspire the people who were assembled at the foot of the mountain with a salutary dread of His terrible majesty, of the fiery zeal of His wrath and love, which consumes whatever opposes it (Ex. 19:16). But now the Lord was not in these terrible phenomena, to signify to the prophet that He did not work in His earthly kingdom with the destroying zeal of wrath, or with the pitiless severity of judgment. It was in a soft, gentle rustling that He revealed Himself to him.[53]

The wind, the earthquake, and the fire were awesome displays of God's power, but these were not His instruments of revelation to Elijah; rather, God spoke to His prophet in a still, quiet voice. The former things probably prompted the prophet's awe, but God did not choose to reveal His mind to Elijah by dreadful sounds, quivering ground, or brilliant flames. Just as God was not confined to one agency in dealing with Elijah, neither was He limited to using one prophet to confront His wayward people. Elijah was just one of many agencies available to God; accordingly, Elijah should not think of himself as being the only tool in God's hand, but one of many. To think otherwise would be limiting God's omnipotence and omniscience.

God also showed Elijah that He was not limited in what He used either. For example, He could use a still, quiet voice to accomplish more than an earthquake could, as in Elijah's case. In fact, God delights in using weak and foolish things to do His bidding, as there is obviously no question as to who was responsible for the feat (1 Cor. 1:27-29).

Only the gentle voice of love could cause Elijah to realize what God wanted him to learn. George Williams explains: "He should have recognized that there was no difference between his heart and that of the nations; and, that as coercion failed to make him leave his cave, so it failed, and must fail, to compel men to leave their sins."[54] Truly, Elijah was not different than his fathers; indeed, all of us share the same rebellious nature inherited from Adam (1 Kgs. 19:4)!

Hearing God's soothing voice accomplished what the spectacular displays could not. When Elijah heard the Lord speaking in this fashion, *"he wrapped his face in his mantle and went out and stood in the entrance of the cave"* (1 Kgs. 19:13). Having gained the attention of His discouraged servant, the Lord again asked Elijah, *"What are you doing here, Elijah?"* Elijah repeats his earlier response of informing the Lord of Israel's desperate spiritual condition, and that he is the only one left in Israel loyal to Him (1 Kgs. 19:14).

Depressed people rarely think straight. Had Elijah forgotten about Obadiah and the one hundred prophets of Jehovah that he was secretly caring for? No servant of the Lord is excluded from suffering spiritual depression. It happens when we believe we have done our best for the Lord, but our expectations for our own ministry are not met. Even Moses, the meekest man on the earth, whom God spoke with face to face, suffered despair (Num. 11:10-15). The unbelief, murmuring, and demands of the people prompted Moses to have an emotional breakdown. But as with Elijah, Moses received the Lord's kindness, not a rebuke, to encourage and strengthen him. And as with Moses, it was not the Lord's plan to take Elijah's life, nor to remove him from his responsibility.

Elijah was finally moving in the right direction towards restoration – He came before the Lord. When we are before the Lord, it is hard to have high thoughts of ourselves or our ministries. Contact with God's majesty and greatness causes us to blush before our Creator, and like Elijah, we too want to hide our faces in our mantles. Every servant of the Lord must realize that He alone is to direct, to empower, and to be honored in what we do for Him.

Consequently, the Lord's solution was to get Elijah's focus off himself and his expectations and back on the Lord and doing His bidding. Servants of the Lord are not responsible for the results of what they do; they are just to be obedient and faithful to the One who calls them to serve. The Lord then commanded Elijah to return by the way of the Wilderness of Damascus (1 Kgs. 19:15). He was to anoint Hazael to be king of Syria, Jehu to be king of Israel, and Elisha to be Elijah's replacement (1 Kgs. 19:16-17). In the future, God would be using these three men to chasten Israel for her idolatry and to purge Baal worship from the land. This exercise would teach Elijah that he was not indispensable; the Lord could use whomever He chose to accomplish His work.

Lastly, the Lord informed Elijah that he was not the last Jehovah worshiper in Israel: *"Yet I have reserved seven thousand in Israel, all whose knees have not bowed to Baal, and every mouth that has not kissed him"* (1 Kgs. 19:18). It was true; most of Israel had not responded appropriately to God's discipline, the vast majority remained rebellious. But, praise be to God; no matter how spiritually dark things appear, He always has a witness for Himself on the earth (1 Kgs. 19:18; Acts 14:17; Rom. 11:5). While agreeing with this, C. H. Mackintosh further observes that true revivalists have also been rare among redeemed:

> There were seven thousand in Israel who had not bowed the knee to Baal, and who, we may suppose, were only waiting for some vigorous hand to plant the standard of truth. No one amongst them would seem to have had power for such a bold step, but they would no doubt rejoice in Elijah's boldness and ability to do so. This has often been the case in the history of the people of God. In times of greatest darkness there have always been those whose spirits mourned in secret over the widespread evil and apostasy, who longed for bursting in of spiritual light, and were ready with joy to welcome its earliest beams. God has never left Himself without a witness; although it is only here and there we can perceive a star of sufficient magnitude and brilliancy to pierce through the clouds of night and enlighten the benighted Church in the wilderness, yet we know, blessed be God, that let the clouds be ever so dark and gloomy, the stars have been there in every age, though their twinkling has been but little seen. Thus it was in the days of Elijah; there were seven thousand such stars whose light was obscured by the thick clouds of idolatry – who

> would not yield to the darkness themselves, though they lacked power to enlighten others yet was there but one star of sufficient power and brightness to dispel the mist and create a sphere in which others might shine. This was Elijah the Tishbite.[55]

The revelation of 7,000 fellow Jehovah worshipers greatly encouraged Elijah; things were not as bleak and hopeless in Israel as he thought – the Lord was completely aware of Israel's condition and was working to resolve it. And praise the Lord, we hear no more complaints from Elijah.

This was all a humbling lesson for Elijah. On three previous occasions the prophet had obeyed the Lord's command to "go" (1 Kgs. 17:3, 9, 18:1), but while suffering from depression he had failed to comply at Horeb (1 Kgs. 19:3). After being encouraged by the Lord, Elijah immediately obeyed the Lord's fifth command to "go" and he returned by the same way he had come to Horeb (1 Kgs. 19:15). Retracing our steps which led us into failure back to the place where we stepped out of God's will is always the safest route to restoration.

Meditation

> Our love for God and our appreciation of His love and forgiveness will be in proportion to the recognition of our sin and unworthiness.
>
> — Dave Hunt

> Sin forsaken is one of the best evidences of sin forgiven.
>
> — J. C. Ryle

Elisha Is Called

1 Kings 19:19-21

Elijah had learned that he was one of many in the Lord's work of confronting Israel's apostasy. He would now largely withdraw from public ministry. God would use him only twice more as His messenger: once to confront evil Ahab over Nabal's vineyard and once to rebuke wicked Ahaziah on his sickbed.

After receiving his new marching orders at Mount Horeb, Elijah departed for Abel Meholah to find his successor, Elisha:

> *So he departed from there, and found Elisha the son of Shaphat, who was plowing with twelve yoke of oxen before him, and he was with the twelfth. Then Elijah passed by him and threw his mantle on him. And he left the oxen and ran after Elijah, and said, "Please let me kiss my father and my mother, and then I will follow you." And he said to him, "Go back again, for what have I done to you?" So Elisha turned back from him, and took a yoke of oxen and slaughtered them and boiled their flesh, using the oxen's equipment, and gave it to the people, and they ate. Then he arose and followed Elijah, and became his servant* (1 Kgs. 19:19-21).

Apparently, Elijah liked the idea of passing on the prophet's mantle (i.e. his ministry) to someone else, as he did not anoint Hazael or Jehu, but rather immediately searched out Elisha, his own successor. Elijah was disheartened and no longer wanted to be a prophet; in fact, he just wanted to die, but God did not grant that request. Passing along his mantle and the responsibility that went with it suited him just fine.

Notice that when Elijah found Elisha plowing in the field, he did not say anything to him, but literally threw the mantle on Elisha and quickly departed. Elisha actually had to run after Elijah in order to speak with him. Elisha as a mentee demonstrates several admirable qualities, which we would do well to notice and ponder if we want to develop profitable mentor/mentee relationships with others.

Principles for Embracing the Mantle

The following seven principles are drawn from the biblical narrative relating to Elisha's calling, training, and commissioning as God's prophet (three more principles will be drawn from 2 Kgs. 2).

1. **God calls working people into His work.** Elisha was plowing a field with twelve yoke of oxen – he was a working man. There is no example in the Bible of God calling a lazy or irresponsible person into ministry. Rather, He uses those who have first been proven faithful in what they have been given to do. David was attending his father's sheep when he was anointed king over Israel. Gideon was threshing wheat when called to be the judge of God's people. Peter, Andrew, James, and John were fishing or cleaning their nets when the Lord summoned them to be His disciples.

   Whether chores at home, classes at school, or tasks in the workplace, all that we do is a proving ground for what God wants to accomplish next in our lives. The Lord Jesus put the matter this way: *"He who is faithful in what is least is faithful also in much; and he who is unjust in what is least is unjust also in much"* (Luke 16:10-11). Those who are faithful to do what they are supposed to do are being prepared for greater responsibilities, challenges, and honor.

2. **Elisha was in a right relationship with authority.** Elisha requests that he be allowed to first go home and inform his parents of God's calling for his life and to kiss them good-bye. Apparently, he was a young, unmarried man still living under his father's authority. It is good to remain under authority in whatever station God has put us, until God clearly repositions us under new authority. It is a mark of a false teacher to despise authority and to speak evil of dignitaries (2 Pet. 2:10).

   The centurion speaking to the Lord Jesus on behalf of his sick servant understood that one must be under authority to have authority (Luke 7:8). Since the Lord Jesus had authority over diseases, the centurion knew that the Lord Jesus was under authority and could therefore heal his servant, which the Lord did. Until God called Elisha into the ministry, he remained under the authority structure in which God had placed him. It is a good principle for us all to follow while we wait on the Lord for new marching orders.

The Lord rebuked those who used family ties as an excuse to delay commitment to Him (Luke 9:61-62). Elisha is not doing that; he is rather ensuring that a transition from God-ordained authority (his parents) to another God-ordained authority (the prophet Elijah) occurred properly. This is similar to a daughter receiving permission from her father to leave his authority to be bound to her husband and to remain under his authority, care, and protection. Elisha's purpose in going home first was to sever the tie that presently bound him to serve his parents.

3. **The mantle is to be handed over with care.** The mantle represented the work of the Lord and is thus precious to God. The Hebrew word *shalak* is translated "threw" in verse 19 and literally means "to throw" or "to hurl." Elijah was in such a poor emotional state when he found Elisha that he just threw his cloak on Elisha and left. Elisha, however, understood that having the mantle itself did not equip him to be a prophet; he needed instruction. It takes time to mentor others in righteous living and practical ministry. The mantle cannot be thrown; the work of the Lord must be carefully committed to the next generation.

   Elisha would eventually receive Elijah's mantle and continue the work of God. The Hebrew word *addereth* is translated "mantle" and is used five times during the interactions of Elijah and Elisha. *Addereth* describes a cloak made of fur or fine material. Elijah wore a prophet's cloak which marked him as God's spokesman; this same cloak would later be passed on to Elisha. Though it was a great privilege to wear this cloak, it also reminded the prophet of his responsibility to speak only the words of God and his accountability to God if he failed to do so.

4. **Elisha wanted the mantle.** Elisha ran after Elijah. He appreciated the opportunity to serve with and learn from Elijah. It is especially

important for young people to understand that it is a privilege to be mentored by others; it is not a right. Nor should the mentoring relationship be viewed as some program one finishes to achieve some church position or spiritual status. Close interaction with a mature believer, someone who genuinely cares about the mentee, is a wonderful provision from the Lord to promote spiritual growth. Count it a great blessing if someone is willing to invest their time and resources to enhance your future.

Wrong attitudes, however, will make mentoring drudgery. If you desire to be mentored for Christ, but no one has approached you, why not ask a mature believer (of the same gender) to spend some regular time with you in Bible study and answering questions? Take the initiative and see what happens.

5. **Elisha assisted Elijah in the Lord's work.** Mentoring relationships are often thought to be unidirectional – the mentor serves the mentee, but that is not a correct understanding. Elisha ministered to Elijah (1 Kgs. 19:21). A few years later, it would be Elisha, on behalf of Elijah, who would anoint Jehu and Hazael, the tasks given Elijah at Mount Horeb. Long after Elijah had departed heavenward in a whirlwind, Elisha was still known as *"Elisha ... who used to pour water on the hands of Elijah"* (2 Kgs. 3:11). Certainly, Elijah taught Elisha much, but Elisha showed his appreciation for his mentor by selflessly serving him also.

   Paul instructed the believers in Galatia in the same principle: *"Let him who is taught the word share in all good things with him who teaches"* (Gal. 6:6). He also told the Gentile believers at Rome that it was their duty to give financially to the poor saints at Jerusalem, for the Jews had brought the gospel message to them (Rom. 15:26-27). If someone blesses you in the name of Christ, consider how you might bless them in return. This is not a "payback" per se, but rather a unique opportunity to refresh someone who has helped you.

6. **Elisha encouraged Elijah.** Elijah's name means "God is my God." His name aligns with his ministry of calling an apostate nation back to the Lord. It was a hard and discouraging calling. Elijah needed a friend, and who better than Elisha, whose name means "God is

Salvation," to strengthen Elijah. Elisha was a companion of Elijah for about ten years and helped him regain his courage and faithfulness in speaking for the Lord. God would again send Elijah to confront Ahab and Jezebel and pronounce judgment on them (1 Kgs. 21:17-26). Elijah and Elisha's relationship was mutually beneficial; they needed each other. Mentors need encouragement also, and Elisha is a good example of a supportive mentee.

7. **Elisha made a sacrifice to be mentored.** After informing his parents that he would be departing with Elijah, Elisha slaughtered a yoke of oxen and burnt his implements in order to cook the meat for the people. More than being gracious to others, he was effectively closing the door on his former life. By removing the possibility of returning to farming, he was showing his dedication to Elijah and his commitment to learn from him. Likewise, mentees should understand that some activities will have to go by the wayside in order to have the time to be mentored properly. Mary had to say "no" to some legitimate activities in order to have time to sit at the Lord's feet and learn from Him (Luke 10:38-42). Although she was misunderstood by her sister Martha, the Lord complimented her in front of everyone for making the best choice. It is not just the mentor who sacrifices himself or herself; the mentee must also be committed to the mentoring process.

Elijah had a rough start in effectively passing the precious work of the Lord on to Elisha, but apparently he did well in the end. Elisha demonstrated many good attitudes in the mentoring relationship; these we would do well to copy in our own lives.

The development of mentoring relationships requires that both the mentor and the mentee maintain a proper perspective of their ministries to each other. Maturity in the mentee both endorses the mentor's ministry and prepares the mentee to be able to teach others in the future. Good mentoring relationships are active and will ultimately develop into a peer type of mentality, where counsel is given when required, but the ongoing interaction is not needed. This dynamic will be witnessed in the relationship of Elijah and Elisha in the coming narrative, until Elijah's work is complete and he is taken home in 2 Kings 2.

Meditation

> Christianity without discipleship is always Christianity without Christ.
>
> — Dietrich Bonhoeffer

> Only a disciple can make a disciple.
>
> — A. W. Tozer

King Ahab's Syrian Campaigns

1 Kings 20

The historian leaves the prophets Elijah and Elisha to their own affairs and refocuses our attention on King Ahab. At this juncture, Israel was being threatened by the Syrians led by Ben-Hadad II. King Asa of Judah had earlier hired Ben-Hadad I, the present aggressor's father, to attack King Baasha of Israel (1 Kgs. 15:18-20). Ahab and Ben-Hadad II will face off in battle three times; the first two of those confrontations are recorded in this chapter and the third is in 1 Kings 22. The Lord will show kindness to his wayward people by demonstrating His providential authority and power to protect them.

Ahab's Victories Over the Syrians (1 Kgs. 20:1-30)

Ben-Hadad II came with the armies of thirty-two neighboring city-kings to besiege King Ahab in Israel's capital city, Samaria (1 Kgs. 20:1). Ben-Hadad sent messengers to offer terms of surrender to Ahab, which the king accepted, seeing no other way to save the people in the city: *"Your silver and your gold are mine; your loveliest wives and children are mine"* (1 Kgs. 20:2-4). This was perhaps the noblest act that Scripture affords Ahab; he was willing to sacrifice his wealth and family to save those under his authority.

Apparently, Ben-Hadad regretted not demanding more from Ahab, so he sent his messengers back with new terms of surrender, even though Ahab had already agreed to his previous offer (1 Kgs. 20:5). Ben-Hadad said that tomorrow his men would enter the royal palace and the homes of his officials and would take whatever they delighted to have (1 Kgs. 20:6). After hearing this message, Ahab summoned the elders and the people together and informed them of his efforts to save them, and the deceitful dealings of Ben-Hadad. He observed that the Syrian king could not be trusted, and if they permitted Ben-Hadad's troops to enter the city unchecked, there would be no means of stopping a massacre. After hearing about the situation and the king's selfless efforts to protect them, they agreed with Ahab not to consent to Ben-Hadad's terms (1 Kgs. 20:8).

Ahab sent Ben-Hadad's messenger back to him to affirm that he would honor their first agreement, but not the modified version regarding the terms of their surrender (1 Kgs. 20:9). The Syrian's pride swelled up within him at this defiance and vowed, *"The gods do so to me, and more also, if enough dust is left of Samaria for a handful for each of the people who follow me"* (1 Kgs. 20:10). After hearing the Syrian king's response, Ahab answered back, *"Let not the one who puts on his armor boast like the one who takes it off"* (1 Kgs. 10:11). This taunt implied that Ben-Hadad was full of threats, but was afraid to back them up in battle.

Obviously, Ahab's reply did not deescalate the situation, but rather prompted Ben-Hadad to assemble his troops for war (1 Kgs. 20:12). It was at this moment that the Lord sent an unnamed prophet to Ahab with a message, *"Have you seen all this great multitude? Behold, I will deliver it into your hand today, and you shall know that I am the Lord"* (1 Kgs. 20:13). Ahab inquired as to how the Lord would gain the victory, and the prophet answered that he was to order the battle lines and that the young leaders of Israel's provinces would fight valiantly to defeat the large Syrian army (1 Kgs. 20:14). The fact that the Lord would use a small number of young (non-battle hardened) fighters to gain the victory would prove to everyone that He was behind Syria's defeat.

Ahab obeyed the prophet's command and gathered up 232 young leaders and 7,000 men of Israel to follow after them at a distance (1 Kgs. 20:15-16). A scouting party reported to Ben-Hadad that a band of men from Samaria was coming out of the city, but it was not Samaria's army (1 Kgs. 20:17). Clearly, the Syrian king was not anticipating an attack by only a few hundred men against his army and therefore commanded that the band of Israelites be brought before him to understand their intentions (1 Kgs. 20:18). But Israel wanted war; the young princes of Israel fought valiantly, each killing a Syrian in combat (1 Kgs. 20:19). This unexpected setback caused the Syrian army to turn on its heels and then all of Israel's troops joined in the slaughter, including disposing of much of Ben-Hadad's cavalry and war-chariots (1 Kgs. 20:20-21). After this victory, the prophet returned to Ahab and told him to strengthen himself, for in the spring of the next year Ben-Hadad would return to attack Israel again (1 Kgs. 20:22).

Ben-Hadad's servants theorized why they had been defeated by Israel in the previous engagement: *"Their gods are gods of the hills. Therefore they were stronger than we; but if we fight against them in the plain, surely we will be stronger than they"* (1 Kgs. 20:23). His advisors then counseled the Syrian king to reorganize his army with better trained soldiers and this time to engage Israel on flat ground to gain the victory over Ahab (1 Kgs. 20:24-25). This meant that many more war-chariots and cavalry would be brought to the battlefront and thus his victory over Ahab was guaranteed. Ben-Hadad agreed with this plan.

As the prophet had predicted the previous year, Ben-Hadad brought his troops back into Israel to battle Ahab, but this time the conflict would be in the plain near Aphek, not in the hills of Samaria (1 Kgs. 20:26). Ahab gathered his small number of troops and encamped opposite the Syrians. The writer notes the contrast; Israel's camp was *"like two little flocks of goats, while the Syrians filled the countryside"* (1 Kgs. 20:27).

The same prophet, "a man of God," delivered a third message to Ahab from the Lord: *"Because the Syrians have said, 'The Lord is God of the hills, but He is not God of the valleys,' therefore I will deliver all this great multitude into your hand, and you shall know that I am the Lord"* (1 Kgs. 20:28). The Lord was going to grant Israel a second victory over the large Syrian army because of their insult and also to prove to His wayward people that He was the only true God of Israel – their idols could not save them.

On the seventh day, the standoff ended and the battle was engaged with Israel slaughtering 100,000 Syrian troops in a single day (1 Kgs. 1:29). Twenty-seven thousand surviving Syrians (including Ben-Hadad) fled to the fortified city of Aphek to evade their pursuing attackers, but the Lord caused the city's wall to fall on Ben-Hadad's troops to conclude their retreat (1 Kgs. 20:30). The Syrian king and some of his officials secured themselves within an inner chamber located inside the city.

Ahab's Treaty with Ben-Hadad (1 Kgs. 20:31-43)

Ben-Habad's advisors suggested that they humble themselves by wearing sackcloth and putting ropes around their bodies and heads and then appearing before Ahab to plead for mercy (1 Kgs. 20:31-32). Ahab did grant them mercy and even called Ben-Hadad "his brother" and invited him up into his chariot (1 Kgs. 20:33). Both the expression and the gesture symbolized that a new treaty now existed between the two kings. Ben-Hadad promised to restore all the cities of Israel that his father had taken during King Asa's rule and that Ahab was free to establish trade in Damascus (1 Kgs. 20:34). Although the Lord had honored His word and delivered Ahab's enemy into his hand, Ahab agreed to Ben-Hadad's offer and let him go free, which angered the Lord. Ahab wanted to maintain a strong Syria to better buffer Israel from the growing Assyrian threat.

According to an ancient record of King Shalmaneser III (Assyrian King from 859-824 B.C.) now maintained at the British Museum, Ahab and Ben-Hadad successfully repelled an attack by Assyria at Qarqar located on the Orontes River in Syria. According to the record, Ahab supplied 2,000 chariots and 10,000 soldiers to support Syria's defense.[56] While this battle is not recorded in Scripture, archeological evidence once again verifies the historical accuracy of the book of Kings.

The Lord's displeasure was felt by His prophets also, as one prophet moved by the word of the Lord said to another, *"Strike me, please"* (1 Kgs. 20:35). But the man refused to strike his fellow prophet; therefore the first prophet foretold that because he had not obeyed the Lord, a lion would kill him as soon as he departed, which is what happened (1 Kgs. 20:36).

The first prophet said to another man, "Strike me, please"; that man obeyed and wounded the prophet (1 Kgs. 20:37). Then the wounded prophet departed, waited for Ahab by the roadside, and disguised himself with a bandage over his eyes (1 Kgs. 20:38). When Ahab drew near to him, he pretended to have been in the recent battle and told the king his sad story. In his illustration, he supposedly had been entrusted with guarding a captured Syrian soldier on pain of paying a large sum of money or suffering death if the man escaped (1 Kgs. 20:39). The captured soldier did escape and his only way of avoiding death was to pay a talent of silver; obviously a poor soldier like himself did not have that kind of wealth, but the king did. In summary, he faced the death penalty for his negligence unless a talent of silver could be paid on his behalf. Thus he appealed to the king for assistance.

But the king showed no mercy. He judged that the man knew the consequences for negligence and therefore should die for letting the

Syrian soldier escape, as he had been in full control of the situation (1 Kgs. 20:40). Obviously, given the implications of what had just happened, Ahab condemned himself by his own decree.

The prophet then removed the bandage about his eyes and Ahab recognized him as a prophet of Jehovah (1 Kgs. 20:41). The prophet had acted out what Ahab had done in letting Ben-Hadad go and so had secured the king's own ruling of condemnation against himself. The prophet then affirmed God's word to Ahab: *"Because you have let slip out of your hand a man whom I appointed to utter destruction, therefore your life shall go for his life, and your people for his people"* (1 Kgs. 20:42). The Lord was holding Ahab responsible for not completing the immense victory that He wanted to secure for His people by removing Israel's chief nemesis. The king of Israel then returned to his house in Samaria displeased and bad-tempered because of the prophet's decree (1 Kgs. 20:43).

Meditation

> Ahab had one thing to do by the command of God, and while he did a hundred things, he neglected the one. What a revelation of a perpetual reason and method of failure! We are given some one responsibility by God, some central, definite thing to do. We start to do it with all good intentions, and then other things, not necessarily wrong in themselves, come in our way. We get "busy here and there" doing many things and we neglect the one central thing.[57]

Naboth's Vineyard and Ahab's Death

1 Kings 21-22; 2 Chron. 18

Ahab Steals Naboth's Vineyard (1 Kgs. 21:1-16)

Ahab coveted a lush vineyard owned by Naboth that was situated next to his royal palace in Jezreel (1 Kgs. 21:1). The king offered to buy this property, or to trade Naboth for it, so he could have a vegetable garden near his house (1 Kgs. 21:2). But honorable Naboth declined to sell Ahab what he had inherited from his fathers and was to be passed down to his children (1 Kgs. 21:3).

The king was distraught over Naboth's decision and resorted to not eating and sulking in his bed (1 Kgs. 21:4). Queen Jezebel inquired as to why the king was melancholy and he explained the situation concerning the desired vineyard to her (1 Kgs. 21:5-6). She told the king of Israel to arise, eat, and be merry, for she would find a way to secure the vineyard for him (1 Kgs. 21:7).

Jezebel's solution was to plot evil against just Naboth. She sent sealed letters to the elders and nobles of Naboth's city to ask them to proclaim a fast and to be sure to seat Naboth in the place of honor (1 Kgs. 21:8-9). They also were to seat two men, scoundrels, before him to bear witness of his blasphemy against God and the king and then take Naboth outside and stone him (1 Kgs. 21:10). In short, Jezebel's plan to gain the vineyard for her husband was to murder an innocent man and then steal his possession. We learn later that she also had Naboth's sons executed so there would be no lawful heir to the vineyard (2 Kgs. 9:26).

Jezebel clearly understood the inheritance laws governing land in Israel, but chose to abuse justice to get what she wanted. Moses had laid down strict regulations for confirming the truth through the testimony of multiple witnesses, so that no one would be found guilty of a crime by the mouth of a single witness (Deut. 19:15). False witnesses (often for personal gain or to settle a vendetta) also plagued Israel's history, as observed in the story. For this reason, Moses said that the priests and magistrates were to carefully examine the testimony of a witness against an accused person to ensure the testifier was not lying (Deut. 19:16-18). If the witness was found to be false, then that person was to suffer the punishment he sought to inflict on the innocent party (Deut. 19:19). This example would make others think twice about committing perjury in a court of law (Deut. 19:20). According to the Law, the city's leaders and the two false witnesses deserved the death penalty for their crime against Naboth.

The local leaders executed Jezebel's plan flawlessly and then informed her that Naboth had been stoned and was dead (1 Kgs. 21:11-14). After hearing this news, she informed the king that Naboth, who refused to sell his property to him, was dead and he could now seize his vineyard, which the king did (1 Kgs. 21:15-16). But the thing that Jezebel and Ahab had done angered the Lord.

Ahab Condemned (1 Kgs. 21:17-29)

Elijah, now emotionally restored, was training Elisha at this time. The Lord instructed Elijah to deliver a message of condemnation to Ahab for murdering innocent Naboth to steal his vineyard (1 Kgs. 21:17-18). Elijah told Ahab that, because he had murdered and stolen the deceased's possession, dogs would lick his blood in the same place that they licked Naboth's after he was stoned (1 Kgs. 21:19).

The prophet not only told the king that his death was imminent, but dogs licking one's blood indicated that he would suffer a shameful demise. Instead of expressing remorse for what he had done, Ahab rebuffs Elijah, *"Have you found me, O my enemy?"* (1 Kgs. 21:20). But the prophet counters that he is not Ahab's enemy, but rather was sent by the Lord to rebuke the king for abusing his God-given authority (1 Kgs. 21:21). For his crime the Lord promised to *"cut off from Ahab every male in Israel, both bond and free"* to end his dynasty (1 Kgs. 21:21). Even though God had delivered Ahab from the Syrians twice, Ahab had not drawn near to the Lord, but rather had caused His name to be blasphemed in Israel because of his evil deed concerning Naboth.

Elijah also prophesied concerning Jezebel, the instigator of Naboth's murder: the dogs shall eat Jezebel's body by the wall of Jezreel (1 Kgs. 21:23). In fact, the bodies of those in Ahab's household would be feasted on by dogs if in the city and by the birds if in the open fields (1 Kgs. 21:24). This was a fitting end for the most wicked king to sit on Israel's throne – *"there was no one like Ahab who sold himself to do wickedness."* His evil wife continually stirred him up to do what God hated, especially to worship abominable idols (1 Kgs. 21:25-26).

The prophet's message keenly affected Ahab's conscience; the king tore his clothes, put sackcloth on his body and then mourned and fasted (1 Kgs. 21:27). God observed Ahab's humility and informed Elijah that, because the king had humbled himself, He would not bring the prophesied calamity on Ahab's household in his lifetime, but in the days of his son, the next ruler of Israel (1 Kgs. 21:28). However, in the next chapter it is obvious that Ahab's heart had not really softened towards the Lord, even after receiving God's mercy.

The Lord's response to Ahab's contrition is a wonderful illustration of what the prophet Ezekiel would tell the Jews centuries later: God does not enjoy punishing the wicked, but rather His holy character demands that He must avenge evil. God's preference is that the wicked repent and be saved: *"I have no pleasure in the death of the wicked, but that the wicked turn from his way and live"* (Ezek. 33:11). The Israelites should not think that the Lord derived pleasure in being wrathful; rather, He longs to joyfully interact with those choosing to honor Him through obedience. No person should think that he or she has gone so far down the wide path leading to destruction that he or she cannot be rescued – no one is hopelessly lost unless he or she chooses not to repent and turn to the Lord for forgiveness and mercy.

In the end, all will acknowledge Christ's lordship (Phil. 2:9-10), but we should never think that He receives pleasure from casting the wicked into the Lake of Fire. Interestingly, everlasting *hell fire* was not originally prepared for mankind but rather for Satan and the other rebellious angels (Matt. 25:41). However, God will use this abode of torment to also punish those who continue the devil's rebellion by rejecting God's offer of salvation in Christ. The Lord longs for all men to repent and to turn to Him by faith that they might be declared righteous in His sight (Ezek. 33:12). However, those laboring to establish their own righteousness before God through their own doings remain unforgiven for their iniquities (Ezek. 33:13-14; Rom. 10:1-3). Conversely, if a sinner repents and seeks forgiveness from the Lord, he or she will be forgiven; such an individual will be known by their continuance in works of righteousness afterwards (Ezek. 33:15-16).

Ahab Is Warned (1 Kgs. 22:1-28; 2 Chron. 18:1-27)

After three years of peace with Syria, the king of Judah, Jehoshaphat, visited Ahab, who *"killed sheep and oxen in abundance"* and hosted a great feast (1 Kgs. 22:1-2; 2 Chron. 18:2). During the feasting, Ahab suggested that they work together to liberate Ramoth in Gilead from Syrian occupation (1 Kgs. 22:3). Ramoth was one of the three Cities of Refuge on the eastern side of the Jordan River (Deut. 4:43). The city was about thirty miles east of the Jordan River and was under the control of Syria.

In response to Ahab's invitation to fight beside him for this noble religious cause, Jehoshaphat answered, *"I am as you are, my people as your people, my horses as your horses"* (1 Kgs. 22:4). While a polite statement acknowledging their ethnicity, it was not true from a spiritual standpoint; wicked pagans and Jehovah-fearing worshipers can never enjoy brotherly communion with each other. Jehoshaphat had surrendered his personal identity with Jehovah to be reckoned as one with Ahab, but a child of God and a child of the devil can never be one. When believers identify with the wicked, they will undoubtedly become averse to God's people and to the things important to Him.

Christians are chosen in Christ to receive God's goodness, but it is not because of their personal righteousness that they receive God's favor. It is, however, because of their holy standing in Christ. They must be a holy people and have no fellowship with unrighteousness, especially in association with children of the devil. For this reason, Paul admonishes the carnal believers at Corinth to consecrate themselves to the Lord:

> *Do not be unequally yoked together with unbelievers. For what fellowship has righteousness with lawlessness? And what communion has light with darkness? And what accord has Christ with Belial? Or what part has a believer with an unbeliever? And what agreement has the temple of God with idols? For you are the temple of the living God. As God has said: "I will dwell in them and walk among them. I will be their God, and they shall be My people." Therefore "Come out from among them and be separate, says the Lord"* (2 Cor. 6:14-17).

Likewise, being chosen and redeemed by God, the Jewish nation also received a holy standing before God that no other nation enjoyed.

Such an unmerited position of favor demanded Israel's holiness to God and no close association with wicked idolaters.

Jehoshaphat was a godly king who responded to his wealth and honor by continuing to follow after the Lord (2 Chron. 17:3-6); however, he often associated with those who were not and suffered for it (as witnessed in this chapter). Ahab's gifts and feast in his honor had softened Jehoshaphat's good sense in repudiating what God had not endorsed. If Satan had tried to ensnare Jehoshaphat with a clearly ungodly scheme, he would have detected it, but he was less suspicious of the evil hidden within a religious cause. Perhaps Jehoshaphat thought that, though God was not with Ahab, what could be wrong with joining with the ungodly king to recapture a city with religious significance? However, the king of Judah will learn that the only safeguard against evil is to remain in communion with the Lord, for *"evil company corrupts good habits"* (1 Cor. 15:33).

Dear believer, be aware that the devil often lures the godly into unnatural unions with his own people through religious causes. These things are often valued by churchianity, but not by the Lord. Satan uses benevolent objects and religious grounds to influence God's people to leave a true work of God for what is not. The busy work of religion is a poor substitute for Spirit-led ministry that counts for eternity! Just because well-known people are connected with some activity does not make it a God-honoring investment of time and resources.

Although the king of Judah wrongly claimed a kindred spirit with Ahab and Israel, he also desired that a prophet of the Lord confirm the matter before they engage the Syrians in battle (1 Kgs. 22:5). Amazingly, the godly king petitions the wicked king, whom God has rejected, *"Please inquire for the word of the Lord today"* (2 Chron. 18:4). Though godly Jehoshaphat's conscience is clearly at work, it is utter mockery of God's authority to solicit His counsel and assistance when we have already determined what we are going to do. As C. H. Mackintosh rightly surmises, such conduct honors God with our lips and not our hearts:

> We must be really brought to the end of everything with which self has aught to do, for until then God cannot show Himself. But we can never get to the end of our plans until we have been brought to the end of ourselves.[58]

The king should have reviewed Scripture for direction, sought godly counsel, and most importantly asked the Lord to confirm the right course of action, but Jehoshaphat did not do that.

The king of Israel was happy to oblige the king of Judah's request, so he asks his own four hundred prophets whether the Lord would grant them victory over the Syrians, if they worked together to retake Ramoth Gilead (1 Kgs. 22:6). The false prophets of Ahab all confirmed that God would grant Israel victory for this noble cause. However, Jehoshaphat was not convinced and asked Ahab, *"Is there not still a prophet of the Lord here, that we may inquire of Him?"* (1 Kgs. 22:7). So as not to offend Ahab, Jehoshaphat equates the counsel of Ahab's idolatrous prophets with that of a true prophet of God. Though acknowledging that Ahab's 400 prophets are not of the Lord, he still bestows honor and respect that they do not deserve. Those who walk with the Lord should never give equality to world religions, which have their basis in satanic propaganda. The ministers of God and those who serve the devil have nothing in common and should be kept distinct.

Although the king of Judah remained courteous, he was clearly apprehensive about the situation he had become entangled in. Paul tells believers to proceed in questionable matters (i.e., those not specifically addressed by Scripture) only when one has complete conviction from the Lord to do so, *"for whatever is not from faith is sin"* (Rom. 14:23). H. L. Rossier notes that the Spirit of God may cause believers to be unsettled about a particular activity to dissuade them from it in the same way that He is grieved within a believer who chooses to sin (Eph. 4:30):

> There is a spiritual sense that warns a true heart, though perhaps not being able to account for it, that certain spiritual manifestations do not have the Spirit of God as their agent. …The child of God feels ill at ease in an environment opposed to God, ill at ease in presence of certain discourse which claims to come from religious tongues but lacks the divine character, ill at ease confronted with such vaunting as that which takes place here before the king of Israel. So it was with Jehoshaphat, too, for after having been present at the scene brought on by his request to Ahab, *"Inquire, I pray thee, this day of the word of Jehovah"* (v. 5), he finds himself obliged to add: *"Is there not here a prophet besides, that we might inquire of him?"* (v. 7).[59]

Ahab then remembered that there was one prophet of the Lord, Micaiah, that they might inquire of, but Ahab hated him because Micaiah always spoke against him (1 Kgs. 22:8). Of course, Jehoshaphat knew that a true prophet of Jehovah would speak out against the wickedness of Ahab, but he made light of Ahab's comment urging that they should seek Micaiah's counsel also. So Ahab sent for Micaiah. Ahab's false prophets continued predicting victory while Ahab and Jehoshaphat sat waiting on two thrones at the entrance to Samaria (1 Kgs. 22:10, 12).

One of these prophets, Zedekiah (the son of Chenaanah), even made iron horns to illustrate how the kings of Israel and Judah would gore the Syrians in battle (1 Kgs. 22:11). The messenger who was tasked with bringing Micaiah before the kings was informed of all that had transpired and told Micaiah that he should agree with the other prophets (1 Kgs. 22:13). However, Micaiah, understanding his accountability before the Lord to speak only the truth, replied: *"As the Lord lives, whatever the Lord says to me, that I will speak"* (1 Kgs. 22:14). No wonder Ahab did not appreciate Micaiah's prophecies, he spoke for the One who detested Ahab's behavior.

Once Micaiah arrived, Ahab asked him if they should go to war to retake Ramoth Gilead from the Syrians (1 Kgs. 22:15). Having gone through this exercise previously, Micaiah initially responds sarcastically to emphasize the true message that he will reveal in time: *"Go and prosper, for the Lord will deliver it into the hand of the king!"* Ahab discerns that he is being mocked and commands Micaiah to swear in the name of the Lord and only say the truth (1 Kgs. 22:16). It is noteworthy that Micaiah is the third prophet that Jehovah has sent to warn King Ahab and each did so multiple times. Elijah and an unnamed prophet had previously addressed Ahab. Ahab received more revelation as to the will of God than any other king of Israel and yet did the most evil regardless.

While clearly a pagan like Ahab did not value invoking the Lord's name in such matters, Micaiah did and complied. With the needful rebuffing of sarcasm being past, the prophet delivered Jehovah's message: *"I saw all Israel scattered on the mountains, as sheep that have no shepherd. And the Lord said, 'These have no master. Let each return to his house in peace'"* (1 Kgs. 22:17). The phrases, "no shepherd" and "no master" signified Ahab's coming death. Ezekiel will use the same terminology to affirm that, in his day, Israel had no true king-shepherd who spiritually fed God's hungry people (Ezek. 34:5-8). The Lord Jesus said that Israel was suffering from the same spiritual deficiency during His earthly sojourn (Matt. 9:36). Scripture reveals that there will be no such shepherd-king like David in Israel again until the Son of David appears to restore and rule over Israel during the Kingdom Age.

Understanding that this prophecy was against him, Ahab turns to Jehoshaphat to bemoan the matter: *"Did I not tell you he would not prophesy good concerning me, but evil?"* (1 Kgs. 22:19). The prophet of Jehovah continued by revealing the scene in heaven related to their circumstances (1 Kgs. 22:20-23). To accomplish his judgment against Ahab, the Lord permitted fallen angels to speak seductively through Ahab's prophets to cause Ahab to attack the Syrians so that he might die. We see another example of the sovereign affairs of God being accomplished by false prophets in Ezekiel's day centuries later. Ezekiel foretold that God would prevent true prophets from answering Israel's idolatrous leaders when the time of Judah's judgment should be realized, but that He would permit false prophets to do so (Ezek. 14:9). God promised to punish both Judah's idolatrous leaders and those false prophets who spoke in His name to deceive them; this act of vindication would serve to summon His wayward people back to Him in purity (Ezek. 14:10-11).

Zedekiah did not appreciate Micaiah's prophecy and struck him on the cheek, and then publicly mocked his message, *"Which way did the spirit from the Lord go from me to speak to you?"* (1 Kgs. 22:24). Micaiah then delivered a prophecy against Zedekiah for his insolence: there was a day coming when he would try to hide from the Syrians, but he would not be able to escape God's judgment through them (1 Kgs. 22:25).

Ahab commanded that Micaiah be taken to Amon, the governor of the city, and be imprisoned with only a meager ration of bread and water until Ahab returned safely from battling the Syrians (1 Kgs. 22:26-27). But Micaiah used Ahab's own statement to reaffirm God's word – if Ahab returned in peace, then Micaiah had not spoken on behalf of the Lord (1 Kgs. 22:28).

Regrettably, Jehoshaphat continued on with Ahab, though he knew what the word of the Lord was. When a believer associates himself with the world, he will do so thoroughly, for Satan will relentlessly use every effort possible to force that saint out of communion with God.

Ahab Dies (1 Kgs. 22:29-40; 2 Chron. 18:28-34)

So Ahab and Jehoshaphat combined their armies and went across the Jordan together to retake Ramoth Gilead from the Syrians (1 Kgs. 22:29). Ahab said that he wanted to take part in the conflict instead of being a royal spectator, so he requested that Jehoshaphat wear his royal robes and represent him, while he fought with his men (1 Kgs. 22:30). However, since Ahab was breaking his treaty with Syria, and knew Ben-Hadad would be exceedingly angry with him, the tactic seems to be more based on self-preservation. Matthew Henry further explains Ahab's treachery:

> Ahab adopts a contrivance by which he hopes to secure himself and expose his friend (v. 30): "I will disguise myself, and go in the habit of a common soldier, but let Jehoshaphat put on his robes, to appear in the dress of a general." He pretended thereby to do honor to Jehoshaphat, and to compliment him with the sole command of the army in this action. He shall direct and give orders, and Ahab will serve as a soldier under him. But he intended,
>
> 1. To make a liar of a good prophet. Thus he hoped to elude the danger, and so to defeat the threat, as if, by disguising himself, he could escape the divine cognizance and the judgments that pursued him.
>
> 2. To make a fool of a good king, whom he did not cordially love, because he was one that adhered to God and so condemned his apostasy.[60]

Jehoshaphat agreed to Ahab's plan without knowing the dire situation that he was entering. Ahab was correct. Ben-Hadad was furious with him and had instructed the thirty-two captains of his chariots to ignore the main battle and go after the king of Israel (1 Kgs. 22:31).

There is a lesson here: the man of God had so thoroughly associated himself with the world that he resembled a child of the devil and not a child of God. As the king of Judah will soon learn, when a believer chooses to commune with children of the devil to do the work of the devil, he is in jeopardy of losing everything, even his life.

Once the battle was engaged, the Syrian captains thought they recognized Israel's king in the royal chariot and pursued him (1 Kgs.

22:32). Jehoshaphat quickly realized that his life was in peril and cried out to the Lord for help (1 Kgs. 22:33). The captains then discerned that Jehoshaphat was an imposter since he fled from them instead of engaging them in battle. So they returned to the battlefront in search of the real king of Israel.

In a random shot, a Syrian archer struck Ahab between the joints of his armor. While the archer had not been aiming at the chink in the king's armor per se, the Lord guided the arrow to its mark to fulfill His word spoken through Micaiah. The king commanded his driver to withdraw from the battle because he had been wounded (1 Kgs. 22:34). The battle was fierce, so Ahab, in order not to discourage his men from fighting, propped himself up in his chariot the remainder of the day while he slowly bled out – he died that evening (1 Kgs. 22:35). Hearing of the king's death, Israel withdrew from the conflict and Jehoshaphat, thankful to be alive, journeyed back to Jerusalem (1 Kgs. 22:36).

Ahab was buried in Samaria, and the dogs licked up his blood as it was being washed from his chariot in a public place (where the harlots bathe), fulfilling the word of God spoken through the imprisoned prophet (1 Kgs. 22:37-38). This was also a partial fulfillment of Elijah's prophecy concerning Ahab's death, as this event took place in Samaria, instead of Jezreel (1 Kgs. 21:19). The Lord also honored His word spoken by His unnamed prophet against Ahab after the Syrian treaty (1 Kgs. 20:42). Jehovah had brought three of His prophets to warn Ahab by foretelling his death, yet the king of Israel would not turn to the Lord.

Ahab had been industrious in his construction projects, even building for himself an ivory house, but in the end his wickedness brought a divine wrecking ball to his household (1 Kgs. 22:39). (Archeologists have found more than 200 ivory figures, panels, and plaques in excavations of Samaria.[61]) Ahab's son Ahaziah reigned as king in Israel and would be the last of Ahab's dynasty.

Indeed, the Lord judged Ahab, but thankfully, He also moved to save godly Jehoshaphat from his life-threatening predicament. *"The Lord knows how to deliver the godly out of temptations and to reserve the unjust under punishment for the day of judgment"* (2 Pet. 2:9). The king of Judah, realizing his desperate need, cried out to the Lord to save him from the Syrians. In contrast, wounded Ahab did not humble himself before the Lord, but rather tried to hide his weakness by propping himself up in his chariot to encourage his men to keep fighting. Jehoshaphat knew where his strength resided – in the Lord, but proud Ahab chose a facade of power and to perish in his sins. Our fallen nature will cause us to make poor choices at times, but man's greatest travesty is to not immediately confess our failures to God when we know we have done wrong. His deliverance awaits the humble, but His wrath will be poured out on the proud.

Meditation

> The conscience that can let pass without reproof things from which it would formerly have shrunk is much to be feared. Instead of being under the action of the truth of God, it is under the hardening influence of the deceitfulness of sin.
>
> — C. H. Mackintosh

King Jehoshaphat of Judah

1 Kings 22:41-50; 2 Chronicles 17, 19-20

We were previously introduced to King Jehoshaphat because of his unfortunate interaction with King Ahab in 2 Chronicles 18. Jehoshaphat, the son of Asa, became Judah's king in the fourth year of Ahab; he was thirty-five years old at that time and reigned twenty-five years in Jerusalem (873-848 B.C.; 1 Kgs. 22:41-42). His mother's name was Azubah the daughter of Shilhi. The writer summarizes Jehoshaphat's reign: *"He walked in all the ways of his father Asa. He did not turn aside from them, doing what was right in the eyes of the Lord. Nevertheless the high places were not taken away, for the people offered sacrifices and burned incense on the high places"* (1 Kgs. 22:43).

Building Up the Kingdom (2 Chron. 17)

After coming to the throne, Jehoshaphat strengthened himself against Israel by placing troops in all the fortified cities of Judah, and establishing garrisons in Judah and in the buffer cities of Ephraim which his father Asa had captured (2 Chron. 17:1-2). Because Jehoshaphat walked in the Lord's commandments and purified Judah of idols and removed their shrines in the high places, the Lord blessed and established his kingdom (2 Chron. 17:4-6).

Additionally, Jehoshaphat strengthened the people by ensuring that the priests and Levites visited and taught God's law to the people throughout Judah (2 Chron. 17:7-9). Because Jehoshaphat feared the Lord and wanted those he ruled to reverence Him also, God caused the surrounding nations to fear Jehoshaphat (2 Chron. 17:10). Because the king sought the Lord, he was blessed with a peaceful and a prosperous reign. Even his enemies gave him presents and paid him tribute (2 Chron. 17:11).

Besides establishing many fortifications throughout Judah and on the border of Ephraim, Jehoshaphat built up Judah's army. He appointed five captains to oversee 780,000 soldiers from Judah and 280,000 soldiers from Benjamin (2 Chron. 17:12-19).

Rebuke for Unnatural Unions (2 Chron. 19:1-3)

Although the writer of Kings alludes to the many positive things that Jehoshaphat accomplished for Judah, he also notes that *"Jehoshaphat made peace with the king of Israel"* (1 Kgs. 22:44). We have already observed the consequences of this in the previous narrative (1 Kgs. 22; 2 Chron. 18).

To summarize, Ahab conned Jehoshaphat into forging an alliance with him in order to retake Ramoth, a City of Refuge in the Transjordan, which was under Syrian control. Ahab was an evil king and godly Jehoshaphat should have known better than to unite with Ahab, especially in a meaningless cause that God had not sanctioned. The king of Judah enjoyed prosperity and had fortified his kingdom against military invasion, but not his heart against the assault of allurement.

The result of this union nearly cost Jehoshaphat his life, but he cried out to the Lord and God saved him. After Jehoshaphat returned to Jerusalem, the prophet Hanani rebuked the king for his alliance with Ahab, *"Should you help the wicked, and love them who hate the Lord?"* (2 Chron. 19:2). Though Jehoshaphat had done many good things for the Lord, the king would suffer for affiliating with wicked Ahab. For example, the marriage alliance he established with Ahab (Jehoshaphat's son Jehoram married Ahab's wicked daughter Athaliah) resulted in rampant idolatry in Judah after Jehoshaphat's death.

Satan has used this tactic of *unnatural unions* on many throughout Biblical history. Joshua fell prey to the Gibeonites' trickery in Canaan: *"we are your servants ... we know your God ... make a peace treaty with us"* (Josh. 9). He listened to the enemy, did not seek God's counsel on the matter, and paid a high price for the deception. Indeed, one of Satan's most successful strategies against God's people throughout the ages is the use of "unnatural unions." C. H. Mackintosh wrote regarding this in the mid-19th century:

> There is great danger, at the present day, of compromising truth for the sake of union. This should be carefully guarded against. There can be no true union attained at the expense of truth. The true Christian's motto should be, "Maintain truth at all cost; if union can be promoted

in this way, so much the better, but maintain the truth." The principle of expediency, on the contrary, may be thus enunciated: "Promote union at all cost; if truth can be maintained as well, so much the better, but promote union." This latter principle can only be carried out at the expense of all that is divine in the way of testimony.[62]

How many Christians today are reaping God's judgment for teaming up with the unregenerate to accomplish some religious cause or to support some charitable activity? If children of God and children of the devil are working together harmoniously, it is not God who is glorified in the endeavor, but the one who has wanted God's glory and station from the beginning (Isa. 14:12-15).

After rebuking the king for his involvement with Ahab, the prophet Hanani ends his message on a consoling note: *"Nevertheless good things are found in you, in that you have removed the wooden images from the land, and have prepared your heart to seek God"* (2 Chron. 19:3). Thankfully, failures are never final unless we make them so – God wants us to succeed.

Further Reforms (2 Chron. 19:4-11)

While we remain on the earth, failures are not final unless we determine them to be so. The Lord desires that His people learn from their failures, rise up in newly acquired wisdom, and move forward with Him in grace. So falling is not what makes one a failure, but wallowing in self-pity and choosing to stay down does: *"For a righteous man may fall seven times and rise again, but the wicked shall fall by calamity"* (Prov. 24:16). Jehoshaphat rises again! After being restored, he takes on the work of the evangelists and goes out to where the wayward and wicked resided in an attempt to see them restored to the Lord also: *"He went out again through the people from Beer-sheba to mount Ephraim, and brought them back unto the Lord God of their fathers"* (2 Chron. 19:4).

Likewise, the Lord Jesus and His disciples moved about Galilee, Samaria and Judea seeking the lost sheep of Israel. Our Savior did not expect wayward sheep to visit His family's carpentry business in Nazareth to learn about the Good Shepherd; rather, He went out seeking what was lost to Him. This was His evangelistic example, what He taught and then commanded His disciples to do after His departure (Matt. 28:19-20; Acts 1:8).

To ensure that God was honored in Judah, Jehoshaphat appointed godly judges who would render righteous decisions without being persuaded otherwise by partiality or bribery (2 Chron. 19:5-7). He also established a supreme court of sorts in Jerusalem to handle the weightier matters of justice throughout the kingdom (2 Chron. 19:8-11). Amariah the high priest was in authority over the religious cases and the Levite Zebadiah, the civil cases. A number of Levites assisted these officers in the judicial supervision of the court system.

Defeat of the Foreign Alliance (2 Chron. 20:1-30)

Not long after the failed attempt to secure Ramoth Gilead, the Moabites, the Ammonites, and the Meunites (an Arabian tribe residing in Edom) united against Jehoshaphat (2 Chron. 20:1). If the Syrians could repel the united armies of Israel and Judah, then these Transjordan factions probably thought that they could defeat the king of Judah if they combined their forces. Jehoshaphat soon learned that this alliance had gathered at Hazazon Tamar (En Gedi) on the western shore of the Dead Sea and would soon be assaulting Jerusalem (2 Chron. 20:2).

Fearing this invasion, Jehoshaphat sought the Lord on the matter and proclaimed a fast throughout all Judah. Jews from across Judah poured into Jerusalem to seek the Lord with their king (2 Chron. 20:3-4). Given the size of Judah's army, the congregation, which included *"all Judah, with their little ones, their wives, and their children,"* would have been enormous (2 Chron. 20:13). They stood before the Lord with their king. Jehoshaphat led the congregation in prayer:

> *O Lord God of our fathers, are You not God in heaven, and do You not rule over all the kingdoms of the nations, and in Your hand is there not power and might, so that no one is able to withstand You? Are You not our God, who drove out the inhabitants of this land before Your people Israel, and gave it to the descendants of Abraham Your friend forever? And they dwell in it, and have built You a sanctuary in it for Your name, saying, "If disaster comes upon us -- sword, judgment, pestilence, or famine -- we will stand before this temple and in Your presence (for Your name is in this temple), and cry out to You in our affliction, and You will hear and save." And now, here are the people of Ammon, Moab, and Mount Seir – whom You would not let Israel invade when they came out of the land of Egypt, but they turned from them and did not destroy them -- here*

> *they are, rewarding us by coming to throw us out of Your possession which You have given us to inherit. O our God, will You not judge them? For we have no power against this great multitude that is coming against us; nor do we know what to do, but our eyes are upon You* (2 Chron. 20:5-12).

This is a lovely prayer in which the king first extols the immense power of their sovereign God. He then recalls God's past goodness shown to them as Abraham's descendants by giving them their homeland and also a central sanctuary to worship Him in. Because of the Lord's command, the Israelites had spared the three nations now threatening them while journeying from Egypt to Canaan. So now they requested the Lord's help since they had honored His decree.

Jehoshaphat then recalls God's friendship with Abraham, reminding the Lord that His people before Him now wanted to enjoy the same kind of communion with Him that Abraham did. Besides 2 Chronicles 20:7, Scripture twice more refers to Abraham as "the friend of God" (Isa. 41:8; Jas. 2:23). Abraham delighted in the Lord and also enjoyed the Lord's fellowship, blessing, and protection (e.g., Gen. 18). This was what the king desired for Judah at that present time.

After the king finished praying, the Spirit of the Lord came upon Jahaziel the son of Zechariah, a Levite of the sons of Asaph who was in the midst of the assembly (2 Chron. 20:14). He told the king and his countrymen not to be afraid, for the battle with the approaching enemy was not theirs, but the Lord's (2 Chron. 20:15). He then told them to go out to meet, not to fight, the enemy the next day. They would find them coming from the Ascent of Ziz and at the end of the brook before the Wilderness of Jeruel (Desert of Tekoa; 2 Chron. 20:16).

Because the battle was the Lord's, they were to take up a position opposite the enemy and then *"stand still and see the salvation of the Lord"* (2 Chron. 20:17). There was no need for them to fear the enemy because the Lord was with them and would protect them. When Jehoshaphat and the people heard this prophetic word, they all bowed their faces to the ground and worshiped the Lord (2 Chron. 20:18). The Levites from the clan of Kohath then stood up and praised the Lord with exuberant singing (2 Chron. 20:19).

The next morning, the people gathered to march out into the Wilderness of Tekoa to meet the enemy as God had commanded the previous day (2 Chron. 20:20). The king charged the people, *"Believe in the Lord your God, and you shall be established; believe His prophets, and you shall prosper"* (2 Chron. 20:20). To demonstrate their faith in the Lord, the king positioned the Levite singers in front of the army and the people, so that they could "praise the beauty of holiness" as they moved forward (2 Chron. 20:21). The Levites sang, *"Praise the Lord, for His mercy endures forever."*

This sight may have stunned the enemy marching towards Jerusalem, as it was not a normal military strategy to posts musicians and singers as your first wave of combatants in a military engagement. The Lord added to their confusion and set ambushes against the soldiers of Ammon, Moab, and Mount Seir by causing the Ammonites and Moabites to attack and utterly destroy those from Edom (2 Chron. 20:22). Afterwards, the Lord caused the Ammonites and Moabites to destroy each other (2 Chron. 20:23). It was a total massacre, leaving the wilderness littered with innumerable dead bodies (2 Chron. 20:24).

Judah had fully trusted in the Lord and, as a result, not only was the threat totally removed, but the people were rewarded with the vast spoil of their enemy which took three days to gather (2 Chron. 20:25). On the fourth day after their deliverance, Judah assembled in the Valley of Berachah to bless the Lord and then Jehoshaphat led his countrymen back to Jerusalem. They praised the Lord as they went (2 Chron. 20:26-27). After returning to Jerusalem, praises to God continued to be offered by musicians and singers at the temple (2 Chron. 20:28).

Not only did the Lord deliver His people from an enormous invading army and bless them with the spoils of His war, He also blessed them with peace by causing the surrounding countries to fear the God of the Jews, who fought for His people (2 Chron. 20:29). Afterwards, *"the realm of Jehoshaphat was quiet, for his God gave him rest all around"* (2 Chron. 20:30).

The Lord longs to show Himself strong to those who are in a right relationship with Him and realize that He is their strength. King Jehoshaphat's prayer conveyed this realization on behalf of the nation: *"O our God, will You not judge them? For we have no power against this great multitude that is coming against us; nor do we know what to do, but our eyes are upon You"* (2 Chron. 20:12). God responded to their faith in Him by completely wiping out the advancing armies without one Jew lifting his sword. Dear believer, God is able!

Jehoshaphat's Final Days (1 Kgs. 22:41-50; 2 Chron. 20:31-37)

Jehoshaphat reigned in Judea for twenty-three years and walked in the godly ways of his father Asa during his entire tenure (2 Chron. 20:31). He did what was right in the sight of the Lord; although he did not remove the high places used to traditionally worship Jehovah (he did remove all the pagan shrines in high places; 2 Chron. 20:32-33).

The writer of Kings mentions that *"there was no king of Edom"* (1 Kgs. 22:47) to underscore Edom's subjugation to Judah. This opened the way to the Red Sea through the Gulf of Aqaba and permitted Jehoshaphat to pursue an ambitious merchant marine enterprise.

The historian closes his account of the life of Jehoshaphat by again highlighting his propensity to forge unnatural unions with wicked people (2 Chron. 20:34-37). In his later years as king, Jehoshaphat allied himself with Ahab's wicked son Ahaziah, the king of Israel, on a commercial venture to Tarshish. However, the ships they were building in Ezion Geber for this enterprise never set sail because the Lord destroyed them. The Lord brought the prophet Eliezer to rebuke Jehoshaphat: *"Because you have allied yourself with Ahaziah, the Lord has destroyed your works."*

Jehoshaphat was a good king, but he had a tendency to associate with wicked people. He aligned himself with evil Ahab to recapture a religious city, and the endeavor almost cost Jehoshaphat his life. Often the Lord will bring us into painful situations to pry us out of the world's grip. God hates worldliness in the believer's life and will take drastic measures to ensure that the believer feels His jealousy (Jas. 4:4).

Meditation

> Nothing exposes religion more to the reproach of its enemies than the worldliness and hard-heartedness of its professors.
>
> — Matthew Henry

> A true revival means nothing less than a revolution, casting out the spirit of worldliness and selfishness, and making God and His love triumph in the heart and life.
>
> — Andrew Murray

King Ahaziah of Israel

1 Kings 22:51-53; 2 Kings 1

Ahaziah, the oldest son of Ahab, became king over Israel in Samaria in the seventeenth year of Jehoshaphat king of Judah (1 Kgs. 22:51). He reigned in Israel less than two years (853-852 B.C.) and walked according to the evil ways of his parents (Ahab and Jezebel; 1 Kgs. 22:52). The historian summarizes his foul legacy: he *"made Israel sin for he served Baal and worshiped him, and provoked the Lord God of Israel to anger"* (1 Kgs. 22:53).

Ahaziah and Elijah (2 Kgs. 1)

Ahab's father Omri had imposed taxation on Moab, but after the death of Ahab, the Moabites led by Mesha rebelled against Israel, now ruled by young Ahaziah (2 Kgs. 1:1, 3:4-8). Perhaps the shock of this insurrection caused Ahaziah to suffer a serious injury in his home after falling to the ground through a lattice covering over a window (2 Kgs. 1:2). Being a devout Baal worshiper, he sent messengers from Samaria to the Philistine city of Ekron (40 miles to the southwest) to inquire of the pagan deity concerning his recovery.

Baal-zebub was believed to have special healing power. The Syrian deity was actually named Baal-zebul (meaning the "Lord of life"), but the Israelites mocked him by calling him Baal-zebub (or the "Lord of the flies").[63] Sadly, the king mocked his own name by seeking Baal's assistance; Ahaziah means "who Jehovah sustains."

In response to Ahaziah's pagan thinking, the Angel of the Lord (i.e., a theophany of preincarnate Christ) appeared to Elijah again and commanded the prophet:

> *Arise, go up to meet the messengers of the king of Samaria, and say to them, "Is it because there is no God in Israel that you are going to inquire of Baal-Zebub, the god of Ekron?" Now therefore, thus says*

the Lord: "You shall not come down from the bed to which you have gone up, but you shall surely die" (2 Kgs. 1:3-4).

Elijah obeyed the Lord and intercepted Ahaziah's messengers en route to Ekron and delivered the Lord's message to them. Ahaziah's servants then immediately returned to Samaria and conveyed the prophet's words to the king, who was surprised by their unexpectedly quick return (2 Kgs. 2:5-6). Apparently, Elijah did not identify himself, nor did Ahaziah's servants know him, so the king inquired as to what the unnamed prophet looked like (2 Kgs. 2:7). They replied that he was *"a hairy man wearing a leather belt around his waist"* (2 Kgs. 2:8). By this description the king knew that the disturbing message had come from Elijah the Tishbite.

After learning where Elijah had met with his servants, Ahaziah sent one of his captains with fifty soldiers to arrest Elijah. Coming to the prophet's last known location, they found him sitting on top of a hill, as though he was waiting for them to arrive. In the king's name, the captain demanded that Elijah come down to them: *"Man of God, the king has said, 'Come down!'"* (2 Kgs. 2:9). The title "Man of God" in the historical books was often associated with God's prophets; hence, the expression is applied to both Elijah and Elisha more than thirty times.

Elijah replied to the captain, *"If I am a man of God, then let fire come down from heaven and consume you and your fifty men"* (2 Kgs. 2:10). Fire came down from heaven and consumed the captain and his fifty men (2 Kgs. 2:10). This judgment may seem unnecessarily harsh to the reader, but we must remember that Ahaziah had rejected God's word spoken through Elijah, and by demanding his arrest, had shown contempt for Elijah's God. Matthew Henry summarizes the scene before us:

> Elijah calls for fire from heaven, to consume this haughty daring sinner, not to secure himself (he could have done that some other way), nor to avenge himself (for it was not his own cause that he appeared and acted in), but to prove his mission, and to reveal the wrath of God from heaven against the ungodliness and unrighteousness of men. This captain had, in scorn, called him a man of God: "If I be so," says Elijah, "thou shalt pay dearly for making a jest of it." He valued himself upon his commission (the king has said, "come down"), but Elijah will let him know that the God of Israel is superior

> to the king of Israel and has a greater power to enforce his commands. It was not long since Elijah had fetched fire from heaven, to consume the sacrifice (1 Kgs. 17:38), in token of God's acceptance of that sacrifice as an atonement for the sins of the people; but, they having slighted that, now the fire falls, not on the sacrifice, but on the sinners themselves.[64]

Seeing that his men failed to return, Ahaziah sent another captain with fifty men to arrest Elijah (2 Kgs. 2:11). Arriving at Elijah's location, the second captain also relayed the king's command to the prophet: *"Man of God, thus has the king said, 'Come down quickly!'"* Again Elijah answered the second captain as he had the first and fire came down and consumed another fifty-one men (2 Kgs. 2:12). Again, some have criticized Elijah's actions as callous – 102 men dead just to avoid arrest? But not only had Ahaziah shown contempt for God's word and his prophet, we also must remember the dispensational truth that Elijah represents – the unyielding judgment of the Law. Albert Barnes explains:

> Ahaziah had, as it were, challenged Yahweh to a trial of strength by sending a band of fifty to arrest one man. Elijah was not Jesus Christ, able to reconcile mercy with truth, the vindication of God's honor with the utmost tenderness for erring men, and awe them merely by His presence (John 18:6). In Elijah the spirit of the Law was embodied in its full severity. His zeal was fierce; he was not shocked by blood; he had no softness and no relenting. … He continued the uncompromising avenger of sin, the wielder of the terrors of the Lord, such exactly as he had shown himself at Carmel. He is, consequently, no pattern for Christian men (Luke 9:55), but his character is the perfection of the purely legal type. No true Christian after Pentecost would have done what Elijah did. But what he did, when he did it, was not sinful. It was but executing strict, stern justice.[65]

Not undeterred by the deaths of his men, the king sent a third captain with fifty soldiers to arrest Elijah. However, upon arriving at Elijah's location, and probably noticing the 102 charred bodies about the prophet, the third captain did not convey the king's command, but rather fell on his knees and pleaded with Elijah for mercy on behalf of himself and his men:

> *Man of God, please let my life and the life of these fifty servants of yours be precious in your sight. Look, fire has come down from heaven and burned up the first two captains of fifties with their fifties. But let my life now be precious in your sight* (2 Kgs. 1:13-14).

The third captain feared God, and with a contrite position and a sincere approach before a holy God, he pleaded for mercy. Those who genuinely cast themselves upon the mercy of God will never do so in vain! The Lord granted his request and instructed Elijah to go with them and not to be afraid (2 Kgs. 2:15). Notice that a man who truly fears the Lord is the only kind of man to whom God would entrust the care of His servant Elijah.

Elijah was brought before King Ahaziah and immediately delivered the Lord's rebuke: *"Because you have sent messengers to inquire of Baal-Zebub, the god of Ekron, is it because there is no God in Israel to inquire of His word? Therefore you shall not come down from the bed to which you have gone up, but you shall surely die"* (2 Kgs. 2:16). Elijah affirmed the previous message of the king's imminent death, but also explained why – he had sought help and counsel from Baal and not from the true God of Israel. Ahaziah did not recover from his injuries, but died as Elijah had foretold. Because Ahaziah had no sons, his younger brother Joram (Jehoram) ruled over Israel after his death (2 Kgs. 2:17-18).

Elijah was personally directed by the Lord throughout the events of this chapter. Because the prophet completely obeyed the word of the Lord, he was protected from harm and the king of Israel was reproved. Rebuking Ahaziah will be Elijah's last official task before ascending in a fiery chariot to be with the Lord (2 Kgs. 2).

Meditation

O Word of God incarnate, O Wisdom from on high,
O Truth, unchanged, unchanging, O Light of our dark sky!
We praise Thee for the radiance that from the hallowed page,
A lantern to our footsteps, shines on from age to age.

— William Walsham How

Elisha Succeeds Elijah

2 Kings 2

The Mentoring Relationship of the Prophets

We have not heard anything about Elisha since his prophetic calling recorded in 1 Kings 19, although we know that he continued to minister to Elijah during his prophetic training (1 Kgs. 19:21; 2 Kgs. 3:11). Elijah and Elisha enjoyed about a ten-year mentor-mentee relationship. The lack of specifics about their association suggests that the nature of the mentoring ministry is a private and personal experience.

Elijah's prophetic ministry draws to a close in this chapter and Elisha will take his place as the premier prophet in Israel at this time. The prophets were similar in that both were appointed by the Lord and evidently both instructed the "sons of the prophets" as a leading teacher (2 Kgs. 2:3, 4:38). Both men were empowered by God to do extraordinary miracles.

The differences between Elijah and Elisha are more obvious. Elijah came from rustic Gilead beyond the Jordan River, and thus likely grew up in a poorer home. Elisha, on the other hand, came from Abel Meholah in Israel proper, and appears to have had a wealthy upbringing (i.e. plowing with twelve yoke of oxen). Elijah was prone to mood swings, but Elisha seems to be more even-tempered. Elijah was a hairy man (2 Kgs. 1:8), while Elisha was bald (2 Kgs. 2:23).

Elijah's ministry was more public, as he was confronting an apostate nation, whereas Elisha's ministry was more personal and compassionate. Elisha labored to turn his countrymen from idolatry by showing them that only Jehovah could meet their needs. Yet, Elisha's ministry superseded Elijah's in duration and in the number of miracles performed. Elijah's miracles were dramatic (e.g. a severe drought and fire coming down from heaven on three different occasions). By contrast, Elisha's miracles were modest and personal – he was a champion of the people. In this sense, Elisha's ministry typifies that of the Lord Jesus, while Elijah's confrontational ministry represents the forerunning work of John to prepare wayward Israel for their Messiah's coming.

Although Elisha did more miracles and showed compassion to individuals, it is Elijah, not Elisha, who is predominant in the New Testament. There, Elijah is referenced by name twenty-nine times, while Elisha is mentioned briefly and only once. These men were vastly different in social upbringing, emotions, and ministries, but their mentor-mentee relationship enabled each one to wonderfully serve the Lord. This indicates that God may bring polar opposites together in such relationships, and also serves as a reminder that the goal of mentoring is not to recreate ourselves in those we mentor, but to enable the mentee to understand and fulfill his or her divine calling.

The Home-Call of Elijah (2 Kgs. 2)

In this chapter, the historian recounts what Elijah was doing just before the Lord took him into heaven in a whirlwind departure. Both Elijah and Elisha were in Gilgal and Elijah told his apprentice to wait there, for the Lord had called him to Bethel (2 Kgs. 2:1-2). If this reference is to the original Gilgal, Bethel would have been an uphill, 15-mile walk to the northwest. If the original location refers to the modern Jiljiliah as some commentators believe[66], then that would have been a 7-mile walk to the southwest. Given the direction of Jericho (their next stop) and the distance one could travel on foot in a day, the latter option seems more likely, as the two prophets would have walked 22 to 23 miles in one day. If the original Gilgal is in view, the distance would be over 30 miles and nearly a complete backtrack of their route.

The Lord had already revealed to Elisha that his mentor would be leaving him that very day. The Lord had divulged this information to the sons of prophets at Bethel and Jericho also (2 Kgs. 2:3, 5). For this reason, Elisha declined to stay in Gilgal, but remained with Elijah; he did not want to miss his mentor's exit. The two journeyed to Bethel, but after arriving, Elijah said that the Lord had directed him to Jericho. The elder prophet again instructed Elisha to remain behind, but again the younger prophet declined (2 Kgs. 2:6).

After passing through Jericho, the two men came to the Jordan River, with fifty men of the sons of the prophets following some distance behind them (2 Kgs. 2:7). Two groups of the sons of the prophets had already foretold that Elijah would be taken up to heaven that very day. They served as God's witnesses of the event from a distance, for later they will be unable to find Elijah's body and will also declare: *"The spirit of Elijah rests on Elisha"* (2 Kgs. 2:15).

Shortly before ascending into heaven from the Mount of Olives, the Lord Jesus told His disciples that they would be witnesses for Him in the world after He departed (Acts 1:8). Like the sons of the prophets long ago, Christians today are Christ's witnesses at a distance (His ambassadors on earth representing the Lord in heaven; 2 Cor. 5:20). As His witnesses, we proclaim the resurrection and ascension of Christ (i.e., His body is nowhere to be found on earth). And like the prophets of old, believers (true witnesses) today recognize and rely upon the direction of the Holy Spirit within them.

Elijah took his mantle, rolled it up, and struck the water with it and the river divided before them. The two prophets crossed on dry ground (2 Kgs. 2:8). This was Elijah's seventh and last miracle. His others included starting and ending a drought, the nonempty barrel of flour and jar of oil, fire from heaven consuming the altar at Carmel, the resurrection of a dead boy, and fire from heaven twice upon his would-be captors.

After crossing the Jordan, Elijah asked his faithful friend and helper Elisha, *"Ask! What may I do for you, before I am taken away from you?"* Elisha answered, *"Please let a double portion of your spirit be upon me"* (2 Kgs. 2:9). The elder prophet said, *"You have asked a hard thing. Nevertheless, if you see me when I am taken from you, it shall be so for you; but if not, it shall not be so"* (2 Kgs. 2:10). It was a hard thing, because it was not Elijah's to give, so he gave Elisha a confirming sign if God chose to grant his request. While they were still talking, a chariot of fire suddenly appeared with horses of fire, and separated the two of them; and Elijah went up by a whirlwind into heaven (2 Kgs. 2:11).

Seeing the spectacular sight, Elisha cried out, *"My father, my father, the chariot of Israel and its horsemen!"* (2 Kgs. 2:12). In a split second, Elijah was gone and his mentee would see him no more. Elisha tore his garment in two and picked up Elijah's mantle that had fallen from him as he was being whisked away (2 Kgs. 2:13). The young prophet had just witnessed the vital connection between Elijah's mantle and God's glory. The mantle, which pictures God's authority over His work, is precious to Him. Furthermore, Elisha observed that God rewards those who honor Him by using the mantle properly. By picking up the mantle, Elisha was illustrating that he valued God's work, the privilege of representing God in the work, and also sharing in God's glory after the work was finished. May believers today also value ministry appreciated by the Lord Jesus, the honor of serving Him, and *"the glory which shall be revealed in us"* through Him (Rom. 8:18).

When Elisha took up Elijah's mantle, he had nothing but God and He would prove to be all Elisha needed. Elisha then walked back to the Jordan River and struck the water with Elijah's mantle in the same way his master had moments earlier and said, *"Where is the Lord God of Elijah?"* The waters divided as before and Elisha crossed back over the dry riverbed (2 Kgs. 2:14).

When the sons of the prophets from Jericho saw him, they affirmed, *"The spirit of Elijah rests on Elisha"* and bowed down before him in respect for the prophetic office (2 Kgs. 2:15). Then they requested that Elisha give them leave to search for the body of Elijah to ensure he received a proper burial in case the Lord had abandoned his body in some remote place (2 Kgs. 2:16). Initially, Elisha denied their request, for he knew that Elijah's body was not on the earth, but after they continued to press him, he gave them leave to search (2 Kgs. 2:17). After three days, the fifty men returned to Jericho, where Elisha was, and confirmed that the body of Elijah was nowhere to be found. Elisha reminded them that he had previously told them that they would not find his body (2 Kgs. 2:18).

More Mentoring Principles

Seven principles for guiding the mentee's relationship and attitudes towards his or her mentor were previously drawn from 1 Kings 19:19-20. Three more principles derived from the narrative in 2 Kings 2 are now added to the original list:

1. **The mentor must go for the mentee to grow.** There came a time when it was beneficial for Elisha and Elijah to part ways. As long as the mentor is available, there will be the tendency for the mentee to rely on him or her for solutions to their problems. Doing what a mentor says is easier than applying what one knows to be true to one's own life and learning through personal experience, which includes gleaning lessons from one's mistakes. Normally, children grow, mature, and eventually leave the safety of their parents' care

to marry and begin their own families, or pursue education or employment, or to engage in some ministry for the Lord. Just as the development of a local church can be hindered by a missionary or church-planter who stays there too long, the same is true of a close mentoring relationship. Paul instructed Timothy, *"And the things that you have heard from me among many witnesses, commit these to faithful men who will be able to teach others also"* (2 Tim. 2:2).

While a mentor may provide lifelong counsel to a mentee, their close mentoring interaction will be short-lived if it follows the biblical model. The most time Paul invested in teaching a particular group of believers was about three years at Ephesus; he normally only spent a few weeks or months at any one church. If new converts are properly cared for, it would not be unusual for many of them to be teaching others after a year or two. This expediency was certainly evident at places such as Philippi and Thessalonica. It is important for the mentee to become a mentor of others in order to pass along what he or she has learned. As the Lord Jesus taught, this is an important aspect of making disciples – teaching new believers all that the Lord taught His disciples (Matt. 28:20).

2. **Elisha wanted to go further than his mentor.** When given the opportunity to request a blessing from his master, Elisha requested a double portion of Elijah's spirit. What did Elisha desire from Elijah? I believe that his request relates directly to what the firstborn son received from his father under the Law. According to Deuteronomy 21:17, the firstborn son received a double portion of the family inheritance and became the rightful successor of the family. Elisha had become so identified with his master Elijah that he wanted Elijah to consider him as his son; he wanted to represent Elijah in his ministry and proceed with his God-given blessing and power to do so. Elijah had accomplished great things for God, but Elisha has a heart to do even more than his mentor.

   After Elijah went to heaven, Elisha picked up the cloak that had fallen from Elijah – Elisha desired to do the work of the Lord as Elijah's successor. His first statement after receiving the mantle reflects this truth: "*Where is the Lord God of Elijah?*" Elisha watched Elijah use the mantle previously to part the Jordan River, and he was determined to use it in the same manner and in Elijah's name. As a result the Jordan River parted and Elisha crossed over on dry land; by this miracle God endorsed Elisha as His new prophet. A record of Elisha's ministry confirms that he did receive a double portion of Elijah's spirit. Elijah did seven miracles during his ministry, one of which was restoring life to a dead boy. Elisha did fourteen miracles, two of which related to raising the dead back to life. The second resurrection occurred after a dead man was thrown on Elisha's bones in an impromptu burial by the pallbearers to avoid capture by an approaching enemy army.

3. **Elisha was not a clone of Elijah.** Elisha was called to a very different type of prophetic ministry than that in which Elijah had engaged. Elijah had confronted an apostate nation and pronounced divine judgments on Israel and its leadership. Conversely, Elisha would be a champion of the people. God would use him to perform acts of kindness and to bless the brokenhearted. Elisha was appointed to be a prophet of God, but he was not called to be an Elijah; God had given him a unique ministry. Yet, with this said, he carried within him the spirit of Elijah in doing the work of the Lord which he had been given to do. As mentors, we don't want to clone ourselves; rather, we want to see those we mentor go further than we have gone. We desire them to recognize, develop, and use their spiritual gift(s) to edify the body of Christ and serve others in His name. Success is being faithful to God's calling for your life, and is not related to how you compare to others or how much approval you get from them. Each believer is a unique creation of God and requires tender care and sincere respect to reach his or her full potential for Christ.

Elisha provides us with several good principles to follow in establishing and maintaining good mentoring relationships with others:

- Be faithful to what God has given you to do – God calls working people into His work.
- Maintain a right relationship with God-ordained authority.
- Respect the work of the Lord; it cannot be received without proper preparation.

- Desire to be mentored by mature believers.
- Assist those who are mentoring you to perform the work that God has given them to do.
- Encourage your mentor.
- Be willing to make personal sacrifices in order to be mentored.
- Pursue growth in order to mentor others; mentoring relationships are dynamic.
- Desire to do more for the Lord than what your mentor has done.
- Pursue the ministry God has given you; it is probably quite different than your mentor's.

Elisha's Second Miracle (2 Kgs. 2:19-22)

The leaders of Jericho came to Elisha to inform him that the city's water supply was bad and the surrounding ground was barren (2 Kgs. 2:19). Geological surveys have shown that certain springs in the region have come in contact with radioactive strata which can cause sterility.[67] It is possible that the unstable strata around Jericho had channeled radioactive material into the water supply, resulting in widespread ramification.

Elisha requested a new bowl filled with salt be brought to him (2 Kgs. 2:20). After he received the bowl of salt, Elisha went to the city's well, cast the salt into it, and said, *"Thus says the Lord: 'I have healed this water; from it there shall be no more death or barrenness.'"* (2 Kgs. 2:21). So the water in the well was healed that day and remained fresh afterwards (2 Kgs. 2:22). While this miracle appears to be in chronological order, the historian's record of Elisha's miracles is not necessarily so.

The new bowl represented Elisha as being God's new instrument to direct His affairs after Elijah's departure. Normally, adding salt to water renders it unusable for human consumption, but applying what was known to worsen water to make it better further heightened the spectacular nature of the miracle. This demonstration was to show Baal worshipers at Jericho that Baal, the supposed god of fertility, was a phony and that only Jehovah could remove their barrenness.

Elisha's Third Miracle (2 Kgs. 2:23-25)

Elisha's third miracle was in association with disrespect shown to his prophetic office. While ascending from Jericho to Bethel, several youths mocked him by saying, *"Go up, you baldhead! Go up, you baldhead!"* (2 Kgs. 2:23). It is possible that Elisha may have suffered from baldness, and the youths were mocking him because lepers, being forced to shave their heads, were socially scorned. Perhaps the youths were scoffing at the particular style in which the prophets were known to clip their hair. Another possibility was that these youths were Baal worshipers and were demeaning Elisha as God's prophet: "If you were truly a great prophet of Jehovah, you would be able to ascend up into heaven like Elijah did." The youths may have been mocking the idea of Elijah's ascension altogether.

Whatever the slur, the youths had shown disrespect to one of their elders and a prophet of Jehovah. A slur against God's representative is also an insult to Him. Accordingly, Elisha turned and pronounced a curse on them in the name of the Lord. Immediately, two female bears came out of the woods and mauled forty-two of these mocking young people (2 Kgs. 2:24). Elisha continued his journey westward to Mount Carmel and then returned to Samaria (2 Kgs. 2:25).

Meditation

God of the prophets, bless the prophets' sons;
Elijah's mantle over Elisha cast.
Each age its solemn task may claim but once;
Make each one nobler, stronger, than the last.

— Denis Wortman

The remains of great and good men, like Elijah's mantle, ought to be gathered up and preserved by their survivors; that as their works follow them in the reward of them, they may stay behind in their benefit.

— Matthew Henry

King Joram (Jehoram) of Israel

2 Kings 3

Moab's Rebellion

After Ahab's death, his son Jehoram became king of Israel in the eighteenth year of Jehoshaphat king of Judah (2 Kgs. 3:1). He reigned from Samaria for twelve years (852-841 B.C.) and did evil in the sight of the Lord, but not to the extent of his wicked parents or brother (2 Kgs. 3:2). Although still promoting idolatry in Israel, Jehoram did *"put away the sacred pillar of Baal that his father had made"* (1 Kgs. 3:2). None of Israel's kings led the Northern Kingdom back into the Levitical worship of Jehovah at Jerusalem, but there were some that were less evil than others. Joram and later Jehu and Hoshea would be examples of such kings.

Moab had been sending 100,000 lambs and the wool of 100,000 rams in annual tribute to Israel, but Mesha, the king of Moab, rebelled against Israel after Ahab's death (2 Kgs. 3:4-5). Jehoram rallied Israel's forces and sought permission from Jehoshaphat to travel through Judah, as he wanted to encircle the Dead Sea and attack Moab from the south, instead of the expected, shorter, eastern route. Jehoshaphat not only granted Jehoram's request but also agreed to accompany and to assist the king in suppressing Moab's rebellion (2 Kgs. 3:6). Jehoshaphat said, *"I will go up; I am as you are, my people as your people, my horses as your horses"* (2 Kgs. 3:7). The king of Judah's response to Jehoram is baffling, given that the Lord had spared his life after he united with wicked Ahab in a battle God had not endorsed and then was rebuked by the prophet Hanani for his alliance with Ahab, *"Should you help the wicked, and love them who hate the Lord?"* (2 Chron. 19:2). Jehoshaphat was a godly king, but he was prone to unnatural unions with those who opposed the Lord.

Jehoshaphat inquired as to the battle plan, and was told that they should assemble their combined forces by way of the Wilderness of Edom. Edom was under Judah's control at this time, so forces from Edom, whose land they would be traversing to reach Moab from the south, joined the armies of Judah and Israel. As planned, all three armies merged and marched together seven days en route to Moab, but they ran out of water somewhere on the eastern side of the Dead Sea (2 Kgs. 3:9). The situation was desperate and Jehoram bemoaned that the Lord was delivering their forces into the hands of the Moabites by withholding water from them (2 Kgs. 3:10).

Jehoshaphat inquired if there was a prophet of Jehovah to consult. As a loyal Jehovah-worshiper, Jehoshaphat had wrongly taken up company with the children of the devil in an activity that God had not endorsed. In His fathomless goodness, the Lord then sent a distressing trial to awaken His man to that very fact and to bring out the true life that was within him. Having put the operations of the flesh aside, Jehoshaphat now has a renewed spiritual focus to his thinking – he wants to know the mind of the Lord. Indeed, *"the Lord knows how to deliver the godly out of temptations and to reserve the unjust under punishment for the day of judgment"* (2 Pet. 2:9). What a comfort God's faithfulness is to all believers: *"If we are faithless, He remains faithful; He cannot deny Himself"* (2 Tim. 2:13).

In response to Jehoshaphat's inquiry, one of Jehoram's servants said, *"Elisha the son of Shaphat is here, who poured water on the hands of Elijah"* (2 Kgs. 3:11). Given Elisha's forthcoming response, it is doubtful that he was traveling with the three armies, but rather, the Lord had directed him to a nearby location so that he would be available when summoned. Jehoshaphat affirmed that the Lord spoke through Elisha and his counsel should be sought (2 Kgs. 3:12). The kings of Judah, Israel, and Edom then journeyed an unknown distance to speak to Elisha and receive direction from the Lord.

Elisha's Fourth Miracle – Water and Blood (2 Kgs. 3:13-27)

Elisha initially shunned and censured the king of Israel, suggesting that he should seek counsel from the pagan prophets of his parents (2 Kgs. 3:13). Jehoram responded to Elisha's terse statement by accusing Jehovah of apparently giving Moab victory over their combined forces. Not put off by Jehoram's blame-shifting, Elisha again snubs him, but does agree to seek the Lord on their behalf only because Jehoshaphat was among them, *"As the Lord of hosts lives, before whom I stand, surely were it not that I regard the presence of Jehoshaphat king of*

Judah, I would not look at you, nor see you" (2 Kgs. 3:14). But being hindered from prophesying, Elisha requested a musician be brought before him (2 Kgs. 3:15).

We might think that this prophetic block was caused by the presence of two evil kings, but that had never hindered a prophet from delivering God's message previously. We must then assume that the Spirit of God in Elisha was grieved, not by the presence of two wicked kings, but because a godly king was in their company. What a rebuke to Jehoshaphat! What a warning to us too – our carnal behavior can actually hinder the Holy Spirit from using others we labor with from serving the Lord! Let us never think that secret sin affects only the guilty party. Sin amongst God's people injures the local church and the body life of the Church.

A musician was summoned, and while he played calming music, the word of the Lord came to Elisha. The prophet then informed the three kings what they should do if they wanted to survive and to achieve victory over the Moabites:

> *"Make this valley full of ditches." For thus says the Lord: "You shall not see wind, nor shall you see rain; yet that valley shall be filled with water, so that you, your cattle, and your animals may drink." And this is a simple matter in the sight of the Lord; He will also deliver the Moabites into your hand. Also you shall attack every fortified city and every choice city, and shall cut down every good tree, and stop up every spring of water, and ruin every good piece of land with stones* (2 Kgs. 3:16-19).

The armies of Judah, Israel, and Edom would be delivered from their thirst and from the Moabites, if they acted in faith to God's word as declared by Elisha. The ditches were dug to retain the water that God would soon provide (i.e., to collect some of the water before it flowed out of the valley). The next morning, a sudden rush of water came by the way of Edom, and filled the ditches they had dug with water (2 Kgs. 3:20).

After learning of the three armies coming to war with them, the Moabites gathered all their forces (including those normally considered too old to fight) at their border to defend Moab (2 Kgs. 3:21). As the sun rose the next morning the red glare of the sunlit sky reflecting off the pools of water caused the Moabites to think that the armies had slaughtered each other in the night and the valley before them was full of blood (2 Kgs. 3:22). They knew that the valley was dry, so what else could cause a red reflection, but blood?

Believing that their supposed invaders were all dead, the Moabites rushed into the open to despoil their lifeless bodies (2 Kgs. 3:23). But the illusion had been permitted by the Lord so that Judah, Israel, and Edom would be able to attack an unsuspecting and unprepared Moabite army. In order to carry away the most plunder, the Moabites may have entered their enemies' encampments without their weapons, shields, and armor.

The Moabites suffered a great slaughter as they retreated into Moab with the allies hotly pursuing and destroying their cities along the way. The attackers filled farmland with debris from the conquered cities, plugged wells and springs, and also cut down good trees to make Moab desolate (2 Kgs. 3:24-25). With slingers pounding Kir Haraseth, the king of Moab realized he could not withstand the attack. He gathered 700 swordsmen and tried to punch through Edom's lines (thinking that Edom was the weakest of the three armies), but his escape attempt failed (2 Kgs. 3:26). The Moabite king retreated into the city, and offered his oldest son (who was to be the next king of Moab) on the city's wall as a burnt offering to Chemosh.

The sight of a human sacrifice unnerved the Israelites, who immediately ceased hostilities and retreated back to their homeland (2 Kgs. 3:27). The expression that there *"was great indignation against Israel"* is not explained. Since God had enabled the three armies to attack Moab by performing a miracle, it seems doubtful that this statement refers to the Lord's anger. Rather, Judah was probably angry with Israel for pressing their vengeance against Moab beyond reason, thus prompting the king to offer his son to his god in a last-ditch effort to save himself. Human sacrifices were an abomination to any God-fearing Israelite, and clearly the Lord used the appalling event to smite the consciences of His people: If you are deeply convicted by Mesha's pagan act, why not be shocked by your own idolatry?

Interestingly, after the hostilities were ended, Mesha wrote the record of this battle on the Moabite Stone and praised his god for delivering him from Israel. Though clearly defeated, the Moabite king had survived the attack and Kir Hareseth had not been captured; therefore, Mesha praised Chemosh for the deliverance.

The Moabite Stone, which dates back to 850 B.C., was discovered by a German missionary in 1868 at Dibon, Jordan. This four-foot-high by two-foot-wide basalt monument documents Moabite attacks on Israel, as recorded in 2 Kings 1 and 3. Mesha was the king of the Moabites who was forced to pay tribute to Israel. The Bible states that the Moabite tribute suddenly stopped; *"Mesha, king of Moab, rebelled against the king of Israel..."* (2 Kgs. 3:5). Mesha's account of his rebellion against Israel is found on this large stone. Prior to this finding, the existence of the Moabite people had not been confirmed through archeological evidence.[68] Today, there are over 150,000 archeological records, such as the Moabite Stone, substantiating the historicity of the Old Testament!

This story reminds us that God will always send the water if we will be faithful to dig ditches when He commands. There is not much glamor in forcing our shovels into hard, dry ground or throwing dirt from one place to another, but obedience, especially in what seems mundane or unreasonable, demonstrates the kind of faith that God honors. God used a small thing like digging a ditch to demonstrate His great power to the soldiers of Israel and Edom, who did not respect Him. We should not expect God to do great things in our lives if we are not willing to be faithful in the little things, such as shoveling a little dirt when asked to! To dig a ditch in the valley of shadows shows our faith in God's coming provision.

Meditation

> If we cannot believe God when circumstances seem to be against us, we do not believe Him at all.
>
> — Charles Spurgeon

Elisha's Prophetic Ministry – Four More Miracles

2 Kings 4

Second Kings 4 through 8 focus our attention on the prophetic ministry of Elisha rather than on the reign of any particular king.

Elisha's Fifth Miracle – the Widow's Oil (2 Kgs. 4:1-7)

A widow of one of the sons of the prophets informed Elisha that a creditor planned to take her two sons into slavery until her debt was paid off (2 Kgs. 4:1). Proving herself to be a woman of faith, she brought her dire situation to the attention of Jehovah's chief prophet. The location of this story is unrevealed, but it is likely that the widow lived in or near one of the cities associated with the schools of the prophets (i.e., Bethel, Gilgal, or Jericho).

The Lord's compassion on this woman, the former wife of one of His prophets, is touching. Elisha asked what she would like him to do about it and also what assets she still retained in the house (2 Kgs. 4:2). She told the prophet that all she had in the house was a jar of oil. Elisha told her to borrow as many empty vessels from her neighbors as she could and bring them into her house; then she was to shut the door behind her and her sons (2 Kgs. 4:3-4).

The widow did what Elisha told her to do. After closing the door, she poured from her jar of oil and filled all the containers that she had brought into the house and then the supply of oil ceased (2 Kgs. 4:5-6). As instructed by Elisha, the widow then sold the oil and paid off the creditor who was threatening to enslave her sons (2 Kgs. 4:7). J. G. Bellett observes two practical applications from this story:

> First, as long as the poor widow produced her vessels, the pot produced its oil. The oil waited on the vessels. Vessels were the measure of the oil. In other words, divine power waited on faith – faith measured the active resources of God on the occasion. Second, the prophet said, *"What do you have in the house?"* Jesus afterward

> said to His disciples, *"How many loaves have you?"* or, as he said to Moses, *"What is that in your hand?"* For it is suitable that whatever we have should be put to use. It may be quite unequal to the necessity; but whatever it be, it should be occupied. It may be but a shepherd's staff, and Israel to be redeemed; it may be but a pot of oil, and the creditor, who has a right to sell children and all, has to be paid; it may be but five loaves, and five thousand hungry ones have to be fed. But still, let what there is be available for God's use.[69]

The magnitude of this miracle depended on the widow's faithfulness to use what she had and to borrow vessels from others. The more she gathered, the greater God's blessing would be. Little in our hands is immeasurable in God's. At Calvary, the blessed Savior was stripped of all he had and nailed to a tree. All that was available to Him was the nails in His feet and hands, so He used those to accomplish that most tremendous feat humanity would ever witness, God's incarnate Son bearing the weight of the world's sin. God is able to use the most insignificant things to accomplish immense good.

If the widow chose to gather many common vessels, she would not only escape her debts, but also have adequate means to care for her sons afterwards. We often do not experience God's greatness because we think too little of Him; we decline to ask Him for great things.

Napoleon's army fought hard to secure a certain island in the Mediterranean Sea. During a victory celebration for his chief of staff a young lieutenant boldly approached the emperor and saluted him. Napoleon asked him what he wanted, and the lieutenant replied, "Give me this island; it is my boyhood home." This seemed to everyone else a ludicrous request, for many men had lost their lives in gaining the victory; yet, without hesitation Napoleon deeded the island to the lieutenant. When Napoleon was asked later why he had done such a thing, he replied, "He honored me by the magnitude of his request."[70] Likewise, the magnitude of our prayer requests indicate just how big we believe our God to be.

While the inheritance of all believers is in Christ in heavenly places, each believer must labor to possess what divine providence agrees to confer. The Lord desires us to ask Him for our portion that we might obtain abundant grace. Hence, we read of the Lord Jesus exhorting His disciples to petition His Father in His name for that which is lacking or needful:

Ask, and it will be given to you; seek, and you will find; knock, and it will be opened to you. For everyone who asks receives, and he who seeks finds, and to him who knocks it will be opened (Matt. 7:7-9).

Therefore I say to you, whatever things you ask when you pray, believe that you receive them, and you will have them (Mark 11:24).

Most assuredly, I say to you, whatever you ask the Father in My name He will give you. Until now you have asked nothing in My name. Ask, and you will receive, that your joy may be full (John 16:23-24).

Years later, James informed carnal believers that they lacked essential spiritual resources because they failed to pray: *"Yet you do not have because you do not ask"* (Jas. 4:2). The Lord's liberality eagerly anticipates our righteous prayers! If we thirst for the abundant springs of heavenly life, we shall find them inexhaustible where we sojourn now, for *"He satisfies the longing soul"* (Ps. 107:9).

Elisha's Sixth Miracle – The Resurrection of the Shunammite's Son (2 Kgs. 4:8-37)

The narrative now shifts to circumstances occurring in the city of Shunem located about five miles south of the Hill of Moreh in the Jezreel Valley. This is where the Philistines had gathered to fight King Saul, whose army was assembled at Mount Gilboa (1 Sam. 28:4). Saul and three of his four sons died on Gilboa in that confrontation.

A notable and spiritually-minded woman at Shunem offered Elisha an open invitation to eat at her house any time he was in the area (2 Kgs. 4:8). Elisha must have regularly taken advantage of her hospitality, for she suggested to her husband that they create a small, upper room on the wall of their home for the prophet when he was passing through (2 Kgs. 4:9). This was accomplished.

The furnishings of the prophet's chamber show that the woman understood the modest lifestyle a humble servant of the Lord preferred. The prophet's chamber was small and contained no lavish items. Only the essential items of a bed, a table, a chair, and a lampstand were in the room (2 Kgs. 4:10).

On one particular visit, Elisha asked his servant Gehazi to express his appreciation for her care of them, and also to ask what he might do for her in return (2 Kgs. 4:11-12). Perhaps Elisha thought the woman would be more likely to share her needs with his servant than with himself. The well-known prophet was prepared to speak to the king or the commander of the army on her behalf, but she responded that she enjoyed a peaceful life among her people (2 Kgs. 4:13).

Gehazi reported the matter to Elisha, who then inquired of his servant, *"What then is to be done for her?"* Gehazi answered, *"Actually, she has no son, and her husband is old"* (2 Kgs. 4:14). Immediately, it was revealed to the prophet what the Shunammite woman's most secret desire was – to have a child of her own. By her earlier response, she clearly thought the matter was impossible, and for that reason, probably never mentioned her deep longing to anyone else. But the Lord knew all about it. Because she was a pious woman, she was willing to accept the circumstances that God's providence had placed her in and bear such emptiness in faith. She believed that her God was a good God who does good in the way He knows is best. God rewards faith that rests in His character and attributes, even when it seems unreasonable to do so. This is why Paul exhorted believers to *"rejoice always, pray without ceasing, in everything give thanks; for this is the will of God in Christ Jesus for you"* (1 Thess. 5:16-18).

After Elisha heard that the woman had no son, he summoned her (2 Kgs. 4:15). When she arrived at the prophet's chamber, Elisha said, *"About this time next year you shall embrace a son"* (2 Kgs. 4:16). Culturally speaking, Hebrew women viewed childbearing as an expression of God's approval and barrenness a mark of His disfavor. Consequently, married Hebrew women with children were esteemed and barren women were scorned (e.g., Rachel and Hannah). So while the Shunammite woman would have been delighted by the news, she did not believe the matter possible and was therefore guarded in her response. Perhaps Elisha was merely jesting with her; the woman did not want to get her hopes up only to be disappointed again. However, she did conceive and delivered a son at the appointed time, just as the prophet predicted (2 Kgs. 4:17).

Several years later when the child went out to see his father who was reaping with others, he complained of a severe headache (2 Kgs. 4:18). The father instructed one of his servants to carry the lad back to his mother (2 Kgs. 4:19). His wife sat the boy on her knees and held him until he died at noontime (2 Kgs. 4:20). She carried the child upstairs and laid him on Elisha's bed and then left the prophet's chamber, closing the door behind her (2 Kgs. 4:21).

The woman then asked her husband for a donkey to ride on and a servant to accompany her to find Elisha and bring him back to their home (2 Kgs. 4:22). Apparently, she did not tell her husband that their son had died, because he did not understand why she would be seeking the prophet when it was not a religious day, such as a New Moon or a Sabbath (2 Kgs. 4:23). She probably feared that her husband would not let her go if he knew their only son was dead.

The previous narrative has shown that all the spiritual initiation in this family has come through the Shunammite woman, not her husband. His response to his wife's request is not characteristic of a man of faith, but of a member of formalized religion: "Why would you seek God's prophet other than a day that was on the religious calendar?" Many in Christendom today would not consider any religious activity appropriate other than attending a Sunday morning formality or perhaps celebrating some supposedly important Christian holiday. However, the Church is the spiritual body of Christ and is to be a living expression of His life each and every day within those who are His.

The woman told the servant with her to drive on hard and not to worry about her comfort unless she said otherwise – she needed to find Elisha as soon as possible (2 Kgs. 4:24). Elisha was at Mount Carmel, which was about a twenty-mile journey west of Shunam (or Shunem). When Elisha saw the Shunammite woman coming to meet them, he commanded Gehazi to run and meet her to determine if her household was well (2 Kgs. 4:25-26). To preclude any delay in expressing her need to Elisha, she declined to tell Gehazi her plight, simply answering him, "It is well." However, when she came to Elisha she fell to the ground and grasped his feet. Gehazi was going to push the woman away from his master, but Elisha said to Gehazi, *"Let her alone; for her soul is in deep distress, and the Lord has hidden it from me, and has not told me"* (2 Kgs. 4:27).

The woman reminded him that giving her a son was his idea. She had not requested a child and she had also asked not to be deceived in the matter (2 Kgs. 4:28). She was implying that Elisha had fooled her by giving her a son, but only for a short time. Time was critical, so Elisha told Gehazi to quickly journey to the Shunammite's home without any distractions and lay his staff on the face of the boy; he and the mother would arrive afterwards (2 Kgs. 4:29-30).

Gehazi did as Elisha commanded, but the child did not revive after placing the prophet's staff on the child. So he returned to his master to give the report (2 Kgs. 4:31). While the staff was a symbol of the prophet's authority, God would not use it to revive the child. His people, immersed as they were in a pagan culture, would have then viewed the prophet's staff as magical, rather than ascribing the miracle to Jehovah.

Elisha, already knowing this, wanted to teach the Shunammite woman, who had placed much dependence upon him, to learn to rely on the Lord alone. By sending his servant ahead with his staff to place on the child, he had raised her expectations, but at the same time taught her that he also had to fully rely on the Lord.

After seeing the dead child on his bed, Elisha closed the door to the chamber behind him and Gehazi (2 Kgs. 4:32-33). By this time, the boy had likely been dead for two days. No doubt Elisha had tender thoughts towards this lad, for he was God's answer to his prayers and he would have been pleased to watch the boy grow and to delight his mother's heart. After praying to the Lord, the prophet stretched out his body over the lad's body – face to face and hand to hand (2 Kgs. 4:34). Although this action warmed the boy's body, he did not revive. After walking back and forth in the house (likely while pleading with the Lord in prayer), the prophet returned to again stretch himself over the boy's body (2 Kgs. 4:35). The child then sneezed seven times and opened his eyes. Elisha instructed Gehazi to summon the Shunammite woman, *"so he called her"* (2 Kgs. 4:36). H. L. Rossier reviews how this woman's faith responded to all three calls of the prophet in this chapter:

> How the Shunammite must have been moved at this new call! The first time (v. 12) the prophet had called her to prove the precious faith that she possessed; the second time (v. 15) to give her the child of promise, an object for her heart. The third time – what would he give her when mourning was filling her soul? Ah! She does not doubt; he would give her her son, clothed in an entirely new character: her resurrected son. Oh, joy that cannot be expressed in words! Her heart is too full to express itself; she bows herself silently and worships God![71]

After arriving, Elisha told her to *"pick up your son."* But seeing her son alive, she first fell at his feet to express her gratitude, then she lifted up her son and departed from the chamber (2 Kgs. 4:37).

Elisha's Seventh Miracle – Purifies a Pot of Stew (2 Kgs. 4:38-41)

Elisha returned to the school of the prophets at Gilgal during a time of famine. He commanded that a large pot of stew be provided for the sons of the prophets. Food was scarce, so various herbs and wild gourds were gleaned from nearby fields and added to the pot. Unbeknown to the cooks, some of the gourds were poisonous. Jamieson, Fausset, and Brown suppose the culprit to be colocynth, whose leaves, stems, and cucumber-like fruit resemble that of a wild vine. The "gourds," or fruit, are of the color and size of an orange, bitter to the taste, causing colic, and exciting the nerves; largely eaten, they could cause such a derangement of the stomach and bowels as to result in death.[72]

The stew was served, but upon eating it the men cried out, *"Man of God, there is death in the pot!"* (2 Kgs. 4:40). The context of the narrative indicates that the stew was harmful to eat. There should have been life in the pot, but instead there was death. But Elisha had a solution; he asked for some flour to be brought, which he added to the pot to purify its contents. He then commanded that it be served to the sons of the prophets and no one suffered any ill effects after eating it. Thomas L. Constable explains the miracle's meaning:

> In Elisha's day a spiritual famine had resulted from the people's turning from God and His law. The people were hungry spiritually. In an effort to satisfy need, they had imbibed a false religion called Baalism. It looked harmless enough but proved disgusting and deadly. God's prophets helped counteract the deadly effects of Baalism in Israel.[73]

Given this understanding of the miracle's spiritual significance, C. A. Coates applies the same truth for those in the Church Age:

> I believe the ministry of the Spirit during the last century has been largely a casting of meal into the pot. I have no doubt that the Lord is by the Spirit bringing in what will counteract the working of what is wrong. I believe the meal is the truth as ministered by the Spirit in contrast with what has been ministered by the mind of man. There is divine substance in it which is corrective. It is not exactly emptying the pot and starting afresh, but the Spirit giving a divine setting forth

of the truth to correct a merely natural apprehension of it. All that we know of divine things we have either taken up by the Spirit or in our natural minds; there is no vital power in the latter.[74]

Only God can displace death (i.e., that which is apart from Him) with life (which is in Him alone). Previously Elisha cast salt into the toxic well at Jericho to accomplish the same purification that the flour worked in the poisonous stew in this chapter. Moses cast a tree into the bitter waters at Marah so the Israelites could drink and not perish in the wilderness. The salt, the flour, and the tree all picture what the Lord Jesus Christ did to offer us eternal life in place of death. He cast Himself into death, so that those who would partake of Him would receive life:

Then Jesus said to them, "Most assuredly, I say to you, Moses did not give you the bread from heaven, but My Father gives you the true bread from heaven. For the bread of God is He who comes down from heaven and gives life to the world." ... "I am the bread of life. He who comes to Me shall never hunger, and he who believes in Me shall never thirst." ... "And this is the will of Him who sent Me, that everyone who sees the Son and believes in Him may have everlasting life; and I will raise him up at the last day" (John 6:32-35, 40).

Like the sons of the prophets, our first parents gathered up for themselves wild fruit with deadly repercussions. Because they ate it, death intruded into God's creation and all humanity died in Adam (Rom. 5:12). The good news is that the Lord Jesus Christ experienced the death we deserved so we can experience His life. Praise be to God!

Elisha's Eighth Miracle – Feeds One Hundred Men (2 Kgs. 4:42-44)

A man from Baal Shalisha brought Elisha the firstfruits of his harvest – twenty loaves of barley bread and a sack of newly ripened grain. Elisha commanded that it be given to the people to eat, but his servant scoffed at the idea of placing such a small provision before a hundred hungry men. But Elisha insisted, saying that everyone would eat and there would be some food left over. So the bread was set before the people, they ate as much as they desired, and there was bread remaining, just as the prophet had foretold.

The Lord Jesus did a similar miracle twice. First, He fed about 20,000 people by multiplying a boy's sack lunch of two fish and five loaves. Second, He likely fed over 15,000 people with a few small fishes and seven loaves, and yet there were many baskets of food remaining after both miracles (Matt. 14:17-21, 15:32-38).

Elisha's miracles demonstrated that though Baal was supposedly "the lord of the earth," it was Jehovah alone who controlled earth's resources and could multiply such resources to bless His people. Likewise, when believers share with others and leave the implications with God, He is able to bless our generosity and cause us to flourish:

> *There is one who scatters, yet increases more; and there is one who withholds more than is right, but it leads to poverty. The generous soul will be made rich, and he who waters will also be watered himself* (Prov. 11:24-25).

> *Cast your bread upon the waters, for you will find it after many days* (Eccl. 11:1).

Because Jehovah controls all things, He alone is able to satisfy all our needs, even after we have been His instrument to bless others. The more God enables us to help others, the more we will be blessed.

Meditation

Thou art coming to a king, large petitions with thee bring,
For His grace and power are such, none can ever ask too much!

— John Newton

Elisha's Prophetic Ministry – Naaman's Leprosy

2 Kings 5

Elisha's Ninth Miracle – Naaman Healed of Leprosy (2 Kgs. 5:1-19)

We are now introduced to Naaman, a powerful and honorable commander in the Syrian army who had an incurable case of leprosy (2 Kgs. 5:1-2). A young Israelite girl had been captured during a Syrian raid into Israel and was now serving Naaman's wife (2 Kgs. 5:3). The maiden must have been treated well, for she wanted to help her master. She told her mistress that there was a great prophet in Samaria (Elisha) who could heal her husband's leprosy, that is, if he would seek his help (2 Kgs. 5:4). This was quite a statement of faith in Jehovah and His prophet, as there had never been a leper healed by any prophet previously – a fact that the Lord Jesus confirmed (Luke 4:27). D. L. Moody observes:

> A little maid said a few words that made a commotion in two kingdoms. God honored her faith by doing for Naaman, the idolater, what he had not done for any in Israel (Luke 4:27). How often has the finger of childhood pointed grown-up persons in the right direction. The maid boasted of God that He would do for Naaman what He had not done for any in Israel, and God honored her faith.[75]

The servant's girl's claim was reported to Naaman, who then received his king's permission to go to Samaria to see if it were true. The king of Syria wrote a letter to the king of Israel asking him to assist his trusted servant's quest for healing.

Naaman left Syria with ten talents of silver, 6,000 shekels of gold, and ten changes of clothing (2 Kgs. 5:5). He delivered the king of Syria's letter to the king of Israel, but, after reading it, the king tore his clothes and said, *"Am I God, to kill and make alive, that this man sends a man to me to heal him of his leprosy? Therefore please consider, and see how he seeks a quarrel with me"* (2 Kgs. 5:6-7). Clearly there was no power to heal Naaman among the idolaters at the palace. After hearing that the king had torn his clothes over the situation, Elisha sent a message to the king: *"Why have you torn your clothes? Please let him come to me, and he shall know that there is a prophet in Israel!"* (2 Kgs. 5:8).

The king of Israel sent Naaman to Elisha. The Syrian commander arrived at the prophet's house in his chariot and then stood at his front door (2 Kgs. 5:9). Elisha did not come to the door to meet Naaman, but rather sent a messenger to him, who instructed him to *"go and wash in the Jordan seven times, and your flesh shall be restored to you, and you shall be clean"* (2 Kgs. 5:10). Naaman was furious that he had come so far and that the prophet did not want to meet him and wave his hand over him while calling on Jehovah, his God (2 Kgs. 5:11). Furthermore, he reasoned that the rivers Abanah and Pharpar in Damascus were better than any river in Israel. Could he not have washed in them instead of traveling such a long distance to bathe in the inferior Jordan River (2 Kgs. 5:12)?

It seems likely that Elisha was with the sons of the prophets at Jericho at this time, which meant the Jordan River was nearby. Given the distance Naaman had already traveled, going to the Jordan to bathe would be at most a brief inconvenience. Regardless, Naaman departed the prophet's house enraged. Not only did the commander suffer from the ailment of leprosy, he also was infected with the deadly disease of pride. God would prove that He was able to deal with both of Naaman's debilitating conditions.

Thankfully, Naaman's loyal servants reminded him that if the prophet had asked him to do something great to be healed he would have done it; consequently, washing seven times in a small river should not infuriate him if he wanted to be healed (2 Kgs. 5:13). Naaman heeded this counsel and washed himself seven times in the Jordan River. His flesh was not only healed but restored to child-like smoothness (2 Kgs. 5:14). *Seven* is the number of completion in Scripture and thus washing seven times typified the complete healing of Naaman that God would accomplish in response to his faith. The commander's skin condition was better than anything he could have imagined – it was a perfect healing indeed! Naaman swallowed his pride and God took away his leprosy.

A now contrite Naaman, with his servants, returned to Elisha's house to give him a gift, but the prophet refused to accept it (2 Kgs. 5:15-16). Elisha had not performed the miracle for a reward, but in obedience to God's word, therefore he would not profit from what God had done. If Elisha had taken a reward for what only God could accomplish, it would have lessened what Naaman needed to understand about spiritual cleansing – God's grace cannot be purchased or earned; it is a gift received through faith (Eph. 2:8-9). The purpose of the miracle was to introduce Naaman to the only One who could meet his need and make him whole again, Jehovah. Naaman then confessed that Israel's God was now his God!

Leprosy was a general term for various skin diseases, including the most prominent and feared, Hansen's disease. Leviticus 13 identifies two main types of leprosy that infected people: leprosy of the flesh and leprosy of the head. Spiritually speaking, these relate to two classes of deadly sins. Leprosy of the flesh refers to fleshly lusts and includes gluttony, drunkenness, fornication, lasciviousness, etc. Leprosy of the head speaks of lusting in the mind which results in pride, unbelief, arrogance, envy, humanism, etc.

There are two biblical examples of proud individuals whom God smote with leprosy. The first was Miriam, the sister of Moses, who with Aaron spoke against her brother, God's chosen leader for the people (Num. 12:1-4). Because Aaron was the high priest, he was spared judgment, as that would have cut off the nation from Jehovah, but Miriam was punished with leprosy and was unclean with the disease for seven days (Num. 12:9-11). Because Aaron quickly recognized the leprosy in his sister, even though she was veiled, it is likely that the disease appeared on her face, thus representing the sin of pride.

Besides Miriam, King Uzziah was also struck in the head with leprosy because of his pride (2 Chron. 26:16-21). When King Uzziah served the Lord obediently, he was blessed. Yet, when he went his own way, God humbled him. God demonstrated His hatred of pride by judging both Miriam and King Uzziah with leprosy on the head. They were struck with a deadly disease that had no cure at that time. In mercy, God healed a humbled Miriam, but King Uzziah died proud and leprous.

Similarly, those spiritually dying of the deadly disease of sin can be healed only by God. Since no price can be put on the shed blood of

Christ which makes cleansing and forgiveness possible, God extends the offer of healing without cost to those who submit themselves to Him. Salvation is a gift of God and must be received by faith in His word (Rom. 10:9-10). This is why Elisha would not receive any compensation for a work that only God could do.

The commander then told Elisha that he would no longer offer personal burnt offerings and sacrifices to other gods, but only to the Lord. To demonstrate his change of heart, he desired that two mules be loaded with earth from Israel so that after he returned to Syria, he could erect an altar to honor Jehovah (2 Kgs. 5:17). Naaman's polytheistic thinking was that no god could be worshipped but in his own land; therefore, Naaman wanted to bring some Israel back with him – so he could worship Jehovah, the God of Israel. Of course, this was all superstitious hogwash, but it demonstrated the sincerity of his new faith (though he obviously still lacked understanding). Only a sincere heart would be willing to transport several bags of soil all the way back to Syria.

Naaman did foresee a difficulty, though, once he returned to Syria: how could he honor Jehovah when in the presence of his king who revered pagan deities? Therefore, he asked Elisha to forgive him when he had to accompany his master into the temple of Rimmon and bow down with his king in the temple (2 Kgs. 5:18). Elisha neither approved nor disapproved of Naaman's proposal, but rather sent him away in peace (2 Kgs. 5:19). The commander then began the long journey home with his servants and with a story of his healing that would spread Jehovah's fame throughout Syria.

God's grace had been wonderfully experienced by an unclean Gentile outside the covenant promises of God with Israel, because he demonstrated faith in the message of healing announced by Israel's God. Paul acknowledges this same situation existed between Jew and Gentile at the time of Christ's first advent (Eph. 2:11-12). But then the apostle explains how unclean Gentiles in the Church Age can be cleansed and blessed by Israel's God:

> *If indeed you have heard of the dispensation of the grace of God which was given to me for you ... that the Gentiles should be fellow heirs, of the same body, and partakers of His promise in Christ through the gospel, of which I became a minister according to the gift*

> *of the grace of God given to me by the effective working of His power* (Eph. 3:2-7).

Every Gentile today who suffers from the deadly disease of sin experiences the same type of cleansing and healing that Naaman did when he or she trusts in the gospel message of Jesus Christ. All such cleansed lepers are brought into the Body of Christ, where Jew and Gentile alike enjoy all the rich blessings promised to Abraham long ago – forever!

Elisha's Tenth Miracle and Gehazi's Greed (2 Kgs. 5:20-27)

Elisha's servant Gehazi did not understand why his master had not received anything from the man wanting to show his gratitude for being healed (2 Kgs. 5:20). Eager to profit from the situation before Naaman got too far away and the opportunity would be lost, Gehazi decided to run after him. Noticing Gehazi in pursuit, Naaman halted and got down from his chariot to ask Elisha's servant if all was well (2 Kgs. 5:21). Gehazi then spun his yarn, *"All is well. My master has sent me, saying, 'Indeed, just now two young men of the sons of the prophets have come to me from the mountains of Ephraim. Please give them a talent of silver and two changes of garments"* (2 Kgs. 5:22).

Naaman was more than happy to oblige, but pressed Gehazi to take two talents of silver and two changes of garments (2 Kgs. 5:23). This sounded good to Gehazi. Naaman then sent two of his servants to carry the silver and the garments back to the citadel they had just departed. Gehazi then took the articles and hid them in the house and released the men to return to Naaman (2 Kgs. 5:24).

Believing his entire enterprise had been covert, Gehazi went in feigning innocence and stood before his master (2 Kgs. 5:25). Elisha then asked him, *"Where did you go, Gehazi?"* But Gehazi lied to cover up his sin, *"Your servant did not go anywhere."* Elisha then revealed the subterfuge and pronounced judgment on his servant:

> *Did not my heart go with you when the man turned back from his chariot to meet you? Is it time to receive money and to receive clothing, olive groves and vineyards, sheep and oxen, male and female servants? Therefore the leprosy of Naaman shall cling to you and your descendants forever* (2 Kgs. 5:26-27).

Notice that Elisha does not rebuke Gehazi for his falsehoods to Naaman or to himself. The weightier offense was of a spiritual nature, not a moral one. Elisha's rebuke therefore centered on the question, "Is it time to receive money?" Since God had just taught Naaman about salvation being solely by His grace, was it the proper time to take his money and confuse God's message of obtaining life? MacDonald writes: "Gehazi had sinned greatly in giving the Syrians occasion to think that God's free gift of grace was not free at all."[76]

Furthermore, many false prophets were fleecing their countrymen of their money with empty messages and under false pretenses, but a true servant of God should never be motivated by personal greed, but rather by God's glory. Those who honor the Lord will be cared for by the One who controls everyone's purse, but those who do not will be punished. Was it time to behave like the false prophet who desired personal gain and not God's honor? No. It was for this same reason that Paul did not take anything from the Corinthians while He was preaching the gospel to them. The apostle did not want them to question his motives or think that God's salvation through Christ could be purchased (2 Cor. 11:7-15).

In retribution for Gehazi's abominable deed, his skin immediately turned as white as snow and he went out from his master's presence leprous. Not only would he be unclean the remainder of his life, but leprosy would perpetually cling to his descendants also. This meant that Gehazi must have already been married and had children, as he would not be able to marry and have children as a leper. Not only had he brought terrible judgment on himself and his family, but he was now disqualified from serving the Lord as Elisha's helper.

Because of his privileged ministry, he had witnessed God's power and authority in ways others had not. In God's economy, higher responsibility also results in higher accountability. The more God entrusts us with, the greater the consequences if we neglect what is important to Him. No doubt for years to come, Gehazi deeply regretted that moment when greed caused him to undermine God's word.

Yielding to just one carnal whim can ruin a lifetime of good testimony. Let us count the cost ahead of time – a few temporal trifles or moments of passion are not worth the long and hard consequences that follow: *"Do not be deceived, God is not mocked; for whatever a man sows, that he will also reap. For he who sows to his flesh will of the flesh reap corruption, but he who sows to the Spirit will of the Spirit reap everlasting life"* (Gal. 6:7-8).

Meditation

It ill becomes the servant to seek to be rich, and great, and honored in that world where his Lord was poor, and mean, and despised.

— George Mueller

That which is won ill, will never wear well, for there is a curse attends it which will waste it. The same corrupt dispositions which incline men to sinful ways of getting will incline them to the like sinful ways of spending.

— Matthew Henry

Elisha's Prophetic Ministry – Enemy Blinded and Healed

2 Kings 6

Elisha's Eleventh Miracle – The Floating Ax Head (2 Kgs. 6:1-7)

The living quarters for the sons of the prophets at Gilgal had become too small (2 Kgs. 6:1). It is quite understandable how this situation developed. Young men seeking to know God's word better would have flocked to wherever the premier prophet of Israel was residing. After obtaining Elisha's approval, it was decided that each man should go to the Jordan and harvest timber for constructing a new residence large enough for their needs at that location (2 Kgs. 6:2).

The men were not seeking cedar, marble, or stone for construction material, but, rather, each man was to hew his beam. This meant that they were erecting a simple, no-frills structure barely adequate for housing (a large shack of sorts). The sons of the prophets requested that Elisha accompany them, which he agreed to do (2 Kgs. 6:3-4).

While trees were being felled at the Jordan, an iron axe head flew off its handle into the river (2 Kgs. 6:5). The woodsman cried out to Elisha that the axe had been borrowed. This loss was doubly sorrowful, for not only was it needed for the construction project, but the poor prophet probably did not have the funds to replace it either. It is one thing to live in poverty with an honest mind, but quite another to be burdened with the guilt of debt towards those who have our affection.

Sympathizing with the loss, Elisha asked the man where the axe head had been lost. After the prophet was shown the place, he cut off a stick and threw it in the water, which caused the iron head to float upwards to the surface (2 Kgs. 6:6). Elisha then told the man to snatch it out of the water, which he did (2 Kgs. 6:7).

We might think of this incident as a little miracle in comparison to reviving the Shunammite's dead son, but that would be incorrect. We must remember that nothing in God's creation is harder for Him to control physically than anything else. Not only did the Lord create all things that exist, He also holds together all things (Col. 1:16-17). All that we observe consists only because God maintains it.

True miracles occur when God invades and defies the natural order that He put in place to govern creation. So, it would be no less difficult for God to cause the molecular processes within a non-functioning body to begin again than to change the molecular structure of iron to make it lighter than water. This is why the Lord could pose the question to His servant Abraham: *"Is anything too hard for the Lord?"* (Gen. 18:14). If there is nothing too hard for the Lord, it stands to reason that there is nothing too easy for Him either, meaning He is not in any way challenged by or limited in managing His creation – He is God.

Elisha's Twelfth Miracle – the Syrian Army Blinded (2 Kgs. 6:8-19)

The king of Syria devised plans to covertly attack Israel, but Elisha repeatedly alerted Israel's king of the enemy's tactics, which thwarted the Syrian attacks (2 Kgs. 6:8-10). This greatly troubled the Syrian king, who suspected a traitor among his military staff (2 Kgs. 6:11). But one of the king's servants informed his master that this was not a matter of treachery, but, rather, there was a prophet in Israel named Elisha who was telling the king of Israel what they spoke about in secret (2 Kgs. 6:12).

The king then ordered a reconnaissance mission into Israel to determine Elisha's location, so that he could be captured. This would prevent, he thought, any further hindrance to his invasion plans. The king somehow thought that Elisha would not be aware of his kidnapping plan in spite of his previous knowledge, or would be powerless to foil it. Elisha was in Dothan, so the king of Syria sent a great army, including cavalry and chariots, to surround the city during the night (2 Kgs. 6:13-14).

Elisha's servant arose early and discovered that the city was surrounded by the enemy. He quickly informed his master, and then anxiously inquired as to what they should do (2 Kgs. 6:15). Elisha responded by reassuring his servant, *"Do not fear, for those who are with us are more than those who are with them"* (2 Kgs. 6:16). Elisha then prayed, *"Lord, I pray, open his eyes that he may see."* The Lord granted this prayer and the young man was enabled to see the host of angelic forces in fiery chariots that surrounded them (2 Kgs. 6:17; Ps.

68:17; Heb. 1:7). This was not a new sight for Elisha; he had witnessed his mentor being carried up into heaven by such a chariot drawn by horses of fire (2 Kgs. 2:11). Though normally invisible to the eye, Elisha knew by faith that God's angelic protectors were with him.

"Fear not" are often God's first words of comfort and reassurance to troubled believers in Scripture. Nearly everything we connect with in this sin-cursed world inspires some level of anxiety in feeble beings like ourselves. Additionally, there is the ongoing hostility of the devil against those who represent Christ and the believer's daily struggle of mortifying fleshly impulses by yielding to God's Spirit. Besides all this, there is the overshadowing reality that each of us must stand before the Lord and give an account of all that we have done! Who can answer these things and calm the agitation within the believer's heart? Only the Lord can – His grace is sufficient for every trial and every necessity in life! We find true, lasting peace and mental tranquility only in the Lord Jesus Christ!

Hence, John's charge concerning the enemy lurking about to devour us is most encouraging, *"greater is He that is in you, than he that is in the world"* (1 Jn. 4:4; KJV). The Lord with anyone is a majority. Actually, the Lord alone is a majority! Elisha's servant discovered this truth when God opened his eyes to see the horses and chariots of fire that filled the surrounding mountains. He was terrified of the Syrian army that had surrounded them at Dothan because they were intent on killing Elisha. But Elisha did not fear the enemy; his only concern was to do the will of God. His example is one we should follow too; we must do God's will, and not be anxious about anything else.

The Syrians advanced against Dothan and Elisha asked the Lord to strike the Syrian forces with blindness, which He did (2 Kgs. 6:18). This was a disorienting blindness similar to what the angels inflicted on those surrounding Lot's house in Genesis 19. This blindness was not connected directly with sight, but a condition that left the victim disoriented, for even a blind man can find the door of a house. But the Sodomites outside of Lot's home fumbled about as dizzy children that had been quickly spun about and then left to walk unaided.

Elisha then promised to guide the bewildered Syrians to the man they sought to arrest, not knowing that it was he who was speaking to them. Elisha led them to the capital city of Israel, Samaria, about eight miles south-southwest (2 Kgs. 6:19). Their journey in the opposite direction of

Syria also suggests how debilitating their blindness was; otherwise, they would have sensed the sun warming their faces instead of the backs of their heads and would have known they were moving away from their homeland. The sight of thousands of soldiers grasping the shoulder of the man in front of them and slowly walking blindly into the heart of their enemy's territory would have been comical. Nothing is too hard for the Lord and He was in complete control of this situation. He was not only ensuring the safety of His prophet and his servant, but also working to bring peace to Israel.

Elisha's Thirteenth Miracle – Blind Syrians Healed (2 Kgs. 6:20-23)

After arriving at Samaria, Elisha asked the Lord to open the eyes of the Syrian soldiers, which He did (2 Kgs. 6:20). What a shock to learn that they were prisoners in the stronghold of Israel. The king of Israel thought this would be an easy score against their enemy, so he asked Elisha if he could slaughter them where they stood (2 Kgs. 6:21).

However, the Lord's intention was not to deliver His wayward people's enemy to them, but for all to see, including the Syrians, that the God of Israel was the one true God. Accordingly, Elisha told the king that he should not kill those whom he had captured without warfare; rather, he should feed them and give them drink and permit them to return to their master (2 Kgs. 6:22). The king of Israel then prepared a great feast for the Syrians and sent them in peace back to their king. That act of kindness caused the Syrian marauders to cease from raiding Israel (2 Kgs. 6:23).

J. Herbert Livingston explains that in the Ancient East, a covenant was bridged between two factions when they agreed to eat a meal together under one roof.[77] By demonstrating selfless love for their enemies, Israel was blessed with peace. The same outcome can occur today. Paul later emphasized the powerful testimony of God's grace when believers choose to do good to their oppressors:

> *Beloved, do not avenge yourselves, but rather give place to wrath; for it is written, "Vengeance is Mine, I will repay," says the Lord. Therefore, "if your enemy is hungry, feed him; if he is thirsty, give him a drink." ... Do not be overcome by evil, but overcome evil with good* (Rom. 12:19-21).

If you have people problems, resort to the powerful weapon of love as your first response to the difficulty.

Elisha's Double Portion

Elijah had told Elisha that he would receive a double portion of his spirit if he witnessed his departure into heaven, which he did (2 Kgs. 2). Elijah performed seven miracles, one of which was raising his host's son from the dead. Elisha was responsible for fourteen miracles, two of which were resurrections of the dead. The second instance actually occurred after his death when a dead man touched his entombed bones (2 Kgs. 13:21). In time, the prophecy of Elijah was fulfilled; Elisha received a double portion of Elijah's spirit.

Meditation

Now our heavenly Aaron enters,
With His blood, within the veil;
Joshua now is come to Canaan,
And the kings before Him quail.

Now He plants the tribes of Israel
In their promised resting place;
Now our great Elijah offers
Double portion of His grace.

He has raised our human nature
In the clouds to God's right hand;
There we sit in heavenly places,
There with Him in glory stand.

Jesus reigns, adored by angels;
Man with God is on the throne;
Mighty Lord, in Thine ascension
We by faith behold our own.

— Christopher Wordsworth

Elisha's Prophetic Ministry – Samaria Besieged

2 Kings 6:24-8:15

Syria Besieges Samaria (2 Kgs. 6:24-33)

The events of this story likely occurred before those of the previous chapter. King Ben-Hadad of Syria had plundered Israel and besieged the capital city of Samaria so securely that it created famine-like conditions for its inhabitants (2 Kgs. 6:24). A donkey's head was sold for eighty shekels of silver, and one-fourth of a kab of dove droppings for five shekels of silver (2 Kgs. 6:25). "Dove droppings" was the name of a plant that produced a white edible bulb. (Today, the plant is referred to as Orithogalum umbellatum, *the Star of Bethlehem.*)

One day the king of Israel was walking on the city's wall when a woman cried out for his help (2 Kgs. 6:26). Before hearing her situation, the king vented his frustration with a sarcastic rant against the Lord: he could not provide her grain, wine or oil, for he was not greater than God (i.e., what he considered God to be; 2 Kgs. 6:27). His indictment implied that God was either incapable or unwilling to care for His people – if Jehovah was truly the God of Israel, He would do something about their misery.

The king (likely Joram, though his name is not mentioned) was not prepared for the woman's request. She had entered an agreement with another mother on the previous day: if she killed and boiled her son so that they both could eat, then the other mother would do the same the following day to her son (2 Kgs. 6:28). The woman speaking to the king had held up her end of the deal (i.e., both women had eaten her son), but the second mother had now betrayed their agreement and was hiding her son (2 Kgs. 6:29).

When the king heard her appeal, he was both alarmed and grieved. He tore his clothes and as he walked away, the people below saw that the king was wearing sackcloth underneath his torn royal attire (2 Kgs. 6:30). The king then said, *"God do so to me and more also, if the head of Elisha the son of Shaphat remains on him today!"* (2 Kgs. 6:31).

Although wearing scratchy sackcloth was a sign of repentance, Joram's attitude towards God's representative, Elisha, demonstrated the shallow nature of his self-abasement. By blaming God's messenger for Israel's distress, the king was charging God with wrongdoing. He rejected the idea that the nation's suffering was God's just recompense for their idolatry.

Moses had promised the Israelites that God would punish their wickedness by sending widespread famine and death, invasion, and dispersion. Moses foretold that their cities and idolatrous high places would be destroyed, and that severe famine-like conditions would drive them to cannibalism to survive (Lev. 26:29-31). As shown by this narrative, there were times when the Israelites resorted to cannibalism to avoid starvation (e.g. Lam. 4:10).

The king sent a messenger (an executioner) to find Elisha and end his life. Elisha, who was sitting in his home with several elders, spoke just before the king's assassin arrived: *"Do you see how this son of a murderer has sent someone to take away my head? Look, when the messenger comes, shut the door, and hold him fast at the door. Is not the sound of his master's feet behind him?"* (2 Kgs. 6:32). The man arrived while Elisha was still speaking, and his mission was abruptly averted. The king then promptly arrived and confronted a still-living Elisha, *"Surely this calamity is from the Lord; why should I wait for the Lord any longer?"* (2 Kgs. 6:33).

Elisha Predicts End of Famine (2 Kgs. 7:1-20)

Apparently, the prophet had already informed the king why the famine was occurring and that he should suffer patiently under God's chastening and not surrender to Ben-Hadad. Joram had heeded this command, but now was ready to take matters into his own hands. But the prophet preempted Joram's intentions by declaring a new message from the Lord, one of deliverance: *"Tomorrow about this time a seah of fine flour shall be sold for a shekel, and two seahs of barley for a shekel, at the gate of Samaria"* (2 Kgs. 7:2). One of the king's high ranking officers rejected the prophet's declaration saying, "*If the Lord would make windows in heaven, could this thing be?"* (2 Kgs. 7:2). Elisha rebuffed the officer's skepticism with a second prophecy, *"In fact, you shall see it with your eyes, but you shall not eat of it"* (2 Kgs. 7:3).

The king's heart changed from vengeance towards Elisha to anticipation and hope. As Solomon rightly observed, the hearts of kings are under God's control: *"The king's heart is in the hand of the Lord, like the rivers of water; He turns it wherever He wishes"* (Prov. 21:1). Whether through kings of Israel (like Saul or Joram), or Gentile kings (like Pharaoh, Nebuchadnezzar, or Cyrus), God is the one who ensures all His sovereign purposes are accomplished perfectly.

There were four lepers at the city gate who reasoned that they should surrender to the enemy rather than starve to death where they were or with their countrymen within the city (2 Kgs. 7:4). So at twilight they departed for the Syrian camp. But they found the camp outskirts deserted (2 Kgs. 7:5). The historian then explained that the Lord had caused the Syrians to hear the noise of charging horses and chariots. Believing that Israel had hired Hittite mercenaries from the north and Egyptians from the south to attack them, they abandoned their camp. The panic was so intense that they left their tents, horses, donkeys, and supplies behind (2 Kgs. 7:6-7). In 2 Kings 6 the Lord distorted the eyesight of the Syrians to bring Israel peace; here the Lord distorts the hearing of the Syrians to again liberate His people. God may turn the heart of kings, or manipulate the human senses, or perform other supernatural miracles to ensure every outcome conforms to His will.

The four lepers went into one tent and ate and drank their fill. They then carried off some of the silver, gold, and clothing. Afterwards, they despoiled a second tent and hid its contents also (2 Kgs. 7:8). But one leper had a guilty conscience about what they were doing and expressed the matter to his friends, *"We are not doing right. This day is a day of good news, and we remain silent. If we wait until morning light, some punishment will come upon us. Now therefore, come, let us go and tell the king's household"* (2 Kgs. 7:9). The other lepers agreed, so they all returned to Samaria and told the gatekeeper about the deserted Syrian camp. He promptly reported the information to the king (2 Kgs. 7:10-11). The assessment of the lepers also issues a challenge to believers today: Should not those who have tasted the Lord's goodness be faithful to herald the good news of Jesus Christ, so that others who are spiritually starving can be satisfied also?

But the king believed the report to be a Syrian trap to lure the starving Israelites out of the city in order to vanquish them (2 Kgs. 7:12). Clearly, he did not believe Elisha's prophetic promise had come to pass. But one of the king's servants encouraged his master to let several men take five of the remaining horses to search out the camp to determine if it was a trap or whether the Syrians had suffered some tragedy (2 Kgs. 7:13). The king then sent two two-horse-drawn chariots to investigate the camp (2 Kgs. 7:14). These scouts not only found the camp deserted, but also discovered that the road eastward to the Jordan River was littered with discarded items such as garments and weapons (2 Kgs. 7:15).

The scouts returned to the city and gave the king their report. The news swept through the city like wild fire and the inhabitants raced to the Syrian camp to plunder it (2 Kgs. 7:16). Because of the great abundance of food, *"a seah of fine flour was sold for a shekel, and two seahs of barley for a shekel."* Furthermore, the officer who doubted God's word the previous day was trampled by the people rushing out of the city to get the Syrian spoil; the king had put him on gate-keeping duty (2 Kgs. 7:17-20). Hence, God's word, as spoken by Elisha, was fulfilled on both counts.

The King Restores the Shunammite's Land (2 Kgs. 8:1-6)

Elisha warned the Shunammite woman (whose son he had raised from the dead) to leave the land for a more suitable location because there was going to be a severe famine for seven years in Israel (2 Kgs. 8:1). (This hardship may have occurred during the events of the previous chapter.) The woman is clearly a widow at this time, for her husband is not mentioned and the prophet directly addressed her *"you and your household."* The woman heeded the prophet's counsel and moved her household to the land of the Philistines and then returned to Israel after the famine was over (2 Kgs. 8:2). However, when she returned, she found that others had taken up residence in her home. So she decided to ask the king for the return of her property (2 Kgs. 8:3).

At that same time she arrived to petition the king, Gehazi, in response to the king's request, was informing him about the great things he had witnessed Elisha do (2 Kgs. 8:4). It seems doubtful that the king would have permitted a leprous Gehazi into his presence, meaning the events in this chapter occurred before Naaman's healing. It has been suggested that the various miracles Elisha performed are not recorded in strict chronological order, but rather are arranged to best convey God's overall warning to Israel concerning her idolatry.

Just as Gehazi was telling the king about Elisha raising the Shunammite's son back to life, she appeared before the king and Gehazi identified her as the mother of the boy (2 Kgs. 8:5). The king promptly restored all that was hers plus all the proceeds of her property since she departed from Israel (2 Kgs. 8:6). God's providential care of this faithful woman, now a widow, is astounding. He protected her from the famine and then blessed her afterwards. He controlled the timing of Gehazi's visit with the king and the stories that he told. Furthermore, the Lord softened the heart of a king who was not loyal to Him. Nothing is too hard for the Lord (Gen. 18:14)!

J. N. Darby suggests that God's interaction with the Shunammite woman through Elisha provides a picture of His dealings with Israel through Christ:

> The history of the woman, whose son Elisha had raised to life again, gives us a little picture of all God's dealings with Israel. During long years, as determined by Jehovah, Israel is deprived of everything; but God has preserved all for them, and in the day of blessing all will be restored to them; and they shall receive double the fruit of their years of affliction. It is the son restored to life that brings blessing. Nevertheless the judgments of God are being accomplished.[78]

Ben-Hadad Dies (2 Kgs. 8:7-15)

Afterwards Elisha went to Damascus to fulfill the task of anointing Hazael given to Elijah at Sinai years earlier. When Ben-Hadad, the king of Syria, heard that Elisha was in Damascus, he instructed Hazael to take a present to him and to inquire if he would recover from his illness (2 Kgs. 8:7-8). Since Naaman was a captain in Ben-Hadad's army, and the king had drafted a letter to the king of Israel on his behalf, the Syrian king would have certainly known of Naaman's healing (2 Kgs. 5). This story indicates that Elisha had gained a certain level of notoriety beyond Israel's borders.

Hazael obeyed the king's command and took forty camels bearing the good things of Damascus to Elisha. Given the Ancient Near East culture, the forty camels were probably more for gift display than for load-bearing purposes (i.e., each camel may have been carrying a single gift, but that sight of a long camel convoy afforded a grander presentation). After arriving, Hazael relayed the king's inquiry to the prophet concerning his medical condition (2 Kgs. 8:9).

Elisha told Hazael to go and tell the king, *"You shall certainly recover."* However, the prophet then told Hazael that God had shown him that actually the king would soon die (i.e., be assassinated before he could fully recover his health). Afterwards Elisha stared at Hazael for an uncomfortable period of time before beginning to weep (2 Kgs. 8:11). When Hazael asked why he was weeping, Elisha told him: *"Because I know the evil that you will do to the children of Israel: Their strongholds you will set on fire, and their young men you will kill with the sword; and you will dash their children, and rip open their women with child"* (2 Kgs. 8:12).

Hazael flatly rejected Elisha's declaration, saying, *"Is your servant a dog, that he should do this gross thing?"* (2 Kgs. 8:13). There are at least two possible understandings of his statement: Hazael may have implied that only a dog could do such a monstrous thing and that he was incapable of such a despicable deed. Or he may have been belittling the idea that he, being of low social position, could ever sit on Syria's throne. The Hebrew grammar suggests the latter understanding is more likely (i.e., it was not the atrocity that startled him, but the idea of his greatness). The Hebrew *gadowl* rendered "gross" by implication in the NKJV literally means "high," "great," or "noble." It is rendered "great" in the KJV, NASV, ESV, and Darby's translation of the Bible.

In either case, Hazael's mock humility and hypocrisy are evident. Future events prove that he had already been planning his ascension to the throne and did not care about the welfare of his master. Additionally, his actions after becoming king, proved that he was unconcerned for the welfare of the Israelites. Elisha countered his statement with a second prophetic decree: Hazael had been chosen by the Lord to rule over Syria (2 Kgs. 8:13). Probably because he was a Gentile, Elisha merely announced Hazael's appointment, without the symbolic gesture of anointing him with oil.

Hazael returned to Ben-Hadad with Elisha's good news – he would not die from his illness. However, the next day Hazael suffocated Ben-Hadad with a thick, wet cloth. This method of killing the king would make it look like Ben-Hadad had died of natural causes. Hazael became the king of Syria just as Elisha had predicted (2 Kgs. 8:14-15). He reigned from 841 to 801 B.C., through the reigns of Ahaziah, Athaliah, and Joash in Judah and of Joram, Jehu, and Jehoahaz in Israel. Israel suffered much during Hazael's reign, but the Northern Kingdom was able to withstand Syrian oppression after his son, Ben-Hadad III, replaced him on the throne. It is ironic that Hazael named his son after the man he had murdered; perhaps his appalling deed haunted his conscience for years afterwards.

Meditation

> Inordinate desires commonly produce irregular endeavors. If our wishes be not kept in submission to God's providence, our pursuits will scarcely be kept under the restraints of His precepts.
>
> — Matthew Henry

King Jehoram (Joram) of Judah

2 Kings 8:16-23; 2 Chronicles 21

Jehoram was the oldest son of Jehoshaphat; his brothers were Azariah, Jehiel, Zechariah, Azaryahu, Michael, and Shephatiah (2 Chron. 21:1-2). Jehoshaphat gave his sons silver, gold, precious things, and fortified cities (2 Chron. 21:3). Jehoshaphat's near-death excperience at Ramoth Gilead happened about the same time that he made his son Jehoram coregent of Judah in 853 B.C. (2 Kgs. 8:16). Perhaps Jehoshaphat was planning to be away from Jerusalem on military campaigns for some time and wanted his son to oversee the nation's domestic affairs in his absence.

After his father's death five years later (in 848 B.C.), Jehoram began to rule Judah alone, which coincided with Joram's fifth year over Israel (Joram was the son of Ahab and unfortunately is also referred to as Jehoram; 2 Kgs. 8:16). Jehoram was thirty-two years old when he became king of Judah, and he reigned eight years in Jerusalem (853-841 B.C.; 2 Kgs. 8:17).

The alliance between Jehoshaphat and Ahab resulted in Jehoram marrying Athaliah, the pagan daughter of Ahab and Jezebel (2 Kgs. 8:18). Her wicked influence in the king's life proved to be stronger than the godly heritage he had received from his father. *"He made high places in the mountains of Judah, and caused the inhabitants of Jerusalem to commit harlotry, and led Judah astray"* (2 Chron. 21:11). Jehoram did more evil before the Lord than any previous king of Judah.

Although he purposely led God's covenant people into idolatry, *"yet the Lord would not destroy Judah, for the sake of His servant David, as He promised him to give a lamp to him and his sons forever"* (2 Kgs. 8:19). Athaliah's evil influence on Jehoram is evident in one of his first acts of office after his father died – he slaughtered all six of his brothers (the sons of Jehoshaphat) to prevent any rivals to the throne (2 Chron. 21:4). While kings of Israel had engaged in such barbaric measures, no king of Judah had dared murder their kin to secure their kingdom.

The Edomites rebelled against Judah's authority and recognized their own king. The Edomites had come under Judah's rule after their defeat during Jehoshaphat's reign (2 Chron. 20). Jehoram took Judah's army, including a full contingent of chariots, to confront the Edomites at Zair (probably Seir; 2 Kgs. 8:21). Because the enemy had surrounded Jehoram's encampment, he led his troops on a night-time raid which proved unsuccessful. In fact, he and many of his men were fortunate to escape with their lives. The historian then notes that Libnah (a region near the border of Philistia southwest of Judah) also rebelled against Jehoram's rule (2 Kgs. 8:22). Judah had become weak and politically isolated.

Because Jehoram's father Jehoshaphat had wholly followed the Lord, He caused the surrounding nations to fear Judah's God, thus blessing Jehoshaphat with peace and with the tribute of other kingdoms. However, the Lord was not with Jehoram because he pursued evil. Hence, the surrounding nations turned on him – the fear of the Lord no longer constrained Judah's enemies.

The prophet Elijah delivered God's word to Jehoram through a brief letter to Jehoram:

> *Because you have not walked in the ways of Jehoshaphat your father, or in the ways of Asa king of Judah, but have walked in the way of the kings of Israel, and have made Judah and the inhabitants of Jerusalem to play the harlot like the harlotry of the house of Ahab, and also have killed your brothers, those of your father's household, who were better than yourself, behold, the Lord will strike your people with a serious affliction – your children, your wives, and all your possessions; and you will become very sick with a disease of your intestines, until your intestines come out by reason of the sickness, day by day* (2 Chron. 21:12-15).

Then, to accomplish His Word, the Lord stirred up the Philistines and the Arabians near Ethiopia to invade Judah (2 Chron. 21:16). Judah suffered heavy losses. The enemy even raided the king's house and carried away his possessions, his sons and his wives. Only the youngest son Jehoahaz remained (2 Chron. 21:17). Because of Jehoram's idolatry, God permitted all the seed royal to be destroyed, except for one, Jehoahaz (also called Ahaziah). Regrettably, Jehoram's evil wife Athaliah was not captured, but this also was part of God's providential purposes to chasten Judah.

After these foreign raiders departed from Judah, the Lord struck Jehoram in his intestines with an incurable disease (2 Chron. 21:18). After two full years, the king's agonizing disease overtook him, his intestines came out and he died (2 Chron. 21:19). The people did not mourn at his funeral fires. They buried him in the City of David, but not in the tombs of the kings (2 Chron. 21:20). His youngest and only remaining son Ahaziah reigned in his place.

Meditation

> Verily, we know not what an evil it is to indulge ourselves, and to make an idol of our will.
>
> — Samuel Rutherford

> Now we may infer from any defeat of ours that it is due either to lack of faith or failure to obey. No other reason can suffice.
>
> — Watchman Nee

King Ahaziah of Judah

2 Kings 8:25-29; 2 Chron. 22:1-9

At the age of twenty-two, Ahaziah (also called Jehoahaz and Azariah), the youngest son of Jehoram, began to reign in Judah (2 Kgs. 8:25; 2 Chron. 22:6). This coincided with the twelfth year of Joram's (Ahab's son and Ahaziah's brother) rule over Israel (842 B.C.). (Both Judah and Israel had kings named Ahaziah and Jehoram within the span of a few years, but both Ahaziahs reigned only about a year and not at the same time.) Ahaziah's mother was Athaliah, the daughter of King Ahab (the granddaughter of King Omri; 2 Kgs. 8:26). It should be no surprise that Ahaziah did evil in the sight of the Lord, for his wicked mother Athaliah and his father's advisor counseled him in royal matters (2 Chron. 22:3-4).

Most likely to avenge his grandfather's death, his counselors encouraged Ahaziah to align with King Joram (Jehoram) in Israel (his uncle) and to attack the Syrians (2 Chron. 22:5). The king's advisors probably thought that Syria was more vulnerable, having just experienced a change in authority; Hazael had just murdered Ben-Hadad II to secure the throne (2 Kgs. 8:14-15). Ironically, Joram, the king of Israel, was wounded by the same enemy and in the same vicinity that his father Ahab was mortally wounded, Ramoth Gilead. He went to Jezreel to recover from his wounds and while there, his nephew Ahaziah, the king of Judah visited him (2 Chron. 22:6).

The Lord had determined to judge Ahaziah through Jehu during this visit. Jehu had already been anointed by Elisha as Israel's next king in order to end Ahab's dynasty, as foretold by the prophet Elijah (2 Kgs. 9:1-10; 2 Chron. 22:7). While Jehu was executing judgment on the house of Ahab at Jezreel, he found the princes of Judah (sons of Ahaziah's brothers) who served Ahaziah and killed them also (2 Chron. 22:8).

Ahaziah escaped the slaughter, but after Jehu's men thoroughly searched the region, he was found hiding in Samaria (2 Chron. 22:9).

Ahaziah was captured and, apparently, while being brought back to Jehu at Jezreel, was able to escape his captors, but not before being mortally wounded by Jehu's men. He later died in Megiddo of his injuries (2 Kgs. 9:27). Though a wicked king, who reigned for only one year, Ahaziah was given a proper burial because he was *"the son of Jehoshaphat, who sought the Lord with all his heart."* In actuality, Ahaziah was Jehoshaphat's grandson, but the expression of lineage indicates how much the people appreciated godly Jehoshaphat's reign. Ahaziah had no adult son to assume the throne of Judah, so this gave his evil mother Athaliah the opportunity to take control of the Southern Kingdom (2 Chron. 22:9).

Meditation

> *Do not be deceived, God is not mocked; for whatever a man sows, that he will also reap. For he who sows to his flesh will of the flesh reap corruption, but he who sows to the Spirit will of the Spirit reap everlasting life* (Gal. 6:7-8).

King Jehu of Israel – Rise to Power

2 Kings 9

Jehu Anointed King of Israel (2 Kgs. 9:1-13)

Being anointed with oil by a prophet marked God's man for a task whether as prophet, priest, or king in Israel (Ex. 30:30; 1 Kgs. 19:16). Kings were generally anointed only when there was a new dynasty, as shown by David's (1 Sam. 16:13) and Jehu's anointing. Solomon's anointing would be an exception.

Elisha instructed one of the sons of the prophets to take a flask of oil to Ramoth Gilead, find Jehu the descendant of Nimshi, and then privately anoint him with oil as the next king of Israel (2 Kgs. 9:1-2). After pouring the oil over Jehu's head, the man was instructed to immediately flee and return without delay (2 Kgs. 9:3-4). The young prophet did as Elisha said and found Jehu sitting with other captains in Israel's army. He spoke to Jehu while among his comrades, *"I have a message for you, Commander."* Jehu said, *"For which one of us?"* Elisha's emissary clarified, *"For you, Commander"* (2 Kgs. 9:5). The two left the group and went into the house where Jehu was privately anointed king of Israel (2 Kgs. 9:6). Jehu was then given a prophetic message from the Lord:

> *I have anointed you king over the people of the Lord, over Israel. You shall strike down the house of Ahab your master, that I may avenge the blood of My servants the prophets, and the blood of all the servants of the Lord, at the hand of Jezebel. For the whole house of Ahab shall perish; and I will cut off from Ahab all the males in Israel, both bond and free. So I will make the house of Ahab like the house of Jeroboam the son of Nebat, and like the house of Baasha the son of Ahijah. The dogs shall eat Jezebel on the plot of ground at Jezreel, and there shall be none to bury her* (2 Kgs. 9:7-10).

The Law deemed dogs as unclean animals; hence, to be eaten by wild dogs and not to receive a proper burial was reprehensible to an

Israelite. The young prophet then opened the door and fled the scene as instructed by Elisha. This was for his protection, as the upheaval during a coup often inflicts harm on bystanders unaware of what is happening.

The other captains inquired what the prophet had told Jehu, but he deflected their request saying, *"You know the man and his babble"* (2 Kgs. 9:11). But his companions sensed a seriousness about the encounter and requested that Jehu tell them the truth about the prophet's message. Jehu then told the other captains that the Lord had chosen him to be king over Israel (2 Kgs. 9:12). Then each man quickly took off his outer garment and put it under him on the platform above the steps and they blew trumpets to announce that God had selected Jehu as the king of Israel instead of Joram (2 Kgs. 9:13). There is no evidence that Jehu had considered rebelling against his king until after he was anointed by God to do so.

After the anointing of Jehu, the prophet Elisha fades into obscurity for over four decades. Other than one brief conversation with Israel's king Jehoash (Joash) just before his death, Scripture is silent about Elisha's final years.

King Joram of Israel Killed (2 Kgs. 9:14-26)

Jehu then began to conspire against Joram who had returned to Jezreel to recover from wounds received while defending Ramoth Gilead against Hazael king of Syria (2 Kgs. 9:14). Jehu instructed his comrades not to let anyone leave the city; this would ensure that King Joram would not be warned before he arrived at Jezreel (2 Kgs. 9:15). The historian then informs us that Ahaziah, the king of Judah, had come to Jezreel to visit his recovering uncle, King Joram (2 Kgs. 9:16).

Jehu took a group of fellow-supporters and hastened quickly to Jezreel, about a 45-mile journey west. A watchman in a tower at Jezreel saw the group approaching the city and informed the king, who sent out a messenger on horseback to inquire if they were coming in peace (2 Kgs. 9:17). The king's horseman inquired of Jehu if he had come in peace, but Jehu responded sharply, *"What have you to do with peace? Turn around and follow me"* (2 Kgs. 9:18). The messenger complied and the tower watchman reported his observations to the king who sent a second rider to ask the intentions of the approaching group (2 Kgs. 9:19). Jehu answered the second rider as he had the first and he too joined the group. This incident was also reported to the king, with the additional observation that the breakneck speed of the leading chariot was like the driving of Jehu; apparently Jehu already had a reputation as a speedster (2 Kgs. 9:20).

When both messengers did not return to the palace, Joram concluded that Jehu must be bearing bad news of the conflict at Ramoth Gilead. In haste to have their curiosity satisfied, both Joram and Ahaziah mounted separate chariots to intercept the approaching Jehu (2 Kgs. 9:21). They converged on the property of Naboth the Jezreelite, which Joram's father Ahab had previously gained through murder and theft. The king of Israel immediately asked Jehu, *"Is it peace, Jehu?"* Jehu's response to Joram is one of the most insightful declarations ever uttered by a ruler of the Northern Kingdom: *"What peace, as long as the harlotries of your mother Jezebel and her witchcraft are so many?"* Israel could have no peace with God as long as the nation pursued what He abhorred.

Hearing Jehu's response, Joram called out to Ahaziah, "Treachery," and turned his chariot around to scramble back to Jezreel, but Jehu drew his bow and shot him in the back. The arrow passed through his heart and came out his chest (2 Kgs. 9:24). In their haste to meet Jehu, neither king had thought to put on his armor – they were not expecting warfare.

The king of Israel sank to the floor of his chariot. Jehu commanded Bidkar to retrieve his body and cast it out on the ill-gotten property that had been Naboth's (2 Kgs. 9:24). Jehu then reminded Bidkar that they had both heard the word of Lord spoken by Elijah against Ahab: *"Surely I saw yesterday the blood of Naboth and the blood of his sons and I will repay you in this plot"* (2 Kgs. 9:25). In accordance with God's word, Jehu commanded that Joram's body should be thrown on the same plot of ground which Ahab gained by murdering its owners (2 Kgs. 9:26). Jehu had fulfilled the prophecy of Elijah and ended Ahab's dynasty (2 Kgs. 9:1-10; 2 Chron. 22:7). Jehu's reign over Israel began with Joram's death in 841 B.C.

King Ahaziah of Judah Killed (2 Kgs. 9:27-29)

After seeing what happened to his uncle Joram, Ahaziah fled south by the road to Beth Haggan (2 Kgs. 9:27). Jehu commanded his men to pursue Ahaziah, who apparently was wounded by an arrow near Ibleam. The details of Ahaziah's final hours are sketchy. The king of

Judah was apparently able to elude his assassins while hiding in Samaria (likely the region, not the city), but was eventually found by Jehu's men (2 Chron. 22:9). He may have been captured and while being taken to Jehu at Jezreel was able to escape his captors, but not before being mortally wounded by archers at the Ascent of Gur. Apparently, Ahaziah sought protection at the high-walled chariot city of Megiddo, but died there of his injuries shortly after arriving (2 Kgs. 9:27).

While Jehu was executing judgment on the house of Ahab at Jezreel, he found the princes of Judah (sons of Ahaziah's brothers) who served Ahaziah and he killed them also (2 Chron. 22:8). Ahaziah had no adult son to assume the throne of Judah, which allowed his evil mother Athaliah to take control of Judah (2 Chron. 22:9).

Jezebel's Death (2 Kgs. 9:30-37)

After learning of her son's death and that Jehu was approaching Jezreel, Jezebel painted her eyes and adorned her head (2 Kgs. 9:30). After observing Jehu pass through the city's gate, she called out to him through an open window, *"Is it peace, Zimri, murderer of your master?"* (2 Kgs. 9:31). Clearly, Jezebel was aware of the coup d'état and linked Jehu with the assassination of the house of Baasha. She was pointing out that just as Zimri had no peace after murdering his master, neither would Jehu. Jehu did not respond to the wicked woman's indictment, but rather called out, *"Who is on my side?"* Two or three eunuch servants indicated their allegiance to Jehu (2 Kgs. 9:32). Jehu then commanded them to through her out the window, which they did (2 Kgs. 9:33). Some of her blood splattered on the wall and the horses when she hit the ground and then Jehu trampled her body under his horse.

After several days of breakneck travel and slaughter, Jehu and his men paused to feast and to celebrate the end of Ahab's dynasty and Jehu's coronation as Israel's new king. Because she was the king's daughter, Jehu later commanded some of his men to go back, collect, and bury the accursed woman's body (2 Kgs. 9:34). Jehu had temporarily forgotten about Elijah's earlier prophecy (1 Kgs. 21:23) which had been confirmed to him again at Ramoth Gilead.

When Jehu's burial detail returned to the location of Jezebel's death, they found only her skull, feet, and the palms of her hands, for wild dogs had eaten or dragged away the rest of her body (2 Kgs. 9:35). The men reported the matter to Jehu, who then promptly recalled God's word spoken through Elijah: *"On the plot of ground at Jezreel dogs shall eat the flesh of Jezebel and the corpse of Jezebel shall be as refuse on the surface of the field, in the plot at Jezreel, so that they shall not say, 'Here lies Jezebel'"* (2 Kgs. 9:36-37). Jehu was acknowledging that God had honored His promise to judge Jezebel.

There would be no grave to bring to remembrance the evil woman who had popularized the worship of Baal and Ashtoreth in Israel. In addition to their idolatry, Ahab and Jezebel had perverted justice and oppressed the righteous, but God held them accountable and passed judgment on them. Our all-knowing and all-powerful God is righteous and just! This assures us that every deed which affronts His character will be properly attended to – none can escape the consequences of unrepented sin.

Meditation

> If you take care of yourself and walk with integrity, you may be confident that God will deal with those who sin against you. Above all, don't give birth to sin yourself; rather, pray for those who persecute you. God will one day turn your persecution into praise. … Yes, let God be the Judge. Your job today is to be a witness.
>
> — Warren Wiersbe

King Jehu of Israel – Further Cleansing

2 Kings 10

Ahab's Seventy Sons Killed (2 Kgs. 10:1-11)

Jehu then wrote and sent letters to the elders and rulers of Samaria who were caring for Ahab's seventy sons (2 Kgs. 10:1). In short, Jehu suggested that since they were harboring Ahab's sons, they should recognize the best of his sons as king and prepare their best warriors and war-chariots to defend him in battle (2 Kgs. 10:2-3). Jehu was intent on wiping out the house of Ahab and this tactic was designed to speed up the process. His strategy worked, as Samaria's leaders were afraid of Jehu because he had already overcome two kings (2 Kgs. 10:4). They decided not to defend Ahab's dynasty by recognizing a new king, but rather to side with Jehu and be his servants (2 Kgs. 10:5).

After understanding their intention to capitulate, Jehu wrote a second letter to them, testing their allegiance: *"If you are for me and will obey my voice, take the heads of the men, your master's sons, and come to me at Jezreel by this time tomorrow"* (2 Kgs. 10:6). The leaders then decapitated Ahab's seventy sons and sent their heads in a basket to Jehu at Jezreel (2 Kgs. 10:7). Jehu then ordered the messenger bearing the basket to place them in two piles at the entrance of the gate; the spectacle displayed Jehu's dominance over Ahab's dynasty (2 Kgs. 10:8).

The next morning, Jehu went to the gate of the city and addressed the people:

> *You are righteous. Indeed I conspired against my master and killed him; but who killed all these? Know now that nothing shall fall to the earth of the word of the Lord which the Lord spoke concerning the house of Ahab; for the Lord has done what He spoke by His servant Elijah* (2 Kgs. 10:9-10).

First, Jehu took full responsibility for the death of his master (King Joram), but denied any involvement in killing Ahab's sons (though he had instigated it). Second, he absolved the people listening to him of any responsibility for the death of Ahab's sons. Through this tactic, Jehu gained a psychological benefit in the minds of the people. Because Jehu had willfully confessed to the first slaying, the people believed him when he claimed he had not participated in the latter murders. He thus implied that since none of them was responsible for their deaths, God must be the one responsible (i.e., He had fulfilled His word as spoken by Elijah). Third, having absolved the people of all guilt, he reiterated that they were siding with the Lord by siding with him, for the prophecy of Elijah concerning Ahab had been completely fulfilled. Having no responsibility for what had happened and knowing that it was what God wanted to happen caused the people to embrace Jehu as their new king.

Jehu used the infallibility of the word of God to justify his conduct, but his murder of Ahaziah was beyond what God had sanctioned, as was his next action in removing all potential challengers in Israel. Jehu killed all who remained of the house of Ahab in Jezreel, and also his chief officers, close acquaintances, and his pagan priests (2 Kgs. 10:11). While cleansing away the wickedness of Israel did honor the Lord, the slaying of innocent people (those not Ahab's heirs or pagan priests) angered Him. The prophet Hosea later pronounced God's judgment on Jehu for these offenses (Hos. 1:4).

Ahaziah's Forty-Two Brothers Killed (2 Kgs. 10:12-14)

Regrettably, Jehu's holy zeal for cleansing wickedness from Israel went beyond the scope of what had been commanded by the Lord, and thus too far! On the way from Jezreel to Samaria, Jehu met relatives of King Ahaziah of Judah at Beth Eked of the Shepherds (2 Kgs. 10:12). They obviously were not aware of the events surrounding Ahaziah's death and answered Jehu truthfully, *"We are the brothers of Ahaziah; we have come down to greet the sons of the king and the sons of the queen mother"* (2 Kgs. 10:13). The Queen Mother was Jezebel, perhaps their grandmother or extended family through marriage. Jehu commanded that the forty-two relatives of Ahaziah be seized. They were all taken to the well of Beth Eked and executed there (2 Kgs. 10:14).

As Ahaziah's actual brothers had all been slain by the Arabs prior to his royal accession (2 Chron. 21:17, 22:1) we understand the meaning of the Hebrew word *'ach* translated "brothers" to here mean "brethren" (as translated in the KJV). *'Ach* is often used in Scripture to speak of kin in the general sense (e.g., Num. 25:6, Deut. 1:16). In this case, the deceased were extended family of Ahaziah (e.g., nephews, cousins, etc.); they were the "princes of Judah" (2 Chron. 22:8).

The Remainder of Ahab's Family Slain (2 Kgs. 10:15-17)

Afterwards, Jehu departed and met Jehonadab the son of Rechab coming towards him. Jehu greeted him and inquired, *"Is your heart right, as my heart is toward your heart?"* (2 Kgs. 10:15). Jehonadab answered that it was, so Jehu extended his hand to lift him up into his chariot and then invited him to witness his *"zeal for the Lord"* (2 Kgs. 10:15). After they arrived in Samaria, Jehu destroyed everyone remaining in the household of Ahab to fulfill the prophetic word of God given through Elijah (2 Kgs. 10:16-17). Whether Jehonadab took part in the slaughter or merely observed it with approval is unknown; however, he did later assist Jehu in removing Baal-worship from Israel (2 Kgs. 10:15-27). His righteous example then passed down to subsequent generations, which the prophet Jeremiah acknowledged more than two centuries later.

Jeremiah used the example of the nomadic Rechabites, Jehonadab's descendants, who had faithfully followed their forefather's instructions not to drink wine, nor build houses, nor plant fields or vineyards, to reprove Judah for being disobedient to their heavenly father (Jer. 35:6-10). Interestingly, we learn from 1 Chronicles 2:55 that the Rechabites were Kenites from Hemath, but were numbered with the children of Judah. Yet, these Jewish proselytes passed down a godly heritage to their children.

The piety of his father Rechab is expressed in the name given to his son Jehonadab, which means, *"Jehovah freely gave."* Rechab had taught Jehonadab to fear the Lord and to respect God-ordained authority. This heritage had been passed down from generation to generation in their clan (Jer. 35:13). God honors those who are in a right relationship with His authority; He teaches us submission to Him through His various earthly authority structures. The Rechabites had obeyed the directions of their forefather Jonadab, and God promised to bless them because they had. Jeremiah did not affirm that Jonadab's prohibition of drinking wine and dwelling in houses was correct, but rather the prophet commended his descendants for their submission to his command. This is a good example for God's people to follow no matter what time period they sojourn in.

It is evident from the narrative that Jehu already knew Jehonadab and his reputation as a devout worshiper of Jehovah who loathed idolatry. Although in the company of this zealous but cruel king, Jehonadab, as we soon will see, is not willing that one true servant of Jehovah should mingle with Baal worshipers of Samaria.

Baal Worshipers Killed (2 Kgs. 10:18-31)

Jehu then sets a trap for Baal worshipers in Israel by declaring that he would worship Baal even more than Ahab did (2 Kgs. 10:18). The ruse was to gather all the servants of Baal in one place to have a great sacrifice to the Canaanite deity so that they could all be slaughtered (2 Kgs. 10:19-20). A public decree was sent throughout Israel for all Baal worshipers to gather at his temple on a particular day (2 Kgs. 10:21).

When the day arrived, the temple of Baal was completely full. Jehu then ordered the keeper of the wardrobe to ensure all Baal worshipers received the proper vestments for the ceremony (2 Kgs. 10:22). This was done not for religious fanfare, but so those identifying with Baal by wearing the pagan robes (probably of white byssus) would be executed. To further ensure that only the wicked were killed, Jehu and Jehonadab went into the pagan temple and told the Baal worshipers to search for any servants of Jehovah that might be hiding among them (2 Kgs. 10:23).

Jehu and Jehonadab were in the temple at the time the sacrifices and burnt offerings to Baal began. Jehu had positioned eighty armed men outside the temple with orders to kill all pagan worshipers trying to escape the temple and they would forfeit their own lives if any escaped (2 Kgs. 10:24). After the offerings were made, Jehu commanded his guard and captains, *"Go in and kill them; let no one come out!"* (2 Kgs. 10:25). None of the worshipers of Baal escaped. The captains then went into the inner temple and brought the sacred pillars out of the temple and burned them (2 Kgs. 10:26). They tore down the sacred image of Baal and reduced his temple to a pile of rubble (2 Kgs. 10:27). In one day, *"Jehu destroyed Baal from Israel"* (2 Kgs. 10:28).

Although Jehu had fulfilled God's word and had been zealous for the Lord, the historian reminds us that he continued in the sins of Jeroboam the son of Nebat, who caused Israel to worship the golden calves that were at Bethel and Dan (2 Kgs. 10:29): *"Jehu took no heed to walk in the law of the Lord God of Israel with all his heart; for he did not depart from the sins of Jeroboam, who had made Israel sin."* True, Baal and Ashtoreth worship had been removed from Israel, but Jehu still promoted the idea of worshiping Jehovah outside of Jerusalem and honoring the golden calves created to represent Jehovah; it was idolatry just the same.

But at this point, Jehu had done more to please the Lord than any other king of the Northern Kingdom. The Lord commended Jehu for what he had done correctly, *"Because you have done well in doing what is right in My sight, and have done to the house of Ahab all that was in My heart, your sons shall sit on the throne of Israel to the fourth generation"* (2 Kgs. 10:30). It pleased the Lord that Jehu put away evil, but that is not the same as heeding the law of God and setting your mind on what is good. Jehu did the former, but neglected the latter; hence, God's favor on the line of Jehu would be short-lived.

Furthermore, Jehu's merciless attack on the godly line of David was not commanded by the Lord and therefore would not go unpunished. The Lord confirmed this when He told Hosea to name his wife's first child Jezreel: *"Call his name Jezreel, for in a little while I will avenge the bloodshed of Jezreel on the house of Jehu, and bring an end to the kingdom of the house of Israel"* (Hos. 1:4). The significance of Jezreel here is not in the meaning of the name, but as it relates to where blood was wrongly shed. Righteous Naboth, the Jezreelite, was murdered by Ahab through a wicked plot by his evil wife Jezebel to obtain a vineyard that Ahab wanted to own (1 Kgs. 21). Ironically, a century later, Jehu ordered the bloody massacres of the house of Ahab and of the house of David on the property of Naboth (2 Kgs. 9-10).

While the judgment against the house of wicked Ahab had been predicted by Elijah (1 Kgs. 21:21-24), commanded by Elisha (2 Kgs. 9:1-10), and approved by the Lord (2 Kgs. 10:30), Jehu's massacre of Ahaziah and his relatives and innocent associates of Ahab in Israel was not. Jehu's slaughter of Baal worshipers and priests in Israel was appropriate (2 Kgs. 10:18-28), but his brutal carnage of David's wayward descendants was not sanctioned by God and would be judged. Jehu was not motivated for the glory of God, but rather by pride and selfish ambition. Because Jehu acted on his own behalf, God would judge his house for the unsanctioned bloodshed at Jezreel.

This prophecy was fulfilled in 752 B.C. when Shallum killed Zechariah and ended Jehu's dynasty in the fourth generation (2 Kgs. 15:10). The Lord informed Hosea that the fulfillment of this prophecy would signal the complete collapse of the Northern Kingdom, as symbolized by Israel's defeat in the valley of Jezreel. The later event occurred in 733 B.C. when Tiglath-Pileser III of Assyria overtook the plain of Jezreel, which led to the fall of Samaria in 722 B.C. Israel then became a province of Assyria and many of her surviving inhabitants were exiled.

Syria's Invasion of Transjordan (2 Kgs. 10:32-35)

While there had been a cleansing of evil in Israel, it had been tainted by Jehu's carnal zeal; as a result, no true revival occurred among the people. This brought God's chastening upon Israel, thus Jehu's reign was one of turmoil and decline. The Lord began to dismantle Israel's possessions and territory at that time. To fulfill His word through Elisha (2 Kgs. 10:32), He permitted Hazael to conquer the Israelites in the Transjordan where the tribes of Gad, Reuben, and Manasseh resided. The Syrians then occupied Gilead and Bashan to the rivers Aroer and Arnon (2 Kgs. 10:33). Although not stated in the narrative, the Black Obelisk discovered in 1846 reveals that Assyria under Shalmaneser III's leadership received tribute from Jehu.[79]

Although God had raised up Hazael to punish His errant people, the Syrian king's brutality exceeded God's intentions. Accordingly, He moved the prophet Amos to foretell that He would punish Damascus, *"because they have threshed Gilead with implements of iron"* (Amos 1:3). The Syrians not only conquered Gilead, but also massacred many Israelites by running over them with threshing implements. Albert Barnes describes Syria's ruthless behavior:

> The instrument, Jerome relates here, was "a sort of wain [wagon or cart], rolling on iron wheels beneath, set with teeth; so that it both threshed out the grain and bruised the straw and cut it in pieces, as food for the cattle, for lack of hay." A similar instrument, called by nearly the same name, is still in use in Syria and Egypt. Elisha had

> foretold to Hazael his cruelty to Israel: *"Their strongholds thou wilt set on fire, and their young men wilt thou slay with the sword, and wilt dash their children, and rip up their women with child"* (2 Kgs. 8:12).[80]

Pulling threshing implements over people would both crush them and cut their bodies to shreds. Such disregard for human life and brutality was a war crime that would not go unpunished. The Lord promised that Syria would be invaded, their cities would be captured and burned, their king killed, and many of their inhabitants enslaved and exiled to Kir (Amos 1:4-5). The Assyrians, led by Tiglath-Pileser III, fulfilled this prophecy in 732 B.C.

The Death of Jehu (2 Kgs. 10:34-36)

Hosea pronounced judgment on Jehu for his overzealous brutality inflicted on those beyond Elijah's prophecy (the nobility of Judah and various associates and extended family of Ahab; Hos. 1:4). True, Jehu had fulfilled his divine commission, but he served himself in doing so. Jehu reigned over Israel from Samaria for twenty-eight years (841-814 B.C.) and was buried in Samaria with his fathers. His son Jehoahaz ruled in his place. Jehu's failure poses a lesson for us to learn from. It is possible to have great zeal for the Lord, but if we go beyond the boundaries of God's Word in serving the Lord, we cause His name to be dishonored.

Jehu was the best king that the Northern Kingdom would ever have, but he settled for something less than God's best and, accordingly, spiritual revival did not overtake the nation even after his efforts to purge paganism. Merely leading people away from what God hates is not the same as leading them into joyful communion with Him. There are many ills to be avoided in the world, but that alone does not constitute a victorious Christian life – only living for Christ in the power of the Holy Spirit and in accordance with God's Word does that.

Meditation

When we walk with the Lord in the light of His Word,
What a glory He sheds on our way!
While we do His good will, He abides with us still,
And with all who will trust and obey.

Israel's Kings

Not a shadow can rise, not a cloud in the skies,
But His smile quickly drives it away;
Not a doubt or a fear, not a sigh or a tear,
Can abide while we trust and obey.

— John H. Sammis

Godly Jehoiada and Wicked Athaliah

2 Kings 11; 2 Chronicles 22:10-23:21

Athaliah was a granddaughter of King Omri, the daughter of King Ahab and Queen Jezebel, the sister of King Joram and King Ahaziah of Israel, the wife of King Jehoram of Judah, and the mother of King Ahaziah of Judah.

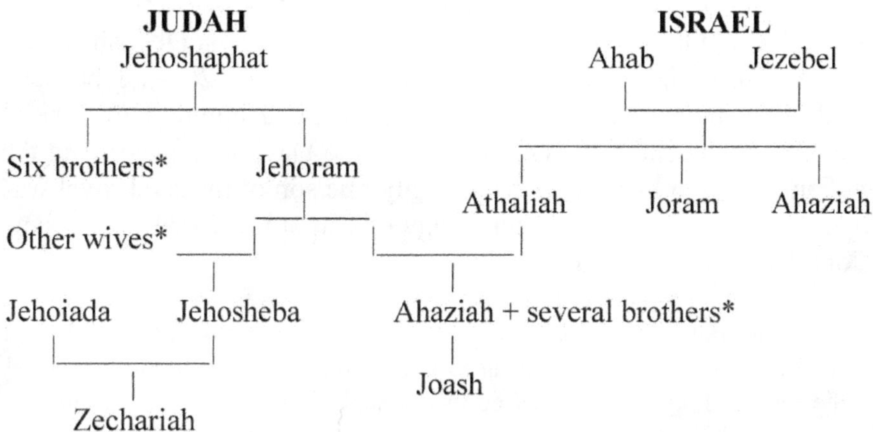

Ahaziah's forty-two brethren may have been descendants of *

In fulfillment of Elijah's prophetic word, Athaliah's parents, her brother Joram, and extended family had all been executed. Her husband Jehoram, her brother Ahaziah, and all her sons (except Ahaziah) had been judged by the Lord through disease, injury, or foreign raiders. Additionally, Jehu had murdered Athaliah's closest associates and friends in Israel. Jehu slaughtered Athaliah's only remaining son, Judah's King Ahaziah, and forty-two of his brethren (i.e., members of her extended family, probably several grandsons). The historian then reveals how this exceedingly evil woman responded to these losses.

Because Ahaziah left no son able to take the throne of Judah, Athaliah decided to butcher all remaining potential royal heirs, so that she could rule Judah without being contested (2 Kgs. 11:1). Those murdered would include any male descendants of her dead husband Jehoram through other wives and any of her own grandsons that Jehu did not kill. Athaliah's barbaric act directly opposed God's covenant with David that decreed that one of David's descendants should be on the throne of Judah forever. Though clearly motivated by personal ambition, she was striking back at God for the deaths of her family the only way she could.

Thankfully, *"Jehosheba, the daughter of King Jehoram, sister of Ahaziah, took Joash the son of Ahaziah, and stole him away from among the king's sons who were being murdered; and they hid him and his nurse in the bedroom, from Athaliah, so that he was not killed"* (2 Kgs. 11:2). We learn from 2 Chronicles that Jehosheba (Jehoshabeath) was the wife of Jehoiada the high priest (2 Chron. 22:11). Jehosheba would have been Ahaziah's half-sister (King Jehoram had several wives). For a second time, God permitted the Davidic dynasty (and the Messianic line) to hang by a thread; only one son of the seed royal was alive. While considering the genealogy of Christ presented in Matthew 1, John Heading observes:

> In 2 Chronicles 22:10, we have noted that Athaliah destroyed all the seed royal – evidently Satan used this woman to attempt to destroy the line leading to Christ. Of course, Joseph, in this line, was not the natural father of the Lord Jesus, so this refers to His legal and regal authority, stemming from the lesser to the greater, from David to Christ. By contrast, priestly influence caused a faithful wife to preserve the line leading to Christ (2 Chron. 22:1)! This reflects upon believers today; we must preserve what the religion of the world wants to destroy, whereas we destroy what the world wants to build (Gal. 2:18).[81]

Joash was hidden for six years by Jehoiada and Jehosheba in the unused temple while wicked Athaliah reigned over Judah (2 Kgs. 11:3). God can use anything to accomplish His will, even the closing of His temple by Joash's evil father so that the last of David's royal line is protected. Jehoiada was a godly priest whose tenure reached as far back as the reforms of Asa and Jehoshaphat. He was probably born during

Rehoboam's reign and was therefore likely over ninety years of age when these circumstances unfold.

Joash Crowned King of Judah (2 Kgs. 11:4-12; 2 Chron. 23:1-11)

In the seventh year, Jehoiada was ready to displace Athaliah by publicly revealing Joash's existence and crowning him as the rightful heir to the throne of David (2 Kgs. 11:4). Jehoiada summoned five captains of the bodyguards to the temple. These were men whom the priest believed would not be loyal to the queen: Azariah the son of Jeroham, Ishmael the son of Jehohanan, Azariah the son of Obed, Maaseiah the son of Adaiah, and Elishaphat the son of Zichri (2 Chron. 23:1). These men, under oath, agreed to gather Levites and chief fathers of the cities of Judah and bring them to Jerusalem to form a large bodyguard to protect Joash, and escort him safely from the temple to the place of his public coronation (2 Chron. 23:2).

The Levites and priests coming to Jerusalem would be divided into three groups on the Sabbath; one group would be positioned at the king's house, another at the Gate of Sur, and the third at the gate behind the accompanying escort (2 Kgs. 11:5-6). The ceremony was planned to occur at the changing of the guard on the Sabbath which ensured the temple area would be crowded with people (2 Kgs. 11:7). Because the guards being relieved were not to leave the temple complex, twice as many bodyguards would be able to protect Joash (2 Kgs. 11:9). These armed bodyguards were challenged to lay down their lives to protect the king while he was escorted from the temple to the courtyard to be anointed. Anyone approaching the boy was to be killed (2 Kgs. 11:8).

To the captains of the hundreds, leading the Levite guardsmen, Jehoiada gave spears and shields that had belonged to King David which had been stored in the temple (2 Kgs. 11:10). The captains also commanded their own soldiers attached to them (e.g., the Kerethites). Surrounded by an armed escort, Joash was brought from the temple to the Bronze Altar in the courtyard. There he was anointed, and crowned the king of Judah (2 Kgs. 11:11). Joash was also given the written Testimony – the Law of the Lord for His people. The people clapped their hands and shouted, *"Long live the king!"* (2 Kgs. 11:12). It was necessary to publicly anoint Joash as there had been a challenge to the Davidic dynasty for the throne of Judah.

The Death of Athaliah (2 Kgs. 11:13-21; 2 Chron. 23:12-21)

Athaliah heard the loud cheering from the temple and went to investigate (2 Kgs. 11:13). She was shocked to hear the people rejoicing and the trumpeters announcing a new king, Then she saw little Joash wearing a crown and standing by the high pillar at the eastern gate of the inner temple courtyard, as was customary for newly crowned royalty (2 Kgs. 11:14; 2 Chron. 23:13). Athaliah tore her clothes and cried out, *"Treason! Treason!"*

Jehoiada commanded the captains of the hundreds, the officers of the army to remove Athaliah from the temple area under heavy guard and slay her outside the temple complex (2 Kgs. 11:15). She was arrested and escorted out of the temple (by the route the horses enter the king's palace) and was executed (2 Kgs. 11:16). (To clarify, this was the Horse Gate into the palace complex, not the Horse Gate into the city.)

Jehoiada then made a covenant between the Lord, the king, and the people, that they should be the Lord's people (2 Kgs. 11:17). Afterwards a great multitude of the people stormed the temple of Baal. They broke the altars and the images in pieces, killed the pagan priest Mattan before the altars, and then tore down the structure (2 Kgs. 11:18).

Jehoiada then reinstated the oversight of the house of the Lord as previously assigned by David to the courses of priests and Levites (2 Chron. 23:18). Now burnt offerings would be again offered with rejoicing and singing in accordance with the Law of Moses. Jehoiada also set trustworthy gatekeepers at the gates of the temple to ensure no unclean person could enter the house of the Lord (2 Chron. 23:19).

Then the people escorted the king from the temple to the king's house and he sat on the throne of Judah (2 Kgs. 11:19). The people rejoiced over the death of wicked Athaliah and that a seed of David still existed to reign over them (2 Kgs. 11:20). Joash was seven years old when he became king (2 Kgs. 11:21).

Since the first prophecy foretelling that a Victor would come through the seed of the woman and would defeat Satan (Gen. 3:15), the devil's primary mission has been against Messiah (more specifically the person of Jesus Christ). This attack has come on three main fronts.

First, Satan tried to destroy the family line through which the Deliverer would come. Examples include: his effort to pervert the godly line of Seth in Genesis 6 and Athaliah's attempt in this chapter to kill the entire royal seed to obtain the throne. However, Jehosheba protected the only remaining son of Ahaziah, permitting Joash to be listed in the official genealogy of Christ recorded in Matthew 1.

Second, when preventing the birth of Messiah was unsuccessful, direct attempts on the life of the Lord Jesus were made. When the Lord Jesus was a child in Bethlehem, Herod attempted to kill Him by murdering all the boys in the vicinity who were two years old and younger (Matt. 2). Later, attempts would be made on the Lord's life as an adult in Nazareth, when distraught Jews tried to push Him over a cliff (Luke 4:29) and when the religious leaders sought to stone Him (John 8:59, 10:31) for His alleged blasphemies.

Third, having failed to stop Christ from completing His redemptive work and resurrection, Satan now concentrates on casting doubt on the Person of Christ, on slandering His name, and seducing worshipers into idolatry or heresy. May we be wise to the devil's deceitful ways and not be duped into any activity or conversation which would undermine the person, the work, or the glory of the Lord Jesus Christ.

Meditation

Jesus the mighty conqueror, now rises from the tomb,
His resurrection glory dispels its chilling gloom.
While, from its open portals, an angel, clad in light,
Doth reveal to mortals the triumphs of His might.

Death's power forever is broken, God's saints no longer mourn;
Its sting can bring no torture, for Christ the curse hath borne;
His glorious exaltation let men and angels sing;
Jesus, mighty conqueror! In earth and Heaven is King.

— William Wilbor

King Joash (Jehoash) of Judah

2 Kings 12; 2 Chronicles 24

Joash Repairs the Temple (2 Kgs. 12:1-16; 2 Chron. 24:1-14)

Joash became king of Judah when he was seven years old and reigned forty years in Jerusalem; his mother's name was Zibiah of Beersheba (2 Kgs. 12:1). He would be the first of four relatively good kings who would rule Judah for the next century. However, Joash, Amaziah, Uzziah, and Jotham were not of the same caliber of king as Asa, Jehoshaphat, Hezekiah, and Josiah, who had instigated religious reform to some degree in Judah.

As long as Joash's godly mentor, the high priest Jehoiada, was alive, Joash did what was right in the sight of the Lord. He did not, however, remove the high places where the people sacrificed and burned incense to the Lord, probably because the paramount concern initially was reinstating proper temple worship (2 Kgs. 12:2-3). Jehoiada took two wives for him, and he had sons and daughters (2 Chron. 24:3).

As a young man, Joash became grieved that the house of the Lord, his nursery and sanctuary when a child, had fallen into disrepair. Having spent six years of his childhood living in the temple, he would have been well aware of its rundown condition. His early formative years among God's priests and in God's house caused Joash to feel a certain sorrow for the temple's neglected state. The king commanded the priests to collect three types of funds: *"All the money of the dedicated gifts that are brought into the house of the Lord – each man's census money, each man's assessment money – and all the money that a man purposes in his heart to bring into the house of the Lord"* (2 Kgs. 12:4).

The census money was connected with the half a shekel offering to the Lord as acknowledgement of His atonement (Ex. 30:13). These funds were designated for the temple (the tabernacle originally). The assessment money related to the redemption (with a twenty percent increase in evaluation) of anything that had been dedicated to the Lord (Lev. 27:1-8). Then there were the ongoing free-will offerings of the people, as compared to the first two gifts which were to be collected annually (2 Chron. 24:5).

The priests and Levites were to travel throughout the cities of Judah to gather appropriate funds from each household to ensure the expedient repair and ongoing maintenance of the temple (2 Kgs. 14:4; 2 Chron. 24:4-5). This is the first time since the temple was erected by Solomon (about 150 years earlier) that there has been any mention of repair work on the temple. Nonetheless, the priests did not quickly enact the king's command; rather, they diverted the funds that were collected to their own needs and temple operating expenses.

The renovation impasse came to a head in the twenty-third year of Joash's reign. The king called the chief priest Jehoiada to answer for his negligence in obeying his decree to properly keep up the temple, which he reminded Jehoiada was required by the Law of Moses (2 Kgs. 14:6; 2 Chron. 24:6). The historian then informs us that the sons of Athaliah had broken into the house of God, doing much damage to it and taking the holy things to Baal's temple, which had been destroyed (2 Chron. 24:7).

Since solicitation and compulsion to support the work of the Lord had utterly failed, Joash decided to try a new tactic in gaining funds to repair the house of the Lord – freewill offerings. The king commanded that a chest be constructed and that a hole be bored in its lid so that the people could place their gifts in the chest anonymously. The chest was to be set outside the gate of the temple (2 Chron. 24:8). A proclamation was then made throughout Judah for those wanting to honor the collection that Moses had imposed on Israel to support the upkeep of God's dwelling place (2 Chron. 24:9).

This matter delighted the people, who with their leaders contributed liberally and joyfully (2 Chron. 24:10). There was no collection agency, no forced giving, no personal solicitations, no fund-raising campaigns, only voluntary giving as each person was exercised by the Lord. This is the spiritual pattern of giving emphasized in Scripture (1 Cor. 16:2). Hence, Paul exhorts believers, *"So let each one give as he purposes in his heart, not grudgingly or of necessity; for God loves a cheerful giver"* (2 Cor. 9:7). The Jews in Joash's day resented being compelled to give, but delighted in contributing to the work of the Lord when permitted to do so freely. God's work, done God's way, will never lack His resources.

After all had an opportunity to contribute, the Levites brought the chest before the king and opened it. There was much money in the chest, which was collected, counted, and the amount recorded by the king's scribe and the high priest's officer. The chest was returned to its location at the gate, and the process was repeated each day. An abundance of money was collected by this procedure (2 Chron. 24:11). The example of two witnesses counting and recording the funds received shows the importance of good procedures both to ensure proper accountability of what is important to the Lord and that righteous servants of the Lord do not get blamed for wrongdoing.

The Levites then paid masons, stonecutters, carpenters, and builders from the money collected to repair the temple (2 Kgs. 12:11-12). However, there was not enough money initially to hire craftsmen to create the various holy articles of gold and silver, such as spoons, trimmers, sprinkling-bowls, various vessels, and trumpets (2 Kgs. 12:13). Thankfully, those hired to repair the temple were honest men who gave their best efforts for what they were paid to do; thus, no money was wasted in the restoration effort (2 Kgs. 12:14-15).

Only the free-will offerings were used to repair the temple; the money from the sin and trespass offerings was not used for this work, as those funds belonged to the priests (2 Kgs. 12:16). The sin offering dealt with the offense of sin and the trespass offering with the damages of sin, which is why the latter offering included the payment of an additional one-fifth in excess of the indebted amount. Restitution for past sins occurred per the Law, and the offering priests benefitted from the people's desire to be right with God. Today, the Body of Christ benefits from every believer who repents from sin, is reconciled with Lord, and continues to walk in holiness with Him.

The Apostasy of Joash (2 Chron. 24:15-22)

Jehoiada the priest died at 130 years of age and was buried in the City of David among the kings (2 Chron. 24:15). This means that Jehoiada was about one hundred years old when young Joash first came to the temple – there was about a century in age between them.

Why did Jehoiada enjoy such a long life? Because the Lord knew the heart of Joash to be unreliable. Without accountability to Jehoiada,

Joash would have been prone to waver spiritually and morally, a reality that becomes evident shortly. God's mercy to His people is therefore shown by extending Jehoiada's lifespan beyond any person during the previous seven hundred years of biblical history (Aram, the great-grandson of Jacob and father of Moses, lived to be 137 years old; Ex. 6:20).

Jehoiada followed the Lord his entire lifetime. And the historian reminds us that this is why his countrymen greatly honored him after his death: *"he had done good in Israel, both toward God and His house"* (2 Chron. 24:16).

Sadly, Joash soon proved to be a follower and not a true leader. Shortly after his godly mentor died, certain elders in Judah influenced Joash to cease worshiping Jehovah at the temple and to bow to wooden images and various idols (2 Chron. 24:17-18). The Lord sent prophets to warn the king and his people of the consequences of their sin, but they would not listen (2 Chron. 24:19).

One such prophet was Zechariah the son of Jehoiada the priest. As inspired by the Holy Spirit, he stood up among the people and delivered a stern warning from the Lord: *"Why do you transgress the commandments of the Lord, so that you cannot prosper? Because you have forsaken the Lord, He also has forsaken you"* (2 Chron. 24:20). After hearing this message, the king commanded that Zechariah be stoned, even though he was standing in the courtyard of the temple (2 Chron. 24:21).

Joash did not remember the kindness which Jehoiada had shown him. Not only did the high priest save his life as an infant, but he had raised him as his own son. How did Joash show his gratitude to Jehoiada? He ordered that Jehoiada's son, Zechariah, be murdered in the court of the Lord's house. Zechariah would have been like a brother to Joash. John Heading explains that Joash's act was doubly offensive to God because it occurred at His house:

> This should be contrasted with Solomon's act when Joab was slain by the altar of the tabernacle (1 Kgs. 2:29, 34), the difference being that the tabernacle had previously been forsaken by the Lord (Ps. 78:60). In the case of Joash, all his memories of hiding in the house, and rebuilding the house, had no effect on him. He used holy things with which to commit sin contrary to the commandments of God. Sin in the house is objectionable, and should be compared with the sin that

> the Lord found in the house (John 2:14). The Scriptures summarize the situation, *"the king remembered not the kindness which Jehoiada his father had done to him"* (2 Chron. 24:22); here was a man without a heart.[82]

It is hard to imagine a colder heart than Joash's at this juncture, but his apostasy did not stop with the stoning of Zechariah at the temple. The king further mocked the Lord afterwards, saying, *"The Lord look on it, and repay!"* (2 Chron. 24:22). And as Joash would soon learn, the Lord would repay Joash for his appalling crime.

It is noteworthy that the Lord Jesus later used Joash's example to rebuke the stiff-necked rebellious attitude of the Jewish lawyers (Luke 11:51). The Lord said that blood from all the prophets (i.e., from the first, Abel, to the last, Zechariah) would be required of that guilty generation. As Chronicles is the last book in the Hebrew Bible and Genesis is the first, the Lord was saying that the shed blood of all the Old Testament martyrs would be avenged.

Hazael Threatens Jerusalem (2 Kgs. 12:17-18)

Hazael, the king of Syria, conquered Gath and then was determined to conquer Jerusalem (2 Kgs. 12:17). Because he was away from the Lord, the king did not seek Jehovah's help or counsel. Instead, he took the sacred things that were his fathers' – Jehoshaphat, Jehoram, and Ahaziah – and all the gold in the temple treasuries and sent them to Hazael. The king of Syria was satisfied with the gift and turned his army away from Jerusalem.

The Death of Joash (2 Kings 12:19-21; 2 Chron. 24:23-27)

However, sometime later, that Syrian army invaded Judah and Jerusalem again; it was springtime (2 Chron. 24:23). Although the Syrian army was much smaller than Judah's, the Lord permitted the Syrians to slay Judah's leaders and despoil the people because the people had forsaken Him (2 Chron. 24:24). Apparently, the Syrians left Joash severely wounded and then his own servants Zabad (also called Jozachar) and Jehozabad conspired against him because of the innocent blood he had shed in Jehoiada's family; they killed Joash while in his bed (2 Chron. 24:25-26). Joash died in the house of the Millo which goes down to Silla (2 Kgs. 12:20).

Joash was buried in the City of David, but he was not buried in the tombs of the kings, as Jehoiada was. He was the youngest king to ever sit on Judah's throne and reigned forty years in Jerusalem (835-796 B.C.). Joash's son Amaziah reigned in his place (2 Chron. 24:27). Joash started well for the Lord, but finished poorly and was not respected by his countrymen. The apostasy of the king caused the entire nation to drift from the Lord and then to suffer under His chastening.

Lot did well when he followed consecrated Abraham, but when he separated from the man of faith, he became enamored with Sodom. Though his soul was vexed daily by the sins of that place, he still remained there. As a result, Lot lost his testimony and eventually everything he had, except for his two immoral daughters. When Jehoiada died, the godly influence guiding Joash was gone. He was on his own, and what he really was soon became evident – a carnal man without true conviction. He lost everything also, even his life at forty-seven years of age.

MacDonald suggests an application for believers: "It is vital that we persevere in godliness lest we hinder the kingdom of God. Jehoiada, a shining example! Joash, a solemn warning!"[83] Thank God for godly people who influence us to do well for the Lord, but how it must thrill the heart of God for people to choose to follow Him because they really love Him and want to.

Meditation

> Be more concerned with your character than your reputation, because your character is what you really are, while your reputation is merely what others think you are. The true test of a man's character is what he does when no one is watching.
>
> — John Wooden

Kings Jehoahaz and Jehoash of Israel

2 Kings 13

Jehoahaz Reigns in Israel (2 Kgs. 13:1-9)

Jehu's son Jehoahaz became Israel's king in the twenty-third year of Joash, king of Judah (2 Kgs. 13:1). He reigned in Samaria for seventeen years (814-798 B.C.). Jehoahaz did evil in the sight of the Lord and caused Israel to continue in the sins of his father who upheld the religious system of Jeroboam (2 Kgs. 13:2).

Israel's rebellion provoked God's anger, so He permitted Syria, ruled by Hazael and then his son Ben-Hadad II, to overcome the Northern Kingdom (2 Kgs. 13:3). The situation was bleak, for the Syrians had reduced Jehoahaz's army to a token force of only fifty horsemen, ten chariots, and ten thousand foot soldiers (2 Kgs. 13:7). This severe oppression caused King Jehoahaz to plead with the Lord, who listened to him and gave Israel an unnamed deliverer to end Syria's invasion (2 Kgs. 13:4-5). The unnamed deliverer might be Adanirari III, the king of Assyria, or perhaps the prophet Elisha who declared God's deliverance. Jamieson, Fausset, and Brown suggest that the "savior" refers to Israel's next two kings succeeding Jehoahaz, "namely, Joash, who regained all the cities which the Syrians had taken from his father (2 Kgs. 13:25) and Jeroboam II."[84]

Even though God had saved them from harm in answer to Jehoahaz's prayer, the people still did not repent from the sins of Jeroboam and maintained a wooden image in Samaria (2 Kgs. 13:6). Jehoahaz died and was buried with his fathers in Samaria. His son Jehoash reigned in his place (2 Kgs. 13:9).

Jehoash (Joash) Reigns in Israel (2 Kgs. 13:10-13)

In the thirty-seventh year of Joash king of Judah, Jehoash the son of Jehoahaz became king over Israel in Samaria (2 Kgs. 13:10). He reigned sixteen years (798 to 782 B.C.) and did evil in the sight of the Lord, for like his father and grandfather, he continued Jeroboam's religion in Israel (2 Kgs. 13:11). Jehoash and his son Jeroboam II shared coregency the last eleven years of Jehoash's rule.

Not much is known about Jehoash, other than he did war with Amaziah, the king of Judah (2 Kgs. 13:12) and had a conversation with the prophet Elisha just before he died (2 Kgs. 13:14-19). Jehoash died and was buried with his fathers in Samaria and his son Jeroboam II sat on the throne of Israel (2 Kgs. 13:13).

The Death of Elisha (2 Kgs. 13:14-21)

We are not told what Elisha had been doing since his last official act of anointing of Jehu four decades earlier (in 841 B.C.; 2 Kgs. 6). We learn in this chapter that Elisha had an illness that would result in his death.

Jehoash (Joash) the king of Israel came down to visit the prophet. The king wept over Elisha, saying, *"O my father, my father, the chariots of Israel and their horsemen!"* (2 Kgs. 13:14). This same expression was uttered by Elisha at Elijah's home-calling to show respect and fondness for the one departing. Jehoash valued the prophet's presence in his kingdom. Elisha had been a loyal guardian of Israel and an honorable servant of the Lord and therefore would be missed (2 Kgs. 2:12). By using the title "father," Jehoash conveyed his deep respect for Elisha, even regarding him as a superior. It is evident that, though Jehoash continued following the precepts of Jeroboam's religion (even naming a son after him), he still respected Jehovah. The prophet responded to the king's grief by rendering one final prophecy.

He told the king to take his bow and some arrows (2 Kgs. 13:15). While the king held his bow, Elisha put his hand on the king's hand holding his bow, then Elisha told him to open the east window (towards Syria) and shoot an arrow through the open window, which the king did (2 Kgs. 13:16). The prophet then responded: *"The arrow of the Lord's deliverance and the arrow of deliverance from Syria; for you must strike the Syrians at Aphek till you have destroyed them"* (2 Kgs. 13:17). Then Elisha told the king to take some arrows and strike the ground with them, which the king did three times (2 Kgs. 13:18). And Elisha then angrily reproved the king for striking the ground only three times, saying that he should have struck five or six times to symbolize a complete defeat of Syria (1 Kgs. 13:19). But since he struck the ground only three times, he would win only three battles against Syria and would not completely overcome Israel's enemy.

Not long after this conversation, Elisha died and was buried in an unnamed location (1 Kgs. 13:20). Elijah anointed Elisha as a prophet during Ahab's reign (which concluded a few years later in 853 B.C.). Elisha died early in the reign of Jehoash of Israel, probably in the 796 to 795 B.C. timeframe. This would indicate that Elisha's total ministry spanned about sixty years, although we are not informed how active he was as a prophet in his later years.

The next spring, marauders from Moab raided Israel. One such raid occurred while several men were carrying a man's body to a burial site. Not wanting to be caught by the Moabite raiders, they hastily placed the dead man's body in Elisha's tomb, but when the corpse touched the bones of Elisha, the man revived and stood on his feet (1 Kgs. 12:21). This would be the fourteenth miracle associated with Elisha, which, as previously mentioned, would be exactly twice the number of miracles performed by Elijah. Indeed, Elisha had received a double portion of Elijah's spirit as Elijah had predicted.

Israel Recaptures Cities (2 Kgs. 13:22-25)

The historian closes the chapter by reporting how Hazael king of Syria oppressed Israel during all the days of King Jehoahaz (2 Kgs. 13:22). Yet, the Lord was gracious to his people and had compassion on them because of His covenant with their forefathers; therefore, He did not destroy them or cast them from His presence (2 Kgs. 13:23).

After Hazael's death, his son Ben-Hadad II reigned on Syria's throne (2 Kgs. 13:24). As foretold by Elisha, Jehoash had a measure of success against Ben-Hadad II and was able to retake cities in Israel that had been captured during his father Jehoahaz's reign (2 Kgs. 13:25).

There is not much to cheer about in this chapter which focuses on the reigns of two pseudo-evil kings in Israel. Although they did not lead Israel into gross idolatry as Ahab did, they were still replacing God-ordained worship with a humanized version of Jehovah worship, which angered the Lord.

God's faithfulness to His covenant people despite all their rebellious doings is comforting and reminds us of what Paul said of the Lord Jesus: *"If we are faithless, He remains faithful; He cannot deny Himself"* (2 Tim. 2:13). Those in Christ are forever secure in Him, even when we do things that grieve His heart. May we be encouraged to live for the Lord; as believers we are on the winning side, the present world is a fading mirage, and there are better things yet to come.

Meditation

> "Great is Thy faithfulness," O God my Father,
> There is no shadow of turning with Thee;
> Thou changest not, Thy compassions, they fail not;
> As Thou hast been Thou forever wilt be.
>
> "Great is Thy faithfulness!" "Great is Thy faithfulness!"
> Morning by morning new mercies I see;
> All I have needed Thy hand hath provided –
> "Great is Thy faithfulness," Lord, unto me!
>
> — Thomas Chisholm

King Amaziah of Judah

2 Kings 14:1-22; 2 Chronicles 25

Amaziah Reigns in Judah (2 Kgs. 14:1-6; 2 Chron. 25:1-4)

Amaziah, the son of Joash, became king of Judah in the second year that Jehoash was reigning over Israel (2 Kgs. 14:1). He was twenty-five years old when he became king and ruled Judah for twenty-nine years (796-767 B.C.); his mother was Jehoaddan of Jerusalem (2 Kgs. 14:2). He did what was right in the sight of the Lord, but *"not like his father David"*; rather, he followed the quasi-good example of his father Joash (referring to his early years as king; 2 Kgs. 14:3). Amaziah was not a reformer, but he did identify with Jehovah. His lukewarm devotion did not lead Judah nearer to the Lord, nor did it cause him to end the offense of worshiping Jehovah in the high places instead of His temple (2 Kgs. 14:4). His foolish veneration of Edom's defeated gods later in his reign was exceptionally offensive to God.

Amaziah's first act in office was to execute his father's servant-assassins (2 Kgs. 14:5). He did not, however, take vengeance out on the families of the two murderers, but rather heeded the Law of Moses which commanded that: *"Fathers shall not be put to death for their children, nor shall children be put to death for their fathers; but a person shall be put to death for his own sin"* (2 Kgs. 14:6).

The War With Edom and Amaziah's Apostasy (2 Kgs. 14:7; 2 Chron.25:5-16)

When Amaziah was approximately thirty-nine years old, he organized a great army with a viable command structure and enlisted men twenty years old and above throughout Judah and Benjamin (2 Chron. 25:5). A force of 300,000 choice soldiers who could handle spear and shield was assembled for the purpose of battling Edom. Not satisfied with this tally, Amaziah also hired 100,000 mercenaries from

Israel for 100 talents of silver to join his offensive against Edom (2 Chron. 25:6). However, God sent a prophet to deliver a message to the king:

> *O king, do not let the army of Israel go with you, for the Lord is not with Israel – not with any of the children of Ephraim. But if you go, be gone! Be strong in battle! Even so, God shall make you fall before the enemy; for God has power to help and to overthrow* (2 Chron. 25:7-8).

When Amaziah complained to the man of God that he had already paid the soldiers from Israel the 100 talents of silver, the prophet told the king, *"the Lord is able to give you much more than this"* (2 Chron. 25:9). Though having already paid the mercenaries, Amaziah heeded the word of God spoken through His prophet and discharged the troops from Ephraim, which greatly angered them (2 Chron. 25:10).

The Lord was with Amaziah as he led his army against Edom in the Valley of Salt. The army of Judah killed ten thousand Edomites and captured another ten thousand alive, but then those prisoners were cast off a high rock to their deaths (2 Chron. 25:11-12). Amaziah also captured Sela (probably Petra) and renamed the city, Joktheel (2 Kgs. 14:7).

This great victory was marred by two events. First, the discharged soldiers from Israel were infuriated by their dismissal and raided several cities in Judah as far north as Beth Horon; they butchered 3,000 people and took much spoil (2 Chron. 25:13). Second, Amaziah brought back to Jerusalem the gods of the Edomites, whom he had just defeated (2 Chron. 25:14). Why he bowed down and burned incense to the very images that were unable to protect their worshipers is unexplainable. Jehovah had just honored His word to deliver the Edomites to Amaziah and the king showed his thankfulness by honoring the false deities of his defeated foes.

The Lord was angry with Amaziah and sent one of His prophets to warn him, *"Why have you sought the gods of the people, which could not rescue their own people from your hand?"* (2 Chron. 25:15). The king rejected the prophet's message and retorted, *"Have we made you the king's counselor? Cease! Why should you be killed?"* So the prophet abruptly ceased imploring Amaziah to repent of his idolatry and ended their discussion with this statement: *"I know that God has determined to destroy you, because you have done this and have not heeded my advice"* (2 Chron. 25:16).

Israel Defeats Judah (2 Kings 14:8-14; 2 Chron. 25:17-24)

The killing and plundering by the mercenaries from Israel prompted Amaziah to send a declaration of war to Jehoash, Israel's king: *"Come, let us face one another in battle"* (2 Kgs. 14:8). Jehoash sent a messenger back to Amaziah with a parable to incite his anger:

> *The thistle that was in Lebanon sent to the cedar that was in Lebanon, saying, "Give your daughter to my son as wife"; and a wild beast that was in Lebanon passed by and trampled the thistle. You have indeed defeated Edom, and your heart has lifted you up. Glory in that, and stay at home; for why should you meddle with trouble so that you fall – you and Judah with you?* (2 Kgs. 14:9-10).

Jehoash's parable highlights the ludicrous behavior of a thistle (a plant of no value) making impertinent demands on a towering cedar. The former image was being ascribed to Judah, and the latter to Israel. Although the message was not conveyed in a spirit of humility, what Jehoash said was basically true. But since the provocation was promped by the Lord to punish Judah, Amaziah did not heed Jehoash's warning (2 Kgs. 14:11).

In 792 B.C., the two armies met at Beth Shemesh in Judah and Amaziah's army was routed by Israel's army led by Jehoash (2 Kgs. 14:12). Jehoash captured Amaziah at Beth Shemesh and then led his army to Jerusalem, where he broke down the city's wall from the Gate of Ephraim to the Corner Gate (about six hundred feet; 2 Kgs. 14:13). The king of Israel then took all the gold and silver found in the temple and in the king's treasuries and returned to Samaria with many hostages (2 Kgs. 14:14). Amaziah remained a prisoner in Israel for twelve years. During this time his young son Azariah ruled Judah.

The Death of King Amaziah (2 Kgs. 14:15-20; 2 Chron. 25:25-28)

Amaziah the son of Joash ruled Judah for fifteen years after the death of Jehoash the son of Jehoahaz, king of Israel, in 782 B.C. (2 Chron. 25:26). Although Amaziah ruled for a total of twenty-nine years, twelve of those years were spent in Israel as a prisoner. Amaziah returned to Jerusalem after being released, but since his victory over Edom years earlier, he had turned away from following the Lord. There was a conspiracy against him which caused him to flee westward to the fortified city of Lachish (2 Chron. 25:27). He was pursued and killed at Lachish, and his body was brought back to the City of David and Amaziah was buried with his fathers (2 Chron. 25:28).

Amaziah started well and was blessed for it, but Judah suffered much after their king became proud and began revering false gods, instead of solely worshiping and relying on Jehovah. It is interesting to note that Matthew passes over Judah's last three disappointing kings when detailing the genealogy of Christ (Matt. 1); Ahaziah, Joash, and Amaziah are not mentioned, because their lives were not honoring to the Lord.

King Solomon warned that the Lord will not tolerate pride, especially in those who rule His people: *"The fear of the Lord is to hate evil, pride and arrogance, and the evil way"* (Prov. 8:13). *"By pride comes nothing but strife"* (Prov. 13:10). *"Pride goes before destruction and a haughty spirit before a fall"* (Prov. 16:18). *"A man's pride will bring him low, but the humble in spirit will retain honor"* (Prov. 29:23). God hated Amaziah's pride and therefore brought him low at great cost to those he ruled over. Beware, dear believer: God hates our pride too (Prov. 6:16)!

Meditation

> I have had more trouble with myself than with any other man.
>
> — D. L. Moody

> None are more unjust in their judgments of others than those who have a high opinion of themselves.
>
> — Charles Spurgeon

King Jeroboam II of Israel

2 Kings 14:23-29

Jeroboam II, the son of Jehoash, became Israel's king in the fifteenth year of Amaziah; he ruled from Samaria for forty-one years (793-753 B.C.; 2 Kgs. 14:23). Jeroboam II was coregent with his father Jehoash for about twelve years. He followed his father's legacy of holding to the doctrines of the first Jeroboam, who caused Israel to sin before the Lord (2 Kgs. 14:24).

Under Jeroboam II, Israel's affluence was at its apex; Israel had a strong military and enjoyed economic and political prosperity. He even restored Israel's previously lost territory in the Transjordan. This was between the entrance of Hamath about 150 miles northeast of the Sea of Galilee to the Sea of the Arabah (the Dead Sea), in the south (2 Kgs. 14:25).

The historian notes that Jonah (from Gath Hepher) had a prophetic ministry during Jeroboam's reign before the Lord sent him to Nineveh (2 Kgs. 14:26). The Northern Kingdom was enjoying a time of wonderful prosperity because the Lord had seen their previous affliction and was determined to alleviate it. The Lord would also affirm His word to the Northern Kingdom by a number of His prophets during this era (2 Kgs. 14:27).

Besides Jonah, we also know that Hosea and Amos served the Lord as prophets during Jeroboam II's reign. Isaiah delivered messages to the Southern Kingdom during this time also. Hosea's prophetic ministry to the Northern Kingdom occurred *"in the days of Uzziah, Jotham, Ahaz, and Hezekiah, kings of Judah, and in the days of Jeroboam the son of Joash, king of Israel"* (Hos. 1:1). Since King Jeroboam II ruled over Israel from 793-753 B.C. and Hezekiah sat on Judah's throne from 715-686 B.C., Hosea's ministry would have lasted a minimum of 39 years and more likely in the sixty-year range.

The prophet Amos also delivered God's messages to the Northern Kingdom during the reigns of Jeroboam II in Israel and Uzziah in

Judah, about two years before an earthquake struck the region in 860 B.C. (Amos 1:1). Amos mentions that living conditions in Israel had drastically improved under Jeroboam II's reign. Instead of the shacks the Israelites were forced to live in under foreign rulers, many now had comfortable houses of hewn stone (Amos 5:11). As today, the accumulation of wealth and luxurious living are often followed by moral decline and spiritual degeneracy; such was the case in Jeroboam's reign.

Hosea warned Jeroboam II of Israel's coming judgment through a botanical metaphor in Hosea chapter 10. The Israelite nation bore some refreshing fruit for the Lord during those early years together in the wilderness, but that was not the situation now (Hos. 9:10). Hosea rightly assesses: *"Israel empties his vine; he brings forth fruit for himself"* (Hos. 10:1). Centuries earlier, Asaph spoke of Israel as a vine brought out of Egypt that had once flourished because of God's care, but because of the nation's unfaithfulness had been repeatedly trampled on by invaders (Ps. 80). Hosea employs the same imagery and message for the Northern Kingdom here, as will Isaiah, Jeremiah, and Ezekiel in later warnings against the Southern Kingdom (Isa. 5:1; Jer. 8:13, 12:10-13; Ezek. 15). This prophetic choir resounded God's assessment of the Israelite nation: Israel was a worthless vine/vineyard because of its fruitless disposition towards God.

Although the Northern Kingdom was presently enjoying prosperity, from God's perspective Israel had only lush foliage, but its fruit was worthless because it was self-produced for itself. It was not from God or for God. At a glance, the vine appeared prosperous and healthy during Jeroboam's reign, but the more God blessed Israel materially, the more she became self-absorbed, yielding corruption. God's vine had produced nothing valuable to Him – it was empty and needed to be uprooted.

The prophet Amos delivers a similar message to the Northern Kingdom, by delivering a eulogy about their demise (although Israel had not yet been judged; Amos 5:1). How shocked his countrymen must have been to hear a grief-stricken Amos reading their obituary aloud. While Amos' dirge must have had a jaw-dropping effect on his happy-go-lucky audience, no spiritual revival occurred in Israel. They were experiencing wonderful affluence under Jeroboam's leadership: Why should they be concerned about following the Lord? Indeed this is a debilitating mindset that hinders many people from following the Lord today.

Jeroboam died and was buried with the kings of Israel in Samaria and his son Zechariah reigned in his place (2 Kgs. 14:28-29). Turbulent years were ahead for Israel, as four of Israel's next kings would be assassinated (between 752-732 B.C.).[85] Israel's economy would rapidly decline and the Northern Kingdom would experience invasion, defeat, and wide-scale death and dispersion over the next thirty years. Israel's glory days were over and the wrath of God was coming.

Meditation

God is longsuffering, slow to anger, and quick to forgive,
Yet we must do as He commands without neglect or delay.
Someday there will be no more todays for Him to give.
So let us not linger between now and never, but swiftly obey.

— W.A.H.

King Uzziah (Azariah) of Judah

2 Chronicles 26; 2 Kings 15:1-7

Uzziah Reigns in Judah (2 Kgs. 15:1-4; 2 Chron. 26:1-15)

Uzziah (Azariah) became the king of Judah at the age of sixteen after his father Amaziah was taken prisoner to Israel by Jehoash. This event happened in the twenty-seventh year of Jeroboam II's reign in Israel (790 B.C.; 2 Kgs. 15:1). (Note that Jeroboam II ruled twelve of these twenty-seven years with his father Jehoash.[86]) Jehoash died in 782 B.C. and sometime afterwards Amaziah returned from Israel to Judah and shared the regency with Uzziah until Amaziah's death in 767 B.C. Uzziah's mother's name was Jecholiah of Jerusalem and he ruled Judah altogether for fifty-two years (790-739 B.C. ; 2 Kgs. 15:2). After he became a leper, Uzziah shared regency with his son Jotham.

King Uzziah was better than many kings who ruled over the Southern Kingdom: "*King Uzziah did what was right in the sight of the Lord, according to all that his father, Amaziah, did*" (2 Chron. 26:4). The historian is comparing the early part of both king's reigns, for neither man finished well. Like his father Amaziah, Uzziah was not a reformer; nor did he remove the high places of worship. He was, however, blessed for following the Lord, for "*as long as he sought the Lord, God made him prosper*" (2 Chron. 26:5). The king was fortunate to experience the meaning of both his names: Azariah means "Jehovah has helped" and Uzziah means "Jehovah is my strength."

His leadership brought Judah economic prosperity, technological improvements, and vast military strength. He won victories against Gath, Jabneh, and Ashdod and then tore down the walls of those cities and built fortified garrisons about them (2 Chron. 26:6). Not only did God give him victories against the Philistines, but He also helped Uzziah against the Arabians at Gur Baal and against the Meunites (2 Chron. 26:7). The Ammonites brought tribute to Uzziah and the fame of his military might spread all the way to Egypt (2 Chron. 26:8).

Uzziah also fortified Jerusalem's defenses by building towers at the Corner Gate, the Valley Gate, and at the corner buttress of the wall (2 Chron. 26:9). Even in times of prosperity and blessing, it is wise to attend to the protection of God's people, as the enemy often strikes when least expected. Paul told the Ephesian elders that they must always be alert to properly guard those in their care:

> *Therefore take heed to yourselves and to all the flock, among which the Holy Spirit has made you overseers, to shepherd the church of God which He purchased with His own blood. For I know this, that after my departure savage wolves will come in among you, not sparing the flock. Also from among yourselves men will rise up, speaking perverse things, to draw away the disciples after themselves. Therefore watch* (Acts 20:28-31).

Additionally, the king built surveillance and communication towers in the desert, dug many wells, and had much livestock, farmland and vineyards (2 Chron. 26:10).

Uzziah's army had 2,600 chief officers (all mighty men) who commanded 370,500 well-equipped and well-trained soldiers (2 Chron. 26:10-13). Besides the shields, spears, helmets, body armor, bows, and slings for his soldiers, he built catapults on the towers to shoot arrows and throw large stones (2 Chron. 26:14). The writer then summarized the height of Uzziah's popularity: *"His fame spread far and wide, for he was marvelously helped till he became strong"* (2 Chron. 26:15).

Uzziah's Pride (2 Kings 15:4; 2 Chron. 26:16-20)

Uzziah's accomplishments, however, caused him to think more highly of himself than he did of his God: *"But when he was strong his heart was lifted up, to his destruction, for he transgressed against the Lord his God by entering the temple of the Lord to burn incense on the altar of incense"* (2 Chron. 26:16). In arrogance he brought a censer into the temple to offer worship to Jehovah. This was an intrusion upon the priesthood which God had strictly forbidden (i.e., only Levitical priests could perform such tasks and then only according to the Law). What happened next was astounding:

> *So Azariah the priest went in after him, and with him were eighty priests of the Lord – valiant men. And they withstood King Uzziah,*

> *and said to him, "It is not for you, Uzziah, to burn incense to the Lord, but for the priests, the sons of Aaron, who are consecrated to burn incense. Get out of the sanctuary, for you have trespassed! You shall have no honor from the Lord God." Then Uzziah became furious; and he had a censer in his hand to burn incense. And while he was angry with the priests, leprosy broke out on his forehead, before the priests in the house of the Lord, beside the incense altar. And Azariah the chief priest and all the priests looked at him, and there, on his forehead, he was leprous; so they thrust him out of that place. Indeed he also hurried to get out, because the Lord had struck him. King Uzziah was a leper until the day of his death. He dwelt in an isolated house, because he was a leper; for he was cut off from the house of the Lord* (2 Chron. 26:17-21).

When King Uzziah served the Lord obediently, he was blessed. Yet, when he went his own way, God humbled him. King Uzziah was struck with leprosy on his forehead to symbolize the sin of pride (Lev. 13:29). The Lord will not tolerate pride, especially in those ruling His people. God's judgment immediately fell on Uzziah while he was in God's house. This reminds us of Peter's exhortation: *"For the time has come for judgment to begin at the house of God; and if it begins with us first, what will be the end of those who do not obey the gospel of God?"* (1 Pet. 4:17). During the Church Age, the house of God is a spiritual temple that He is building one living stone at a time (1 Pet. 2:5). When the Church upholds the righteousness of God by judging sin within its members, the power of the gospel message is accurately conveyed in both word and deed. A carnal church has no power to preach the gospel, but rather her hypocrisy numbs the consciences of the lost by endorsing their sin.

There was no cure for leprosy in Old Testament days; it brought social isolation and a slow, agonizing death. Its damage to the nervous system often prevented individuals from being properly treated for injuries, as typically no pain was felt when injury occurred.

Like Uzziah the leper, Israel's ongoing sin had made them numb to the pangs of their conscience, and they were further injuring their souls through idolatry. Pain is generally a good thing because it alerts us to what needs attention, but Israel was ignoring the warnings given by God's prophets. Hence, the nation, like Uzziah, was isolated, suffering, and heading towards death. This is likely the reason Isaiah ties his prophetic calling to Uzziah's death and not to his life – there is no life apart from God (Isa. 6:1). Today there is a cure for leprosy and, thankfully, there is a cure for the sin it represents – the Lord Jesus Christ.

Uzziah's Death (2 Kgs. 15:5-7; 2 Chron. 26:21-23)

King Uzziah was a leper until the day of his death. He lived in an isolated house, and, as a leper, was prohibited from coming before the Lord at the temple (2 Chron. 26:21). He co-reigned over Judah with his son Jotham for about thirteen years (2 Kgs. 15:5), his son being the one who actually judged the people. Uzziah died and was buried in a field associated with the tombs of the kings of Judah because he was a leper (2 Chron. 26:22). Jotham continued ruling over Judah after his father's death for about four more years (2 Chron. 26:23).

Meditation

> Pride springs from desire. Man aspires to obtain a place for himself that he may feel honored before men. He loves to hear praising voices and considers them just and true. He also attempts to elevate himself in his work, whether in preaching or in writing, for his secret self-motive goads him on. In a word, this one has not yet died to his desire of vainglory. He is still seeking what he desires and what can inflate him. ... Do not be taken in or flattered by your own success or fame. Only what has gone through the cross matters.
>
> — Watchman Nee

Kings Zechariah, Shallum, Menahem, Pekahiah, and Pekah of Israel

2 Kings 15:8-31

The thirty-year era of Israel's final six kings (752-722 B.C.) was marked by political upheaval, foreign subjection, and desolation, culminating in Assyrian invasion and captivity. Israel's ally at this time, Syria, served as a buffer state against the strengthening Assyrian Empire. After Syria fell to Assyria in 732 B.C., Israel was vulnerable and ripe for invasion. As predicted by the prophets Amos and Hosea years earlier, the Northern Kingdom fell to Assyria. This occurred in 722 B.C.

Zechariah Reigns in Israel (2 Kgs. 15:8-12)

Zechariah the son of Jeroboam II gained the throne of Israel in Samaria in the thirty-eighth year of Uzziah (Azariah) king of Judah (2 Kgs. 15:8). He reigned for six months in 753 B.C. and did evil in the sight of the Lord – he continued Jeroboam I's religious system in Israel (2 Kgs. 15:9). Shallum, the son of Jabesh, conspired against Zechariah and murdered the king in front of the people; he reigned over Israel in his place (2 Kgs. 15:10).

The historian then noted that this event fulfilled God's word to Jehu, *"Your sons shall sit on the throne of Israel to the fourth generation"* (2 Kgs. 15:11-12). This prophecy was fulfilled in 752 B.C. when Shallum killed Zechariah and ended Jehu's dynasty in the fourth generation (2 Kgs. 15:10). Furthermore, the fulfillment of Hosea's prophecy concerning God's vengeance on Jehu for the innocent blood shed at Jezreel would signal the complete collapse of the Northern Kingdom (Hos. 1:3-5). Tiglath-Pileser III of Assyria overtook the plain of Jezreel and defeated Israel in 733 B.C., which led to the fall of Samaria in 722 B.C. Afterwards, Israel became a province of Assyria and many of her surviving inhabitants were exiled.

With the end of Jehu's dynasty, Israel's glory days were over; the nation rapidly deteriorated economically, politically, and militarily. The quick succession of kings, often through assassination, brought chaos to the Northern Kingdom. The time had come for God to severely judge Israel's two and a half centuries of idolatry.

Shallum Reigns in Israel (2 Kgs. 15:13-16)

Shallum, the son of Jabesh, reigned only one month (in 752 B.C.) during the thirty-ninth year of Uzziah king of Judah before being assassinated by Menahem from Tirzah (2 Kgs. 15:13-14). In the uprising to overcome Shallum, Tiphsah would not surrender, so Menahem destroyed the city and treated its inhabitants brutally, even to ripping open all the pregnant women (2 Kgs. 15:15-16). His harsh dealings with Tiphsah would serve as a deterrent to other cities from opposing his kingship.

Menahem Reigns in Israel (2 Kgs. 15:17-22)

Menahem the son of Gadi became king over Israel, and reigned ten years in Samaria (752-742 B.C.; 2 Kgs. 15:17). He did evil in the sight of the Lord and continued the idolatrous system of Jeroboam (2 Kgs. 15:18). Menahem was from Tirzah, the original capital of Israel until Omri moved it to Samaria in the seventh year of his reign (2 Kgs. 15:14). Historical information indicates that there was a growing hostility between the western part of the Northern Kingdom (referred to as "Ephraim") and the eastern portion, called "Israel," during the final years before the Assyrian invasion.[87] The Northern Kingdom was unraveling – spiraling downward to its destruction.

Pul, the king of Assyria, invaded Israel, and Menahem gave him 1,000 talents of silver to maintain his position on the throne, and to hopefully gain Assyria's assistance in the future if needed (2 Kgs. 15:19). However, Assyria would not be helping Israel any time soon; rather, God would use the nation to sternly chasten His people.

This large amount of silver was gained through heavy taxation of the people, especially the wealthy, as each man was forced to pay fifty shekels of silver to the king of Assyria. Pul did withdraw from Israel without a war, but Menahem's tactic only delayed the inevitable – Israel would be conquered and taken into exile by Assyria (2 Kgs.

15:20). Menahem died and his son Pekahiah reigned in his place (2 Kgs. 15:21-22).

Pekahiah Reigns in Israel (2 Kgs. 15:23-26)

Pekahiah, the son of Menahem, became king over Israel in the fiftieth year of Uzziah (Azariah) king of Judah (2 Kgs. 15:23). He reigned two years in Samaria (742-740 B.C.) and did evil in the sight of the Lord, *"he did not depart from the sins of Jeroboam the son of Nebat, who had made Israel sin"* (2 Kgs. 15:24). One of Pekahiah's officers, Pekah, led an insurrection, along with Argob and Arieh and fifty men from Gilead. They successfully assassinated the king in the citadel of the king's house in Samaria (2 Kgs. 15:25-26).

Pekah Reigns in Israel (2 Kgs. 15:27-31)

Pekah, the son of Remaliah, became king over Israel in Samaria in the fifty-second year of Uzziah (Azariah) king of Judah (2 Kgs. 15:27). He reigned twenty years and caused Israel to continue in the sins of Jeroboam (2 Kgs. 15:28). There is a chronological difficulty with this statement because if Pekah became king of Israel in 740 B.C. and reigned twenty years, that would be two years past the fall of the Northern Kingdom to Assyria in 722 B.C. Furthermore, Hosea (Israel's last king) ruled for nine years after Pekah's reign. McNeely suggests that the most plausible explanation is "that Pekah, the easterner, ruled over the eastern area of Gilead, not as a coregent, but as a contemporary of Menahem and his son Pekahiah."[88] This would mean that Pekah's rule began in 752 B.C. and ended in 732 B.C. and hence overlapped the reigns of Menahem and Pekahiah, until Pekah executed Pekahiah in 740 B.C.

Tiglath-Pileser III (Pul), king of Assyria, invaded Israel and captured Ijon, Abel Beth Maachah, Janoah, Kedesh, Hazor, Gilead, and Galilee, and all the land of Naphtali in 734-732 B.C. (2 Kgs. 15:29). Tiglath-Pileser took many Israelites back to Assyria as slaves. In the twentieth year of Jotham the king of Judah (732 B.C.), Hoshea led a conspiracy against Pekah and reigned in his place after murdering him (2 Kgs. 15:30-31).

Meditation

The world's corruption is a result of its defiance.

— Warren Wiersbe

Nothing hath separated us from God but our own will, or rather our own will is our separation from God.

— William Law

King Jotham of Judah

2 Kings 15:32-38; 2 Chronicles 27

Jotham, the son of Uzziah, began to reign in Judah in the second year of Pekah, the king of Israel (2 Kgs. 15:32). Jotham was twenty-five years old when he became king, and he reigned sixteen years in Jerusalem; his mother's name was Jerusha the daughter of Zadok (2 Kgs. 15:33). Twelve to thirteen years of his reign were as coregent with his father Uzziah; he became the sole king of Judah in 740 B.C. after his father's death. The prophet Micah began his ministry during Jotham's reign.

Jotham followed his father's godly example (though he did not enter the temple inappropriately as his father had done; 2 Chron. 27:2). Jotham *"did what was right in the sight of the Lord,"* but he did not remove the high places in Judah where the people continued to sacrifice and burn incense to Jehovah (2 Kgs. 15:34). Although this matter was considered trivial by most of Judah's kings, it did not go unnoticed by the Lord.

Not much is said about Jotham in Scripture, perhaps because he was a good king who enjoyed a successful and prestigious reign. This may explain why the prophet Isaiah did not deliver any messages from the Lord to him; he did not need to be rebuked. His notable accomplishments include: building the Upper (north) Gate of the house of the Lord, building up the wall of Ophel, and erecting fortified cities and towers throughout the mountains and forests of Judah (2 Chron. 27:3-4). This was necessary because Tiglath-Pileser was making frequent incursions into the region to expand Assyria's borders. We know from the Assyrian Annals that Assyria moved against the west in 743-738 B.C. and again in 736-732 B.C.[89]

Jotham defeated Ammon in battle; they then paid Jotham that year and the next two years: 100 talents of silver, 10,000 kors of wheat, and 10,000 kors of barley (2 Chron. 27:5). The writer of Chronicles then acknowledges why the king fared well during his reign: *"So Jotham became mighty, because he prepared his ways before the Lord his God"* (2 Chron. 27:6). His godly example and productivity stand in sharp contrast to the kings of Israel at this time. However, the writer of Kings notes that *"in those days the Lord began to send Rezin king of Syria and Pekah the son of Remaliah against Judah"* (2 Kgs. 15:27). This was necessary in God's providential care of Judah and dealing with her next king, Ahaz, whose heart would not be right with the Lord.

Jotham was one of Judah's best kings; he left a godly heritage for his children to follow. Jotham died and was buried with his fathers in the City of David and his son Ahaz reigned in his place (2 Chron. 27:9).

Meditation

> A father's responsibility is not to make the child's decisions, but to let the child watch him make his.
>
> — Ed Cole

King Ahaz of Judah

2 Kings 16; 2 Chronicles 28

The prophet Isaiah's ministry was to the southern kingdom, and it extended through the reigns of four kings: Uzziah, Jotham, Ahaz, and Hezekiah (Isa. 1:1). From a political, economic, and military standpoint, all these kings fared well. Three of the kings did largely what was morally right, Hezekiah especially so, but Ahaz *"did not do what was right in the sight of the Lord"* (2 Chron. 28:1). He was the first king of Judah to introduce something idolatrous and corrupting into the service of God at the temple (2 Chron. 28:2). He also was the first Judean king to offer his own children as burnt sacrifices to Baal: *"He burned incense in the Valley of the Son of Hinnom, and burned his children in the fire"* (2 Chron. 28:3). Matthew Henry explains the expression that Ahaz made his children "to pass through the fire" (2 Kgs. 16:3):

> That he made his sons to pass through the fire, to the honor of his dunghill-deities. He burnt them, so it is expressly said of him (2 Chron. 28:3), burnt some of them, and perhaps made others of them to pass between two fires, or to be drawn through a flame, in token of their dedication to the idol.[90]

This vile behavior explains why the contraction "Ahaz" is used in Scripture rather than referring to his given name "Jehoahaz" (as recorded on Syrian inscriptions). "Jeho-" is short for "Jehovah," and there was nothing about Ahaz that exalted Jehovah. Ahaz means "has held" and therefore Baal-ahaz would be a more appropriate name for this Judean king ensnared by gross idolatry.

Ahaz was everything his godly and industrious father was not: administratively, he was weak; politically, he was pro-Assyrian; religiously, he was an idolater. The writer of Kings summarizes his idolatry: *"He walked in the way of the kings of Israel ... he sacrificed and burned incense on the high places, on the hills, and under every green tree"* (2 Kgs. 16:3-4). This is probably why the historian breaks his introductory protocol of listing the king's mother's name; it would seem that the Lord was sparing Ahaz's mother the shame of being associated with her evil son. Ahaz reigned sixteen years in Jerusalem (732-715 B.C.).

The Israel-Syrian Alliance (2 Kgs. 16:5-6; 2 Chron. 28:5-15)

At the time that Ahaz reigned over Judah, Pekah was the king of Israel, and Rezin, the king of Syria. Pekah and Rezin were gathering their armies to launch a second invasion into Judah. Although Israel's alliance with Syria had been established for several years, and though their previous attempt to take Jerusalem had failed (2 Kgs. 16:5), the fresh amassing of troops along Judah's border was frightening to Ahaz (Isa. 7:2).

It was at this point that Isaiah visited Ahaz and challenged him to believe that what God had said would come true: *"If you will not believe, surely you shall not be established"* (Isa. 7:9). The horrific trial that Ahaz was facing was a faith-building opportunity for him to draw closer to God, which is what God desired him to do. God was willing to work a miracle to help Ahaz understand that Jehovah was the only God of Israel and to prompt him to trust in His word declared by Isaiah. Overall, Ahaz failed to properly represent God to the people; this was his opportunity to be spiritually revived by exercising faith in God's Word and by experiencing the wonder of God.

God wanted Ahaz to believe that both of Isaiah's date-specific prophecies (Isa. 7) would be fulfilled; the Israel-Syrian alliance in Ahaz's day would soon fail, followed by a total collapse of the Northern Kingdom within sixty-five years. Obviously, Ahaz would not be alive to see the latter fulfilled, so Isaiah offers Ahaz an opportunity to see a supernatural sign of his choosing to affirm that Isaiah was speaking for the Lord. This would hopefully bolster Ahaz's resolve to exercise faith in all God had spoken through Isaiah.

Amazingly, Ahaz declines Isaiah's offer for God to work a spectacular sign: *"I will not ask, nor will I test the Lord"* (Isa. 7:12)! While it is wrong to request a sign from God in order to trust in Him (Matt. 12:38-39; John 6:30), it is also a mistake to reject Him when He offers to demonstrate His glory. J. N. Darby writes: "Ahaz, feeling the proximity of God, shrinks, under the form of piety, from the offered sign, and God takes up the matter in grace as to Messiah, but in the revelation of judgment."[91]

The king's mock piety demonstrates that he was unwilling to abandon his trust in Assyria for protection. Matthew Henry suggests that Ahaz's response indicates the reality of his dissatisfaction with God: "Secret disaffection with God is often disguised with the color of respect to him; and those who are resolved that they will not trust God, yet pretend they will not tempt him."[92] Ahaz had drifted so far from the Lord that he just did not care what God had to say or would do. Sadly, rather than seeking Jehovah's help, Ahaz sought Baal's favor by offering his own children as burnt sacrifices.

Because Ahaz forsook the Lord, He permitted the king of Syria to defeat Ahaz in battle and a great multitude of Jewish captives were brought to Damascus (2 Chron. 28:5). Additionally, the Lord delivered Ahaz into the hand of King Pekah of Israel, whose army killed 120,000 valiant men in Judah in one day (2 Chron. 28:6). Additionally, a mighty soldier of Ephraim named Zichri killed Maaseiah the king's son, Azrikam the officer over the king's house, and Elkanah who was second to the king (2 Chron. 28:7). Israel not only despoiled Judah, but carried away 200,000 women and children of their brethren back to Samaria (2 Chron. 28:8).

However, the Lord sent the prophet Obed to confront the returning army over their savagery in Judah and their enslaving of their brethren:

> *Look, because the Lord God of your fathers was angry with Judah, He has delivered them into your hand; but you have killed them in a rage that reaches up to heaven. And now you propose to force the children of Judah and Jerusalem to be your male and female slaves; but are you not also guilty before the Lord your God? Now hear me, therefore, and return the captives, whom you have taken captive from your brethren, for the fierce wrath of the Lord is upon you* (2 Chron. 28:9-11).

Leaders from the tribe of Ephram, Azariah, Berechiah, Jehizkiah, and Amasa, heeded the prophet's warning and opposed the bringing of Jewish captives into Israel, lest God judge them for doing so (2 Chron. 28:12-13). The armed men left the captives and the spoil before the leaders, who took of the spoil to properly clothe, care for, and even transport the feeble back to Jericho in Judah (2 Chron. 28:14-15).

Besides these devastating attacks by Syria and Israel, the Edomites were raiding villages in Judah and carrying away captives and the Philistines had conquered and were occupying a number of cities in southern Judah (2 Chron. 28:17-28). The historian pauses to explain why there was suddenly so much suffering and tragedy in Judah: *"The Lord brought Judah low because of Ahaz king of Israel, for he had encouraged moral decline in Judah and had been continually unfaithful to the Lord"* (2 Chron. 28:19). Although God had intervened to return Israel's captives to Judah unharmed, Ahaz still did not turn to the Lord, but rather he went to the Assyrians for help.

Judah Seeks Help From Assyria (2 Kgs. 16:7-9; 2 Chron. 28:16-21)

Although the Lord promised to deliver Judah from the Syrian-Israeli alliance, Isaiah told Ahaz that an even greater military threat was looming over Judah – Assyria. Yet that is where Ahaz turned for aid (2 Chron. 28:16; Isa. 7:17). Ahaz sent a message to the king of Assyria, *"I am your servant and your son. Come up and save me from the hand of the king of Syria and from the hand of the king of Israel, who rise up against me"* (2 Kgs. 16:7). To prove his sincerity, Ahaz took the silver and gold from the house of the Lord and from king's and other leader's treasuries and sent it as a present to the king of Assyria (2 Kgs. 16:8; 2 Chron. 28:21).

The king of Assyria heeded Ahaz and conquered Damascus and took many captives to Kir and killed King Rezin (2 Kgs. 16:9). But as Albert Barnes explains, the horrific events which prompted Ahaz to seek Assyrian assistance only served to better position Assyria against Ahaz:

> In this calamity, Ahaz stripped the temple of its treasures and ornaments, and sent them to Tiglath-pileser, king of Assyria, to induce him to come and defend him from the united arms of Syria and Ephraim. The consequence was, as might have been foreseen, that the king of Assyria took occasion, from this, to bring increasing calamities upon the kingdom of Ahaz. He first, indeed, killed Rezin, and took Damascus (2 Kgs. 16:7). Having subdued the kingdoms of

> Damascus and Ephraim, Tiglath-pileser became a more formidable enemy to Ahaz than both of them.[93]

Ahaz went to Damascus to congratulate Tiglath-Pileser after his victory over Syria. Ahaz did much in an attempt to persuade Tiglath-Pileser to support him in Judah (2 Chron. 28:21). However, in the coming days, the Assyrians would inflict on Judah the worst attacks that they had experienced in three centuries. Tiglath-Pileser levied heavy tribute on Judah during Ahaz's reign, and later Sennacherib invaded northern Judah and would have slaughtered Hezekiah (Ahaz's son) and his entire army if God had not miraculously intervened (Isa. 36-37). Hezekiah would initially seek help against the Assyrians from the waning Egyptian Empire, but God would not permit that to happen; His solution was far better!

Ahaz's Further Apostasy and Death (2 Kgs. 16:10-20; Chron. 28:22-27)

While in Damascus Ahaz saw a pagan altar that impressed him. He commanded the priest Urijah (Uriah) to note its pattern and to construct one like it in Jerusalem (2 Kgs. 16:10). Urijah obeyed the king and built the altar on which Ahaz then offered sacrifices, and grain and drink offerings (2 Kgs. 16:11-13). Previously (before the attack on Jerusalem), Isaiah had spoken favorably of the priest Uriah (Isa. 8:2). However, being an accomplice to the king's evil plan shows that Uriah lacked devotion to the Lord in his later years.

In an attempt to influence the Assyrian king, Ahaz removed the Bronze Altar from its place in the temple courtyard to the north side of his new pagan altar (2 Kgs. 16:14). Ahaz then commanded the priests to put the morning and evening offerings, and the various burnt, meal, and peace offerings of the people, on the new altar (2 Kgs. 16:15-16). He would use the Bronze Altar merely as a talisman for purposes of divination – to inquire of it. Or, as some commentators believe, Ahaz was merely saying, "It will be for me to inquire (or to consider) what I shall do with it." In other words, he did not know what to do with the Bronze Altar, but would figure it out later.

Ahaz further transgressed the Lord by cutting off the panels of the carts and removing the lavers from them; and also he took down the huge Bronze Sea (the Laver) from the bronze oxen that were under it, and put it on a pavement of stones (2 Kgs. 16:17). Additionally, in honor of the king of Assyria, Ahaz removed the Sabbath pavilion in the temple, and he removed the king's outer entrance from the house of the Lord.

The divine chastening that Ahaz had experienced from various military foes did not cause him to repent, but rather to be increasingly unfaithful to the Lord (2 Chron. 28:22). In open defiance of Jehovah, he sacrificed to the gods of Damascus which he believed had previously defeated him, saying, "*Because the gods of the kings of Syria help them, I will sacrifice to them that they may help me*" (2 Chron. 28:23). His idolatry not only ruined him, but brought down the entire Southern Kingdom.

Ahaz went so far as to gather the Lord's holy articles from His temple, to have them cut to pieces, and then to have the doors of the house of God barred (2 Chron. 28:24). He erected pagan altars throughout Jerusalem and pagan worship centers on the high places throughout Judah (2 Chron. 28:4). Despite his godly heritage, Ahaz was one of Judah's worst kings; he did much to provoke God's anger against His people.

Because of his wickedness, Ahaz (like apostate Joash before him) was buried in Jerusalem, but not in the tombs of the kings (2 Chron. 28:26-27). Ahaz's son Hezekiah reigned in his place. Ahaz was a failure because he rejected God's Word and would not trust in the Lord for deliverance – the very opposite would be true of Hezekiah.

Meditation

> If there be, therefore, perpetual failure in your life, it cannot arise from any weakness or impotence in the Mighty God; but from some failure on your part. That failure may probably be discovered in one of three hiding places--imperfect surrender, deficient faith, or neglected communion. But when the intention of the soul is right with God, without doubt He will save.
>
> — F. B. Meyer

King Hoshea of Israel

2 Kings 17

Israel's Final King (2 Kgs. 17:1-4)

In the twelfth year of Ahaz king of Judah (732 B.C.), Israel recognized her final king, Hoshea the son of Elah (2 Kgs. 17:1). He reigned in Samaria nine years and did evil in the sight of the Lord, but not to the extent of the kings before him (2 Kgs. 17:2). The historian does not mention Hoshea continuing in the sins of Jeroboam I. Jewish tradition suggests that Hoshea permitted Israelites in the declining Northern Kingdom to return to Jerusalem to worship the Lord. Although all the kings of Israel were evil to some extent, Hoshea was likely Israel's second best king behind Jehu. But the nation had slipped too far into wickedness, and such modest improvements came too late, to stay Israel's coming judgment.

Shalmaneser, king of Assyria, came up against Hoshea and Israel became a vassal state paying annual tribute money to Assyria (2 Kgs. 17:3). However, this changed after the king of Assyria uncovered a conspiracy by Hoshea, for he had solicited the help of Egypt against Assyria and ceased paying the annual tribute to Assyria. The king of Assyria responded by imprisoning Hoshea, which left Israel without a king in her final days. Archeologists have found a description of the fall of Samaria (as recorded in 2 Kgs. 17:3-6, 24, 18:9-11) inscribed on the palace walls of Sargon II, the king of Assyria.

Israel Enslaved and Exiled to Assyria (2 Kgs. 17:5-23)

The historian then supplies more details about the invasion. Assyria swept through the Northern Kingdom taking whatever they wanted and putting the capital city of Samaria under siege in the sixth year of Hoshea's reign (2 Kgs. 17:5). In 722 B.C., after a three-year siege, Samaria fell and many Israelites were enslaved and transported to Assyria; they *"placed them in Halah and by the Habor, the River of Gozan, and in the cities of the Medes"* (2 Kgs. 17:6).

The writer then pauses to explain why Israel had suffered such shocking judgment. God's covenant people had aroused God's wrath because of their deep-seated idolatry and for following the statutes of the Gentiles instead of His Law given to them by Moses (2 Kgs. 17:7-12). The Lord had been longsuffering, even sending many prophets to warn them and to call them to repentance (2 Kgs. 17:13-14). But stiff-necked Israel abandoned God's Law for pagan rituals and chose to honor dumb idols instead of Jehovah (2 Kgs. 17:15-16). The Israelites even *"caused their sons and daughters to pass through the fire, practiced witchcraft and soothsaying, and sold themselves to do evil in the sight of the Lord, to provoke Him to anger"* (2 Kgs. 17:17). Therefore the Lord became furious with Israel, and *"removed them from His sight; there was none left but the tribe of Judah alone"* (2 Kgs. 17:18).

Judah was not innocent either; at times she had *"walked in the statutes of Israel,"* which caused the Lord to chasten the Southern Kingdom also (2 Kgs. 17:19). The Lord was still willing to go on with Judah, but the time had come to utterly reject Israel, to deliver her to the plunderers, and to remove her from the land (2 Kgs. 17:20).

God had torn the northern tribes from the house of David after the death of Solomon because of Rehoboam's sin (2 Kgs. 17:21). Under Jeroboam's leadership Israel departed from the Lord and had continued to practice the evil of his self-concocted religious system for two and a half centuries (2 Kgs. 17:22). The time had now come for the Lord to fulfill His word spoken by the prophets and to remove Israel from the land and out of His sight (2 Kgs. 17:23). Many in the Northern Kingdom were either slaughtered, or taken away and enslaved by the Assyrians.

Assyria Resettles Samaria (2 Kgs. 17:24-41)

After removing many of the Israelites from the land, the king of Assyria brought people from Babylon, Cuthah, Ava, Hamath, and Sepharvaim to settle and possess the region of Samaria (2 Kgs. 17:24). In time, the Israelites who remained in the land intermarried with these new inhabitants, which meant that their Israelite identification was lost. Their descendants became known as the Samaritans and were despised by the Jews of the Southern Kingdom because of their mixed ethnicity.

One of the first cultural clashes between the Jews and the Samaritans occurred about two centuries later when approximately 50,000 Jews returned from Babylonian exile to rebuild the temple in Jerusalem. The descendants of those who had been forcibly relocated in northern Israel in the eighth century B.C. came to the Jewish leader Zerubbabel with a request: *"Let us build with you; for we seek your God"* (Ezra 4:2). But this was merely a tactic of the devil to infiltrate God's people and to confound the work of rebuilding a testimony for the Lord. Zerubbabel recognized this and would have nothing to do with these pagans.

The historian here states that the Samaritans had no fear of the Lord. Therefore, the Lord sent lions among them and some died (2 Kgs. 17:25). This matter was reported to the king of Assyria:

> *The nations whom you have removed and placed in the cities of Samaria do not know the rituals of the God of the land; therefore He has sent lions among them, and indeed, they are killing them because they do not know the rituals of the God of the land* (2 Kgs. 17:26).

The king of Assyria then commanded that one of the captured Israelite priests should return to Samaria and teach the people *"the rituals of the God of the land"* (2 Kgs. 17:27). A single priest, an idolatrous priest following the religion of Jeroboam, was sent back to Samaria. He lived in Bethel and taught the people that they should fear Jehovah, but the people were merely exposed to humanized religion, not to the truth of the Law. Although much of the priest's teaching was erroneous, the people did gain a certain reverence for the Lord (2 Kgs. 17:32-33). Yet, what they were taught did not keep them from worshiping the gods of their homeland as before (2 Kgs. 17:28-29). They revered Israel's God, but only as one among many gods.

As a result, pagan shrines were erected on the hills of Samaria according to the origin of the people settling a particular city. As examples, *"the men of Babylon made Succoth Benoth, the men of Cuth made Nergal, the men of Hamath made Ashima, and the Avites made Nibhaz and Tartak; and the Sepharvites burned their children in fire to Adrammelech and Anammelech, the gods of Sepharvaim"* (2 Kgs. 17:30-31). Again, as time passed, these pagan groups intermarried with the remaining Israelites in the land and became known as the Samaritans.

It should be no surprise, then, that the Samaritans practiced a blended religion which combined pagan rituals with certain elements of Judaism. Obviously the Lord was unimpressed with their humanistic approach of honoring Him, for He said to the Samaritan woman: *"You worship what you do not know; we know what we worship, for salvation is of the Jews"* (John 4:22). God desired His covenant people to comply with His Law, which meant that they must worship Him alone and in the way He decreed (2 Kgs. 17:34-40). Even at the time of Christ's earthly sojourn, the Samaritans practiced a religion of divided affections. Much of the professing Church is crippled by the same half-hearted disposition today.

Because the Lord had repeatedly displayed His holy character in all His gracious dealings with Israel through the centuries, He should have been feared and His name alone revered in Israel – for *"holy and awesome is His name"* (Ps. 111:9). The psalmist stated the foundational principle for understanding human existence and obtaining spiritual awareness: *"The fear of the Lord is the beginning of wisdom"* (Ps. 111:10). This implies that those who have a proper disposition towards the Lord will have the wisdom to do His commandments and praise His name! Israel did not have such a heart for God, even though they cried out to God, *"We know You"* (Hos. 8:2). It was evident that they neither knew nor feared God because they were blatant covenant violators who suffered from divided affections.

Consequently, the prophet Hosea, speaking for the Lord, declared: *"My people are destroyed for lack of knowledge"* (Hos. 4:6) and *"people who do not understand will be trampled"* (Hos. 4:14). Commitment entails being given over to a cause without any reservation and is what the Lord demands of those who identify with His name: *"If you abide in My word, you are My disciples indeed. And you shall know the truth, and the truth shall make you free"* (John 8:31-32). Israel had no such commitment to revealed truth; therefore, God permitted the Assyrians to trample them. The Northern Kingdom would never be an autonomous nation again!

Meditation

> When it comes to God's commands, the issue is not clarity; it's commitment.
>
> — Woodrow Kroll

King Hezekiah of Judah – Religious Reform

2 Kings 18:1-8; 2 Chronicles 29-31

The reign of Hezekiah was a fresh oasis for Judah after the long spiritually parched rule of Ahaz. John Heading offers this outline for the next four chapters which span Hezekiah's reign:

Chapter 29: Purification of the house of the Lord.
Chapter 30: Participation in the house of the Lord.
Chapter 31: Provision for the house of the Lord.
Chapter 32: Protection of the house of the Lord.[94]

Hezekiah Reigns in Judah (2 Kgs. 18:1-3, 5-8; 2 Chron. 29:1-2)

Hezekiah began to reign in Judah as coregent with his father Ahaz in the third year of Hoshea, king of Israel (2 Kgs. 18:1). The year was 729 B.C. and he was twenty-five years old. After the death of Ahaz in 715 B.C. (fourteen years later), Hezekiah ruled Judah alone, and then as coregent with his young son Manasseh for eleven years until Hezekiah died in 686 B.C. In all he ruled Judah about forty-three years, but was considered the leading authority in Judah for only twenty-nine of those years. His mother's name was Abijah, the daughter of Zechariah (2 Kgs. 18:2). Unlike his father, Hezekiah did what was right in the sight of the Lord and he trusted the Lord (2 Kgs. 18:5). No king since Solomon has a fuller and more positive biblical record than Hezekiah.

Two further accolades identify Hezekiah as Judah's second greatest king after David. First, the historian states that he did *"all that his father David had done"* (2 Kgs. 18:3). There had been several good kings of Judah since David, but none received such an outstanding commendation. Second, the writer submits that he was above all other kings before and after him because he held fast to the Lord and did not depart from the Lord's commandments delivered by Moses (2 Kgs. 18:6).

Because of his dedication, the Lord was with Hezekiah and prospered whatever he did (2 Kgs. 18:7). He rebelled against the king of Assyria and did not serve him and he also subdued the Philistines, as far as Gaza (2 Kgs. 18:8). This partially fulfilled Amos' prophecy against Philistia which was more completely achieved during the Maccabean period in second century B.C. (Amos 1:7-8).

Hezekiah Cleanses the Temple (2 Chron. 29:3-19)

Kings briefly refers to Hezekiah's religious reforms, but the writer of Chronicles catalogs three chapters' worth of information. In Hezekiah's first month as king, he repaired and reopened the doors of the temple which his father Ahaz had closed (2 Chron. 29:3). Next, he gathered the priests and Levites in the East Square and said to them (2 Chron. 29:4):

> *Hear me, Levites! Now sanctify yourselves, sanctify the house of the Lord God of your fathers, and carry out the rubbish from the holy place. For our fathers have trespassed and done evil in the eyes of the Lord our God; they have forsaken Him, have turned their faces away from the dwelling place of the Lord, and turned their backs on Him. They have also shut up the doors of the vestibule, put out the lamps, and have not burned incense or offered burnt offerings in the holy place to the God of Israel. Therefore the wrath of the Lord fell upon Judah and Jerusalem, and He has given them up to trouble, to desolation, and to jeering, as you see with your eyes. For indeed, because of this our fathers have fallen by the sword; and our sons, our daughters, and our wives are in captivity. Now it is in my heart to make a covenant with the Lord God of Israel, that His fierce wrath may turn away from us. My sons, do not be negligent now, for the Lord has chosen you to stand before Him, to serve Him, and that you should minister to Him and burn incense* (2 Chron. 29:5-11).

The Levites responded favorably to Hezekiah's request and leaders from all three Levitical sects (six from the Kohathites and four each from the Gershonites and Merarites) responded by gathering and sanctifying their brethren in order to cleanse the temple (2 Chron. 29:12-15). Inappropriate debris was removed from the house of the Lord and carried to the Brook Kidron (2 Chron. 29:16). It took eight days to consecrate everything outside the temple and another eight days for the articles inside the temple – including the items that Ahaz had used in pagan rituals (2 Chron. 28:24, 29:17-19).

Hezekiah Restores Proper Worship at the Temple (2 Chron. 29:20-36)

Moses had established a purification precedent before and after the tabernacle was constructed and erected: The blood of a bullock and of a ram was used to purify the priests and the altar of sacrifice (Ex. 24:6-8, 29:12-21). Likewise, before reinstituting temple sacrifices and worship, King Hezekiah had the priests, the temple and all of its articles ceremonially cleansed by blood. The priests also offered at that time sacrifices of reconciliation for the nation to make restitution to God for their past paganism (2 Chron. 29:20-24).

The next day, after the cleansing was completed, King Hezekiah rose early, gathered the rulers of the city, and went up to the temple (2 Chron. 29:20). Under sanctified conditions, there will always be a work of the Lord to be accomplished, and the Lord's servants should not tarry in their performance of it. Often in the book of Jeremiah, God is depicted as rising early to speak urgently through His prophets to His wayward people. Also, the Lord Jesus was ready "early in the morning" to teach those who eagerly came to hear God's word (Luke 21:38). Likewise, believers in the Church Age should maintain practical sanctification so that they can be available to refresh and honor the Lord at His earliest prompting.

The priests then offered seven bulls, seven rams, and seven lambs as burnt offerings, and seven male goats as sin offerings on the Bronze Altar for the kingdom, for the sanctuary, and for Judah (2 Chron. 29:21-24). The blood of these animals was sprinkled on the altar to atone for Judah's sin. Hezekiah also followed the practice of David and positioned priests with trumpets and Levites with cymbals and various stringed instruments in the temple when the Ark was moved to Jerusalem (1 Chron. 15:16-19).

All the assembly worshiped, the singers sang, and the trumpeters sounded; this continued until the burnt offering was finished (2 Chron. 29:28). Afterwards, the king and all who were present with him bowed and worshiped before the Lord (2 Chron. 29:29). The Levites sang the psalms of David and of Asaph with gladness and reverence before the Lord (2 Chron. 29:30).

With the temple consecration ceremony over, Hezekiah instructed the people to bring their sacrifices and thanksgiving offerings to the Lord (2 Chron. 29:31). The people responded to this summons with willing hearts, and seventy bulls, one hundred rams, and two hundred lambs were offered as burnt offerings to the Lord. This offering meant that the entire animal (other than the skin) was placed on the altar to the Lord and completely consumed by fire. The burnt offering was the offering most appreciated by God because it typified the complete sacrifice and submission of God's Son at Calvary (2 Chron. 29:32).

In addition to the burnt offerings, there were drink offerings and six hundred bulls and three thousand sheep offered as peace or fellowship offerings (2 Chron. 29:33). The offerer, the offering priest, and the Lord all received portions of these offerings as part of a festive feast. There were not enough sanctified priests at that time to perform all the sacrifices, so the Levites helped them until more priests could be consecrated to the Lord (2 Chron. 29:34-35).

The service of the house of the Lord was set in order according to the Law and David's subsequent instructions. Hezekiah and all the people rejoiced that God had prepared their hearts to rejoice in their God the way that He appreciated. Everyone knew that this was a work of the Lord, for all these *"events took place so suddenly"* (2 Chron. 29:36). May we see many more such works of God in our midst today!

Hezekiah Keeps the Passover (2 Chron. 30)

While coregent with his wicked father Ahaz, who had shut down temple worship, there had been no opportunity to keep the Feasts of Jehovah which had not been observed by the Jews for many years. But after Hezekiah became the sole ruler in Judah, he was exercised to keep the Passover. However, there were several difficulties to overcome. First, it was already the sixteenth day of the first month before the house of the Lord was cleansed and reopened and the Passover was to be kept on the fourteenth day of the first month of the Hebrew calendar (2 Chron. 30:1-3). Second, the Passover lambs were to be set aside on the tenth day of the month to be observed and tested. Third, there was a lack of consecrated priests. Fourth, many of those he wanted to attend the Passover lived a considerable distance from Jerusalem.

Hezekiah did not want to wait an entire year to hold the Passover. But the Law had made provision for those not able to keep the Passover in the first month to do so on the fourteenth day of the second month (Num. 9:10-11). The king made a decision that Judah would observe the Passover the following month and that would permit any remaining Israelites from the northern tribes to attend also (2 Chron. 30:4-5).

We pause to draw an important truth from the narrative that has a practical application for believers in the Church Age. The two reasons that God's covenant people could not offer acceptable worship to Him during the days of Ahaz were: the doors of the house of God were closed and there was no cleansed priesthood. How lovely to realize that in the Church Age such obstacles have been eternally dealt with – worship can be offered by believer-priests any time. Peter explains why this is possible: *"Coming to Him as to a living stone, rejected indeed by men, but chosen by God and precious, you also, as living stones, are being built up a spiritual house, a holy priesthood, to offer up spiritual sacrifices acceptable to God through Jesus Christ"* (1 Pet. 2:4-5). The Church is the spiritual house to God and the believers composing it are positionally holy in Christ (i.e., the Church is a house of sanctified priests). This means that believers walking with the Lord can offer acceptable worship to Him at any time. What a blessing to our own souls! We have an eternal privilege that we can actually enjoy now – right now!

Messengers were sent from city to city throughout the northern tribes with a message to repent and be restored: *"Children of Israel, return to the Lord God of Abraham, Isaac, and Israel; then He will return to the remnant of you who have escaped from the hand of the kings of Assyria"* (2 Chron. 30:6). They were reminded that they had suffered God's displeasure because their forefathers had been stiff-necked and did not obey His Law and did not come to His sanctuary to worship (2 Chron. 30:8). The Israelites in the northern tribes were challenged not to continue in the rebellion of their fathers; rather, they had an opportunity to experience the Lord's mercy and compassion, instead of His fierce wrath (2 Chron. 30:8-9).

Many laughed at Hezekiah's messengers, but some from Ephraim, Asher, Manasseh, Issachar, and Zebulun humbled themselves and came to Jerusalem as requested (2 Chron. 30:10-11, 18). The mixed religion of the Samaritans scoffed at what God appreciated. Likewise today, humanized Christianity will always work to lead people away from Christ and into sin. Because the hand of God was on Judah, those of the Southern Kingdom responded uniformly to the king's request and with singleness of heart obeyed the Lord and came to Jerusalem (2 Chron. 30:12).

A great assembly gathered in Jerusalem to keep the Passover on the fourteenth day of the second month and the seven-day Feast of Unleavened Bread afterwards (2 Chron. 30:13). After the Feast of Unleavened Bread ended, the people rose up and purged Jerusalem of its incense censers and altars and cast them in the Brook Kidron (2 Chron. 30:14).

Ashamed over their past sins and their complacency in not being sanctified when the temple was first cleansed (2 Chron. 29), more priests and Levites got right with the Lord and were also sanctified (2 Chron. 30:15-16). Because the feast day had come so soon, there were many in the assembly who were still ceremonially unclean per the Mosaic Law, so sanctified Levites oversaw the slaughtering of the Passover Lambs for those who were unclean (2 Chron. 30:17). Given the uniqueness of the situation – a revival from paganism, Hezekiah prayed that God would look favorably on all those who ate the Passover with a willing heart to honor Him, even though they were not ceremonially clean:

> *May the good Lord provide atonement for everyone who prepares his heart to seek God, the Lord God of his fathers, though he is not cleansed according to the purification of the sanctuary* (2 Chron. 30:18-19).

Although the people had not perfectly followed the Law's stipulations for coming before Him in keeping the Passover (Lev. 15:31; Num. 19:20), the Lord honored Hezekiah's prayer and healed them (2 Chron. 30:20). God did not want to judge those who had already benefitted from past chastening; rather, He wanted the repentant to experience the wonder of His grace. Consequently, the judicial penalty for the offense was not imputed – God's mercy would abound for His people to cover the infraction. God deemed the willing subjection of their hearts as more important than the religious formality.

The children of Israel who kept the Feast of Unleavened Bread in Jerusalem enjoyed seven joy-filled days before the Lord. During the feast, many peace offerings were presented to the Lord and Hezekiah encouraged the priests and Levites to fulfill their official duties by singing songs of praise and playing musical instruments unto the Lord (2 Chron. 30:21-22).

There was so much excitement and gladness among the congregation that they decided to continue the festivities another seven days (2 Chron. 30:23). Hezekiah donated a thousand bulls and seven thousand sheep, and the leaders another thousand bulls and ten thousand sheep for peace offerings to support the extra week of feasting before the Lord (2 Chron. 30:24). A great number of priests were sanctified during this time and the entire assembly, including those who came from Israel and sojourners in the land, rejoiced in the Lord's presence (2 Chron. 30:25).

The historian then notes that Jerusalem had not experienced such joy since King Solomon dedicated the temple two and a half centuries earlier (2 Chron. 30:26). When the fifteen days of celebration concluded, the priests and the Levites prayed for the people. These petitions were heard by the Lord in His holy, heavenly habitation and He responded by blessing His people (2 Chron. 30:27).

Hezekiah's Further Reform (2 Kgs. 18:4; 2 Chron. 31)

God's people had been spiritually revived, and when they departed for their homes, they removed what Jehovah hated from the land:

> *All Israel who were present went out to the cities of Judah and broke the sacred pillars in pieces, cut down the wooden images, and threw down the high places and the altars – from all Judah, Benjamin, Ephraim, and Manasseh – until they had utterly destroyed them all* (2 Chron. 31:1).

The writer of Kings informs us that Hezekiah did his part in the revival by removing the high places, breaking down the sacred pillars, cutting up the wooden images, and even destroying the bronze serpent that Moses had made in the wilderness (Num. 21:6-9). This ancient relic had not been mentioned for about eight centuries, but had somehow survived Israel's turbulent history. Perhaps because of its age and antiquity, the relic took on religious significance in time and the Jews began burning incense to it, even giving it a name – "Nehushtan" (2 Kgs. 18:4).

Interestingly, Nehushtan means "a piece of brass," which means the people knew what it was and still revered it as something more than a piece of brass. We might chuckle at such absurdity, but how many people today identify with Christ while assigning spiritual significance to crosses, candles, incense, water, wooden tables (sometimes called "altars"), church steeples, the church's meeting room (sometimes referred to as "the sanctuary"), etc. However, the only objects in the Church Age which Scripture assigns symbolic significance to are listed in 1 Corinthians 11. These are the bread and wine used during the Lord's Supper to memorialize the Lord's broken body and shed blood at Calvary, and the head covering which affirms divine order by concealing glories that compete with God's glory when His people are before Him (i.e., when speaking to God in prayer or when He is speaking to us through His Word).

Hezekiah felt that ascribing such significance to the serpent distorted the biblical concept of the God of Israel; therefore, he had it destroyed. In summary, Hezekiah was the first king since David to ensure that all Jehovah worship occurred only in His temple, followed Levitical Law, and was performed only by sanctified Levitical servants.

Regarding the Law and the twenty-four Levitical divisions that David instituted, Hezekiah organized the priests and Levites into appropriate divisions to reestablish regular and proper temple worship. He then contributed sacrifices and offerings daily, weekly, monthly, and annually to ensure the proper function of the temple and the support of its servants (2 Chron. 31:2-3). Furthermore, the king encouraged the people to follow his example of liberality, so that the priests and Levites could fully *"devote themselves to the Law of the Lord"* instead of being forced to labor in secular employment to support their families (2 Chron. 31:4). The Law actually prohibited the Lord's servants from such employment, but since the days of Solomon most were not properly sustained by the people (Num. 18:21-24).

Sadly, many of the Lord's servants throughout the Church Age have had this same difficulty. Referring to Deuteronomy 25:4, Paul applies the "not muzzling the ox" principle in the New Testament, that is, those laboring for the kingdom of God were likewise worthy of financial support from those who had benefitted from their preaching (1 Cor. 9:9). The New Testament indicates that Church workers were employed by the Lord, not by local churches. Serving the Lord is not a career to be chosen, but a heavenly calling to be fulfilled! God enables the worker's ministry and is responsible for supporting them financially (Phil. 4:10-19; Col. 4:17). As He most often accomplishes this through

His people, Paul emphasizes that those who had been spiritually blessed by ministry had a "duty" to support those who blessed them (Rom. 15:27). Examples of not muzzling the laboring ox would include the support of the evangelist (1 Cor. 9:14), a teaching elder (1 Tim. 5:17-18), a teacher in general (Gal. 6:6) and commended workers (1 Cor. 9:4).

Gaius provides a good pattern to follow in the care of the Lord's servants. He extended hospitality to itinerant church workers and then did not send them away empty-handed (3 John 5-8; also see Tit. 3:14). At times workers may need to engage in secular employment for financial reasons (Acts 18:3), but nowhere in Scripture do we see them making public appeals for their own financial support. Commended workers serve the Lord (Acts 14:26), and thus the Lord wants His people to freely and abundantly provide for them in His name. This arrangement permits His workers to do His bidding and the Lord to endorse their efforts by attending to their daily needs.

The children of Israel responded to Hezekiah's decree by bringing liberal portions of their firstfruits and tithes to the priests and Levites (2 Chron. 31:5-6). So ample was their giving that the Lord's servants had to set aside the grain, wine, oil and honey in piles during the summer harvest season (2 Chron. 31:7). When the king and the Jewish elders saw the stockpiled goods, they blessed the Lord for His goodness and for the people's generosity (2 Chron. 31:8).

The king inquired if all these supplies would be sufficient to provide for their needs through the winter months. The priests and Levites affirmed that there was plenty to eat, and that there was a splendid surplus of provisions also (2 Chron. 31:9-10). However, Hezekiah wisely discerned that the Levites needed proper storage space to keep the surplus safe for later use. He, therefore, commanded that a storage room at the temple be prepared (2 Chron. 31:11).

Two Levite brothers, Cononiah and Shimei, would oversee ten Levitical supervisors to ensure the proper collection and distribution of goods occurred (2 Chron. 31:12-13). The Levite Kore, the keeper of the East Gate, and six subordinate associates were charged with collecting and distributing the freewill offerings to God (gifts not required by the Law; 2 Chron. 31:14-15).

Careful genealogies of the priests and Levites would guide the distribution of supplies: sons of the priests three years of age and older, and those Levites twenty years and older were entitled to a portion of the gifts received (2 Chron. 31:16-18). Finally, those priests and Levites not living in Jerusalem or in one of the designated priestly cities were not to be overlooked, but also supported (2 Chron. 31:19).

The historian summarizes Hezekiah's leadership in Judah: *"He did what was good and right and true before the Lord his God. And in every work that he began in the service of the house of God, in the law and in the commandment, to seek his God, he did it with all his heart. So he prospered"* (2 Chron. 31:20-21). Six times the writer mentions that Hezekiah served the Lord wholeheartedly and that this was the reason he prospered and those under his rule were richly blessed. May we learn from this example that a half-hearted Christian will never do anything outstanding for the Lord, but those who are fully cleansed and consecrated to Him will be blessed to bless others. God delights in every heart that genuinely beats for Him! Hezekiah was one such faithful, obedient servant of the Lord.

Meditation

With harps and with viols there stand a great throng,
In the presence of Jesus, and sings this new song:
Unto Him who hath loved us and washed us from sin,
Unto Him be the glory forever, Amen!

All these once were sinners, defiled in His sight;
Now arrayed in pure garments in praise they unite:
He maketh the rebel a priest and a king;
He hath bought us and taught us this new song to sing.

How helpless and hopeless we sinners had been,
If He never had loved us till cleansed from our sin:
Aloud in His praises our voices shall ring,
So that others, believing, this new song shall sing.

— A. T. Pierson

King Hezekiah of Judah – Assyrian Invasion

2 Kings 18:9-37; 2 Chronicles 32:1-19

Assyria was now the dominant world power. Assyria's army had recently suppressed a rebellion in Phoenicia and then moved down the Mediterranean coast to bring Philistia into subjection. Sennacherib, the new Assyrian king, was completing the expansion of the Assyrian Empire that his father Sargon II had begun.

Sennacherib, believing he was invincible, then invaded northern and western Judah. The Assyrian king dismissed Israel's God as being no different than other puny gods already defeated in their many territorial conquests. As already foretold by several prophets, God had brought the Assyrians to power not only to be His chastening rod against wickedness in the region, but also, because God detests pride, He would show Sennacherib just how powerful He was. Isaiah allegorically describes Assyria's offense as an axe boasting against the woodsmen who swings it (the Lord in this case; Isa. 10:5-15). Without divine enablement, Assyria could have done nothing to expand their empire!

Two Assyrian Invasions (2 Kgs. 18:9-16; 2 Chron. 32:1-8)

In the fourth year of King Hezekiah, which was the seventh year of King Hoshea of Israel, Shalmaneser, the king of Assyria, invaded Israel and besieged the capital city of Samaria (2 Kgs. 18:9). Samaria fell after a three-year siege in which many Israelites were killed and many more were enslaved and taken to Assyria (2 Kgs. 18:10-11). This judgment, as predicted by God's prophets, came about because of Israel's blatant transgressions against Jehovah over the previous two and a half centuries (2 Kgs. 18:12).

In 701 B.C., seven years after the fall of Samaria, Sennacherib, king of Assyria, invaded the Southern Kingdom and captured many fortified cities in northern Judah (2 Kgs. 18:13). These cities formed a defensive perimeter around Jerusalem. This invasion occurred in the fourteenth year of Hezekiah's reign, a few months after his miraculous healing and shortly after the Babylonian delegation had left Jerusalem.

The attack on Judah's fortifications gave Hezekiah time to bolster Jerusalem's defenses so as to improve their chances of enduring a long siege (Isa. 22:9-11). Hezekiah demolished houses to obtain stones for repairing broken portions of the wall around the City of David (2 Chron. 32:5). He also collected water in the Lower Pool, while stopping up springs in the surrounding area (2 Chron. 32:4). Originally, the Lower Pool (likely located in the southwest of the city) was not protected by a wall, so Hezekiah enclosed the reservoir to protect the water supply from the Assyrians and to reserve it for the city (Isa. 22:11).

However, instead of trying to withstand the Assyrians, whom God had sent to test and to chasten them, the Jews should have realized their helplessness and sought the Lord. Isaiah says they should have pulled out their hair and worn sackcloth, both signs of mourning (Isa. 22:12). Apparently, many Jews did not consider Jehovah powerful enough to rescue them, so instead they became fatalistic: *"Let us eat and drink, for tomorrow we die"* (Isa. 22:13)! And that is what they did. Instead of humbling themselves and requesting deliverance, they chose drunken carousing and feasting – believing the end was near.

Sennacherib directed one of his commanders, Rabshakeh, to move a sizeable portion of his army from Lachish and to surround King Hezekiah at Jerusalem (Isa. 36:2). Lachish was a large city southwest of Jerusalem that had already been captured. Sennacherib's assault on Lachish is recorded in the Annals of the Assyrian king and was depicted on the walls of Sennacherib's palace in Nineveh.[95] Furthermore, an inscription on Sennacherib's Prism extols his military accomplishments in Judea:

> As to Hezekiah the Jew he did not submit to my yoke. I lay siege to forty-six of his strong cities, walled forts, and to the countless small villages in their vicinity. I drove out of them 200,150 people. Himself I made a prisoner in Jerusalem, his Royal residence, like a bird in a cage.[96]

Although having the Assyrian army at Jerusalem's gates was indeed sobering for Judah, Isaiah must have been ecstatic to witness the fulfillment of the prophecy he had uttered thirty years earlier (Isa. 8:5-

10). Hezekiah sent a message to the king of Assyria who was still at Lachish, but was preparing to move the remainder of his troops to attack Libnah (a city about five miles north of Jerusalem; Isa. 37:8). Hezekiah's message to Sennacherib was contrite and concise, *"I have done wrong; turn away from me; whatever you impose on me I will pay"* (2 Kgs. 18:14). The king of Assyria assessed Hezekiah king of Judah three hundred talents of silver and thirty talents of gold.

Hezekiah quickly responded to this request and gave Sennacherib all the silver that was found in the house of the Lord and in the treasuries of the king's house (2 Kgs. 18:15). He also stripped the gold from the doors of the temple and the pillars that he had previously overlaid with gold (2 Kgs. 18:16). However, the ransom Hezekiah paid Sennacherib was not enough and the Assyrian king demanded a complete surrender of Jerusalem. He sent three officers to deliver his demands to Hezekiah, first privately (2 Kgs. 18:17-27) and then publicly to the inhabitants of Jerusalem (2 Kgs. 18:28-37).

Sennacherib Mocks the Lord (2 Kgs. 18:17-37; 2 Chron. 32:9-19; Isa 36:1-22)

Sennacherib sent the Tartan, the Rabsaris, and the Rabshakeh from Lachish with a great army to besiege Jerusalem (2 Kgs. 18:17). Rabshakeh is probably not a proper name, but rather a title denoting high rank – a general, so to speak (similar to the title of Abimelech in Gen. 20:3). For this reason, many commentators refer to him as "the Rabshakeh." Hezekiah sent three distinguished representatives, Eliakim, Shebna, and Joah, to speak with and hopefully to negotiate with Rabshakeh.

This meeting occurred by the aqueduct from the upper pool, on the highway to the Fuller's Field (2 Kgs. 18:17). Isaiah and his son had conversed with King Ahaz at this location about thirty years earlier when Jerusalem was threatened by a Syrian-Israeli alliance (Isa. 7:3). Ahaz did not believe that God would deliver Judah from their attack, but Isaiah told him that within three years the alliance would fail and it did. Now, the same prophet was delivering a similar message to Hezekiah. Would he follow in Ahaz's disbelief or would he put his confidence in the Lord? The historical significance of the meeting location certainly heightened the tension over the outcome of this question.

C. A. Coates suggests the spiritual significance of this meeting place by the upper pool which was on the way to the Fuller's Field (a place for laundering clothes).

> The upper pool suggests purifying influences of an elevated character. If we are not prepared to abide by the pool and the fuller's field where our garments are made white, we shall never form part of the remnant or be able to laugh the Assyrian to scorn. The fuller's field is where the garments are made white. What good are we for testimony if our garments are not purified in the fuller's field?[97]

Those who have been washed by the blood of Christ and then seek to maintain purity as they walk with the Lord in His purposes have nothing to fear on this earth! Isaiah, Hezekiah, and his three ambassadors were such consecrated men and they had nothing to fear from Assyria.

Rabshakeh immediately began to mock the Jews and their God by asking the three Jewish representatives on whom they were depending to defeat Assyria's unbeaten army (2 Kgs. 18:19-25). He suggested that Egypt was like a splintered reed and had no strength to help them (2 Kgs. 18:21). Ironically, on this point Rabshakeh was correct.

The profane Assyrian commander, speaking in Hebrew and in the hearing of Jewish soldiers on the wall, then provided three reasons the Jews should surrender Jerusalem to the Assyrians.

First, he challenged the Jews not to say to him that *"we trust in the Lord our God"* (2 Kgs. 18:22). He wrongly assumed that Hezekiah had angered God by removing all the high places and altars throughout Judah and limiting Jehovah worship to only one altar in Jerusalem. Obviously, the pagan commander did not understand that Hezekiah's reforms pleased the Lord because the king was ensuring that Jewish religious practices were in accordance with God's Law. Hezekiah had purged paganism and reestablished the Levitical priesthood as the only officiants who could offer sacrifices on the Bronze Altar.

Second, Rabshakeh insulted Judah's army as being insignificant and feeble. He offered to give Hezekiah 2,000 horses, if he could find enough cavalrymen to ride them. The gesture implied that Judah was unable to muster up any kind of a legitimate competition (2 Kgs. 18:23). Then, in taunting rhetoric, the commander suggested that even if Judah had 2,000 skilled riders, all of them could not overcome even one low-ranking Assyrian officer in battle (2 Kgs. 18:24).

Third, the Assyrian commander insisted that the Hebrew God, Jehovah, had commanded him to *"go up against this land, and destroy it"* (2 Kgs. 18:25). This implied that God was infuriated with the Jews over the loss of the high places and wanted the Assyrians to punish His people. Obviously, none of this was true, but the Assyrian commander was a master of terrorizing those he wished to conquer. And what better way to demoralize Judah's army than to plant the thought that God was angry with His people and had turned His back on them.

The Hebrew delegation understood the seriousness of the tactic and requested that Rabshakeh speak to them in Aramaic and not in Hebrew during their negotiations (2 Kgs. 18:26). The pompous Assyrian denied their request. He said that he had been sent to communicate his message to the general population, not just to Hezekiah's negotiators, who would likely filter out the nonsensical content of his message (2 Kgs. 18:27). He conjectured that it was important for common soldiers to hear his message, because they would be forced to eat and drink their own waste in order to survive a long siege. So, Rabshakeh spoke with a louder voice so even more Jews would hear his warning (2 Kgs. 18:28):

> *Do not let Hezekiah deceive you, for he will not be able to deliver you; nor let Hezekiah make you trust in the Lord, saying, "The Lord will surely deliver us; this city will not be given into the hand of the king of Assyria"* (2 Kgs. 18:29-30).

Logically speaking, if Jehovah had sent Rabshakeh to punish Judah as he claimed, would not the message from heaven have been to repent and return to Jehovah who loves you, rather than "do not trust in Jehovah"? The weakness of the enemy's position was now revealed. They did not fear the army of Judah, but rather feared that the Jews would put their full confidence in their God.

Such actions of faith by God's people today result in fresh proclamations of the devil's defeat at Calvary. Satan knows that if he can move the believer from the truth of the triumphant ground of Calvary, he can gain a victory. Watchman Nee summarizes this point in his book *Sit, Walk, Stand*:

> Christ's warfare was offensive; He gained the victory over the devil at the Cross. Our warfare is mostly defensive – we war against Satan only to maintain and consolidate the victory which Christ has already gained – we hold what Christ has gained against all challenges. If we fight with the concept of gaining a victory, then we lose the battle at the onset. The Christian walk and warfare draw their strength from sitting before God and resting in Him. Satan's objective is to move us from the perfect ground of triumph, thus our armor (Eph. 6) is essentially defensive.

Satan knows that he can overcome God's people only when they compromise the truth by doubting God's ability and promises. This is why James exhorts believers to *"submit to God. Resist the devil and he will flee from you. Draw near to God and He will draw near to you"* (Jas. 4:7-8). The prophet Ezekiel informs us that before his fall, Lucifer (now referred to as Satan or "the accuser") was a beautiful anointed cherub (Ezek. 28:11-16). He was likely the most powerful being that God created and, thus, is a cunning and dangerous enemy that only God controls. Consequently, believers are not commanded to confront Satan, but rather to resist him by submitting to God in faith.

Believers are to be knowledgeable of the devil's tactics so that he does not gain an advantage over them through ignorance. Paul reminded the Christians at Corinth of this, saying, *"we are not ignorant of his devices"* (2 Cor. 2:11). Because Satan uses the same strategies repeatedly to oppose the things of God, believers are able to become more aware of his evil tactics by studying Scripture. The lesson for us in 2 Kings 18 is that God's people must not compromise the truth no matter what the enemy says – it is best, if possible, not to even listen to what he says.

In the hearing of the Jewish soldiers on the wall, Rabshakeh continued his tirade by promising that if the Jews surrendered, they would receive homes, farms, and vineyards in another land and could get on with their lives in peace (2 Kgs. 18:31-32). Rabshakeh was too shrewd to try to hide Assyria's deportation policy for conquered people; hence, he exaggerates the so-called "opportunity" to make it appear as attractive as possible. Though this may have been appealing as compared to a long siege, it is doubtful that such terms would be honored after their surrender. Even if partially granted, the Jews would still be slaves and under heavy tribute in Assyria.

Rabshakeh concluded his blasphemous rant by again instructing the Jews not to listen to Hezekiah, nor to have confidence in their Jehovah:

> *Do not listen to Hezekiah, lest he persuade you, saying, "The Lord will deliver us." Has any of the gods of the nations at all delivered its land from the hand of the king of Assyria? Where are the gods of Hamath and Arpad? Where are the gods of Sepharvaim and Hena and Ivah? Indeed, have they delivered Samaria from my hand? Who among all the gods of the lands have delivered their countries from my hand, that the Lord should deliver Jerusalem from my hand?* (2 Kgs. 18:32-35).

Reason begs the question, Why would Rabshakeh supposedly obey Jehovah's command to punish the Jewish people if he thought so little of Jehovah, even comparing Him to the gods of Hamath and Arpad in Syria? Furthermore, the Assyrian commander reminded the Jews, that no god had protected anyone in Samaria from being conquered by the Assyrians twenty-one years earlier. Why should they trust in their God now when He did not protect the Northern Kingdom from defeat and exile? Of course, all that had happened to Israel had been prophesied by Isaiah years before as part of God's chastisement for their stubborn idolatry (Isa. 7:8). Judah had been spared a subsequent attack by Assyria largely because of Hezekiah's reforms and his purging of organized idolatry. The situation was much different in Judah than Israel, because Hezekiah was yielding to God's Law and had His favor.

Although the Jewish delegation and soldiers were, no doubt, disturbed and perhaps even terrified after hearing Rabshakeh's taunts, they obeyed the king's command and answered him nothing (2 Kgs. 18:36). Eliakim, Shebna, and Joah returned to Hezekiah with their clothes torn and reported all the Assyrian commander had said to them (2 Kgs. 18:37). The tearing of one's clothes is an ancient Jewish tradition associated with mourning, grief, and loss. Jacob, for example, tore his clothes, put on sackcloth, and mourned many days after being told that his son Joseph had been killed by a wild animal (Gen. 37:34). The men in the envoy were publicly displaying their revulsion over Rabshakeh's irreverence and threats. We will learn of Hezekiah's incredible response of faith to this situation in the next chapter.

Meditation

Encamped along the hills of light ye Christian soldiers rise,
And press the battle ere the night shall veil the glowing skies.
Against the foe in vales below, let all our strength be hurled;
Faith is the victory we know that overcomes the world.

— John H. Yates

King Hezekiah of Judah – Assyrian Defeat

2 Kings 19; 2 Chronicles 32:20-23

Isaiah Assures Hezekiah of Deliverance (2 Kgs. 19:1-13; Isa. 37:1-13)

After King Hezekiah heard the envoy's report, he also tore his clothes, put on sackcloth, and then went to the temple (2 Kgs. 19:1). As previously noted, tearing one's clothes was a dramatic gesture to express outrage or deep grief. Wearing sackcloth was an ongoing expression of brokenness until the distressing situation had passed. Any Jew seeing Hezekiah without his royal attire and earnestly praying in the temple would have been deeply moved. Rabshakeh had blasphemed God and threatened to destroy Judah. Hezekiah knew the situation was desperate and that there was only one remedy – the hand of God.

The king sent Eliakim, Shebna, and the elders of the priests, also covered in sackcloth, to Isaiah with the king's request that he pray with them about this urgent matter (2 Kgs. 19:2). This was significant, as some, like King Ahaz, did not view Isaiah's messages as being divine in origin. However, godly Hezekiah immediately seeks Isaiah's prayers and counsel (2 Kgs. 19:5). Hezekiah likens Jerusalem's situation to a woman who has been in the deep pangs of childbearing for an extended time and has no strength remaining to deliver her baby – meaning that Jerusalem could not deliver herself from this ominous circumstance (2 Kgs. 19:3). The king was hoping that God had taken note of Rabshakeh's profane words and that He would move to vindicate Himself (2 Kgs. 19:4).

Speaking for the Lord, Isaiah assures Hezekiah that God heard every blasphemous word, and that Hezekiah was not to be fearful:

> *Do not be afraid of the words which you have heard, with which the servants of the king of Assyria have blasphemed Me. Surely I will send a spirit upon him, and he shall hear a rumor and return to his*

> *own land; and I will cause him to fall by the sword in his own land* (2 Kgs. 19:6-7).

Rabshakeh had surrounded Jerusalem with a sizeable army, and the Assyrian king, Sennacherib, had moved his remaining soldiers from Lachish to Libnah, a city about five miles north of Jerusalem. At about the same time that Rabshakeh sent a report to Sennacherib on the progress at Jerusalem, the king received another intelligence report that Tirhakah king of Ethiopia was moving north to war with him (2 Kgs. 19:9).

Sennacherib withdrew from the region in order to properly array his troops for combat, but before doing so, he sent a parting message to Hezekiah: *"Do not let your god in whom you trust deceive you, saying, 'Jerusalem shall not be given into the hand of the king of Assyria'"* (2 Kgs. 19:10). He then boasted that no god of any land that he had conquered had been able to deliver anyone from his hand. Sennacherib then supplied a list of key cities throughout the region which had succumbed to Assyria's conquest: Gozan, Haran, Rezeph, Eden, Tel Assar, Hena, and Ivvah (2 Kgs. 19:10-13; Isa. 37:11-13). (Interestingly, some of these cities had fallen over one hundred years earlier.)

Hezekiah's Prayer (2 Kgs. 19:14-19; Isa. 37:14-20)

After Hezekiah received Sennacherib's message, he again went straight to the temple and laid the letter before the Lord to seek the Lord's help through prayer (2 Kgs. 19:14):

> *O Lord of hosts, God of Israel, the one who dwells between the cherubim, You are God, You alone, of all the kingdoms of the earth. You have made heaven and earth. Incline Your ear, O Lord, and hear; open Your eyes, O Lord, and see; and hear all the words of Sennacherib, which he has sent to reproach the living God. Truly, Lord, the kings of Assyria have laid waste all the nations and their lands, and have cast their gods into the fire; for they were not gods, but the work of men's hands – wood and stone. Therefore they destroyed them. Now therefore, O Lord our God, save us from his hand, that all the kingdoms of the earth may know that You are the Lord, You alone* (2 Kgs. 19:15-19; Isa. 37:16-20).

This is a remarkable prayer of faith, a model prayer in many respects. First, notice that Hezekiah did not rush into God's presence frantic and fearful, but he came as a trusting worshiper. He commences his prayer with praise and worship. This is how the Lord Jesus taught His disciples to begin their prayers (Luke 11:2). Hezekiah acknowledges that he is praying to the only true God, the One who dwells in heaven, who created all things, and who controls the kingdoms of the world (2 Kgs. 19:15). To enter God's presence with accolades of praise, expressions of thanksgiving, and heartfelt worship demonstrates to God that we know Him and trust Him. If we believe that God truly controls all things according to His sovereign plan, then we must also believe that time is not a limiting factor for Him to accomplish His best.

Second, Hezekiah asks God to take action against the Assyrians because of Sennacherib's blasphemous words (2 Kgs. 19:16). Notice that Hezekiah did not repeat to God what Sennacherib actually said. The king of Judah understood that an all-knowing, all-seeing, and all-wise God did not need more information. Rather, God is honored when His people are in awe of Him and trust Him. The Lord's people should not waste time supplying God with facts about situations He is already completely aware of – He understands much more than we do anyway. Rather, we should be telling the Lord what we know about Him, giving thanks for what He has done, and expressing our confidence in His attributes and character to achieve the best outcome, even though we do not know what that might be. True faith wants what God wants.

Third, Hezekiah acknowledges the truth of Sennacherib's claim that no people groups (with all their pagan gods) have been able to resist Assyrian aggression (2 Kgs. 19:17-18). This is not to provide God with information, but to acknowledge the incredible prospect that God has to glorify His name. The stage is set, so to speak, and Jehovah has a wonderful opportunity to prove to all Gentile nations that the God of the Jews is indeed Lord of all (2 Kgs. 19:19).

Hezekiah's actions reflect Peter's and James' exhortations to fellow believers in the Church Age when tested by trials:

> *Yes, all of you be submissive to one another, and be clothed with humility, for "God resists the proud, but gives grace to the humble." Therefore humble yourselves under the mighty hand of God, that He may exalt you in due time, casting all your care upon Him, for He*

> *cares for you. Be sober, be vigilant; because your adversary the devil walks about like a roaring lion, seeking whom he may devour. Resist him, steadfast in the faith, knowing that the same sufferings are experienced by your brotherhood in the world* (1 Pet. 5:5-9).

> *God resists the proud, but gives grace to the humble. Therefore submit to God. Resist the devil and he will flee from you. Draw near to God and He will draw near to you. Cleanse your hands, you sinners; and purify your hearts, you double-minded* (Jas. 4:6-8).

The king was literally "clothed with humility" and he humbled himself before the Lord. He effectually "cast his care on the Lord," that is, he laid Sennacherib's letter before the Lord – a gesture meaning, "Lord, you handle this." Walking in faith and truth, Hezekiah fully expected God to honor His name, just as David had three centuries earlier during a threatening situation:

> *Revive me, O Lord, for Your name's sake!*
> *For Your righteousness' sake bring my soul out of trouble.*
> *In Your mercy cut off my enemies, and destroy all those who afflict my soul;*
> *For I am Your servant* (Ps. 143:11-12).

And as we will see shortly, "in due time" God delivered Hezekiah, as He did David. Both Old and New Testaments present the same pattern for victorious living – humility, faith, and obedience.

The King's Prayer Is Answered (2 Kgs. 19:20-34; Isa. 37:21-35)

The Lord God of Israel replied to the king's prayer of faith through Isaiah: *"Because you have prayed to Me against Sennacherib king of Assyria, this is the word which the Lord has spoken concerning him"* (2 Kgs. 19:20-21). The Lord specifically states that He would do three things.

First, the Assyrians would be turned back in such a powerful way that the virgin daughter of Zion (speaking of Jerusalem in poetic parallelism) would mock them (2 Kgs. 19:22). Jerusalem, like a taunting young maiden, would revel over the ineffectual attempts of Sennacherib to take the city. This mocking would rebuff Assyria's blasphemy of Israel's God and their prideful endeavors (2 Kgs. 19:23-25).

The felling of trees (the toppling of nations) and the drying up of brooks for defense (draining moats around cities) metaphorically represented Sennacherib's boasted achievements. But Isaiah likens the nations that Assyria conquered to grass on a flat housetop. These countries were easily overcome because Israel's God had weakened those opposing Assyria, whom He was using to punish them (2 Kgs. 19:26-27). But because of Sennacherib's rage against God, God promised to put a hook in his nose and a bridle in his mouth and to lead him like a captive slave back to Assyria (2 Kgs. 19:28).

The second thing God promised was to maintain a remnant in Judah and to return agricultural productivity back to normal after two years (2 Kgs. 19:29). This sign would dissuade anyone from thinking that the Assyrian withdrawal had happened by chance. The Jews would glean what God caused to spring up naturally in their fields, but in the third year they would be able to sow and reap again. Isaiah then compares this agricultural promise to what God would accomplish spiritually in His people: *"And the remnant who have escaped of the house of Judah shall again take root downward, and bear fruit upward. For out of Jerusalem shall go a remnant"* (2 Kgs. 19:30-31; Isa. 37:31).

There is a lovely application here: believers must root down to bear up fruit to God. Many Christians, often those who are infants in the Lord, are zealous to serve the Lord, but do not want to expend the time to "root downward" first. When Christians try to do something for the Lord without first having a good scriptural foundation, an understanding of their spiritual calling and gifts, and exercising dependence on the Lord, the result is usually harmful to the name of Christ. Young believers desiring to branch out before they are sufficiently rooted in the Lord to sustain the work of ministry will tend to topple over. Thus the wisdom of Isaiah's statement – believers must "take root downward" before they can "bear fruit upward."

To summarize this second decree, some cities had been conquered and vineyards, orchards, etc. had been destroyed by the Assyrians, but all this devastation would be remedied soon. It would take only a couple of years for the rooting down and the bearing up of fruit again. God promised to do this because of His great zeal for Judah.

The third promise of the Lord centered in the protection of Jerusalem and the ultimate destruction of the Assyrian army:

> *"He shall not come into this city, nor shoot an arrow there, nor come before it with shield, nor build a siege mound against it. By the way that he came, by the same shall he return; and he shall not come into this city," says the Lord. "For I will defend this city, to save it for My own sake and for My servant David's sake"* (2 Kgs. 19:32-34; Isa. 37:33-35).

God was long-suffering with Judah because of His unconditional covenant with David. God promised David that one of his descendants would sit on his throne forever, which meant the seed royal had to be preserved. Hence, God informs Hezekiah that Sennacherib will not step foot in Jerusalem. He would not even have time to build a siege ramp because God would turn him back to Assyria by the same route he arrived. Isaiah had already stated that Sennacherib would die by the sword in his own land (2 Kgs. 19:7).

The Trusting King Is Delivered (2 Kgs. 19:35-37; 2 Chron. 32:20-23; Isa. 37:36-38)

The chapter concludes with the fulfillment of much of what Isaiah had previously prophesied concerning the fall of the Assyrians (Isa. 30:27-33, 31:8-9, 33:18-19). Because this is one of the most spectacular defeats in all Scripture of an army threatening Israel, the single verse account seems almost anticlimactic: *"Then the angel of the Lord went out, and killed in the camp of the Assyrians one hundred and eighty-five thousand; and when people arose early in the morning, there were the corpses – all dead"* (1 Kgs. 19:35).

The slaughter by the Angel of the Lord occurred at night. How it was accomplished has been the source of much speculation. It was not likely by pestilence, for the Jews would have been apprehensive about despoiling the dead Assyrian soldiers. Some have suggested that the army was struck by a colossal hailstorm. But that would have damaged the goods and livestock that the Lord was providing for His people through the victory, and also does not explain how Sennacherib survived. We learn from 2 Chronicles 32:21 that the entire Assyrian army was not destroyed, but the Angel *"cut down every mighty man of valor, leader, and captain in the camp of the king of Assyria."* The selective nature of this judgment further substantiates its divine origin (i.e. the Lord disabled the Assyrian army by eliminating all of its leadership and skilled soldiers). Perhaps the best explanation is that the

Lord, who is the essence of all life, simply snuffed out the lives of 185,000 specific men in a single moment of time.

We do know that the next morning the Jews awoke to find 185,000 corpses and that Sennacherib had returned to Assyria with only a remnant of his army (2 Kgs. 19:36). The reason the king was permitted to survive was so that Hezekiah could see that God was in control of every detail of Judah's deliverance. Isaiah had foretold that Sennacherib would return to Assyria and die there by the sword.

Second Kings 19:37 confirms what happened afterwards. Over the next twenty years, Sennacherib engaged in several military exploits, but he never returned to Israel. While the king was worshiping in the house of Nisroch his god in Nineveh, his sons Adrammelech and Sharezer struck him down with the sword. They escaped into the land of Ararat, and Esarhaddon, one of the sons of Sennacherib, ruled in his place.

God permitted Sennacherib several years to reflect on what he had witnessed, that is, much of his army being selectively wiped out without the presence of a visible enemy. Instead of believing that he had actually offended the one true God and lost, he turned to his own gods who did not protect him, nor provide him answers for the calamity. There is an insanity to pride, the ultimate expression being that somehow a man or an angel can overcome his Creator and rule in His place. This was Lucifer's sin which caused his ruin and it is the same mindset that his children, the sons of disobedience, continue to propagate today through a variety of world religions (such as New Age, Mormonism, and Hinduism). Rejecting God, or desiring to be on His throne, never ends well, but humbling ourselves before Him always will.

Assyria was an evil nation, and when they had fulfilled God's purpose, as Isaiah had foretold, God would destroy them by leanness (i.e., pestilence) and by fire (Isa. 10:16-17). The Assyrian soldiers would be consumed like trees in a windblown forest fire; so many would die by fire that even a small child could count the survivors (Isa. 10:18-19). God was true to His word, for when Sennacherib threatened King Hezekiah and Jerusalem in 701 B.C., God sent the Angel of the Lord who slew 185,000 Assyrian soldiers in one night. There were no survivors (none merely wounded; 2 Kgs. 19:35); however, some low-ranking soldiers and Sennacherib were left alive to tell the story of what had happened (2 Chron. 32:21; Isa. 31:8).

Meditation

The Assyrian came down like the wolf on the fold,
His cohorts were gleaming in purple and gold;
The sheen of their spears was like stars on the sea,
When the blue wave rolls nightly on deep Galilee.

Like the leaves of the forest when Summer is green,
That host with their banners at sunset were seen:
Like the leaves of the forest when Autumn hath blown,
That host on the morrow lay withered and strown.

For the Angel of Death spread his wings on the blast,
And breathed in the face of the foe as he passed;
And the eyes of the sleepers waxed deadly and chill,
And their hearts but once heaved, and forever grew still!

And there lay the steed with his nostril all wide,
But through it there rolled not the breath of his pride;
And the foam of his gasping lay white on the turf,
And cold as the spray of the rock-beating surf.

And there lay the rider distorted and pale,
With the dew on his brow, and the rust on his mail:
And the tents were all silent, the banners alone,
The lances unlifted, the trumpet unblown.

And the widows of Ashur are loud in their wail,
And the idols are broke in the temple of Baal;
And the might of the Gentile, unsmote by the sword,
Hath melted like snow in the glance of the Lord.

— George Gordon

King Hezekiah of Judah – Illness and Healing

2 Kings 20:1-23; 2 Chronicles 32:24-26

Hezekiah's Illness and Warning (2 Kgs. 20:1; 2 Chron. 32:24; Isa. 38:1)

Thirty-nine-year-old Hezekiah was sick and near to death when Isaiah visited him and said, *"Thus says the Lord: 'Set your house in order, for you shall die and not live'"* (2 Kgs. 20:1). The prophet had spoken in the name of the Lord, therefore what Isaiah said was sure to come to pass, correct? Isaiah spoke only what God told him to and though the statement conveyed urgency, it did not guarantee imminent death.

Though Hezekiah could probably ensure that the affairs of state were in good order, he apparently did not have a son to set on the throne in his place. Manasseh was born about three years after the events in this chapter; he assumed Hezekiah's throne at the age of twelve (2 Chron. 33:1). As long as Judah had a throne, the Davidic dynasty must not be broken, meaning, Hezekiah needed to have a natural son. Most kings took many wives to ensure they would have plenty of sons and heirs. However, the king had either neglected this matter in his early years (perhaps thinking he had plenty of time to marry and have children), or perhaps he was married, but only daughters had been born to him. The king had been quite occupied with spiritual reform in Judah and with fortifying Jerusalem.

Hezekiah's Prayer (2 Kgs. 20:2-3; Isa. 38:2-3)

After Isaiah delivered his message and departed, Hezekiah turned and faced the wall, tearfully uttering this brief prayer: *"Remember now, O Lord, I pray, how I have walked before You in truth and with a loyal heart, and have done what is good in Your sight"* (2 Kgs. 20:2-3). Why would the king remind God of His integrity and good deeds? In the Old Testament illness and disease were often associated directly with divine punishment for sin. This appears to be Hezekiah's thinking in appealing to the Lord, for later he will connect his deliverance from death with the forgiveness of his sins (Isa. 38:17).

Notice that Hezekiah did not bother to tell God what he wanted; he knew that God was already aware of the desires of his heart. Rather, he reminded the Lord that he had walked in truth and had faithfully led His people to honor Him. He was not a wayward king deserving the death penalty. Few of us could ever pray such a prayer, but the fact that God respected Hezekiah's prayer tells us that it was a true statement – Hezekiah had been a loyal king with high morals and he had brought many reforms to Judah during his tenure. Given that he was the son of a wicked man and had a poor example to follow, this is especially exceptional.

Hezekiah's Answer (2 Kgs. 20:4-6; 2 Chron. 32:25-26; Isa. 38:4-8)

The writer of Kings informs us that Isaiah had not yet departed from the palace before the Lord, responding to Hezekiah's prayer, instructed the prophet to return to the king with a second message (2 Kgs. 20:4):

> *"I have heard your prayer, I have seen your tears; surely I will add to your days fifteen years. I will deliver you and this city from the hand of the king of Assyria, and I will defend this city. And this is the sign to you from the Lord, that the Lord will do this thing which He has spoken: Behold, I will bring the shadow on the sundial, which has gone down with the sun on the sundial of Ahaz, ten degrees backward." So the sun returned ten degrees on the dial by which it had gone down* (Isa. 38:5-8).

One thing that we learn from God's decree is that the events in 2 Kings 20 (Isa. 38 and 39) slightly preceded the events concerning Assyria in 2 Kings 18 and 19 (Isa. 36 and 37). Since Hezekiah died in 686 B.C., the events of this chapter would have occurred early in 701 B.C., just prior to Rabshakeh's advance on Jerusalem recorded in chapter 36. Why is the narrative arranged out of its natural chronology? Isaiah would have written the account first, and he likely placed Hezekiah's folly in showing the Babylon delegation all of Judah's wealth (Isa. 39) in such a way as to preface his prophecies pertaining to Babylon (Isa. 40-48).

Isaiah told Hezekiah that God had heard his prayer and would heal him and add fifteen years to his life. Isaiah also promised Hezekiah that he would be healed quickly. *"On the third day you shall go up to the house of the Lord"* (2 Kgs. 20:5). Why the king asked for a sign from God proving that he would be healed is unknown (2 Kgs. 20:8), but God granted his request. Isaiah asked the king if God should cause *"the shadow go forward ten degrees or go backward ten degrees"* (2 Kgs. 20:9). John A. Martin explains the choices Isaiah was offering Hezekiah:

> Apparently a special stairway had been built as a time device, a kind of sundial. As the sun went down in the west, a shadow would move upward on the staircase so that people could ascertain the time of the day. Interestingly Ahaz had rejected a sign from the Lord (Isa. 7:10-12) but now on a staircase named for him his son Hezekiah was given a sign.[98]

Since it is natural for a shadow to advance as the sun declines in the horizon, Hezekiah chose the latter option. Isaiah promptly petitions the Lord and *"He brought the shadow ten degrees backward, by which it had gone down on the sundial of Ahaz"* (2 Kgs. 20:11). How this miracle was achieved is unknown. It may have been a local phenomenon at the obelisk or one on a grander scale that actually affected the earth's rotation, the sun's disposition, or a redirection of light. What is evident is Isaiah's faith; he did not hesitate to ask God to do what seemed impossible, that is, something beyond what natural law can rationalize.

This all was good news for the king. However, we can only imagine what it was like for Hezekiah to live out his final years knowing exactly when he would die. What effect would that information have on a God-fearing individual? Knowing that you were invincible until God said your time on earth was over might either embolden zeal for the Lord or reckless thrill-seeking. The brevity of our sojourn on earth should cause all believers to evaluate life's priorities and pursue what is best in his or her remaining days.

The psalmists offer many prayers which should encourage us to value each day God has granted to us. For example:

> *O God, You have taught me from my youth; and to this day I declare Your wondrous works. Now also when I am old and grayheaded, O God, do not forsake me, until I declare Your strength to this generation, your power to everyone who is to come* (Ps. 71:17-18).

> *So teach us to number our days, that we may gain a heart of wisdom* (Ps. 90:12).

Paul reminded the Ephesian Christians that the only reason we exist is for *"the praise of His glory"* (Eph. 1:12-14). We were created for God's good pleasure and to accomplish His purposes; nothing beyond that has any value for eternity (Eph. 2:10; Rev. 4:11).

Being healed of a fatal disease and observing a supernatural celestial event likely explains why Hezekiah was prompted to immediately humble himself and to put Sennacherib's threatening letter before the Lord in the temple. Unfortunately, we do not read of Hezekiah doing any other great feats for the Lord in his later years. In fact, the verses following in 2 Kgs. 20 record that Hezekiah was lifted up in pride. He boasted of Judah's great resources to a visiting Babylonian delegation as if they were his.

Hezekiah's Praise (Isa. 38:9-20)

Isaiah 38:9-20 records Hezekiah's song of praise and thanksgiving after being healed. Hezekiah's illness seized him in the prime of his life, so he was very thankful that the Lord had spared his life. Despite the prospect of nearing death, Hezekiah knew that God was in control of his life and had permitted this disease: *"O Lord, I am oppressed; undertake for me! ... He Himself has done it"* (Isa. 38:14-15). Realizing that God was in control of his illness, Hezekiah knew that he should choose to walk carefully and humbly before the Lord.

Whether or not Hezekiah should have requested the Lord's intervention in his medical crisis is debated. From a logical perspective, we might conclude that it would have been better for the king to die from his illness. Hezekiah later fathered Manasseh, the most wicked king to sit on the throne of Judah. Hezekiah brought great religious reform to Judah, even removing the high places, but his son Manasseh plunged Judah into gross idolatry for decades before turning to the Lord near the end of his fifty-plus-year reign. Certainly much heartache for the remnant and for the Lord would have been avoided if Hezekiah had died instead of appealing to the Lord in this chapter.

Yet, all these things are within God's purposes. The Davidic royal line had to continue and Manasseh's wicked ways would test the faithfulness of those loyal to Jehovah and set the stage for a great revival under Josiah. Godly Josiah would cause the Word of God to be heard and honored again in Judah as he ushered in sweeping reforms. If there had been no Manasseh, there would have been no Josiah. In summary, God's ways are above our ways, and Hezekiah's foreknown failure had already been incorporated into God's sovereign plan for refining and restoring His covenant people to Himself. Through Hezekiah's faith, Assyria would be brought down as God said; through Hezekiah's failure, God announced the next phase of Judah's refinement – the Babylonians.

Hezekiah's Healing (2 Kgs. 20:4-11; Isa. 38:21-22)

Isaiah directed the king to apply a poultice of dried figs to his boils or ulcers (2 Kgs. 20:7; Isa. 38:21). This was a common medicinal treatment in those days for such inflammations, but it also offered a test of faith. Isaiah also told Hezekiah that he would be healed in three days (2 Kgs. 20:5). Because of Hezekiah's prayer, God was going to heal him through the poultice, but the king had to act in faith to apply it for three days and wait, which he did. But though Hezekiah was willing to proceed in faith, he also asked for a sign to confirm God's promise of his healing (2 Kgs. 20:8; Isa. 38:22).

Was this request a lapse of faith? It seems more likely that the opposite is true – a supernatural sign would infallibly confirm God's word in the matter. That is, a sign would prove that God had intervened in saving the king's life, and that the king had not been cured just by good medicine. So Hezekiah did not doubt God's word, but rather wanted to confirm it in such a way that no one else would doubt it either. This is a good example of faith-centered prayer, the Lord, and medicine all having their part in the healing process, but the believer must walk wherever the Lord leads in the process!

Meditation

He leadeth me! O blessed thought,
O words with heavenly comfort fraught;
Whate'er I do, where'er I be,
Still 'tis Christ's hand that leadeth me.

Sometimes 'mid scenes of deepest gloom,
Sometimes where Eden's bowers bloom,
By waters still, over troubled sea,
Still 'tis His hand that leadeth me.

— Joseph H. Gilmore

King Hezekiah of Judah – Wealth and Death

2 Kings 20:12-21; 2 Chronicles 32:27-33

Hezekiah's Wealth and Babylon (2 Kgs. 20:12-19; 2 Chron. 32:27-31; Isa. 39)

Because Hezekiah was with the Lord, the Lord prospered whatever he put his hand to. The writer of Chronicles pauses to summarize the wealth that king had accumulated:

> *Hezekiah had very great riches and honor. And he made himself treasuries for silver, for gold, for precious stones, for spices, for shields, and for all kinds of desirable items; storehouses for the harvest of grain, wine, and oil; and stalls for all kinds of livestock, and folds for flocks. Moreover he provided cities for himself, and possessions of flocks and herds in abundance; for God had given him very much property* (2 Chron. 32:27-29).

Second Chronicles 32:30 identifies one of Hezekiah's chief accomplishments: *"Hezekiah also stopped the water outlet of Upper Gihon, and brought the water by tunnel to the west side of the City of David."* In Nehemiah's day, the Fountain Gate was located on the east wall just north of the Dung Gate. There was a man-made pool at this location called the king's pool (Neh. 2:14). This reservoir inside the eastern wall is likely the Pool of Siloam which Hezekiah connected by an underground water tunnel to the Spring of Gihon (northeast of the pool; 2 Chron. 32:30). Gihon was located outside the city and below the steep eastern hill Ophel in the Kidron Valley and thus vulnerable to enemy attack.

Hezekiah had teams of engineers on each end of the tunnel digging through solid rock towards each other. The tunnel is about 1750 feet (533 m) long and maintains a steady 0.6 percent grade the entire length of the channel (i.e., a 10.5-foot drop on a one-third-mile span). The tunnel was a great engineering feat and would supply the city with a robust source of fresh water during a siege. God prospered all that Hezekiah did until he boasted of his wealth to a visiting delegation from Babylon: *"Regarding the ambassadors of the princes of Babylon, whom they sent to him to inquire about the wonder that was done in the land, God withdrew from him, in order to test him, that He might know all that was in his heart"* (2 Chron. 32:31).

God's divine intervention in wiping out the Assyrian army in one night occurred a few months after Hezekiah's healing and likely just after the Babylonian envoy visited him. Merodach-Baladan, the son of Baladan, king of Babylon, heard of Hezekiah's recovery and dispatched an envoy carrying letters and gifts to congratulate the king (2 Kgs. 20:12; Isa. 39:1). Subsequent history suggests that the king of Babylon may have had an ulterior motive in contacting Hezekiah besides just expressing goodwill. John A. Martin explains:

> Merodach-Baladan was Marduk-apal-iddina, the invader. Twice he had tried to break away from the Assyrian Empire, and once had succeeded in taking the city of Babylon. After his second reign (of nine months in 703-702 B.C.), he was deposed by Sennacherib and went to Elam. While there (and while still known as the king of Babylon), he actively tried to form an alliance with other nations to throw off the Assyrian yoke. Undoubtedly his friendly visit after Hezekiah's illness was intended to persuade the king of Judah to join the rebel alliance in the fight against Assyria.[99]

Hence, Hezekiah's showing the Babylonian envoy all *"the silver and gold, the spices and precious ointment, and all his armory – all that was found among his treasures"* was a foolish thing to do (2 Kgs. 20:13; Isa. 39:2). He was trying to impress his pagan visitors by acting as if all the riches of Judah belonged to him, but that was not the case – the wealth of Judah belonged to God.

Isaiah had already stated that Assyria was God's chastening rod on the entire region, so commiserating with those rebelling against God's expressed will (i.e., the Babylonians) was an indiscretion that God did not take lightly. A few months earlier, God had tested Hezekiah's faith through a fatal illness; now he would test the king's heart: *"Regarding the ambassadors of the princes of Babylon, whom they sent to him to inquire about the wonder that was done in the land, God withdrew from him, in order to test him, that He might know all that was in his heart"* (2 Chron. 32:31). In other words, the Lord wanted to show Hezekiah himself the terrible consequences of pride.

Hezekiah's response shows us that we can trust and serve the Lord, but still have pride hiding in our hearts. It is one thing to rest in the Lord and be delivered, but it is an entirely different heart attitude not to rob glory from Him after being blessed. No wonder the Lord often keeps us immersed in trials; it keeps us humble and dependent on Him. Our self-dependence results in the loss of divine blessing and, as Hezekiah would soon learn, is usually harmful to others in our care.

After hearing about the foreign delegation, Isaiah visited Hezekiah and asked him, *"What did these men say, and from where did they come to you?"* (2 Kgs. 20:14; Isa. 39:3). The prophet's questions were not to obtain information, but to assist the king in realizing the gravity of his error. Hezekiah told Isaiah from where they came, Babylon, but not what they had said. This withholding of information may indicate that the Babylonian delegation had indeed solicited Hezekiah's assistance against Assyria (2 Kgs. 20:15; Isa. 39:4-5). After learning that the king had shown the Babylonians all the wealth of Judah, Isaiah issues a twofold prophecy (2 Kgs. 20:16-18):

> *"Behold, the days are coming when all that is in your house, and what your fathers have accumulated until this day, shall be carried to Babylon; nothing shall be left,"* says the Lord. *"And they shall take away some of your sons who will descend from you, whom you will beget; and they shall be eunuchs in the palace of the king of Babylon"* (Isa. 39:6-7).

First, Isaiah said that all Hezekiah had shown the Babylonians would be carried back to Babylon. This seemed unlikely at the time, as Assyria was the dominant world power and the rebel Babylonians were on the run. Second, the prophet told the king that some of his descendants would be made eunuchs and would serve in the royal court of Babylon. These prophecies were fulfilled during three separate main Babylonian invasions in 605, 597, and 588-586 B.C. Each time Judah was despoiled and captives were taken back to Babylon.

More than seventy years into the future (i.e., between 605 and 586 B.C.), every detail of Isaiah's prophecy to Hezekiah was fulfilled. How did the king respond to Isaiah's prophecy, which had been uttered as a rebuke against his foolish pride? The king said, *"'The word of the Lord which you have spoken is good!' For he said, 'At least there will be peace and truth in my days'"* (2 Kgs. 20:19; Isa. 39:8). Although the king accepted God's will, it does not seem that Hezekiah understood the prophet's reproof, nor was he grieved over knowing the appalling future that awaited his great-grandchildren. Rather, the king was just glad that the horrific events prophesied here were not going to happen while he was on the throne. The lack of remorse over foolish behavior is a good indication of how much pride is harboring in the heart.

Hezekiah's Death (2 Kgs. 20:20-21; 2 Chron. 32:32-33)

Hezekiah was not a perfect man, but he did much good for Judah because he clung to the Lord. After his death, he was buried in the upper tombs of the sons of David, and *"all Judah and the inhabitants of Jerusalem honored him at his death"* (2 Chron. 32:33). His father Ahaz did not receive such honor from the people after his death because he did evil in the sight of the Lord. Unfortunately, Judah would be lured back into gross idolatry after Hezekiah's son Manasseh was seated on the throne of Judah.

The chronologer closed his account by noting that there is a threefold record in Scripture testifying of Hezekiah's exemplary life (i.e., in Kings, Chronicles, and Isaiah). John Heading notes: "Only the history of the Lord Jesus exceeds this, by having four Gospels to record His holy life."[100] Hezekiah was an outstanding king of Judah and has been honored as such down through the centuries. He was a brilliant light for God in the midst of intense evil and prevailing darkness.

God delights in honoring those who honor Him, and He is faithful to remember and willing to reward the good that we do: *"For God is not unjust to forget your work and labor of love which you have shown toward His name, in that you have ministered to the saints, and do minister"* (Heb. 6:10).

Meditation

> God's purpose in promising to reward with heavenly and eternal honors the faithful service of His saints is to win them from the pursuit of earthly riches and pleasures, to sustain them in the fires of persecution, and to encourage them in the exercise of Christian virtues.
>
> — C. I. Scofield

Kings Manasseh and Amon of Judah

2 Kings 21; 2 Chronicles 33

Manasseh Reigns in Judah (2 Kgs. 21:1-9; 2 Chron. 33:1-9)

Manasseh, who was born three years after Hezekiah was healed of his illness, began to rule Judah at the age of twelve (2 Chron. 33:1). He reigned fifty-five years in Jerusalem (697-642 B.C.) and did evil in the sight of the Lord, even reverting to the pagan ways of the Canaanite nations conquered by Joshua (2 Chron. 33:2). Five of the six remaining kings of Judah were wicked, but the evil of Manasseh and his son Amon exceeded the other three.

Manasseh's evil was immense; he rebuilt the high places which his father Hezekiah had broken down, raised up altars for Baals, fashioned wooden images, and revered and served all the host of heaven (i.e., star worship) through a variety of pagan means (2 Chron. 33:3). Manasseh's name means "one who forgets," or "forgetting" which well characterizes his reign; he quickly forgot the godly example of his father and the God of his father.

His idolatrous doings went beyond those of any Judean king before him. The king even erected pagan altars for all the host of heaven in the courts of Jehovah's temple – the place that the Lord had said, *"In Jerusalem shall My name be forever"* (2 Chron. 33:4-5). Manasseh caused his sons to pass through the fire in the Valley of the Son of Hinnom and he practiced soothsaying, used witchcraft and sorcery, and consulted mediums and spiritists (2 Chron. 33:6). The king even had the gall to set a carved image that he had made in the Lord's temple, of which God had said to David and to Solomon:

> *In this house and in Jerusalem, which I have chosen out of all the tribes of Israel, I will put My name forever; and I will not again remove the foot of Israel from the land which I have appointed for your fathers – only if they are careful to do all that I have*

> *commanded them, according to the whole law and the statutes and the ordinances by the hand of Moses* (2 Chron. 33:7-8).

We learn from the writer of Kings that it was an image of Asherah that Manasseh placed in Jehovah's temple (2 Kgs. 21:7). Asherah was the Canaanite goddess of fertility. So deeply entrenched was Judah's paganism at this time that even their children worshiped at their altars and before the Asherah poles on high places. Despite experiencing the wonderful revival in the days of Hezekiah, under Manasseh's leadership Judah returned to the idolatry that had marred the reign of King Ahaz, Manasseh's grandfather. Like Ahaz, the people again chose to sacrifice their children, whom God had given them for a heritage to Himself, to false gods (2 Chron. 33:6; Jer. 19:6). For God's people to offer their own children in sacrifice to the god of this age is perhaps the greatest insult that can be committed against the Lord.

Manasseh was so headstrong in enforcing his paganism that he slaughtered those that opposed him. The writer of Kings states, *"Manasseh shed very much innocent blood, till he had filled Jerusalem from one end to another, besides his sin by which he made Judah sin, in doing evil in the sight of the Lord"* (2 Kgs. 21:16). Hezekiah had done more than any other king of Judah to cause God's covenant people to obey and honor the Lord, but his son Manasseh did the exact opposite. The historian summarizes, *"So Manasseh seduced Judah and the inhabitants of Jerusalem to do more evil than the nations whom the Lord had destroyed before the children of Israel"* (2 Chron. 33:9). *He did much evil in the sight of the Lord, to provoke Him to anger"* (2 Chron. 33:6).

Manasseh Repents and Is Restored (2 Kgs. 21:10-16; 2 Chron. 33:10-17)

The Lord sent various prophets, including Isaiah, to warn Manasseh and his people, but they would not listen (2 Chron. 33:10). Jewish tradition says that Manasseh was so furious with Isaiah that he had the prophet sawn in two (Heb. 11:37).[101] What was the message that Manasseh received from the prophets? The Lord said:

> *Because Manasseh king of Judah has done these abominations (he has acted more wickedly than all the Amorites who were before him, and has also made Judah sin with his idols), therefore thus says the*

> *Lord God of Israel: "Behold, I am bringing such calamity upon Jerusalem and Judah, that whoever hears of it, both his ears will tingle. And I will stretch over Jerusalem the measuring line of Samaria and the plummet of the house of Ahab; I will wipe Jerusalem as one wipes a dish, wiping it and turning it upside down. So I will forsake the remnant of My inheritance and deliver them into the hand of their enemies; and they shall become victims of plunder to all their enemies, because they have done evil in My sight, and have provoked Me to anger since the day their fathers came out of Egypt, even to this day"* (2 Kgs. 21:11-15).

Because Manasseh led Judah to commit worse abominations than the Amorites had done, the Lord promised to punish Judah as He had already punished Israel for her idolatry. The imagery of the measuring line and plumb line symbolizes judgment.

The Lord honored His declaration and brought the Assyrian army against Jerusalem. The king of Assyria *"took Manasseh with hooks, bound him with bronze fetters, and carried him off to Babylon"* (2 Chron. 33:11). Like Manasseh, many Jews after him would learn about the ills of idolatry in the capital of Idolatry – Babylon. In his affliction, Manasseh humbled himself, repented, and implored the Lord his God to forgive him (2 Chron. 33:12, 19). The Lord heard and honored Manasseh's prayer and brought him back to Jerusalem and returned his kingdom to him (2 Chron. 33:13). Thankfully, from that day forward, Manasseh knew only Jehovah as his God.

Assyria's incursion into Judah had alerted Manasseh to his need to bolster Judah's defenses. To enclose Ophel, Manasseh built up a high wall outside the City of David on the west side of Gihon (in the valley) and extended it northward to the Fish Gate (2 Chron. 33:14). To better withstand a future invasion, the king ensured that all Judah's fortification had good military leadership.

Having experienced the Lord's forgiveness, a humbled Manasseh was zealous to remove all the foreign gods, idols, and altars that he had built from the temple and Jerusalem; these were cast out of the city (2 Chron. 33:15). He also repaired the altar of the Lord, sacrificed peace offerings and thank offerings on it, and commanded Judah to serve the Lord God of Israel (2 Chron. 33:16). However, the people still sacrificed on high places, but to the Lord only (2 Chron. 33:17). Manasseh had reverted to the reforms of his father Hezekiah, except on this point. Presenting offerings to Jehovah in the high places (instead of the temple alone) occurred throughout most of Judah's history. Only David, Hezekiah, and Josiah honored the Lord's commandment that those who worshiped Him should do so only in His sanctuary (i.e., at the tabernacle and then at the temple).

The Death of Manasseh (2 Kgs. 21:17-18; 2 Chron. 33:18-20)

Manasseh died and was buried in the garden of his own house, in the garden of Uzza (2 Kgs. 21:18). His son Amon reigned in his place (2 Chron. 33:20).

Amon's Reign and Death (2 Kgs. 21:19-26; 2 Chron. 33:21-25)

Amon was twenty-two years old when he became the king of Judah and reigned only two years in Jerusalem (642-640 B.C.; 2 Chron. 33:21). He reverted to the pagan ways of his father Manasseh before his conversion and did evil in the sight of the Lord (2 Chron. 33:22). Amon would not humble himself before the Lord, as his father Manasseh had, but increased in wickedness and transgressions (2 Chron. 33:23). Amon's servants conspired against him, and killed him in his own house (2 Chron. 33:24). The people executed Amon's murderers and placed his son Josiah king on the throne in his place (2 Chron. 33:25).

God had been patient with Manasseh for many years to bring him to repentance, but Amon was more accountable because he had witnessed his father's sins, repentance, and restoration to the Lord. Accordingly, Amon was not permitted the same opportunity as his father, but rather was judged by the Lord. It is a principle that we see throughout Scripture: the more revelation we receive from the Lord, the higher our accountability to God!

Daniel affirmed this reality when he pronounced judgment on wicked King Belshazzar, who had witnessed God humble his father Nebuchadnezzar and bring him to repentance: "*But you his son, Belshazzar, have not humbled your heart, although you knew all this. And you have lifted yourself up against the Lord of heaven*" (Dan. 5:22-23). Likewise, the Lord Jesus, after declaring the message of God, put a curse on some Jewish cities, such as Capernaum, Bethsaida, and Chorazin, for their rejection of God's grace (Luke 10:13-16). They had received the ultimate revelation, their God-given Messiah was standing before them and they had rejected His message. These cities would not receive another opportunity and only the ruins remain today!

Meditation

Great God! to me the sight afford, to him of old allowed;
And let my faith behold its Lord, descending in a cloud.

In that revealing Spirit come down, Thine attributes proclaim,
And to my inmost soul make known, the glories of Thy name.

Merciful God, Thyself proclaim in this polluted breast;
Mercy is Thy distinguished name, which suits a sinner best.

— Charles Wesley

King Josiah of Judah – The Law Is Found

2 Kings 22:1-30, 23:1-2; 2 Chronicles 34

History in Review

Regrettably, Israel's history is characterized by religious waffling from the beginning. Eight centuries before Josiah ascended to Judah's throne, Moses descended from Mount Sinai with a covenant offer from Jehovah. The people, who had just witnessed Jehovah's awesomeness, affirmed their commitment to this covenant: *"All that the Lord has spoken we will do"* (Ex. 19:8), and Moses again ascended the mountain to personally convey their response to God. This may have been the aspiration of their hearts at the time, but their promise to obey Jehovah was self-confident and short-lived, for in just a few days they would construct and worship a golden calf and be judged accordingly.

Indeed, much of Israel's history was marred by rebellion and divine retribution for covenant-failure. During the days of Manasseh, the historian says that the Jews behaved worse than the pagans because they knew God's commandments and chose to commit blatant idolatry anyway (2 Chron. 33:9). The prophet Jeremiah began his ministry thirteen years after Manasseh's death. He described the Jews' propensity to do wickedness this way: their sins had been engraved on their hardened hearts by an iron tool with an unbreakable tip. The people had stony hearts, which directly related to their pagan stone altars. So deeply entrenched was their paganism that even the children worshiped at their altars and before the Asherah poles on high places. Asherah was the Canaanite goddess of fertility.

As previously mentioned, during Manasseh's reign an image of Asherah was actually placed in Jehovah's temple (2 Kgs. 21:7). Although he later removed it (2 Chron. 33:13-15), the image found its way back to the temple because King Josiah had to remove it again (2 Kgs. 23:6). The stony hearts of the people prevailed, and, despite Josiah's sweeping reforms, idolatry returned to Judah. Idols were worshiped by propping up green trees and branches (Asherah poles) before them on the high hills surrounding Jerusalem. It was likely the image of Asherah that Ezekiel spoke of as "the idol of jealousy" being worshiped in the temple in his day (Ezek. 8:5). There would be no more opportunities for repentance; God's patience had given way to wrath. He was going to severely punish His people by despoiling and deporting them. They would be enslaved by their invaders – the Babylonians (Jer. 17:4).

Josiah Reigns in Judah (2 Kgs. 22:1-2; 2 Chron. 34:1-2)

Josiah was only eight years old when he sat on the throne of Judah (2 Kgs. 22:1). His mother's name was Jedidah and he reigned thirty-one years in Jerusalem (640 to 609 B.C.). The writer states that Josiah *"did what was right in the sight of the Lord, and walked in all the ways of his father David; he did not turn aside to the right hand or to the left"* (2 Kgs. 22:2). The only other kings of Judah to receive such a high praise were Asa (1 Kgs. 15:11), Jehoshaphat (2 Chron. 17:3), and Hezekiah (2 Kgs. 18:3-4). However, although Asa and Jehoshaphat removed the pagan high places in Judah, they did not remove those associated with Jehovah worship (1 Kgs. 15:14; 1 Kgs. 22:43) as required by the Law of Moses (Deut. 12:2-14). The prophets Jeremiah and Zephaniah began their prophetic ministries at this time (Jer. 1:2; Zeph. 1:1).

Josiah's Early Reforms (2 Chron. 34:3-7)

The writer of Chronicles provides some specific details of Josiah's spiritual growth and zeal for the Lord (2 Chron. 34:3): The young king began to seek the God of his father David in his eighth year of reign (i.e., Josiah would have then been fifteen years old). In the twelfth year of his reign he had matured sufficiently to begin purging Judah and Jerusalem of the high places, of wooden, carved, and molded images, and to break down the altars of Baal and destroy their associated images (2 Chron. 34:3-4). Interestingly, it was the following year that the Lord called another godly young man named Jeremiah, the son of a priest, to be His prophet (Jer. 1:2). Jeremiah and Josiah no doubt knew each other, as they were approximately the same age and lived only three miles apart (the distance between Jerusalem and Anathoth).

Hilkiah Finds the Law (2 Kgs. 22:3-20; 2 Chron. 34:8-28)

In the eighteenth year of his reign King Josiah sent Shaphan, the scribe, to the temple to make an accounting of freewill offerings received by the doorkeepers and to transfer that money to various faithful craftsmen and workers needed to repair the temple (2 Kgs. 22:3-7). While performing this task, the high priest Hilkiah found *"the Book of the Law in the house of the Lord"* (2 Kgs. 22:8). Hilkiah then gave the book to Shaphan, who read it.

Unknown to God's people, the word of God was in the same place that God's treasure was kept. How sad it is when God's people continue trudging through life ignorant of the great wealth of wisdom and guidance contained in Scripture. The Lord Jesus affirmed that failure is inevitable if we do not know God's Word (Matt. 22:29), and that true disciples long to know and abide in God's Word (John 5:38). May each believer agree with the psalmist, *"I rejoice at Your word as one who finds great treasure"* (Ps. 119:162).

Shaphan then reported to the king that funds from the freewill offerings had been transferred to workers to accomplish temple repair work (2 Kgs. 22:9). Then Shaphan informed the king that Hilkiah had found the book of the Law in the temple and had given it to him; the scribe then read the book to the king (2 Kgs. 22:10). Josiah was shocked at what he heard and tore his clothes to express remorse (2 Kgs. 22:11). The king then commanded five priests, Hilkiah, Ahikam (Shaphan's son), Achbor, Shaphan, and Asaiah to *"go, inquire of the Lord for me, for the people and for all Judah, concerning the words of this book that has been found; for great is the wrath of the Lord that is aroused against us, because our fathers have not obeyed the words of this book, to do according to all that is written concerning us"* (2 Kgs. 22:12-13).

So Hilkiah the high priest, Ahikam, Achbor, Shaphan, and Asaiah went to inquire of Huldah the prophetess, the wife of Shallum, who lived in the Second Quarter (a suburb of Jerusalem; 2 Kgs. 22:14). Why the priests sought counsel from Huldah, instead of Jeremiah or Zephaniah, is not explained, but clearly her gift was highly esteemed in Judah. She also was likely the aunt of Jeremiah (Jer. 32:7). The Lord did not often use a woman to express His mind to His people, but sporadically did so in times of spiritual declension, usually as a means to awaken men to their lack of spiritual fortitude in fulfilling their God-given role as leaders. There are other prophetesses noted in the Bible: Miriam (Ex. 15:20), Deborah (Judg. 4:4), Anna (Luke 2:36), and the four daughters of Philip (Acts 21:9). Though a godly king was on the throne, the long, wicked reign of Manasseh had resulted in the people being ignorant of what God's Law commanded them to do. As to Huldah, Matthew Henry observes:

> The spirit of prophecy, that inestimable treasure, was sometimes put not only into earthen vessels, but into the weaker vessels, that the excellency of the power might be of God. ... It was a mercy to Jerusalem that when Bibles were scarce, they had prophets, as afterwards, when prophecy ceased, that they had more Bibles; for God never leaves Himself without witness, because He will leave sinners without excuse.[102]

Huldah first delivered a message from the Lord to His priests concerning Judah:

> *Behold, I will bring calamity on this place and on its inhabitants – all the words of the book which the king of Judah has read – because they have forsaken Me and burned incense to other gods, that they might provoke Me to anger with all the works of their hands. Therefore My wrath shall be aroused against this place and shall not be quenched* (2 Kgs. 22:15-17).

This was not the only message to be delivered to the king; the prophetess had a personal dispatch to King Josiah from the Lord God of Israel also:

> *Concerning the words which you have heard – because your heart was tender, and you humbled yourself before the Lord when you heard what I spoke against this place and against its inhabitants, that they would become a desolation and a curse, and you tore your clothes and wept before Me, I also have heard you ... Surely, therefore, I will gather you to your fathers, and you shall be gathered to your grave in peace; and your eyes shall not see all the calamity which I will bring on this place* (2 Kgs. 22:18-20).

The five priests then delivered the Lord's two messages to the king.

A Godly Heritage

Before leaving the chapter, we will pause to consider the testimony of the scribe Shaphan, Josiah's trusted secretary, who is mentioned throughout this narrative. Shaphan set a godly example for his children to follow, some of whom were used by the Lord in times of social and religious upheaval.

Ahikam, the son of Shaphan, for example, was determined not to allow the people to murder Jeremiah and, though he risked a social backlash, used his political clout to gain Jeremiah's release (Jer. 26:24). It is also noted that Shaphan's son Gemariah, along with Elnathan, urged Jehoiakim not to burn Jeremiah's scroll (Jer. 36:12, 25). Shaphan's son Elasah hand-carried Jeremiah's letter to the exiled Jews in Babylon (Jer. 29:1-3). Though his son Jaazaniah was a rebel, Shaphan reared up three fine sons who lived for God and, indeed, raised their sons to do the same.

The grandson of Shaphan through Ahikam was Gedaliah, a just and righteous governor over Judah. Micaiah, the grandson of Shaphan through Gemariah, convinced the princes of the importance of Jeremiah's scroll after hearing it read by Baruch (Jer. 36:11-26). It has been observed that the value of parenting is witnessed in one's grandchildren. To this end, Shaphan was a father who obtained a good heritage from the Lord; happy is the man who has a quiver full of such children (Ps. 127:3-5). God used Shaphan's legacy to confront wickedness and to preserve and refresh His servants. May God grant each of us the same heritage.

Meditation

> *Behold, children are a heritage from the Lord, the fruit of the womb is a reward. Like arrows in the hand of a warrior, so are the children of one's youth. Happy is the man who has his quiver full of them; they shall not be ashamed, but shall speak with their enemies in the gate* (Ps. 127:3-5).

The psalmist reminds us we are only stewards, not owners, of the children that God graciously entrusts to our care. If reared in the ways of the Lord, these skillfully sharpened and straight arrows become a rich blessing to all. In ancient days, older children ensured the defense of the family against the attacking enemy. Children must be trained up for the Lord to be a blessing to others and to further the kingdom of God. Untrained children, not surprisingly, remain foolish (Prov. 22:15) and predictably absorb what outside influences fill their void of understanding. Children are natural sponges; they are compelled to learn and to develop an understanding of the world in which they live. God forbid that believing parents through careless neglect should rear up pagans to revile His name. May we count on the Lord and His Word alone to build up our homes!

King Josiah of Judah – The Law Is Obeyed

2 Kings 23:1-30; 2 Chronicles 34:29-34, 35:1-27

The Public Reading of the Law (2 Kgs. 23:1-3; 2 Chron. 34:29-32)

It is good to remember that the events of this chapter occurred when Josiah was approximately twenty-five years old – he was a young man with great zeal for the Lord. The king was keenly affected after Shaphan read him the book of the Law found in the temple. He immediately felt guilt and remorse for the nation's behavior against the Lord. The king wanted the entire nation to be aware of what God expected of them as His covenant people, so he summoned both the leaders and the people of Jerusalem and Judah to come to the temple (2 Kgs. 23:1). Josiah was a young man of 25 or 26 years of age, and yet had great zeal for the Lord.

The priests, the prophets, the leaders, and the common people turned out en masse and the king himself read the Book of the Covenant to the people (2 Kgs. 23:2). Afterwards, the king stood by a pillar and made a covenant with the Lord to do what the Law commanded *"with all his heart and all his soul"* (2 Kgs. 23:3). Additionally, he caused all who were present to stand before the Lord and to enter into a covenant to obey the Law also (2 Chron. 34:32). Six years earlier Josiah had begun to purge the pagan altars from Jerusalem, but now the king had a new zeal to purify the temple, Jerusalem, Judah, and even land of the northern tribes.

Josiah's Further Religious Reforms (2 Kgs. 23:4-20; 2 Chron. 34:33)

Josiah commanded the high priest Hilkiah, the priests of the second order, and the temple doorkeepers to clear out any articles associated with Baal, Asherah, or the host of heaven from the temple. Such items were to be burned outside of Jerusalem near the Kidron and the ashes were to be gathered up and carried to Bethel to defile the long-standing shrine in southern Israel (2 Kgs. 23:4). Albert Barnes suggests why Josiah (and Asa before him) burnt these pagan objects at the brook Kidron: they wanted "to prevent the pollution of the holy city by even the ashes from the burning."[103]

Next, the king *"removed the idolatrous priests whom the kings of Judah had ordained to burn incense on the high places in the cities of Judah and in the places all around Jerusalem, and those who burned incense to Baal, to the sun, to the moon, to the constellations, and to all the host of heaven"* (2 Kgs. 23:5). The wooden images that were purged from the temple were burned and the remaining ash was spread out on the graves of the common people (2 Kgs. 23:6). The ritual booths of the male-cultic prostitutes (where the women wove hangings for the wooden image) were also removed from the temple (2 Kgs. 23:7).

Additionally, Josiah sent the priests throughout Judah to defile the high places where the priests had previously burned incense to the Lord and eaten unleavened bread among their brethren (2 Kgs. 23:8-9). In the future, there would be only two altars used in the worship of Jehovah and both, the Golden Altar of Incense and the Bronze Altar, were in one location – Jehovah's temple in Jerusalem. Josiah's reforms were reminiscent of his grandfather Hezekiah's efforts, which eliminated not only objects of worship offensive to Jehovah, but also the pagan priests who led the people away from Jehovah into corruption.

To this end, Josiah defiled Topheth located on the ridge of the Valley of Hinnom, immediately southwest of Jerusalem. No one would be permitted to offer their children as a burnt offering to Molech again (2 Kgs. 23:10). Then he removed the horses (located at the temple's entrance) and burned the chariots that previous kings of Judah had dedicated to the sun (2 Kgs. 23:11). The altars that were on the roof in the upper chamber of Ahaz and those that Manasseh had made and placed in the two temple courts were torn down, pulverized, and their dust thrown in the Brook Kidron (2 Kgs. 23:12).

The pagan high places east of Jerusalem (on the south side of the Mount of Corruption), which Solomon built for Ashtoreth (the abomination of the Sidonians), for Chemosh (the abomination of the Moabites), and for Milcom (the abomination of the people of Ammon) were destroyed. Pagan images were cut down, and the bones of men were placed at each location to defile the site against future use (2 Kgs. 23:14).

The king's zeal did not stop at the borders of Judah. He had pagan altars, shrines, and images destroyed in the cities of the northern tribes as far north as Naphtali (2 Chron. 34:6-7). After the revival in Hezekiah's day, the people from the northern tribes purged their homeland of pagan altars, yet, twenty years later, the land needed to be purged again. This shows the propensity of the human heart to pull away from what the Lord appreciates, and also our need to be continually revived by the Lord to serve Him wholeheartedly.

One of Josiah's first stops was one of the chief religious sites established by Jeroboam about two and a half centuries earlier which caused Israel to sin against the Lord. (The other altar was located in Dan.) The altar at the high place at Bethel was torn down (2 Kgs. 23:15). Mindful of the earlier prophecy, Josiah saw nearby tombs and ordered that the bones of the dead be burned on the remnants of the pagan altar to desecrate it (2 Kgs. 23:16). However, after finding the tombstone of the man of God who came from Judah to prophesy against Jeroboam and his altar, Josiah told his men not to remove his bones or those of the prophet of Samaria buried with him (2 Kgs. 23:17-18). Both the Jews and the heathen regarded the placement of dead men's bones as a source of perpetual defilement.[104] All the pagan images and articles associated with the shrine were destroyed by fire or smashed to pieces.

Josiah's actions fulfilled the prophecy pronounced by this man of God while Jeroboam was standing by the pagan altar at Bethel:

> *O altar, altar! Thus says the Lord: "Behold, a child, Josiah by name, shall be born to the house of David; and on you he shall sacrifice the priests of the high places who burn incense on you, and men's bones shall be burned on you"* (1 Kgs. 13:2).

The prophet had foretold the name of a future king and what he would do to the altar at Bethel approximately two and a half centuries before it would happen! Godly Josiah, the king of Judah, destroyed the altar at Bethel's shrine, slaughtered the pagan priests associated with it, and then burned the bones of men on the altar's remnants to fulfill this prophecy (2 Kgs. 23:15-20).

Moving northward, Josiah took away all the shrines of the high places that were in the cities of Samaria, destroying and defiling each as he had done to the high place at Bethel (2 Kgs. 23:19). He executed all the pagan priests at these high places and burned the bones of the dead on the altars (2 Kgs. 23:20). Only after purging the abominations among his countrymen of the northern tribes did Josiah return to Jerusalem.

Keeping the Passover (2 Chron. 35:1-19)

Having learned of the required Feasts of Jehovah from reading the Law, and with the temple now repaired, Josiah desired for the nation to celebrate the Passover on the fourteenth day of the first month (2 Chron. 35:1). John Heading describes Josiah's spiritual growth which led to this important point in Israel's history:

> He commenced to reign in his eighth year (2 Chron. 34:3); he began to seek the Lord eight years later (2 Chron. 34:3); in the twelfth year of his reign he began to purge Jerusalem of idols, while six years later we have this Passover. This was growth in grace in an atmosphere of prevailing hostility to the Lord. Since he reigned thirty-one years (2 Chron. 34:1), we conclude that there must have been thirteen Passovers after this great Passover.[105]

The king charged the priests and Levites to perform their required duties at the temple and in accordance with their courses established by David and affirmed by Solomon (2 Chron. 35:2). Furthermore, the priests were not to carry the Ark in any future processional; rather it must remain in the most holy place of the temple (2 Chron. 35:3-4). Just as the Ark had to be in its proper place for acceptable offerings to be presented by the priests to the Lord, the Lord Jesus must have the preeminence in the gatherings of His people in the Church Age for the same to occur (Col. 1:16-17).

Additionally, the priests were to be consecrated and to represent the people to the Lord while slaughtering and presenting the Passover lambs before the Lord (2 Chron. 35:5-6). To ensure that everyone could participate in the Passover and the Feast of Unleavened Bread that followed, Josiah provided, from his royal flocks and herds, 30,000 lambs and young goats, and 3,000 cattle (2 Chron. 35:7). Jewish leaders gave liberally to the people, to the priests, and to the Levites, as did the religious rulers:

> *Hilkiah, Zechariah, and Jehiel, rulers of the house of God, gave to the priests for the Passover offerings two thousand six hundred from the flock, and three hundred cattle. Conaniah, his brothers Shemaiah and Nethanel, and Hashabiah and Jeiel and Jozabad, chief of the Levites, gave to the Levites for Passover offerings five thousand from the flock and five hundred cattle* (2 Chron. 35:8-9).

Such generosity to prompt others to pursue the Lord is evidence of a true work of God. Another mark of legitimacy is order and obedience: *"So the service was prepared, and the priests stood in their places, and the Levites in their divisions, according to the king's command"* (2 Chron. 35:10). The devil attempts to bring disorder or to cause disdain for what God has put in place, but *"God is not the author of confusion but of peace"* (1 Cor. 14:33). The rudiments of human society that God put in place in Genesis 1 and 2, such as the distinction of genders and the procreation of children through the marriage of a man and a woman, are being continually challenged and negated by Satan. Yet, as we observe in the narrative, if we want to experience God's peace, we must first yield to His laws of order.

Because of the sheer volume of lambs to be slaughtered, the Levites did the slaughtering and skinning of the animals and then handed over the collected blood of the animal to the priests who sprinkled it on the Bronze Altar (2 Chron. 35:11). Besides the Passover lambs, burnt offerings were also distributed among the common people so they could give sacrifices to the Lord (2 Chron. 35:12). Because of the generosity of others, everyone had the opportunity to offer worship to the Lord. The Passover lambs were then roasted and boiled as required by the Law (Ex. 12:7-9; 2 Chron. 35:13).

The priests had been so occupied with the burnt offerings that the Levites had to prepare their Passover lambs for them (2 Chron. 35:14). Many of these sacrifices were Peace Offerings (especially the cattle which were not offered during the Passover). These sacrifices provided meat for the offerer and offering priest to eat, as well as a portion for the Lord on the altar. The priests were not able to feast until the evening because they had been busy serving throughout the day.

The singers (the sons of Asaph), the king's prophets (Asaph, Heman, and Jeduthun), and the gatekeepers were all in their proper places performing their commanded functions. The gatekeepers did not have to leave their posts because their fellow Levites prepared food for them (2 Chron. 35:15). The congregation kept the Passover and then the seven-day Feast of Unleavened Bread; sacrifices and praise were offered throughout the entire eight-day festival. This Passover festivity occurred in the eighteenth year of Josiah's reign (2 Chron. 35:16-17).

The historian then reports that there had not been such a keeping of the Passover in Israel since the days of the prophet Samuel four centuries earlier (2 Chron. 35:18). The only other previous Passovers mentioned since Samuel's time were during Solomon's and Hezekiah's reigns. Both of these celebrations probably exceeded this Passover feast in both size and fanfare, but the Lord was particularly pleased with His people's obedience during Josiah's reign. They had been made aware of what they were supposed to be doing, and after hearing the precepts of the Law, they chose to do what God wanted them to do!

Impending Judgment on Judah (2 Kgs. 23:26-27)

Although Josiah had shown great zeal for the Lord in purging the land of abominations, the Lord was not deterred from exercising His fierce wrath for past provocations committed during Manasseh's reign (2 Kgs. 23:26). The Lord had been longsuffering with His people and had shown them much mercy, yet they continued to return to the abominations that angered Him. The Lord declared His resolve in the matter: *"I will also remove Judah from My sight, as I have removed Israel, and will cast off this city Jerusalem which I have chosen, and the house of which I said, 'My name shall be there'"* (2 Kgs. 23:27).

Idolatry originated in Babylon (Gen. 10), so God was determined to take His people with their idols to Babylon, to purify them through chastening, and then to bring them back into the land of promise as a sanctified nation. This cleansing procedure would require seventy years to complete, but was very effective – the Jews never again returned to idolatry after suffering their Babylonian exile. God knew what it would take to refine the affections of His people and was determined to bring it about, yet the coming judgment would not occur during Josiah's reign.

Josiah Dies in the Wrong Battle (2 Kgs. 23:28-30; 2 Chron. 35:20-27)

Josiah's reign occurred during the transition period from the Assyrian Empire to the Babylonian Empire. Pharaoh Necho brought his army north through Israel to aid the king of Assyria positioned at the Euphrates River. However, not appreciating the incursion into his realm, Josiah brassily took his army to the Jezreel Valley to confront Necho, and he did so without consulting the Lord. This king of Egypt then unwittingly became a mouthpiece for the Lord. He sent messengers to Josiah with a warning:

> *What have I to do with you, king of Judah? I have not come against you this day, but against the house with which I have war; for God commanded me to make haste. Refrain from meddling with God, who is with me, lest He destroy you* (2 Chron. 35:21).

Josiah probably thought, "This pagan does not know or speak for my God." However, Josiah was not aware of his own spiritual decline – he was actually the one who was out of step with the Lord in this situation. God had attempted to awaken him to that fact by admonishing him through an unlikely source – the king of Egypt. As already prophesied by Isaiah and Jeremiah, God was gathering all challengers against Babylon together, so that their combined defeat would establish the Babylonian Empire. So in actuality, Josiah was working against the Lord by battling Pharaoh.

Josiah did not heed the warning and he was severely wounded by Egyptian archers at Megiddo in 609 B.C. (2 Chron. 35:24). He apparently died shortly after being transported back to Jerusalem in a second chariot. As Egypt is a symbol of the world throughout Scripture, John Heading reminds us that: "Josiah had interfered with Egypt, so now Egypt interferes with Jerusalem. If Christians interfere with the world, it will interfere with them."[106] Through Moses' leadership, God had brought His covenant people out of bondage and out of Egypt to have communion with Him alone in the wilderness. The blood of the first Passover lamb had marked a difference between them and the Egyptians. Likewise, through the blood of God's Passover Lamb we have been delivered from the bondage of sin and have been carved out of the world to be a people consecrated to God (Gal. 2:20; 6:14).

As God's ambassadors on earth, we are not charged with confronting a wicked world system under the devil's control, but rather with living as pilgrims and strangers in its darkness while manifesting the life and light of Christ. True light always confronts darkness when and where it appears. This means believers are to shine brightly wherever God has put them without regard to personally trying to focus their light only on one thing, which would then diminish illuminating other things.

Josiah's tragic death does not contradict God's word to Josiah; because he was right with the Lord, he went to his grave having peace with God (2 Chron. 34:28). Josiah's servants brought his body back to Jerusalem in a chariot and he was buried in his own tomb. Necho's army was later defeated by the Babylonians at Carchemish in 605 B.C. As the Lord had already foretold through the prophet Isaiah and Jeremiah, He was going to raise up the Babylonians to punish His people and the Assyrians for their brutal atrocities.

Under Josiah's leadership God's people gathered to honor and praise the Lord by keeping the Passover in accordance with His Law. It would be the last festive temple gathering of its kind until the Babylonian captivity was concluded and a new temple was erected in Jehovah's name a century later.

Meditation

Let us sing of the wonderful mercy of God,
Of His constant protection and care;
Let our fervent devotions like incense arise,
When we gather before Him in prayer.

Let us praise and adore Him for all He hath done,
Let us tell of His goodness and care;
Let our fervent devotions like incense arise,
When we gather before Him in prayer.

Let us sing of the wonderful gift of His grace,
That to us He has tenderly shown;
In the blessed communion with Jesus His Son,
That has brought us so near to His throne.

— Fanny Crosby

Kings Jehoahaz, Jehoiakim, and Jehoiachin of Judah

2 Kings 23:31-24:16; 2 Chronicles 36:1-10

Like the Northern Kingdom, the Southern Kingdom's final years (609-586 B.C.) were marked by political chaos, declining prosperity, foreign subjection, and finally invasion, desolation, and captivity. As already prophesied, God's chastening rod against Judah was the Babylonians; He had used the Assyrians to punish Israel. Jehoahaz was captured and taken to Egypt where he died, while the final three kings were captured by Babylon; only Jehoiakim was spared captivity in Babylon.

Following the historical narrative during this era can be challenging, as each of Judah's final four kings is referred to by at least two different names. W. Guftason explains:

> Jehoahaz is also named Shallum (1 Chron. 3:15; Jer. 22:11). The king of Egypt changed the name of Eliakim to Jehoiakim (2 Chron. 36:4). The king of Babylon changed the name of Mattaniah to Zedekiah (2 Kgs. 24:17). Probably both wanted to remind the kings of Judah that they owed allegiance to another, greater, king. … Jehoiachin had also the name of Jeconiah (1 Chron. 3:16) and Coniah (Jer. 22:8).
>
> The author of the Chronicles seems to give the birth order of four of Josiah's sons (1 Chron. 3:15). His firstborn son Johanan may have died before his father or with his father at Megiddo. The records of 2 Kings 23:30 and 2 Kings 24:18, which were eleven years apart, make it clear that when Jehoahaz was 23, Zedekiah, the youngest sibling, was only ten years of age. Jehoiakim, the second oldest, was twenty-five. But in 1 Chronicles 3:15 Shallum is given as the youngest son. Zedekiah and Shallum had the same mother (2 Kgs. 23:41, 24:18), which may explain why they are listed next to each other. One possible solution is that Shallum is put last because his reign was so much shorter than the reigns of Zedekiah and Jehoiakim.[107]

Josiah had four sons, three of whom would rule over Judah in the future (Jehoahaz, Eliakim, and Zedekiah).

The Reign and Captivity of Jehoahaz (2 Kgs. 23:31-34; 2 Chron. 36:1-4)

After Josiah's death, the people chose his middle son Jehoahaz to be the king of Judah. Jehoahaz was twenty-three years old when he became king; his mother's name was Hamutal from Libnah (2 Kgs. 23:31). Jehoahaz chose to follow the ways of his grandfather Amon, instead of his godly father Josiah; he did evil in the sight of the Lord (2 Kgs. 23:32).

Jehoahaz (also called Shallum) only ruled three months (in 609 B.C.) before Pharaoh Necho put him in prison at Riblah in the land of Hamath (2 Kgs. 23:33). Necho placed Jehoahaz's brother Eliakim on the throne of Judah, but changed his name to Jehoiakim (2 Kgs. 23:34). When Pharaoh returned to Egypt, he took Jehoahaz with him. While Jehoahaz was a prisoner in Egypt, Jeremiah foretold that he would never return to Jerusalem (Jer. 22:10-12). Just as Jeremiah had predicted, Jehoahaz died a captive in Egypt.

Jehoiakim Reigns in Judah (2 Kgs. 23:35-24:7; 2 Chron. 36:5-8)

Jehoiakim (Eliakim) was the eldest son of King Josiah. His ascension to the throne came at a great price, as he had to put the people under heavy taxation to pay Pharaoh the silver and gold he demanded (2 Kgs. 23:35). Jehoiakim was twenty-five years old when he became king, and he reigned eleven years in Jerusalem (609-598 B.C.). His mother's name was Zebudah (2 Kgs. 23:36). He also rejected the godly heritage of his father Josiah and followed in the evil of his grandfather Manasseh (2 Kgs. 23:37). Jehoiakim murdered the prophet Urijah and attempted to arrest Jeremiah and his scribe Baruch, but the Lord protected His servants from the king's rage (Jer. 36:23-26).

Unlike his father, Josiah, who cared for the poor and championed righteousness, Jehoiakim was a selfish and corrupt king who oppressed the people and perverted justice for his personal gain (Jer. 22:15-17). As a specific example of his poor leadership, Jeremiah noted Jehoiakim's efforts to construct a prestigious palace of cedar panels for himself while forcing his subjects to build it for him without being paid (Jer. 22:13-14).

Egypt was defeated by Babylon at Carchemish in 605 B.C. Jehoiakim had been paying heavy tribute to Egypt until that time. Babylonian historical records state that Nebuchadnezzar became the king of Babylon in August of 605 B.C. and then invaded Judah the following month. Jeremiah states that Nebuchadnezzar's initial invasion of Jerusalem occurred during the fourth year of Jehoiakim and during Nebuchadnezzar's first year of ascension, thus the 605 B.C. invasion date is confirmed (Jer. 25:1). Apparently, Nebuchadnezzar put Jehoiakim in chains and was set to take him to Babylon as a prisoner (1 Chron. 36:6) when he heard that his father Nebopolassar had died (the date was August 15, 605 B.C.). Realizing that the throne to the empire was in jeopardy, he was forced to reinstate Jehoiakim, who promised loyalty to Babylon as a vassal state. The Babylonian army then took the shortest route possible back to Babylon through the Arabian Desert, so Nebuchadnezzar could secure the throne.

Jehoiakim's agreement to Nebuchadnezzar kept Jerusalem from being destroyed (2 Kgs. 24:1). However, many of the gold and silver vessels from the Jewish temple became the possessions of the conquerors and were transported back to Babylon and stored in pagan temples (2 Chron. 36:7). Nebuchadnezzar also brought to Babylon a number of Jewish captives, including Daniel, and many choice young men of nobility who were unblemished, handsome, intelligent, wise, and quick learners (Dan. 1:3-4).

Three years later, against the word of God delivered by Jeremiah, Jehoiakim rebelled against Babylon (2 Kgs. 24:1). The Lord punished Jehoiakim by sending Chaldean, Syrian, Moabite, and Ammonite marauders against Judah (2 Kgs. 24:2). His rebellion also brought an unhappy Nebuchadnezzar back to Judah; the Babylonians promptly besieged Jerusalem. As the Lord had already proclaimed through His prophets, He was going to use Babylon to severely chasten His people for shedding innocent blood in His land and for their idolatry (2 Kgs. 24:3-4).

Jeremiah prophesied that because Jehoiakim had exploited the people, he would not be mourned when he died but would receive the burial rites of a donkey. When domestic animals died, their carcasses were dragged outside the walls of the city and left to rot and be devoured by scavengers (Jer. 22:19). Normally, after the death of a

Judean king, there was a time of public mourning, an elaborate funeral procession, and then a burial ceremony; however, Jehoiakim would receive none of these honors. Although it is possible that Jehoiakim died from natural causes, it seems more likely that he was assassinated by fellow Jews to appease King Nebuchadnezzar who had journeyed to Jerusalem with his army to put down Jehoiakim's rebellion in 598 B.C. (2 Kgs. 24:10).

After Jehoiakim's death, his eighteen-year-old son, Jehoiachin, ascended the throne (2 Kgs. 24:5-6). Egypt did not return to Judah, for Babylon, now the dominant world power, had captured Egypt's previous territory from the Brook of Egypt to the River Euphrates (2 Kgs. 24:7).

The Reign and Captivity of Jehoiachin (2 Kgs. 24:8-16; 2 Chron. 36:9-10)

Although previously coregent with his father, the eighteen-year-old Jehoiachin ruled Jerusalem solely for just three months before surrendering himself and the city to Nebuchadnezzar in March 597 B.C. (2 Kgs. 24:8). This capture date of Jehoiachin is confirmed by the Babylonian Chronicle as Adar 2, 597 B.C. His mother's name was Nehushta of Jerusalem and *"he did evil in the sight of the Lord"* (2 Kgs. 24:9). Nebuchadnezzar took King Jehoiachin, his mother, his wives, his servants, his princes, and his officers as prisoners to Babylon (2 Kgs. 24:10-12, 15).

After capturing Jerusalem, the Babylonians despoiled the city. They took all the treasure from the temple and the king's house and demolished the remaining articles of gold which Solomon had made for the temple (2 Kgs. 24:13). Nebuchadnezzar also took ten thousand Jewish captives back to Babylon including: 7,000 captains and mighty men of valor and 1,000 craftsmen and blacksmiths (2 Kgs. 24:16). He left the poorest people of the land (2 Kgs. 24:15). The prophet Ezekiel and his family were among the Jewish captives taken to Babylon at this time.

Nebuchadnezzar brought Jehoiachin to Babylon in chains (Ezek. 19:5-9). Jehoiachin remained in prison for most of his life, but after being incarcerated for thirty-seven years, he was released by Amel-Marduk (Evil-Merodach) after he succeeded his father Nebuchadnezzar to the throne of Babylon (2 Kgs. 24:8-17, 25:25-30). However, Jehoiachin never was permitted to return to Israel – he died in Babylon.

Jeremiah foretold that Judah and all her surrounding allies would be defeated by the Babylonians, the result of which would be bitter lamentations throughout the region (Jer. 22:20-22). All that God promised to do through Babylon as foretold by Isaiah, Zephaniah, and Jeremiah was coming true!

The Historical Record Summarized

There were three major Babylonian invasions into Judah from 605 to 586 B.C. Each Jewish defeat was followed by a mass deportation of Jews to Babylon.

The First Invasion: Not long after Josiah's death, Pharaoh Necho replaced Jehoahaz with his brother Jehoiakim. In 605 B.C. the Babylonians came to Jerusalem to confront the Egyptian puppet, Jehoiakim. To save the city, the king pledged allegiance to Babylon, and Nebuchadnezzar took silver and gold from the temple and many captives back to Babylon. The prophet Daniel, and other young men including members of the king's family, were among these early exiles and many were made eunuchs (Dan. 1).

The Second Invasion: King Jehoiakim again switched sides in 601 B.C. to ally with Egypt. Nebuchadnezzar returned to put down his rebellion in 597 B.C. Jehoiakim died during the siege and his son Jehoiachin reigned as king of Judah for three months before the Babylonians conquered Jerusalem. More of Judah's wealth was plundered, and ten thousand Jews were taken to Babylon at that time, among whom were the prophet Ezekiel and his wife (2 Kgs. 24:14).

The Third Invasion: Nebuchadnezzar again returned to Jerusalem in 588 B.C. to suppress Zedekiah's rebellion. (He had also made an alliance with Egypt after pledging loyalty to Nebuchadnezzar.) Jerusalem fell in 586 B.C. after a long siege, and the city and temple were subsequently destroyed. There was a horrendous slaughter of the Jews and tens of thousands of survivors were taken as slaves to Babylon.

There is significant archeological evidence to affirm the historicity of the Old Testament record concerning these events. The fall of Jerusalem to Nebuchadnezzar, the king of Babylon, described in 2 Kings 24:10-14 is also recorded in the Babylonian Chronicles. The

Babylonian Chronicles were found in 1956; these four tablets date back to 600 B.C. The tablets record the historical events associated with the rise of the Babylonians: conquering the Assyrians, the Egyptians and then Judah. All these events are well documented in the books of 2 Kings, 2 Chronicles, Jeremiah, Ezekiel, and Daniel. The Babylonian Chronicles confirm military events such as the battle at Carchemish in 605 B.C. as recorded in Jeremiah 46:2 and 2 Kings 24:7-17. The captivity of King Jehoiachin in Babylon (2 Kgs. 24:15-16) is also recorded on the Babylonian Ration Records.

Meditation

The Bible stands like a rock undaunted
Mid the raging storms of time;
Its pages burn with the truth eternal,
And they glow with a light sublime.

The Bible stands and it will forever,
When the world has passed away;
By inspiration it has been given,
All its precepts I will obey.

The Bible stands every test we give it,
For its author is divine;
By grace alone I expect to live it,
And to prove and to make it mine.

— Haldor Lillenas

King Zedekiah of Judah

2 Kings 24:17-25:30; 2 Chronicles 36:11-23

Zedekiah Reigns in Judah (2 Kgs. 24:17-20; 2 Chron. 36:11-14)

After Nebuchadnezzar conquered Jerusalem and captured and imprisoned King Jehoiachin, the Babylonian ruler appointed Zedekiah as a vassal king of Judah. Zedekiah was Jehoiachin's uncle and the third son of Josiah to reign in Judah (2 Kgs. 24:17). Zedekiah was twenty-one years old when he became king, and he reigned eleven years in Jerusalem (597-586 B.C.); his mother's name was Hamutal, the daughter of Jeremiah of Libnah (2 Kgs. 24:18). Having the same mother, Zedekiah and Jehoahaz were full-blood brothers. Zedekiah did evil in the sight of the Lord, which provoked the Lord to remove His people from the land (2 Kgs. 24:19).

A few years later, Jeremiah warned Zedekiah to yield to God's chastening through Babylon, but Zedekiah caused Judah to align again with Egypt (Pharaoh Hophra) and rebel against Babylon (2 Kgs. 24:20). Nebuchadnezzar responded by invading Judah and putting Jerusalem under siege again in December 589 B.C. (perhaps January 588 B.C.), which was the tenth day of the tenth month of the ninth year of Zedekiah's reign (2 Kgs. 25:1). Despite Hophra's promise, Egypt was unable to subdue the Babylonians and relieve Jerusalem from the siege.

Jeremiah repeatedly declared God's word to Zedekiah, but he refused to obey it. The prophet's message was straightforward: surrender the city and live as captives in Babylon, or resist God's chastening hand and die in Jerusalem (Jer. 21:9). Though Zedekiah may have been rattled by Jeremiah's message, he ignored it because he felt secure within the high walls surrounding Jerusalem. He pompously proclaimed, *"Who shall come down against us? Or who shall enter our dwellings?"* (Jer. 21:13). God would provide answers to those questions shortly.

Simply put, the king had a choice between death and life. Stubborn Zedekiah chose death. That decision had tremendous consequences not only for himself, but also for those he ruled (Ezek. 17:11-21). Before his eyes were put out by the Babylonians, he first met the Babylonian king in person, as prophesied by Jeremiah (Jer. 32:4, 34:3). Then he witnessed the massacre of all his sons (2 Kgs. 25:7). With those hideous images fresh in his mind, he was blinded, chained, and hauled off to Babylon like an animal (Jer. 39:5-7). He never returned to Israel but died as a pitiful captive in a strange land. Just as Ezekiel had prophesied, Zedekiah was brought to Babylon, but did not see that foreign land (Ezek. 12:13).

Besides the king, Jeremiah also warned the priests and common people of Judah not to listen to the false prophets, who were saying that all of the temple vessels that were taken to Babylon with King Jehoiachin would soon be returned (Jer. 27:16-22). Jeremiah countered that not only would the temple vessels stay in Babylon, but all of the remaining temple furnishings would soon be hauled away also. Only after God's judgment was complete would He return the temple vessels to Jerusalem (2 Kgs. 25:13-17; Ezra 1:7-11). The fulfillment of this prophecy would provide the people with irrefutable proof as to who were really God's prophets and who were imposters.

The Fall of Jerusalem (2 Kgs. 25:1-21; 2 Chron. 36:15-20; Jer. 52:4-30)

While we know that Jerusalem fell in the fourth month of the eleventh year of Zedekiah's reign (2 Kgs. 25:1-3), scholars are divided as to whether that occurred in 586 or 587 B.C. The date of Jerusalem's destruction is widely agreed to be in July 586 B.C. The Babylonian Chronicles puts the fall of Jerusalem in the summer of 587 B.C. (the eleventh year of Jehoiachin's captivity), which was the eleventh year and fifth month of Zedekiah's reign (2 Kgs. 25:4-10). Tens of thousands of Jews were slaughtered and the city and the temple were destroyed the following summer (586 B.C.).

The historian emphasizes again that all that happened to Jerusalem was because the Jews were a disobedient people who had repeatedly rejected the pleading of God's prophets to repent to escape wrath (2 Chron. 36:15-16). Because of their stubborn rebellion, God brought the brutal Chaldeans against His people and they showed no mercy to anyone regardless of age, gender, or social status (2 Chron. 36:17).

Babylon despoiled the temple and then burned it. They also broke down the wall of Jerusalem and burned its palaces after plundering the city (2 Chron. 36:18-19). Many Jews were slaughtered and many more were taken to Babylon as captives (2 Chron. 36:20). The writer of Kings noted that seventy-two of the leading citizens of Jerusalem were taken to Nebuchadnezzar at Riblah and were executed there (2 Kgs. 26:18-21).

The Neglected Sabbath Years (2 Chron. 36:21)

The Chaldeans not only destroyed Jerusalem, but also the oil groves and fruit orchards in the region. They stopped up wells and sowed stones in the farmland to make it unprofitable. All this was done so that Jeremiah's prophecy concerning the land having seventy years of rest might be fulfilled (2 Chron. 36:21).

Before the Israelites set foot in the Promised Land, the Lord asserted His ownership of the land (Lev. 25:23). The land was for the good of all of the Jews; it was not to be exploited to gain an advantage over the poor or those suffering hardship (Lev. 25:24). There were two main Laws of the Land that the Jews were to obey: the Year of Jubilee, which released all debts and ensured original inheritances were not lost, and the Sabbath Year, which gave the land rest one year in seven.

The Sabbatical year was to remind the Jews that God owned the land they dwelled in and that they were merely stewards of it. Every seventh year the fields, the olive groves, and the vineyards were to receive a full year's rest. Whatever grew naturally during the Sabbath year was to be freely gleaned by the poor, and anything that remained was considered God's provision for the beasts of the field. To alleviate the Jews' anxiety about not sowing or harvesting crops for two years, the Lord promised an abundant harvest in the sixth year preceding the Sabbath year and in the year of Jubilee to hold them over for those two years (Lev. 25:20-22).

If the Jews heeded His laws of the land, then Jehovah promised to bless them in the land: there would be neither want nor war (Lev. 25:18). Sadly, there is no biblical evidence to indicate the Jews ever obeyed the year of Jubilee statute; in fact, it is not mentioned outside of the Pentateuch. Since the Jews clearly violated seventy straight Sabbath years before their Babylonian exile (2 Chron. 36:20-21), it is doubtful that they ever consistently kept the year of Jubilee command either.

The Jews ignored both Laws of the Land. The Lord kept track of this offense, and, in one lump sum of years, He gave the land its due – seventy years of rest (i.e. one-seventh of the four hundred ninety years the Jews did not honor the Sabbath year; 2 Chron. 36:21). This judgment was prophesied by Jeremiah (Jer. 25:11-12) and realized during the Jews' exile to Babylon, proving once again that there are no loopholes in God's judicial system (Ex. 23:10-13).

Jeremiah confirmed a twofold seventy-year prophecy concerning the nation of Israel: there would be seventy years of Babylonian captivity and seventy years of rest for the land: *"And this whole land shall be a desolation and an astonishment, and these nations shall serve the king of Babylon seventy years"* (Jer. 25:11). The seventy years of captivity began the very year that Jeremiah spoke the prophecy, coinciding with Nebuchadnezzar's first invasion of Judah and first deportation of Jews to Babylon in 605 B.C. The captivity portion of this prophecy was concluded seventy years later when the Babylonian empire fell to the Medes and Persians and the Jewish captives were freed by King Cyrus to return home in 537/536 B.C. This event was foretold two centuries earlier by Isaiah (Isa. 44:28-45:1). The prophet Daniel, who had been in that first group of captives, understood this event to be the fulfillment of Jeremiah's prophecy (Dan. 9:2).

The second portion of the prophecy of seventy years did not begin until Nebuchadnezzar's third invasion, when he besieged Jerusalem during King Zedekiah's reign. In other words, agricultural enterprises in Judah continued from 605 B.C. until the Babylonians besieged Jerusalem for a final time in 589 B.C., even though the seventy-year captivity period had already begun. The prophet Ezekiel recorded the exact date this occurred:

> *Again, in the ninth year, in the tenth month, on the tenth day of the month, the word of the Lord came to me, saying, "Son of man, write down the name of the day, this very day – the king of Babylon started his siege against Jerusalem this very day"* (Ezek. 24:1-2).

The seventy years of desolation ended, according to the prophet Haggai, when the foundation of the temple was laid on the base previously completed. Haggai recorded the exact day that the Lord lifted the forced agricultural rest:

> *Consider now from this day forward, from the twenty-fourth day of the ninth month, from the day that the foundation of the Lord's temple was laid – consider it: Is the seed still in the barn? As yet the vine, the fig tree, the pomegranate, and the olive tree have not yielded fruit. But from this day I will bless you* (Hag. 2:18-19).

This event occurred in the second year of Darius (Hag. 2:10). According to Robert Anderson, the Jews who returned from Babylon began to enjoy the benefits of the land again on December 17, 520 B.C.:

> Now seventy years of 360 days contain exactly 25,200 days; and as the Jewish New Year's day depended on the equinoctial moon, we can assign the 13th December as "the Julian date" of tenth Tebeth 589. And 25,200 days measured from that date ended on the 17th December 520, which was the twenty-fourth day of the ninth month in the second year of Darius of Persia – the very day on which the foundation of the second Temple was laid. (Hag. 2:18, 19.)[108]

God caused one prophet to record the exact starting date and another the precise ending date of the sabbatical period that the land would enjoy in order to prove that His Word stands sure for all time. Although today we do not know the exact date in which the seventy years of agricultural desolation began, if we use consistent parameters the duration of the prophecy can be validated. A Jewish year is 360 days (Rev. 12:6, 14, 13:5; Dan. 12:7), meaning that there are 25,200 days in 70 Jewish years (i.e. 70 x 360 days = 25,200 days). Thus, it seems likely that the seventy-year period of rest that started on December 13, 589 B.C. ended precisely seventy Jewish years later on December 18, 520 B.C., exactly when God restored the land to fruitfulness according to Haggai. Just as Jeremiah predicted, and the writings of Ezekiel and Haggai verify, the land of Israel enjoyed seventy years of rest.

During the revival that occurred under Ezra and Nehemiah's leadership, the people renewed their commitment to honor the regulation of the Sabbatical year (Neh. 10:31).

After the Fall (2 Kgs. 25:22-26; Jer. 40:5-41:18)

Prior to the fall of Jerusalem, the prophet Ezekiel told Jewish leaders that they would not be safe in Jerusalem, for it would be destroyed by foreigners and those surviving the initial attack would be dragged to the borders of Israel and judged by the sword (Ezek. 11:8-12). This was fulfilled when Jewish captives surviving the fall of Jerusalem were later transported to Riblah in Syria and executed (2 Kgs. 25:18-21). To further confirm that this and also Jeremiah's prophecy (Jer. 24) had come true, the writer provides a partial roster of influential Jews who were beaten and then executed in Riblah by Nebuzaradan, the captain of the guard: Seraiah (the chief priest), Zephaniah (the priest next in rank), the three temple doorkeepers, the officer in charge of the soldiers, seven royal advisers, and the chief officer in charge of conscripting the people and sixty of his men (Jer. 52:24-26).

The town of Mizpah had served as a place to assemble the Jewish nation previously when important matters needed to be decided (Judg. 19-21). It was also the location where Samuel presented Saul as Israel's first king (1 Sam. 10:17). Mizpah became the capital of Judah after the Babylonians destroyed Jerusalem in 586 B.C. (2 Kgs. 25:23).

Nebuchadnezzar made Gedaliah the son of Ahikam, the son of Shaphan, governor over the people who remained in the land of Judah (2 Kgs. 25:22). Surviving captains of Judah's army (e.g., Ishmael, Johanan, Seraiah, and Jaazaniah) came out of hiding with their men after hearing that Gedaliah was governor of Judah and offering them amnesty (2 Kgs. 25:23). He understood that God was using Babylon to chasten Judah for her past idolatry and therefore commanded his surviving countrymen to yield to God's will in the matter: *"Do not be afraid of the servants of the Chaldeans. Dwell in the land and serve the king of Babylon, and it shall be well with you"* (2 Kgs. 25:24).

However, this message was not agreeable to Ishmael, who later visited Gedaliah in the seventh month with ten men under a banner of peace. Gedaliah showed hospitality to his visitors by feeding them. It was during or after this dinner that Ishmael and his men struck. Not only did they murder Gedaliah, but they also slew all those in the banquet hall, including the Babylonian soldiers dispatched to protect Gedaliah (Jer. 41:2-3; 2 Kgs. 25:25). The slaughter, likely in the evening, was so complete that it went undetected until the next day (Jer. 41:4).

After news of Gedaliah's death became known, many Jews, against Jeremiah's pleading, fled to Egypt to escape Nebuchadnezzar's presumed wrath (2 Kgs. 25:26). These rebels also took Jeremiah to Egypt against his will. The offense of Gedaliah's murder did bring Nebuchadnezzar back to Jerusalem, which resulted in further suffering for the Jewish survivors.

Jehoiachin Released From Prison (2 Kgs. 25:27-30; Jer. 52:31-34)

Jehoiachin remained in prison for most of his life, but after being incarcerated for thirty-seven years, he was released by Amel-Marduk (Evil-Merodach) after he succeeded his father Nebuchadnezzar to the throne of Babylon (2 Kgs. 25:27). Amel-Marduk was kind to Jehoiachin and gave him a more prominent seat among the captured kings exiled in Babylon (2 Kgs. 25:28). Although Jehoiachin no longer wore prison apparel and ate well at the king's table, he was never permitted to return to Israel – he died in Babylon (2 Kgs. 25:29-30).

The Proclamation of Cyrus (2 Chron. 36:22-23; Ezra 1:1-4)

The historian closes his account by confirming that the Lord had fulfilled various prophecies concerning the fall of the Babylon Empire through the Medes and the Persians. For example, as just explained, Jeremiah foretold that the Jewish captivity in Babylon would last only seventy years (Jer. 25:11-12, 29:10).

Before the Babylonian Empire even existed, Isaiah had prophesied that the Medes would cause it to fall (Isa. 13:17-19). He also provided the name of the Persian king, Cyrus, who would lead the coalition against Babylon. Cyrus would then release the Jews from captivity so that they could return to Jerusalem and rebuild Jehovah's temple (Isa. 44:28-45:1). This detailed prophecy was issued over a century before Cyrus was born and while the Assyrian Empire ruled the world.

The last stronghold of the existing empire, the enormous city of Babylon, fell after a long siege in the autumn of 538 B.C. At that time, the first year of Cyrus king of Persia, the Lord stirred up Cyrus to issue the following decree throughout his kingdom:

> *All the kingdoms of the earth the Lord God of heaven has given me. And He has commanded me to build Him a house at Jerusalem which is in Judah. Who is among you of all His people? May the Lord his God be with him, and let him go up!* (2 Chron. 36:23).

What permitted Cyrus to make this decree and fulfill prophecy? First, God moved in the spirit of Cyrus not only to release the Jews, but also to rebuild God's temple in Jerusalem (2 Chron. 36:22). Second, the Jewish historian Josephus wrote that Cyrus was shown the prophecy of Isaiah and wanted to fulfill it (*The Antiquities of the Jews* 11.1.1). Both the Word of God and the Spirit of God had an effect on Cyrus to accomplish the will of God.

Does this mean Cyrus believed that Jehovah, the God of the Jews, was the one true God? Not likely. The Cyrus Cylinder (538 B.C.) records Persian King Cyrus' conquest of Babylon and his subsequent release of Jewish captives. The Cylinder includes this statement: "May all the gods whom I have resettled in their sacred cities daily ask Bel and Nebo for a long life for me." Cyrus worshiped Bel and Nebo, the gods of Persia. By releasing those who had been in Babylonian captivity and honoring their gods, Cyrus hoped to establish loyal buffer nations on the perimeter of his empire and to ingratiate himself with the gods of these nations, including Jehovah of the Jews. Cyrus thought that by being in good standing with all proclaimed deities of the surrounding nations, it would certainly be well with him. Yet, Jehovah is no man's debtor; in fact, He was acting on behalf of His covenant people to orchestrate the entire matter (Isa. 45:4). Cyrus was merely God's "anointed," or chosen vessel, to accomplish His will (Isa. 45:1).

The many fulfilled prophecies of Scripture, such as those related to this narrative, prove to us that there is one sovereign God who is ultimately responsible for all calamities that occur. At times, He may not be the one performing the work (sometimes he permits others to do it, e.g., Satan). At other times, He may choose not to interfere within the natural order to prevent disasters, which occur as the fallout of original sin (Amos 3:6). Regardless of the agencies God uses to accomplish His will, He alone is in full control of all that happens.

Therefore, we must not think that these final two verses of 2 Chronicles (which are repeated in the opening verses of the book of Ezra) are bizarre or strangely placed. Since Chronicles concludes the Hebrew Bible, we understand how Cyrus' statement is to be understood: God had dealt with His people previously, judged them for their rebellion, and was already working to restore them to Himself, because He is a covenant-keeping God.

The coming days would be horrendous for His people, but God had a providential plan to revive them spiritually and it involved Cyrus, as Isaiah foretold (Isa. 44:28). When the Lord brought His covenant people back to Judah after their captivity, they left their idols in the land from which they originated – Babylon.

Because the Lord created all things, He alone has the right to govern what He has created. Any created thing voicing disapproval of God's ways would be in danger of being destroyed. Therefore, Israel, whom God created, should not question God's corrective discipline of the nation through Babylon or His using Cyrus to end their Babylonian exile (Isa. 45:11-13). Rather, the Jews should rejoice that God loved them enough not to leave them in their carnality. God had been faithful to His covenant with them even though they had not been faithful to Him.

Dear believer, be thankful that God diligently labors to refine and restore those He loves to Himself, so that His goodness can be experienced to the widest extent possible. This is a wonderful and timeless truth no matter when God's people reside on the earth.

Meditation

God moves in a mysterious way His wonders to perform;
He plants His footsteps in the sea and rides upon the storm.
Deep in unfathomable mines of never failing skill,
He treasures up His bright designs and works His sovereign will.

Ye fearful saints, fresh courage take; the clouds ye so much dread
Are big with mercy and shall break in blessings on your head.
Judge not the Lord by feeble sense, but trust Him for His grace;
Behind a frowning providence He hides a smiling face.

His purposes will ripen fast, unfolding every hour;
The bud may have a bitter taste, but sweet will be the flower.
Blind unbelief is sure to err and scan His work in vain;
God is His own interpreter, and He will make it plain.

— William Cowper

Overview of Israelite Kings

Judah's Kings	Israel's Kings	Prosperity	Spiritual	Years	Start/Finish
Saul	Saul	Good	Mostly Evil	40	Good/Evil
David	David	Excellent	Righteous	40	Good/Good
Solomon	Solomon	Excellent	Mostly Right.	40	Good/Evil
Rehoboam		Good	Evil	17	Evil/Evil
	Jeroboam I	Good	Evil	22	Evil/Evil
Abijah (Abijam)		Good	Evil	3	Evil/Evil
Asa		Excellent	Righteous	41	Good/Good
	Nadab	Fair	Evil	2	Evil/Evil
	Baasha	Fair	Evil	24	Evil/Evil
	Elah	Fair	Evil	2	Evil/Evil
	Zimri	Fair	Evil	0	Evil/Evil
	Omri/Tibni	Good	Evil	12/5	Evil/Evil
	Ahab	Good	Evil	22	Evil/Evil
Jehoshaphat		Good	Righteous	25	Good/Good
	Ahaziah	Fair	Evil	2	Evil/Evil
	Joram(Jehoram)	Fair	Mostly Evil	12	Evil/Evil
Jehoram (Joram)		Fair	Evil	8	Evil/Evil
	Jehu	Good	Some Evil	28	Good/Evil
Ahaziah (Azariah)		Fair	Evil	1	Evil/Evil
Athaliah (Queen)		Fair	Evil	7	Evil/Evil
Joash (Jehoash)		Good	Righteous	40	Good/Evil
	Jehoahaz	Fair	Evil	17	Evil/Evil
	Jehoash (Joash)	Fair	Evil	16	Evil/Evil
Amaziah		Good	Mostly Right.	29	Good/Evil
	Jeroboam II	Good	Evil	41	Evil/Evil
Azariah (Uzziah)		Good	Mostly Right.	52	Good/Evil
	Zechariah	Fair	Evil	0.5	Evil/Evil
	Shallum	Fair	Evil	0.1	Evil/Evil
	Menahem	Fair	Evil	10	Evil/Evil
	Pekahiah	Fair	Evil	2	Evil/Evil
Jotham		Good	Righteous	29	Good/Good
	Pekah	Poor	Evil	20	Evil/Evil
Ahaz		Fair	Evil	16	Evil/Evil
	Hoshea	Poor	Mostly Evil	9	Evil/Evil

Judah's Kings	Israel's Kings	Prosperity	Spiritual	Years	Start/Finish
Hezekiah		Good	Righteous	29	Good/Good
Manasseh		Fair	Evil	55	Evil/Good
Amon		Fair	Evil	2	Evil/Evil
Josiah		Good	Righteous	31	Good/Good
Jehoahaz (Shallum)		Poor	Evil	0.25	Evil/Evil
Jehoiakim (Eliakim)		Poor	Evil	11	Evil/Evil
Jehoiachin (Jeconiah)		Poor	Evil	0.25	Evil/Evil
Zedekiah (Mattaniah)		Poor	Evil	11	Evil/Evil

Endnotes

1 William Kelly, 1 and 2 Chronicles (STEM Publishing); 1 Chron. 16-19 http://stempublishing.com/authors/kelly/1Oldtest/chroncls.html

2 James Catron, *Old Testament Law and History* (Emmaus Bible College, Dubuque, IA; 1996), p. 81

3 Edwin R. Thiele, *The Mysterious Numbers of the Hebrew Kings* (Eedrmans, Grand Rapids, MI; 1962), p. 38

4 William MacDonald, *Believer's Bible Commentary* (Thomas Nelson Pub., Nashville, TN; 1990), 1 Chron. 8

5 John Heading, *Understanding 1 & 2 Chronicles – The House of God and Its Service* (Walterick Publishers, Kansas City, KS; 1980), p. 32

6 Robert Jamieson, A. R. Fausset, and David Brown, *Jamieson, Fausset and Brown Commentary* (Electronic Database via Biblesoft; 1997), 2 Sam. 5:9

7 William MacDonald, op. cit., 2 Sam. 23:24-39

8 H. L. Rossier, 2 Samuel (STEM Publishing); 2 Sam. 6 http://stempublishing.com/authors/rossier/2SAMUEL.html

9 Adam Clarke, *Adam Clarke's Commentary* (Electronic Database; 1996 by Biblesoft); 2 Sam. 5:21

10 C. H. Mackintosh, *The Mackintosh Treasury* (Believers Bookshelf Inc., Beamsville, ON; 1999), p. 269

11 John Heading, op. cit., p. 82

12 C. H. Mackintosh, op. cit. , p. 271

13 Eugene H. Merrill, op. cit. p. 465

14 Albert Barnes, op. cit., 2 Sam. 10:4

15 Aharoni, Avi-Yonah, Rainey, and Safrai, *The MacMillan Bible Atlas;* 3rd Edition (MacMillan by Carta; 1993), p. 78

16 Albert Barnes, *Notes on the Old Testament – Exodus to Esther* (Baker Book House, Grand Rapids, MI; reprinted 1851), 2 Sam. 24:1

17 William MacDonald, op. cit., 2 Sam. 24:1

18 John Heading, op. cit., p. 91

19 C. A. Coates, *C. A. Coates Commentary – Second Chronicles* (Kingston Bible Trust, West Sussex, UK), chp. 1

20 C. H. Mackintosh, op. cit., p. 270

21 C. A. Coates, *C. A. Coates Commentary – An Outline of the First Book of Kings* (Kingston Bible Trust, West Sussex, UK), 1 Kgs. 4-6

22 John Heading, op. cit., p. 142

23 Jamieson, Fausset, and Brown, op. cit., 1 Kgs. 2:10

24 John Heading, op. cit., p. 153

25 H. L. Rossier, op. cit., 1 Kgs. 3:16-28

[26] John D. Hannah & Dallas Theological Seminary, *The Bible Knowledge Commentary : An Exposition of the Scriptures* (Victor Books, Wheaton, IL; 1983-1985), p. 104
[27] Jamieson, Fausset, and Brown, op. cit., 1 Kgs. 6:7
[28] Josephus, *Antiquities*; b. viii., chp. iv., sec. 9
[29] Jamieson, Fausset, and Brown, quoting T. O. Paine, op. cit., 1 Kgs. 7:23
[30] Jamieson, Fausset, and Brown, quoting T. O. Paine, op. cit., 1 Kgs. 7:23
[31] Albert Barnes, *The Bible Commentary Vol. 5* (Baker Book House, Grand Rapids, MI; reprinted 1879), p.277
[32] Jamieson, Fausset, and Brown, op. cit., 1 Kgs. 7:27
[33] C. A. Coates, op. cit., 1 Kgs. 4-6
[34] *Keil & Delitzsch Commentary on the Old Testament*: New Updated Edition (Electronic Database via Hendrickson Publishers, Inc.; 1996), 1 Kgs. 8:62
[35] Richard I. McNeely, *First and Second Kings* (Moody Press, Chicago, IL; 1878), p. 53
[36] Thomas L. Constable & Dallas Theological Seminary, *The Bible Knowledge Commentary: An Exposition of the Scriptures* (Victor Books, Wheaton, IL; 1983-1985), p. 505
[37] John Gray, *1 and II Kings* (Westminster, Philadelphia, PA; 1970), pp. 243-244
[38] William Kelly, op. cit., 2 Chron. 7-12
[39] Thomas L. Constable, op. cit., p. 507
[40] Matthew Henry, *Matthew Henry's Concise Commentary on the Whole Bible* (e-Sword, electronic version), 1 Kgs. 11:1-8
[41] Jamieson, Fausset, and Brown, op. cit., 1 Kgs. 11:26
[42] Albert Barnes, op. cit., 1 Kgs. 11:40
[43] John Gray, op. cit., p. 306
[44] John Heading, op. cit., 2 Chron. 11
[45] Thomas L. Constable, op. cit., p. 518
[46] William MacDonald, op. cit., 1 Kgs. 14:25-28
[47] Thomas L. Constable, op. cit., p. 517
[48] C. A. Coates, op. cit., 1 Kgs. 15
[49] C. H. Mackintosh, op. cit., pp. 290, 292
[50] Matthew Henry, op. cit., 1 Kgs. 18:1-16
[51] C. H. Mackintosh, op. cit., p. 304
[52] H. L. Rossier, op. cit., 1 Kgs. 18
[53] Keil & Delitzsch; op. cit., 1 Kgs. 19:11-12
[54] George Williams, *The Student's Commentary on the Holy Scriptures* (Kregel Pub., Grand Rapids, MI; 1956), p. 196
[55] C. H. Mackintosh, op. cit., p. 309
[56] James B Pritchard, *Ancient Near Eastern Texts Relating to the Old Testament* (Princeton University Press, Princeton, NJ; 1955), pp. 278-279
[57] G. Campbell Morgan, *Searchlights From the Word* (Baker Book House, Grand Rapids, MI; 1984), p.100
[58] C. H. Mackintosh, *Genesis to Deuteronomy,* op. cit. p. 122
[59] H. L. Rossier, op. cit., 1 Kgs. 22

60 Matthew Henry, op. cit., 1 Kgs. 22:29-40

61 Thomas L. Constable, op. cit., p. 535

62 C. H. Mackintosh, *Genesis to Deuteronomy* (Loizeaux Brothers, Inc., Neptune, NJ; 1972), p. 47

63 John C. Whitcomb, Jr., *Solomon to the Exile* (Baker Books, Grand Rapids, MI; 1975), p. 64

64 Matthew Henry, op. cit., 2 Kgs. 1:9-18

65 Albert Barnes, op. cit., 2 Kgs. 1:10

66 Thomas L. Constable, op. cit., p. 539

67 John Gray, op. cit., p. 477

68 Testing Worldview/R. Totten/2005, *Archaeology Confirms the Bible Is Historical* [Online] http://worldview3.50webs.com/history.html [Accessed 21 June 2016]

69 J. G. Bellett, *Short Meditations on Elisha – The Serious Christian* series (reprinted by Books for Christians, Charlotte, NC.; no date), pp. 17-18

70 Elmer L Towns and Charles Billingsley, *God Laughs* (Regal/Gospel Light, Ventura, CA; 2011), pp. 147-148

71 H. L. Rossier, *Mediations on the Second Book of Kings* (STEM Publishing); 2 Kgs. 3
http://stempublishing.com/authors/rossier/2KINGS.html#a0

72 Jamieson, Fausset, and Brown, op. cit., 2 Kgs. 4:39

73 Thomas L. Constable, op. cit., p. 539

74 C. A. Coates, op. cit., 2 Kgs. 4

75 D. L. Moody, *Notes From My Bible: From Genesis to Revelation* (Fleming H. Revell, New York, NY; reprint from 1895), 2 Kgs. 5

76 William MacDonald, op. cit., 2 Kgs. 5:20-27

77 J. Herbert Livingston, *The Pentateuch in Its Cultural Environment* (Baker House, Grand Rapids, MI; 1974), p. 157

78 J. N. Darby, *Synopsis of the Books of the Bible Vol. I – Genesis-2 Chronicles* (Stow Hill Bible and Tract Depot, Kingston on the Thames; 1949), p. 406

79 Richard I. McNeely, op. cit., p. 113

80 Albert Barnes, op. cit., Amos 1:3

81 John Heading, op. cit., p. 308

82 John Heading, op. cit., p. 322

83 William MacDonald, op. cit., 2 Kgs. 12:19-21

84 Jamieson, Fausset, and Brown, op. cit., 2 Kgs.13:5

85 R. B. Chisholm Jr., op. cit., p. 1395

86 Edwin R. Thiele, op. cit., p. 79

87 Richard I. McNeely, op. cit., p. 125

88 Richard I. McNeely, op. cit., p. 127

89 Richard I. McNeely, op. cit., p. 135

90 Matthew Henry, op. cit., 2 Kgs. 16:1-4

91 J. N. Darby, *Notes on Isaiah*, STEM Publishing (chp. 5): http://stempublishing.com/authors/darby/NOTESCOM/44005E.html

92 Matthew Henry, op. cit., 2 Kgs. 7:10-16

93 Albert Barnes, op. cit., 2 Kgs. 7:17
94 John Heading, op. cit., p. 333
95 "The Siege of Lachish," *Odyssey Adventures in Archaeology* (Feb. 9, 2012): http://www.odysseyadventures.ca/articles/lachish_slides/lachish_text.htm
96 James B. Pritchard, op. cit.
97 C. A. Coates, op. cit., 2 Kgs. 18
98 John A. Martin, op. cit., p. 1089
99 John A. Martin, op. cit., p. 1090
100 John Heading, op. cit., p. 370
101 According to the non-canonical book of *Assumption of Isaiah*
102 Matthew Henry, op. cit., 2 Kgs. 22:11-20
103 Albert Barnes, op. cit., 2 Kgs. 15:13
104 George William, op. cit., p. 221
105 John Heading, op. cit., p. 385
106 John Heading, op. cit., p. 398
107 W. Gustafson, *What the Bible Teaches – 2 Chronicles* (John Ritchie LTD, Kilmarnock, Scotland; 2015), 2 Chron. 36 intro.
108 Sir Robert Anderson, *The Coming Prince*; Preface to the Tenth Edition http://www.WhatSaithTheScripture.com [last accessed March 28, 2017]

www.ingramcontent.com/pod-product-compliance
Lightning Source LLC
Chambersburg PA
CBHW070337090426
42733CB00009B/1219